AF744026

Property rights and their violations

La propriété violée

Luigi Lorenzetti
Michela Barbot
Luca Mocarelli
(eds/éds)

Property rights and their violations

Expropriations and confiscations, 16th–20th Centuries

La propriété violée

Expropriations et confiscations, XVIe–XXe siècles

PETER LANG
Bern · Berlin · Bruxelles · Frankfurt am Main · New York · Oxford · Wien

Bibliographic information published by die Deutsche Nationalbibliothek
Die Deutsche Nationalbibliothek lists this publication in the Deutsche Nationalbibliografie; detailed bibliographic data is available on the Internet at ‹http://dnb.d-nb.de›.

British Library Cataloguing-in-Publication Data: A catalogue record for this book is available from The British Library, Great Britain

Library of Congress Cataloging-in-Publication Data

Property rights and their violations : expropriations and confiscations, 16th-20th centuries = La propriété violée : expropriations et confiscations, XVIE-XXE siècles / Luigi Lorenzetti, Michela Barbot, Luca Mocarelli (eds/éds).
p. cm.
ISBN 978-3-03-430668-3
1. Property–History. 2. Right of property–History. 3. Eminent domain--History.
4. Confiscations–History. I. Lorenzetti, Luigi, 1964- II. Barbot, Michela. III. Mocarelli, Luca. IV. Title: Propriété violée : expropriations et confiscations, XVIE-XXE siècles.
K720.P7625 2012
346.0409'03–dc23

2012027991

The Editors will express their thanks to the Swiss National Found for the conference's financial support
They would also thank the following institutions for supporting the present publication:
- Fondazione Pasquale Lucchini – Lugano
- Dipartimento di Economia dell'Università degli Studi "Gabriele d'Annunzio", Chieti-Pescara
- Dipartimento di Economia politica dell'Università degli Studi Milano Bicocca
- Università della Svizzera italiana (Accademia di architettura), Mendrisio

And gratefulness to
- Monica Bancalà, for her help in organizing the conference
- Anne Jamison, Raffaella Carobbio, Catherine Derubigny and John O'Callaghan, for the revising and editorial work
- Rosa Congost, Jon Mathieu, Marco Cattini et Jean-François Chauvard, for their help and work in the scientific committee of the Congress

Cover illustration: Expropriations during the extension of Avenue de l'Opera, inhabitants moving from the Butte des Moulins, October 1876, © Bridgeman-Giraudon

Cover design: Thomas Grütter, Peter Lang AG

ISBN 978-3-0343-0668-3 pb. ISBN 978-3-0351-0447-9 eBook

© Peter Lang AG, International Academic Publishers, Bern 2012
Hochfeldstrasse 32, CH-3012 Bern, Switzerland
info@peterlang.com, www.peterlang.com

All rights reserved.
All parts of this publication are protected by copyright.
Any utilisation outside the strict limits of the copyright law, without the permission of the publisher, is forbidden and liable to prosecution.
This applies in particular to reproductions, translations, microfilming, and storage and processing in electronic retrieval systems.

Table of Contents – Table des matières

Introduction – Property and Its Antithesis: Confiscations and Expropriations at the Heart of History

Michela Barbot, Luigi Lorenzetti and Luca Mocarelli

Men more quickly forget the death of their father
than the loss of their patrimony
Niccolò Machiavelli, *The Prince*, Chap. 17.

In recent times the history of the right to property has aroused renewed interest among scholars. In the wake of the frenzy of legal changes introduced by new emerging countries and by the European economies in transition[1], historians and social scientists are once again focusing their investigations on the evolution of one of the cornerstones of capitalism and modernity: the right to private, absolute and exclusive property, as framed in Europe by the 19th century codifications[2].

The formidable number of studies generated on ownership and property have tended to focus mainly on two main questions: the ways in which private and individual property emerged to the detriment of collective property, a concept which a number of scholars believe to be completely inadequate[3], and

1 In particular, we are referring to China or Eastern Europe countries: both of these areas have seen significant changes to their property-rights systems: by way of example see Colombatto Enrico, Macey Johnatan, "Lessons from Transition in Eastern Europe. A Property-Rights Interpretation", in *International Bulletin*, vol. I, n. 1 (1997), pp. 23–29, and Oi Jean, Walder Andrew (eds.), *Property rights and economic reform in China*, Stanford, Stanford University Press, Stanford, 1999.

2 For a thought-provoking reconstruction of the history of property rights from ancient times to the 20th century see Pipes Richard, *Property and Freedom*, New York, Alfred A. Knopf, 1999.

3 Think of the huge amount of literature available on the history of the *Enclosures*, from the classic works of Marc Bloch to more recent studies such as Allen Robert's, *Enclosure and the Yeoman. The Agricultural Development of the South Midlands, 1450–1850*, Oxford, Oxford University Press, 1992; Neeson J. M., *Commoners. Common Right, Enclosures and*

the impact of this process in terms of economic efficiency and improvement of the institutional systems[4].

While not eschewing the important results of these lines of study, they tend to fatally overlook the "other side of the story": the restrictions imposed on the individual's right to property over the centuries to the benefit of the collectivity, a subject which has been the object of decidedly fewer studies[5].

The works gathered in this volume – fruit of an international conference held at Mendrisio in September 2010[6] – attempt to shed light on this little

---

Social Change in England, 1700–1820, Cambridge, Cambridge University Press, 1993; Demélas Marie-Danielle, Vivier Nadine (sous la dir. de), *Les propriétés collectives face aux attaques libérales (1750–1914). Europe occidentale et Amérique latine*, Rennes, PUR, 2003, Alfani Guido, Rao Riccardo (a cura di), *La gestione delle risorse collettive. Italia settentrionale secoli XII–XVIII*, Milano, Franco Angeli, 2011. The debate on the economic efficacy of the *Commons* has been rekindled by the polemic spawned by the theories expounded by Hardin Garrett in "The tragedy of the Commons", in *Science*, 162 (1968), pp. 1243–1248, then discussed in the book by Ostrom Elinor, G*overning the Commons. The Evolution of Institutions for Collective Action*, Cambridge, Cambridge University Press, 1990. For a legal perspective of the question see also Grossi Paolo, *An Alternative to Private Property: Collective Property in the Juridical Consciousness of the Nineteenth century*, Chicago, 1981.

4 The reference is above all to studies carried out within *New Institutional Economics*, of which it is possible to cite Demsetz Harold, "The exchange and enforcement of property rights", in *Journal of Law and Economics*, 7 (1964), pp. 10–26; Id., "Some aspects of property rights", in *Journal of Law and Economics*, 9 (1966), pp. 61–70; Williamson Oliver E., "The Economics of Organization The Transaction Cost Approach", in *The American Journal of Sociology*, 87 (1981), pp. 548–557; North Douglass C., Thomas Robert P., *The Rise of the Western World*, Cambridge, Cambridge University Press, 1973; North Douglass C., *Institutions, Institutional Change and Economic Performance*, Cambridge, Cambridge University Press, 1990.

5 See Jacquot Henri (sous la dir de), *Histoire de l'expropriation du XVIIIe siècle à nos jours, Actes de la Ière Journée d'études historiques du Laboratoire collectivités locales*, Orléans, 13 May 1996, Orléans, Laboratoire collectivités locales, 1997. Although it deals exclusively with France, reference should also be made to the classic work of Halbwachs Maurice, *Les expropriations et le prix des terrains à Paris (1860–1900)*, Paris, Rieder, 1909, and to Lacchè Luigi, *L'espropriazione per pubblica utilità. Amministratori e proprietari nella Francia dell'Ottocento*, Milano, Giuffrè, 1995.

6 The conference, held on 24 and 25 September 2010 at the Laboratorio di Storia delle Alpi at the Università della Svizzera Italiana, was financed by the Swiss National Foundation (SNF), which the organizers thank. The texts published here are a selection of the reports presented on that occasion.

known side of the history of the right to property. The analysis focuses above all on the historical forms of violation of private property through expropriation, attachments, and confiscations by public authorities over a long period of time – from Medieval times to today –, on an extra-European geographic scale and on a wide range of assets, from the stockpiles of wheat in fascist Italy[7] to the slaves freed in the New World[8], and the most classic of all assets expropriated or confiscated, immovable property and land.

We use the word "violation" here in a deliberately provocative way: even although on a regulatory level the procedures discussed in the essays published in this volume were conceived and implemented within the boundaries of each state's legal system, they often gave rise to serious problems of legitimacy and justification for the players involved. Besides, the term "violation" attributes an historical dimension to two actions taken by distinct sectors of governmental power; indeed, while *confiscation* is a coercive measure of a penal nature, *expropriation* is a measure which, to varying degrees in the different historical contexts, combines the administrative sphere with the legal one, supported by the principles of *public interest* (or *necessity)*[9].

Besides this distinction, which certainly leaves room for ambiguity[10], the difficult relationship between *legality* and *legitimacy* emerges most clearly in the essays dealing with the question of compensation paid for expropriation. Just as in the pre-Republican era, in contemporary times it is also, and above all, on the aspect of fair compensation and the ways of calculating it that it may be possible to translate the legality of the procedures into their social consent. Beyond a shadow of a doubt the 19th century codifications and laws helped to standardize the methods of calculating compensation, making them more

7 The fascist stockpiles represent an interesting case halfway between expropriation and confiscation: see the essay by Manuel Vaquero Piñeiro in this volume.

8 The reference is to the essay by Frédérique Beauvois which deals with the case of a form of ownership which is decidedly unusual – slavery –, taking into consideration the debate triggered by its abolition in the colonies of the New World between 1777 and 1888.

9 See Hostiou René, "Deux siècles d'évolution de la notion d'utilité publique", in *Un droit inviolable et sacré. La propriété*, Paris, ADEF, 1990.

10 See the example of the "Confisca reta" illustrated by Dermont Giri, "Note sulla confisca e restituzione delle proprietà private grigioni in Valtellina, Chiavenna e Bormio", in Jäger Georg, Scaramellini Guglielmo (a cura di), *La fine del governo grigione in Valtellina e Contadi: presupposti, modi, effetti*, Sondrio, Tip. Polaris, 2001, pp. 83–88.

objective and less discretionary than before[11]; nevertheless, if observed over a longer period of time, the determination of compensation remains one of the most critical and socially sensitive nodes of every restriction on individual property, invariably abetting tension and conflicts[12]. Even the times, whether rapid or slow, in which compensation is paid do not appear to be impartial but indicate precise priorities and just as precise relationships of power[13]. To use a musical metaphor, we could say that it is the very existence of these relationships of power that makes the history of these procedures more of a polyphony than a solo. Indeed, while not denying the fact that expropriations and confiscations (as the very etymology of the latter – *cum fiscum* – indicates) are closely related to forms of state sovereignty and capitalize on the existence of a strong and authoritative state[14], the essays gathered here also warn us against seeing an overly deterministic and simplistic link between these elements.

On one hand, the legal conventions we are dealing with have a much older history than the admittedly fairly recent one of the nation states[15]; on the other hand, these procedures, even in the context of forms of colonial domination, more than actions unilaterally imposed from above, always appear to imply a

11 The discretionary nature of compensation procedures in the pre-republican era are clearly illustrated in the essay by Claudia Conforti and Francesca Funis and in those by Maria Grazia D'Amelio and Marica Forni who both show how, in Renaissance Florence, 17th century Rome and Milan between the 16th and 19th century the assessments of the experts called on to estimate the value of the assets to be expropriated were all the result of an intricate blend of tangible and subjective criteria.

12 The utmost criticality of the compensation procedures is well documented, for contemporary times, in the essay by Stefano Zaggia on the fascist expropriations in Padua during the 1920s.

13 Emblematic of this is the extremely tardy payment of compensation to the Italian Jews fifty years after the expropriation of their assets and property following the racial laws of 1938 (see Viganò's essay in this volume) and the partial return, only after the Restoration, of the immovable assets confiscated from the emigrant nobles in the French district of Rochefort (1792–1826) discussed in Denis Gandouet's essay.

14 The link between confiscations, taxation and war needs is well documented in the essay by Delleaux on the military confiscations in the French region of Hainaut between the end of the 17th century and the start of the 18th century and by Donatella Strangio who deals with the interesting case of an " inter-state " expropriation following the vicissitudes of the second world war.

15 On the history of the evolution of confiscation in Europe see the exhaustive essay by Annamaria Monti in this volume. For a summary of the principle of expropriation in France see Harouel Jean-Louis, *Histoire de l'expropriation*, Paris, PUF, 2000.

certain degree of negotiation and mediation between the state and the other players involved[16].

Two basic risks are run by attributing solely to the state authorities an active role in the declaration of "public interest" connected to violations of individual property. The first is that of not accounting for the complex relationship forged in the various eras between *public* and *private* property[17]. The second, just as critical risk, is that of disregarding the complex link between general interests and those of the relative territorial areas[18]. Expropriations and confiscations transpire in contexts full of history, and their outcomes inevitably display a marked path dependence on similar contexts. The diverse factors able to impact these outcomes include the legal nature of ownership rights that are concretely subject to restriction. Contrary to the claims made by scholars close to New Institutional Economics[19], the studies presented here suggest that individual, private property does not necessarily represent the best safeguarded and protected legal model and, therefore, the one least exposed to violation risks.

The essays in this volume are clear on this point. In many Medieval and modern Europe societies and in many extra-European colonial contexts, the preponderance of forms of ownership based on actual possession and on fractional and shared ownership (for example, the perpetual lease in its many local forms[20]) even risked translating into a brand-new protection of individual

16 Similar dynamics – oftentimes contradictory – between centre and periphery are described exhaustively by Nicolas Krautberger in his comparative study of public interest expropriations in Algeria and in the French Alps during the 19th century. On the negotiations that expropriations and confiscations can provoke even in totalitarian regimes see Ingold Alice, *Négocier la ville. Projet urbain, société et fascisme à Milan*, Paris, EHESS-Ecole Française de Rome, 2003.

17 The thin line between "public" and "private" is discussed, inter alia, by Daniele Andreozzi in his essay about Trieste in the 18th century.

18 On the local impact of the definition of "public interest" see the case study by Natascia Ridolfi on the expropriations ordered at the end of the 19th century to build the railway network in Abruzzo.

19 Refer above all to the work of Douglass C. North, already cited in footnote 4 of this introduction.

20 On the perpetual lease and forms of dissociated ownership existing in Medieval and modern Europe see, in particular, Faron Olivier, Hubert Étienne (sous la dir. de), *Le sol et l'immeuble: les formes dissociées de propriété immobilière dans les villes de France et d'Italie*, Rome, École Française de Rome, 1993, and, for an even broader overview, Brewer John, Staves Susan (eds.), *Early modern conceptions of property rights*, New York, Routledge, 1996.

rights, playing an unintended role of deterrent and hindrance in the execution of expropriations and confiscations. Nevertheless, the definitive outcome of these dynamics is generally difficult to interpret. In general, where forms of dissociated and shared ownership dominated, expropriation and confiscation inevitably generated huge social costs, expelling entire groups of the population from the community structure and drastically limiting the area of social inclusion[21]. However, in some cases the opposite happened; that is, expropriation of property by the state weakened positions of power and privilege, extending the range of individual rights and helping to reduce social and economic inequalities[22]. These conflicting effects means that it is impossible to draw an overall balance of the redistribution effects of these procedures. In a game of light and shadows, history shows that confiscations and expropriations were able to act contemporarily as powerful instruments of change and tenacious factors of conservation, delineating trends which could only partially overlap the evolution of the forms of ownership they were called on to circumscribe and delimit.

21 The case analyzed by Manoela Pedroza is emblematic of this: the expropriations in Brazil between 1870 and 1910 reinforced the existing social hierarchies, giving even more power to the elite to the detriment of the weaker groups of the local communities. The link between loss of property and loss of the right of citizenship is clearly illustrated by Cerutti Simona, "À qui appartiennent les biens qui n'appartiennent à personne? Citoyenneté et droit d'aubaine à l'époque moderne", in *Annales H.S.S.*, 62 (2007), pp. 355–386.

22 This is what happened when the seditious laws of feudalism were implemented on the feudal lands in the Kingdom of Naples which during the 19th century led to the seizure of part of the property of the former feudal barons, its return to the municipal land and its subsequent allocation to the locals (see the essay by Paola Nardone on this question). For a discussion on this see Voigt Stefan, "On the coexistence of different property rights systems – and its consequences for economic growth and development", in Colombatto Enrico (ed.), *The Elgar Companion to the Economics of Property Rights*, Cheltenham UK, Northampton MA USA, Edgar Elgar, 2004, pp. 154–176.

Introduction – La propriété et son revers: confiscations et expropriations au cœur de l'histoire

Michela Barbot, Luigi Lorenzetti et Luca Mocarelli

Gli uomini dimenticano più presto la morte del padre
che la perdita del patrimonio
Niccolò Machiavelli, *Il principe*, cap. 17

Depuis quelque temps, l'histoire des droits de propriété connaît un nouveau dynamisme. Dans le sillage des tumultueux changements juridiques expérimentés par les pays émergents et par les économies européennes en transition[1], les historiens et les spécialistes des sciences sociales ont renouvelé leurs analyses sur l'un des piliers fondateurs du capitalisme et de la modernité: le droit de propriété individuel, absolu et exclusif tel qu'il avait été tracé en Europe par les codes juridiques du XIXe siècle[2].

Parmi l'imposante quantité d'études conduites autour de ce thème, deux sont les voies d'analyse les plus parcourues: la première insiste sur les modalités de la naissance de la propriété privée individuelle au détriment de la propriété collective – une institution que nombre de chercheurs ont jugé totalement inadaptée au modèle économique libéral[3] –; la deuxième examine les conséquences

1 C'est le cas notamment de la Chine et des pays de l'Europe de l'Est qui ont subi des mutations profondes de leur système de propriété. Voir Colombatto Enrico, Macey Johnatan R., "Lessons from Transition in Eastern Europe. A Property-Rights Interpretation", in *International Bulletin*, vol. I, n. 1 (1997), pp. 23-29; Oi Jean, Walder Andrew (eds), *Property rights and economic reform in China*, Stanford, Stanford University Press, Stanford, 1999.

2 Pour une reconstruction de l'histoire de la propriété de l'Antiquité au XXe siècle, voir Pipes Richard, *Property and Freedom*, New York, Alfred A. Knopf, 1999.

3 Voir l'ample littérature sur l'histoire des enclosures, dont les travaux de Marc Bloch et autres études plus récentes, notamment celles de Allen Robert, *Enclosure and the Yeoman. The Agricultural Development of the South Midlands, 1450-1850*, Oxford, Oxford University Press, 1992; Neeson J. M., *Commoners. Common Right, Enclosure and Social Change in England, 1700-1820*, Cambridge, Cambridge University Press, 1993; Demélas Marie-Danielle, Vivier Nadine (sous la dir. de), *Les propriétés collectives face aux attaques libérales (1750-1914). Europe occidentale et Amérique latine*, Rennes, PUR, 2003; Alfani Guido, Rao

engendrées par ce procès sur l'efficacité économique et sur l'amélioration des systèmes institutionnels[4].

Tout en confirmant les apports décisifs de ce parcours de recherche, relevons toutefois qu'il a inévitablement laissé dans l'ombre « l'autre moitié de l'histoire », à savoir les limitations que le droit de propriété des individus a connu au cours des siècles au profit de la collectivité; un thème qui a fait l'objet d'un nombre inférieur de recherches[5].

Les textes réunis dans ce volume – fruit d'un colloque international qui s'est tenu à Mendrisio en septembre 2010[6] – essayent d'éclaircir ces aspects – à vrai dire encore méconnus – de l'histoire des droits de propriété. Au cœur du sujet il y a les formes, historiquement définies, de la « violation » de la propriété

Riccardo (a cura di), *La gestione delle risorse collettive. Italia settentrionale secoli XII-XVIII*, Milano, Franco Angeli, 2011. Suite à la polémique engendrée par les thèses de Hardin Garrett, le débat sur l'efficacité économique des *Commons* a pris un nouvel élan: voir "The tragedy of the Commons", in *Science*, 162 (1968), pp. 1243-1248. Ces thèses ont été discutées dans Ostrom Elinor, G*overning the Commons. The Evolution of Institutions for Collective Action*, Cambridge, Cambridge University Press, 1990. Pour une perspective juridique sur la question, voir aussi Grossi Paolo, *An Alternative to Private Property: Collective Property in the Juridical Consciousness of the Nineteenth Century*, Chicago, Chicago University Press, 1981.

4 Nous nous référons surtout aux études menées au sein de la nouvelle économie institutionnelle (de l'anglais *New Institutional Economics*). Voir, par exemple, Demsetz Harold, "The exchange and enforcement of property rights", in *Journal of Law and Economics*, 7 (1964), pp. 10-26; Id., "Some aspects of property rights", in *Journal of Law and Economics*, 9 (1966), pp. 61-70; Williamson Oliver E., "The Economics of Organization: The Transaction Cost Approach", in *The American Journal of Sociology*, 87 (1981), pp. 548-557; North Douglass C., Thomas Robert Paul, *The Rise of the Western World*, Cambridge, Cambridge University Press, 1973; North Douglass C., *Institutions, Institutional Change and Economic Performance*, Cambridge, Cambridge University Press, 1990.

5 Cf. Jacquot Henri (sous la dir. de), *Histoire de l'expropriation du XVIII*e *siècle à nos jours, Actes de la I*ère *Journée d'études historiques du Laboratoire collectivités locales*, Orléans, 13 mai 1996, Orléans, Laboratoire collectivités locales, 1997. Même s'ils ne se réfèrent qu'au contexte français, signalons aussi Halbwachs Maurice, *Les expropriations et le prix des terrains à Paris (1860-1900)*, Paris, Rieder, 1909 et Lacchè Luigi, *L'espropriazione per pubblica utilità. Amministratori e proprietari nella Francia dell'Ottocento*, Milano, Giuffrè, 1995.

6 Le colloque, qui s'est déroulé les 24 et 25 septembre 2010 à Mendrisio au Laboratorio di Storia delle Alpi de l'Università della Svizzera italiana, a bénéficié d'un financement du Fond National Suisse pour la recherche scientifique (FNS), que les organisateurs remercient. Les textes figurant dans volume sont le résultat d'une sélection des communications présentées lors de ce colloque.

privée à travers les expropriations, les saisies et les confiscations perpétrées par les autorités publiques dans la longue durée – depuis le Moyen Âge jusqu'à nos jours – à l'échelle européenne et extra-européenne, à l'égard d'une large palette de biens allant de la typologie plus classique des biens expropriés ou confisqués tels que les biens fonciers et immobiliers, aux stocks céréaliers des *ammassi* dans l'Italie fasciste[7] et aux esclaves libérés dans le Nouveau Monde[8].

Nous avons utilisé le mot « violation » dans un but sciemment provocateur: si d'une part, sur le plan normatif, les procédures évoquées dans les contributions de ce volume ont été conçues et mises en œuvre dans des contextes de légalité étatique, très souvent elles ont donné lieu à d'importants problèmes de légitimation et de justification auprès des acteurs concernés. D'autre part, cette expression confère une dimension historique à des actes qui renvoient à des domaines différents du pouvoir public. En effet, alors que la *confiscation* constitue une mesure coercitive pénale, l'*expropriation* est une mesure qui, à différents degrés selon le contexte historique, ajuste le domaine administratif à celui juridique en s'appuyant sur les principes d'*utilité* ou de *nécessité publique*[9]. Au-delà de cette distinction – qui n'est d'ailleurs pas dépourvue d'ambiguïtés[10] – le problème du rapport complexe entre les dimensions de la *légalité* et de la *légitimité* est posé de façon explicite dans les contributions qui abordent la question du dédommagement versé suite à des expropriations. Sous l'Ancien Régime ainsi qu'à l'époque contemporaine, c'est aussi – et surtout – sur le terrain de la juste compensation et des méthodes utilisées pour la calculer que se joue la possibilité de traduire la légalité des procédures en acceptation sociale. Il est certain que les normes juridiques et les législations du XIXe siècle ont contribué à fournir un cadre uniforme et objectif aux méthodes de calcul des

7 Les *ammassi* (réserves de denrées publiques) fascistes représentent un dispositif à mi-chemin entre les expropriations et les saisies. À cet égard, voir dans ce volume le texte de Manuel Vaquero Piñeiro.

8 Nous nous référons à la contribution de Frédérique Beauvois qui analyse l'esclavage en tant que forme de « propriété » particulière. L'article rend compte du débat suscité par son abolition dans les colonies du Nouveau Monde entre 1777 et 1888.

9 Voir Hostiou René, « Deux siècles d'évolution de la notion d'utilité publique », in *Un droit inviolable et sacré. La propriété*, Paris, ADEF, 1990.

10 Voir l'exemple de la *Confisca reta* illustré par Dermont Giri, « Note sulla confisca e restituzione delle proprietà private grigioni in Valtellina, Chiavenna e Bormio », in Jäger Georg, Scaramellini Guglielmo (dir.), *La fine del governo grigione in Valtellina e Contadi: presupposti, modi, effetti*, Sondrio, Tip. Polaris, 2001, pp. 83-88.

compensations, réduisant ainsi leur caractère arbitraire par rapport aux siècles précédents[11]. Néanmoins, dans la longue durée, la détermination de l'indemnité demeure l'un des nœuds critiques et socialement sensibles de la limitation de la propriété individuelle et un facteur potentiel de tensions et de conflits[12].

Même les échéances du paiement de la compensation – qu'elles soient rapprochées ou différées – ne sont pas neutres; bien au contraire, elles révèlent des priorités et des rapports de force précis[13]. Usant d'une métaphore musicale, on pourrait dire que c'est précisément l'existence de tels rapports de force qui fait de l'histoire de ces procédures une polyphonie plutôt qu'un solo. En effet, bien qu'on ne puisse nier que les expropriations et les confiscations (comme l'indique l'étymologie même du mot *cum fiscum*) soient en relation étroite avec les formes de souveraineté étatique et tirent profit de l'existence d'un État fort et autoritaire[14], les contributions qui suivent nous mettent en garde contre l'idée d'un lien immédiat et déterministe entre ces deux éléments. D'une part, les institutions juridiques auxquelles on se réfère possèdent une histoire beaucoup plus ancienne que celle, tout compte fait récente, des États-nations[15]. D'autre part,

11 Le caractère arbitraire des procédures d'indemnisation sous l'Ancien Régime émerge dans le texte de Claudia Conforti et Francesca Funis, ainsi que dans les contributions de Maria Grazia D'Amelio et de Marica Forni. Elles montrent qu'aussi bien à Florence et à Rome aux XVe-XVIe siècles qu'à Milan entre le XVIe et le XIXe siècle les évaluations des experts chargés des estimations des biens expropriés étaient le résultat d'un mélange inextricable de critères objectifs et subjectifs.

12 La complexité extrême des procédures d'indemnisation est illustrée par Stefano Zaggia qui analyse les expropriations fascistes à Padoue dans les années vingt.

13 Un exemple paradigmatique concerne l'indemnisation tardive reconnue aux juifs italiens un demi-siècle après les confiscations de leurs biens perpétrées par le régime fasciste suite aux lois raciales de 1938 (voir la contribution de Marino Viganò dans ce volume) ou encore la restitution partielle, effectuée après la Restauration, des immeubles confisqués aux nobles émigrés dans le district français de Rochefort (1792-1826), mise en lumière dans le texte de Denis Gandouet.

14 Le thème du lien entre confiscations, fiscalité et nécessités de guerre des États est abordé par la contribution de Fulgence Delleaux au sujet des confiscations militaires dans la région française de l'Hainaut entre la fin XVIIe et le début du XVIIIe siècle, et par la contribution de Donatella Strangio, qui présente le cas d'une expropriation « interétatique », faisant suite aux bouleversements de la Deuxième Guerre mondiale.

15 Pour un éclairage juridique sur l'histoire de la confiscation en Europe, voir la contribution d'Annamaria Monti dans ce volume. Pour une synthèse sur l'expropriation dans le contexte français, voir Harouel Jean-Louis, *Histoire de l'expropriation*, Paris, PUF, 2000.

ces procédures, même quand elle se manifestent dans des régimes coloniaux, sont moins des actes imposés par le haut de façon univoque que des processus laissant de la place à un certain degré de négociation et de médiation entre l'État et les autres acteurs engagés[16].

Lorsqu'on attribue au seul pouvoir étatique un rôle actif dans la déclaration de l'« intérêt d'utilité publique » impliquant la violation de la propriété individuelle, on se trouve face à deux pièges majeurs. En premier lieu, on risque de sous-estimer la complexité du rapport qui s'est établi, à travers l'histoire, entre ce qui est d'ordre *public* et ce qui relève de la sphère *privée*[17]. En deuxième lieu – et ce n'est pas le moindre – on risque de laisser dans l'ombre les trames complexes qui relient les intérêts généraux aux intérêts des territoires sur lesquels ils influent[18]. Expropriations et confiscations se manifestent dans des contextes riches du point de vue historique et leurs effets se ressentent inévitablement de cette forte « dépendance au sentier emprunté » (*path dependence*). Parmi les facteurs en mesure d'avoir une incidence sur ces effets, il y a aussi la nature juridique des droits de propriété qui sont l'objet d'une limitation. Contrairement aux propos de l'école néo-institutionnaliste[19], les cas examinés dans ce volume suggèrent que la propriété privée individuelle ne représente pas le modèle juridique le plus garanti et protégé, et de ce fait le moins exposé aux risques de violation.

Les résultats issus des diverses contributions sont explicites: dans de nombreuses sociétés de l'Europe médiévale et de l'époque moderne et dans plusieurs contextes coloniaux extra-européens, la primauté des formes de propriété fondées sur la possession effective et sur la propriété fractionnée et partagée (telle

16 Ces dynamiques – souvent contradictoires – entre le centre et la périphérie sont explicitées par Nicolas Krautberger dans son analyse comparative sur les expropriations d'utilité publique en Algérie et dans les Alpes françaises au cours du XIXe siècle. Sur les négociations que les expropriations et les confiscations peuvent amorcer, même dans un cadre politique totalitaire, voir Ingold Alice, *Négocier la ville. Projet urbain, société et fascisme à Milan*, Paris, EHESS-École Française de Rome, 2003.

17 La démarcation difficile entre « public » et « privé » est soulignée par Daniele Andreozzi dans sa contribution sur la ville de Trieste au XVIIIe siècle.

18 Sur les effets locaux de la définition de l'« intérêt d'utilité publique », voir l'analyse de Natascia Ridolfi sur les expropriations décrétées dans les Abruzzes à la fin du XIXe siècle pour la construction du système ferroviaire.

19 Cf. Douglass C. North, *Institutions, Institutional Change and Economic Performance, op. cit.*

que l'emphytéose dans toutes ses variations locales[20]) a représenté, dans certains cas, un facteur de protection des droits individuels, en jouant le rôle de frein et d'obstacle à l'adoption de mesures d'expropriation ou de confiscation.

Ceci dit, les conséquences de telles dynamiques restent difficiles à saisir dans leur ensemble. De façon générale, là où les formes de propriété dissociée et partagée sont les plus répandues, les expropriations et les confiscations ont fatalement donné lieu à d'importants coûts sociaux, en expulsant de larges pans de la population hors des groupes communautaires et en rétrécissant l'espace de l'inclusion sociale[21]. Dans d'autres cas, toutefois, c'est l'inverse qui s'est produit: l'expropriation décrétée par l'État a parfois permis d'affaiblir des situations de pouvoir et de privilège, en élargissant, par ricochet, la sphère des droits individuels et en contribuant à la diminution des inégalités sociales et économiques[22].

Ces effets ambivalents empêchent de dresser un bilan global des effets de redistribution de ces mesures. Dans un cadre fait de jeux d'ombres et de lumières, à l'épreuve de l'histoire, les expropriations et les confiscations montrent leur capacité à agir à la fois comme de puissants instruments de changement et de tenaces facteurs de conservation, dessinant des trajectoires destinées à se superposer de façon imparfaite à l'évolution des formes de propriété qu'ils sont appelés à circonscrire et à délimiter.

20 Sur l'emphytéose et les formes dissociées de propriété dans l'Europe médiévale et moderne, voir notamment Faron Olivier, Hubert Étienne (sous la dir. de), *Le sol et l'immeuble : les formes dissociées de propriété immobilière dans les villes de France et d'Italie*, Rome, École Française de Rome, 1993, et dans une perspective élargie, Brewer John, Staves Susan (eds), *Early modern conceptions of property rights*, New York, Routledge, 1996.

21 Le cas étudié par Manoela Pedroza est, à cet égard, emblématique: les expropriations décrétées au Brésil entre 1870 et 1910 ont renforcé les hiérarchies sociales en place et consolidé le pouvoir des élites au détriment des groupes les plus faibles des communautés locales. Sur le lien entre la perte de la propriété et la perte des droits de citoyenneté, voir aussi Cerutti Simona, «À qui appartiennent les biens qui n'appartiennent à personne? Citoyenneté et droit d'aubaine à l'époque moderne», in *Annales H.S.S.*, 62 (2007), pp. 355-386.

22 C'est notamment le résultat de l'adoption, au XIXe siècle, des lois subversives de la féodalité sur les fiefs du Règne de Naples. La contribution de Paola Nardone montre que ces lois sont à l'origine de la soustraction d'une partie des propriétés de l'ancienne noblesse féodale au profit du domaine communal, puis de leur répartition parmi la population. Sur ce thème, voir aussi Voigt Stefan, "On the coexistence of different property rights systems – and its consequences for economic growth and development", in Colombatto Enrico (ed.), *The Elgar Companion to the Economic of Property Rights*, Cheltenham UK, Northampton MA USA, Edgar Elgar, 2004, pp. 154-176.

I

Confiscation: An Instrument of the State between Justice, Public Management and Abuse

Les confiscations: un instrument de l'Etat entre justice, gestion publique et abus

Illegitimate Appropriation or just Punishment? The Confiscation of Property in *ancien régime* Criminal Law and Doctrine*

Annamaria Monti

Introduction

In *ancien régime* criminal law, the confiscation of the whole of a property was a punishment for serious crimes, especially for those of a political nature[1]. As Cesare Beccaria wrote, it had been one of the baleful and authorised injustices carried out and approved for centuries, even by educated men and in free republics[2].

It was usually a consequence of conviction of a crime, which was inflicted together with the death penalty or, often, with banishment[3]. It could, however, also be used as a single penalty. Technically, it was a provision of the judicial authority, who seized the guilty party's estate. Confiscation punished the criminal who ostracised himself from the community, by committing a crime: the guilty party was no longer part of the *civitas* and even his family suffered a loss of *status*.

* I would like to thank Professor Laurent Mayali, Director of the Robbins Collection, Boalt Hall School of Law, U.C. Berkeley, for granting me a fellowship to do this research at the Robbins Library, in March 2010. Thank you also to Ed Tyrrell, for helping me with the English text.

1 Pertile Antonio, *Storia del diritto italiano*, vol. V, *Storia del diritto penale*, Torino, Utet, 1892, pp. 228–248; Calisse Carlo, "Svolgimento storico del diritto penale in Italia", in Pessina Enrico (a cura di), *Enciclopedia del diritto penale italiano*, Milano, Società Editrice Libraria, 1905–1906, II, pp. 365–382; Civoli Cesare, "Confisca (Diritto penale)", in *Digesto italiano*, VIII, Torino, Utet, 1896, I, p. 892 s.; Alessandri Alberto, "Confisca nel diritto penale", in *Digesto delle discipline penalistiche*, III, Torino, Utet, 1989, pp. 42–43.

2 Beccaria Cesare, *Dei delitti e delle pene*, a cura di Gianni Francioni, Milano, Mediobanca, 1984, par. XXVI, p. 80.

3 See the critiques by Beccaria, *Dei delitti e delle pene, op. cit.*, par. XXV, pp. 79–80.

Besides acting as a deterrent[4], the so called *publicatio bonorum* was also employed for other reasons, specifically economic; it was used for monetary gains. In fact, confiscation was not only a severe punishment (even if it was not a corporal punishment), it was also an important source of fiscal revenues. From the 12th and 13th centuries, the employment of confiscation clearly showed strong economic interests, in feudal disputes in particular. Similar reasons justified its employment by ecclesiastical authorities and the Spanish and the Italian Inquisitions when fighting heresy[5], according to canon law (X, 5, 7, 10 *Vergentis*; VI, 5, 2, 19, *Quum, secundum leges*)[6].

Moreover, as it dramatically affected the criminal's family, confiscation was an awful and terrifying penalty in *ancien régime* society, which was structured in social orders, bodies and, not least, in families. Niccolò Machiavelli said that men forgot their father's death sooner than the loss of property[7]. During Modern Ages, family honour, prestige and even political power were identified with family estate. That is why the family's patrimony had to be preserved intact from generation to generation and was to be protected at all costs[8].

Furthermore, in relation to the authorities who condemned and seized the estate, confiscation seemed to be more effective in trials against powerful and property-rich political adversaries, guilty of lèse-majesté or high treason, than in prosecuting common and ordinary criminals.

4 Guazzini Sebastiano, *Tractatus de confiscatione bonorum*, Venetiis, Apud Antonium Pinellum, 1611, c. III, pp. 2–3.

5 On medieval Inquisition: Paolini Lorenzo, "Le finanze dell'inquisizione in Italia", in *Gli spazi economici della Chiesa nell'Occidente mediterraneo*, Pistoia, Cissa, 1999, pp. 441–481; Benedetti Marina, "Le finanze dell'inquisitore", in AA.VV., *L'economia dei conventi dei Frati Minori e Predicatori fino alla metà del Trecento*, Spoleto, Cisam, 2004, pp. 363–402. On Roman Inquisition: Prosperi Adriano, *L'Inquisizione romana. Letture e ricerche*, Roma, Edizioni di Storia e Letteratura, 2003. For extended bibliographical references, on Spanish and Roman Inquisition: Maifreda Germano, "Sant'Uffizio, confische e stime nel Cinquecento milanese", in *Quaderni storici*, 135 (2010), pp. 779–824.

6 Alberico da Rosicate, *Commentariorum de statutis, libri IIII*, in *Tractatus universi iuris*, t. II, Venetiis, [s. n.], 1584, lib. I, q. 151, ff. 24v.–25r.; lib. III, q. 18, n. 11, f. 57r.; Deciani Tiberio, *Tractatus criminalis*, Augustae Taurinorum, apud hæredem Nicolai Bevilaquæ, 1593, t. I, l. V, c. 44, pp. 241–244; Farinacci Prospero, *Praxis et theoricae criminalis*, Lugduni, sumpt. Horatij Cardon, 1613, p. I, tit. I, q. 25, n. 12 s.

7 Machiavelli Niccolò, *Il Principe*, Firenze, 1931, cap. 17, p. 78.

8 See *infra*.

At the same time, from a legal point of view, the confiscation of property, or better, of the estate was very difficult to justify as it purposely involved not only the guilty party, but also their family members[9]. Jurists from the 16th and 17th centuries did not expressly criticize this aspect of the *publicatio bonorum* but, when necessary, they consistently took care of the third parties' rights and also of the family members' succession rights.

The polemic against the confiscation of the estate only came to the fore in the second part of the 18th century, clearly demonstrating that this kind of punishment violated one of the most important criminal law principles, i.e. that only the convicted should be penalized. The effects of confiscation were not, in fact, limited to his person, but, as mentioned above, they also affected family members.

Eighteenth century discussions on this penalty concerned how necessary it was and, specifically, its effectiveness. These debates were conducted while the power of punishing itself was being questioned. There were different schools of thought within the Enlightenment movement, relating to the legitimacy of the ancient *publicatio bonorum*, and not all the authors agreed with each other.

Pro delicto alterius puniri

Roman law recognized the confiscation of property. In Roman law, however, the succession rights of the guilty party's wife and children were safeguarded in various ways. The Germanic laws, too, listed confiscation of the estate among the monetary sanctions, as did the written laws of the High Middle Ages, following the late Roman Empire rules.

The *publicatio bonorum* discipline evolved during Roman times[10], but the rules applied during the imperial times were what became a reference for the legislators who followed (such as the barbarian kings), for legal thought in the Middle Ages and also for the jurists to come. Something which is very useful

9 van Damhouder Joost, *Practica rerum criminalium*, Herbipoli, Sumptu Eliae Michaelis Zinck, 1641, cap. LXVI, n. 4, 7–8, p. 212.

10 Kloeckhof Nicolaus, *Historia juris romani de bonis damnatorum*, Genevae, Ap. Frat. Cramer et Cl. Philibert, 1749, p. 149; Ferrini, Contardo "Esposizione storica e dottrinale del diritto penale romano", in Pessina (a cura di), *Enciclopedia del diritto penale*, *op. cit.*, pp. 160–161.

in understanding how confiscation changed in Roman law over the centuries, is consideration of the work of the mid 17th century Dutch jurist, Anton Matthes, who was a late interpreter of humanism and already sensitive to the rationalism of the natural law theories[11]. Some decades later, a colleague of Matthes at Leyden University, Johann Voet, resumed his ideas in his own well known and quoted commentaries on Pandects[12].

And so, according to the rules contained in the so called *libri terribiles* of the Digest, the *publicatio omnium bonorum* was the loss of the whole estate, which was confiscated. The guilty party sentenced to death was also sentenced to the loss of citizenship and liberty and, of course, to confiscation (D 48, 20, 1, l. *Damnatione bona publicantur*; D 48, 20, 8, 3, *Relegati bona per sententiam*). Nevertheless, the emperors Theodosius and Valentinian decided that half of the properties were to be reserved for the descendants (C 9, 49, 4, l. *In metallum damnatum*).

A following 6th century constitution by Justinian, which was generally aimed at mitigating the monetary penalties, changed the rules. If there were ascendants and descendants to the third degree, judges could no longer condemn the guilty party to confiscation. Only if he was guilty of lèse-majesté, could he be sentenced to the *publicatio bonorum*, and all his estate was to be confiscated, with no regard for his family (Nov. 134.13).

In the 12th and 13th centuries, the civil law glossators read Justinian's *Novella* at the bottom of the correspondent title of the *Codex* (auth. *Bona damnatorum* post C, 9, 49 *De bonis proscriptorum*, l. 10 *Quando* = Nov. 134.13). They clearly understood the limitations of confiscation in the more recent Roman laws: the guilty party's estate was devolved to his ascendants, descendants and brothers-in-law to the third degree; judges and officers couldn't profit from it, nor could it be confiscated, except in case of lèse-majesté, according to the ancient laws[13].

Medieval jurists also affirmed that these reforms recognized by the *Authentica* were applicable only if the confiscation of the estate followed, as a consequence,

11 Matthes Anton, *De criminibus ad lib. XLVII et XLVIII Dig. Commentarius*, Amstelodami, Ex officina Johannis a Waesberge, 1661, lib. 48, tit. 18, cap. II, p. 766 f.

12 Voet Johannes, *Commentarius ad Pandectas*, Hagae-Comitum, Apud Abrahamum de Hondt, 1716, t. II, lib. 48, tit. XX, p. 1103 f.

13 Azzone, *Summa super Codicem*, ad C. 9, 49, *de bonis proscriptorum seu damnatorum*, Torino, Ex officio Erasmiana, 1966; Accursio, ad *Auth. Bona damnatorum* C, 9, 49, 10 (=Nov. 134.13), Torino, Ex officio Erasmiana, 1968, f. 291v.

another penalty, such as the death penalty or deportation. On the contrary, these reforms were not applicable if confiscation was inflicted as a single penalty, according to the ancient rules, which imposed, at the same time, precise limitations to the extent of the confiscation itself, to protect both the right of the *legitima*, to be left to the descendants, and third parties' rights[14].

Medieval legal doctrine was therefore conscious of how the Roman emperors limited the extension of confiscation. Jurists started discussing those rules immediately *de iure*[15]. But when they looked at the law in force in their times, they could see a *revival* of this punishment which was largely inflicted by judges, especially in Italian town statute laws (or, as we call them, local laws). The parties guilty of lèse-majesté crimes[16], such as high treason, desertion, conspiracy, forgery of coins, and also of a number of common crimes, such as homicide, rape, robbery and arson were condemned to confiscation by the *statuta*[17]. These convicted parties were usually sentenced both to banishment and confiscation of property.

By quoting Alberico da Rosciate, *magnus practicus* of the 14th century[18], Bartolomeo Cipolla (15th century), Tiberio Deciani, Giulio Claro and Prospero

14 Bossi Egidio, *Tractatus varii*, Venetiis, Apud Dominicum Cavalcalupum, 1581, tit. *de Bonorum publicatione*, n. 1, f. 279r.; Alberico da Rosciate, *Commentariorum de statutis, libri IIII, op. cit.*, lib. III, q. 18, n. 1, f. 56v.; Gambiglioni Angelo, *De maleficiis tractatus*, Venetiis, 1584, *Et eius bona publicamus, et c.*, n. 3, f. 252v.; Claro Giulio, *Volumen alias liber quintus*, Venetiis, apud Ioannem Antonium ab Antoniis, 1570, § *Finalis*, q. 78, par. *Bona damnatorum*; Farinacci, *Praxis et theoricae criminalis, op. cit.*, p. I, tit. I, q. 25, n. 7.

15 Bartolo da Sassoferrato, *Commentaria ... in secunda parte Codicis*, Roma, Il Cigno Galileo Galilei, 1996, ad C. 7, 66, 3, f. 89v.–90r.; Baldo degli Ubaldi, *In VII–XI Codicis libros Commentaria*, Goldbach, Keip, 2004, ad C 7, 66, 3, n. 1–2, ff. 113v.–114r.; ad C 9, 48, *Ne sine iussu Principis, lex unica*, f. 228r.–v.; ad Auth. *Bona damnatorum*, C 9, 49, f. 229v.–230r.; Id., *In Quartum et Quintum Cod. Lib. Commentaria*, Goldbach, Keip, 2004, ad C 4, 17, *Ex delictis defunctorum in quantum heredes conveniantur, lex unica*, n. 7, f. 32r.

16 Sbriccoli Mario, Crimen laesae maiestatis. *Il problema del reato politico alle soglie della scienza penalistica moderna*, Milano, Giuffrè, 1974.

17 Pertile, *Storia del diritto italiano, op. cit.*, pp. 230–231; Kohler Josef, *Das Strafrecht der Italienischen Statuten vom 12.–16. Jahrhundert*, Mannheim, J. Bensheimer, 1897, pp. 72–80; Calisse, "Svolgimento storico del diritto penale in Italia", art. cit., p. 370ss.; Dahm Georg, *Das Strafrecht Italiens im ausgehenden Mittelalter*, Berlin und Leipzig, W. de Gruyter, 1931, pp. 315–317.

18 Alberico da Rosciate, *Commentariorum de statutis, libri IIII, op. cit.*, lib. III, q. 18, n. 13, f. 57r.; Oldrado da Ponte, *Consilia*, Lugduni, [s. n.], 1550, cons. XVII, n. 7, f. 7v.

Farinacci (16th century), among others, said that, in their times, no matter what the Roman law said, usually only a party guilty of heresy or lèse-majesté was sentenced to confiscation, unless local law or customary law provided differently[19]. During 17th century, Matthes echoed their teachings on the use of the punishment according to customs in practice at the time and not to Roman law[20].

In fact, modern legal doctrine was facing a social and juridical reality where confiscation of the estate was largely in use. Across Europe, it was the punishment for more than four hundred crimes, from homicide to forgery of coins, to apostasy[21]. It also reflected the political and institutional changes which occurred in different countries over the centuries.

When *publicatio bonorum* was inflicted by a local law, jurists were very keen on highlighting the limitations of its use. So, if it was a local law which condemned the guilty party to confiscation and it was not a case of heresy or lèse-majesté[22], they said that the rule was to be interpreted strictly and *contra fiscum*, as it derogated from the common law[23].

As also happened in other fields, it seemed that there was a gap between the doctrinal thought emerging from the study of the Code and Digest, and the

19 Cipolla Bartolomeo, *Consilia criminalia*, [Lugduni, Antoine Du Ry, impensis Jacques and Franciscus Giunta, 13 Dec. 1525], cons. 17, *Cum itaque*, f. 38v.; Deciani Tiberio, *Responsorum*, vol. II, Venetiis, apud Hieronymum & Ioannem Zenarios, 1579, resp. 56, n. 61 s., pp. 438–439; Claro, *Volumen alias liber quintus*, *op. cit.*, § *Finalis*, q. 78, par. *Sed certe*; Farinacci, *Praxis et theoricae criminalis*, *op. cit.*, p. I, tit. I, q. 25, n. 10; Damhouder, *Practica rerum criminalium*, *op. cit.*, cap. LXVI, n. 1, p. 212.

20 Matthes, *De criminibus ad lib. XLVII et XLVIII*, *op. cit.*, lib. 48, tit. 20, cap. IV, n. 17 s., p. 894 f.: only the Senate and the echevins from Utrecht inflicted confiscation and only in lèse-majesté cases; Voet, *Commentarius ad Pandectas*, *op. cit.*, t. II, lib. 48, tit. XX, n. 6, p. 1106: according to the noblemen's and towns' privileges, in Holland only a part of the properties was confiscated and only in case of lèse-majesté and forgery of coins.

21 Claro, *Volumen alias liber quintus*, *op. cit.*, § *Finalis*, q. 78, par. *Multa autem*.

22 Cipolla, *Consilia criminalia*, *op. cit.*, cons. 17, f. 34v. s.; Pape Guy, *Decisiones*, Lugduni, officina H. a Porta, sumpt. I. de Gabiano, 1610, q. 346, pp. 317–318; Damhouder, *Practica rerum criminalium*, *op. cit.*, cap. 66, n. 1, p. 212; Farinacci Prospero, *Praxis … pars … quarta*, Norimbergae, Sumptibus Wolfgangi Mauritii Endteri & Johannis Andreae Endteri Haeredum, 1676, q. 116, n. 12 s.; De Angelis Francesco Giuseppe, *Tractatus criminalis … Pars prima*, Venetiis, Ex Typographia Balleoniana, 1736, caput 83, n. 22 s., p. 130.

23 Alberico da Rosciate, *Commentariorum de statutis, libri IIII*, *op. cit.*, lib. I, q. 151, n. 9, f. 24v.; Farinacci, *Praxis et theoricae criminalis*, *op. cit.*, p. I, tit. I, q. 25, n. 21.

law in action. Local laws effectively applied rules contrary to Roman law, which was the common law. By referring to Roman law, doctrinal jurisprudence tried to limit the extent of confiscation according to local and customary laws. In particular, jurists limited the use of confiscation, which often ruined families, by bringing the particular rules back to a multiple-source system, such as the common law system.

To summarize, 16th and 17th century jurists based their opinions on the interpretation of Roman legal sources, by often quoting the same authors, as if they were authorities to follow. Whilst observing the practice of the law in their times, these jurists learned and therefore added their own teachings, which were the most interesting.

One of the most cited authors was Alberto da Gandino, who had studied the *publicatio bonorum malefactorum* according to both Roman and local law. As he had been a judge in medieval Italian towns, he gave some examples of trials which reflected the urban conflicts during the second half of 13th century where confiscation was inflicted.

Amongst his work, he described the case of a man sentenced to confiscation of the estate. The verdict also included that his house was to be destroyed and all the trees to be uprooted[24]. Gandino wondered if the guilty party's wife could have somehow avoided the destruction of the house, by claiming it as part of her dowry. According to Roman law, this would have been possible, but according to the city's customs and local written law, the house, the towers and all the other buildings had to be destroyed. In this situation, in which the wife could not retain her husband's house, she was entitled to receive other properties equal to the claim of her dowry. Gandino said that even if the law was severe, it had to be enforced, because "crimes must not remain unpunished"[25].

Furthermore, judge Gandino wondered what happened when the guilty party's house that was to be demolished had a wall in common with a neighbour's house, or when it was a common property of two brothers and only one

24 Calisse, "Svolgimento storico del diritto penale in Italia", art. cit., p. 380 f.

25 Alberto da Gandino, *Tractatus de maleficiis*, in *Tractatus diversi super maleficiis*, Venetiis, P. Hieronymus Lilius excudebat, 1560, *De bonis malefactorum*, p. 236 f. Regarding women's rights on dowries, Gambiglioni, *De maleficiis tractatus*, *op. cit.*, n. 10, f. 255r. According to 16th century legal doctrine, dowries could not be confiscated: Claro, *Volumen alias liber quintus*, *op. cit.*, § *Finalis*, q. 78, par. *Quaero*; Farinacci, *Praxis et theoricae criminalis*, *op. cit.*, p. I, tit. I, q. 25, n. 111–112.

was condemned. He suggested always trying to avoid demolition of the whole property, "quia non debet alteri per alterum iniqua conditio afferri". Only in cases where separate demolition was impossible, because, for example, when the criminal's property was at the lower floor of a tower, or it was connected to another, the whole building had to be demolished. The justification was always the same, i.e. *ne crimina remaneant impunita*. In this case, however, an innocent party who suffered from the consequences of the punishment could ask the guilty party for compensation. If the guilty party was insolvent, the innocent party could ask the *commune* itself for compensation[26].

I have spoken of what Alberto da Gandino said, because his writings featured the major topics which continued to be discussed by jurists over the following centuries[27]. First of all, the approach to the theme went on to be case by case. Looking for theory as a frame of reference is useless, as legal doctrine was interested in practical cases. The ensemble is very intriguing, and sometimes a bit elusive.

Examples changed, but 16th and 17th century jurists explained, amongst other things, what happened to the guilty party's father's estate, when the son sentenced to confiscation was a *filius familias*. While the father was not responsible for crimes committed by his children, there were debates on the confiscation of children's properties, i.e. the *peculia*[28]. Jurists also discussed if a man was responsible for his wife's crime, and if that crime was punishable with confiscation: Gandino had said that as well as having to provide alimony for his wife, he had to pay the penalty for her, *de aequitate*[29].

Legal doctrine debated on the validity of *donationes*. 12th century jurist Azzone had pointed out three hypothesis. If the *donatio* preceded the crime, it was valid; it was valid even if it preceded the verdict, except in lèse-majesté

26 Alberto da Gandino, *Tractatus de maleficiis*, *op. cit.*, n. 12–13, p. 240.

27 Guazzini, *Tractatus de confiscatione bonorum*, *op. cit.*, *passim*.

28 *Ibidem*, pp. 240–241; Nello da San Gimignano, *De bannitis*, in *Tractatus universi iuris*, vol. XI, pars I, Venetiis, [F. Zilettus], 1584, n. 33, f. 369r.; Gambiglioni, *De maleficiis tractatus*, *op. cit.*, n. 27, f. 257v.; Tartagni Alessandro, *Commentaria in I et II digesti novi*, Venetiis, Apud Iuntas, 1586, ad D 39, 2, 15, 26, *Si de vectigalibus*, n. 44 s.; Claro, *Volumen alias liber quintus*, *op. cit.*, § *Finalis*, q. 78, par. *Praeterea quaero* e s.

29 Alberto da Gandino, *Tractatus de maleficiis*, *op. cit.*, n. 17, p. 241. See also Claro, *Volumen alias liber quintus*, *op. cit.*, § *Finalis*, q. 78, par. *Quaero*; Farinacci, *Praxis et theoricae criminalis*, *op. cit.*, p. I, tit. I, q. 25, n. 113 f.

and heresy cases; if the donation followed the crime and the verdict, it was not valid[30].

Jurists also dealt with transfers of properties and assets, made by the guilty party sentenced to confiscation. They said that third parties' rights were safe, if the transfers were made in good faith[31]. They discussed, too, the possibility of confiscating the estate acquired by the guilty party after committing the crime, during the trial, or after the condemnation, or even after the confiscation itself[32]. Furthermore, jurists debated the confiscation of the estate belonging to a guilty man, who confessed to a crime punishable with confiscation (he could also be *reus convictus*) and then committed suicide fearing the punishment, *ex* C 9, 50, 1[33].

In addition, legal doctrine taught that confiscation could be ordinary or extraordinary. Ordinary confiscation was recognized by local law, or in general, by customary law. It could be inflicted by any judge competent in the territorial jurisdiction, having the *merum imperium ratione territorii*. Confiscation was extraordinary when it was inflicted outside the law, by the prince, using his power, or by supreme judges *in summa potestate positis*. Therefore, a judge could inflict confiscation without following the rules only upon order of the prince, or if he was a supreme judge[34].

30 Alberto da Gandino, *Tractatus de maleficiis*, *op. cit.*, n. 5, p. 237: "Ex ista opinione domini Azonis excogitantur et fiunt quotidie multa baratariae. Nam commissis delictis fiunt tales donationes propter quas communia civitatis et loca perdunt ius suum et ita male cogitantibus paratur via delinquendi".

31 Cipolla, *Consilia criminalia*, *op. cit.*, cons. 17, *Item et ultimo*, f. 39r.; Bossi, *Tractatus varii*, *op. cit.*, n. 44–45, f. 287r.; Claro, *Volumen alias liber quintus*, *op. cit.*, § *Finalis*, q. 78, par. *Solet etiam* e s.

32 There were different opinions, depending on the laws in force: Gandino, *Tractatus de maleficiis*, *op. cit.* n. 15, p. 241; Nello da San Gimignano, *De bannitis*, *op. cit.*, n. 18, f. 367v.; Bossi, *Tractatus varii*, *op. cit.*, n. 80, f. 295v.–296r.; Claro, *Volumen alias liber quintus*, *op. cit.*, § *Finalis*, q. 78, par. *Ulterius*.

33 Pietro Caballo, *Resolutionum criminalium … centuriae tres*, Venetiis, Apud Bertanos, 1672, casus 137, p. 234 f.

34 Oldrado, *Consilia*, *op. cit.*, cons. XVII, n. 10, f. 8r.; Alberico da Rosciate, *Commentariorum de statutis, libri IIII*, *op. cit.*, lib. III, q. 18, n. 8–9, f. 57r.; Gambiglioni, *De maleficiis tractatus*, *op. cit.*, n. 11, ff. 255r.–v.; Cipolla, *Consilia criminalia*, *op. cit.*, cons. 17, *Tertio casu*, f. 38r.; Claro, *Volumen alias liber quintus*, *op. cit.*, § *Finalis*, q. 78, par. *Quaero*; Guazzini, *Tractatus de confiscatione bonorum*, *op. cit.*, c. XII, p. 11 f.

Moreover, the jurists distinguished if confiscation was the punishment inflicted by the law for a single crime, or if it simply followed the condemnation. In the former scenario, any judge who could proceed, could also condemn the guilty party to confiscation. In the latter, where confiscation followed in an automatic way, any judge who could condemn the guilty party to death, could also confiscate the estate, *ex* D 1. 18. 6. 8[35].

The authors also debated if the judge could confiscate real estate in different territories and out of his jurisdiction. Their answer was affirmative if confiscation was inflicted according to common law rules; however, it was negative if it was inflicted by a local law, unless there was a unique *bursa fiscalis*[36].

As all properties, lands and movables could be confiscated, as well as all assets and revenues[37], the position of the guilty party's creditors in front of the fiscal authority had to be cleared. Legal doctrine said that fiscal authority took control of the estate away from the guilty party's heir. It had to give back the dowries, to satisfy the legacies and the *Fideicommissa*, and also the creditors of the inheritance. Therefore, fiscal authority had to pay the debts, but only within the capacity of the confiscated estate, even if an inventory of the estate itself had not been carried out[38].

Finally, in relation to sons, they were less protected compared to wives and creditors. This is not strange at all, confiscation purposely impacted innocent descendants, as a deterrent. Modern Age jurists always said that Roman law reserved half of the properties for the children, *ex gratia et clementia principis*. In their times, on the contrary, *hoc in practica non servatur*, even if some local laws reserved the *legitima* for the children[39].

35 Gambiglioni, *De maleficiis tractatus*, *op. cit.*, n. 11, f. 255r.; Cipolla, *Consilia criminalia*, *op. cit.*, cons. 17, *Secundo casu*, f. 38r.

36 Nello da San Gimignano, *De bannitis*, *op. cit.*, n. 117, f. 366v. s.; Gambiglioni, *De maleficiis tractatus*, *op. cit.*, n. 7, f. 253r–255r.; Cipolla, *Consilia criminalia*, *op. cit.*, cons. 17, *Item aliud dubium*, f. 39r.; Claro, *Volumen alias liber quintus*, *op. cit.*, § *Finalis*, q. 78, par. *Sed hic*; Farinacci, *Praxis et theoricae criminalis*, *op. cit.*, p. I, tit. I, q. 25, n. 94; Novello Iacopo, *Tractatus criminalis*, Venetiis, Ex officina Ioannis Baptistae Somaschi, 1575, n. 7, p. 206; Caballo, *Resolutionum criminalium*, *op. cit.*, casus 138, pp. 239 f.

37 Claro, *Volumen alias liber quintus*, *op. cit.*, § *Finalis*, q. 78, par. *Successive*.

38 *Ibid.*, par. *Sed an*.

39 See *infra*.

Daughters enjoyed a better position. Perhaps this was due to the fact that family was generally identified through the male descendants and male descendants above all had to be impacted through confiscation. However, as I have mentioned before, fiscal authorities had to pay the debts of the estate, as if they themselves were the heir.

As explained above, the rules on confiscation were interpreted in a strict manner, as they derogated from common law and their effects were extended to family members. That is why doctrine affirmed that fiscal authority was obliged to endow the guilty party's daughters, using the confiscated estate, even in lèse-majesté cases[40]. Furthermore, confiscation expressed an irrational hate, it punished someone for a crime committed by someone else[41], and by doing so, it violated a rule of the law. And, of course, it was also for this reason that jurists suggested a restrictive interpretation.

According to some authors, the best remedy for confiscation was to avoid it, so they provided a number of steps to follow, just in case.

Among obvious suggestions, such as not to commit crimes punishable with confiscation, there were more technical pieces of advice. For instance, jurists suggested disinheriting the son who committed a crime, by expressly adding a very important clause to the act of disinheritance, saying that there was no intention to defraud the fiscal authority, instead the only aim was to keep the properties within the family. Another suggestion to avoid confiscation was to establish a *Fideicommissum*[42].

40 Bossi, *Tractatus varii*, *op. cit.*, n. 13, f. 281r.; Claro, *Volumen alias liber quintus*, *op. cit.*, § *Laesae maiestatis*, par. *Hae autem poenae*; Farinacci, *Praxis et theoricae criminalis*, *op. cit.*, p. I, tit. I, q. 24, n. 47; Pellegrini Marcantonio, *De iuribus et privilegiis fisci libri septem*, Coloniae Agrippinae, Apud Ioannem Gymnicum, 1588, V, tit. I, n. 53; Garoni Angelo Stefano, *Commentaria in tit. de Iure et privil. Fisci*, Mediolani, 1629, *Resolutionum fiscalium decas prima*, cap. 7, p. 180 s. See Massetto Gian Paolo, "I reati nell'opera di Giulio Claro", in Id., *Saggi di storia del diritto penale lombardo (Secc. XVI–XVIII)*, Milano, Led, 1994, pp. 184–185.

41 Claro, *Volumen alias liber quintus*, *op. cit.*, § *Laesae maiestatis*, par. *Hae autem poenae*; Farinacci, *Praxis et theoricae criminalis*, *op. cit*, p. I, tit. I, q. 24, n. 47.

42 Guazzini, *Tractatus de confiscatione honorum*, *op.cit.*, c. XXVII, p. 277ss.

Properties and Confiscation

Regarding the estate to be confiscated, the general rule was that everything which is destined for the heir, should go to the fiscal authority. This was a principle of medieval legal doctrine, which 16th and 17th century jurists considered as an *opinio Bartoli*[43]. On the other hand, however, if persons other than the heir had previous interests in a part of the estate, that part could not be confiscated[44]. So, normally, neither feudal possessions, nor *bona emphyteutica*, nor inalienable properties, e.g. because of a specific prohibition, could be confiscated (as *Fideicommissa*)[45].

Feudal law had its own rules concerning confiscation of feudal possessions and so the jurists distinguished. An ancient feud *ex pacto et providentia* could never be confiscated, as the vassal could not dispose of it without permission of the lord and agnates' consent. On the contrary, a new feud transferable, by the lord's consent, could be confiscated: it had to be given back to the lord himself, thereby unifying *dominium utile* and *directum*. Moreover, if the feud was freely transferrable, it could be confiscated: it passed either to the lord, or to the fiscal authority, depending on the crime committed[46]. This was the theory, but the reality was even more complicated[47].

43 Bartolo da Sassoferrato, *Commentaria super prima Digesti novi*, Roma, Il Cigno Galileo Galilei, 1996, ad D 40, 5, 12, l. *Imperator*, f. 79r.: "Res quod est prohibita non potest devenire ad fiscum propter publicationem".

44 Giason del Maino, *In secundam infortiati*, Augustae Taurinorum, Apud Nicolaum Bevilaquam, 1573, ad D 30, 1, 114, 14 (D 30, 1, 117), secunda lectura, *Filius familias*, par. *Divi*, n. 19; Claro, *Volumen alias liber quintus*, *op. cit.*, § *Finalis*, q. 78, par. *Nunc videamus*; Voet, *Commentarius ad Pandectas*, *op. cit.*, t. II, lib. 48, tit. XX, n. 3, p. 1105.

45 Pertile, *Storia del diritto italiano*, *op. cit.*, p. 233 s.; Calisse, "Svolgimento storico del diritto penale in Italia", art. cit., p. 377 f. See also *Constitutio Criminalis Theresiana* [1768], Graz, Akademische Druck- u. Verlagsanstalt, 1993, art. 9, p. 17: *Fideicommissa* and feudal properties were not confiscated, except in lèse-majesté cases.

46 Claro, *Volumen alias liber quintus*, *op. cit.*, § *Feudum*, q. 84; Farinacci, *Praxis et theoricae criminalis*, *op. cit*, p. I, tit. I, q. 25, n. 62 f.; Pellegrini, *De iuribus et privilegiis fisci libri septem*, *op. cit.*, V, tit. I, n. 69 s.; Matthes, *De criminibus ad lib. XLVII et XLVIII*, *op. cit.*, lib. 48, tit. 20, cap. IV, n. 22, p. 898.

47 Decio Filippo, *Consilia sive responsa*, Venetiis, 1570, cons. 252, n. 5, f. 273r.

In general, as Modern Age property law recognized different kinds of ownerships, i.e. a divided ownership of land[48], jurists said that only the *dominium utile*, i.e. the vassal's interest, could be confiscated[49].

The same applied for *emphyteusis*: only the *dominium utile* could be confiscated *ex delicto*[50]. In the case of a clergyman's estate, doctrine argued about its destination[51], since the ecclesiastical property system was also very complicated[52].

What happened to *Fideicommissa*? Andrea Alciato, who was also a lawyer, explained two contrary solutions, both in force in his times. In counselling, he had had recourse to both of them: the first, *communis opinion*, said that a *Fideicommissum* could be confiscated[53]; the second opinion said it could not. The latter was more common in practice[54]: Alessandro Tartagni had based one of his legal opinions on it, saying it had been taught by Bartolus[55].

The practice of the law emerging from the *consilia* was very dynamic: in counselling, doctrine made continuous efforts to safeguard the heirs' rights by always choosing the most suitable jurist's opinion from the past centuries.

48 Grossi Paolo, *Il dominio e le cose. Percezioni medievali e moderne dei diritti reali*, Milano, Giuffrè, 1992. See also Faron Olivier, Hubert Étienne (sous la dir. de), *Le sol et l'immeuble. Les formes dissociées de propriété immobilière dans les villes de France et d'Italie (XIIe–XIXe siècle)*, Rome, Ecole Française de Rome, 1993; Barbot Michela, *Le architetture della vita quotidiana: pratiche abitative e scambi immobiliari nella Milano d'eta moderna*, Venezia, Marsilio, 2008.

49 Tartagni, *Commentaria in I et II digesti novi, op. cit.*, ad D 39, 2, 15, 26, *Si de vectigalibus*, n. 33.

50 *Ibidem*, n. 34–36; Pape, *Decisiones, op. cit.*, q. 438, par. *Circa hoc quaero*, p. 405; Matthes, *De criminibus ad lib. XLVII et XLVIII, op. cit.*, lib. 48, tit. 20, cap. IV, n. 10, pp. 772–773.

51 Oldrado, *Consilia, op. cit.*, cons. XVII, n. 1–2, f. 7v.; Farinacci, *Praxis et theoricae criminalis, op. cit.*, p. I, tit. I, q. 25, n. 50 f.

52 Chittolini Giorgio, "Un problema aperto: la crisi della proprietà ecclesiastica fra Quattrocento e Cinquecento", in *Rivista storica italiana,* (1973), pp. 353–393.

53 Alciato Andrea, *Responsa*, Lugduni, Petrus Fradin excudebat, 1561, resp. 783, f. 467r.–v.: the author said he usually followed this first opinion. See also Oldrado, *Consilia, op. cit.*, cons. XVII.

54 Alciato, *Responsa, op. cit.*, resp. 650, n. 1, f. 429v. See Ruini Carlo, *Responsorum, siue consiliorum tomus quintus*, Venetiis, apud Nicolaum Bevilaquam et socios, 1571, cons. 24, n. 12, f. 30v.; Socini Bartolomeo, *Quarta pars consiliorum*, Lugduni, Compagnie des libraires de Lyon, 1551, cons. 121, n. 1, ff. 161r.–v.; Farinacci, *Praxis et theoricae criminalis, op. cit.*, p. I, tit. I, q. 25, n. 22.

55 Tartagni Alessandro, *Consiliorum … liber primus*, Venetiis, ex officina Iac. Antonii Somaschi, 1597, cons. 23, ff. 33r.–34r.

As a general rule, to guarantee the rights of the other people involved, confiscation was excluded in case of expressed *Fideicommissum*, e.g. when a typical clause in a Will stating *quia volo, quod bona perpetuo conserventur in agnatione, vel familia* prohibited acts of disposition of the estate[56].

On the contrary, if *Fideicommissum* or Substitution only referred to the death of an heir, in theory the fiscal authority might have confiscated the usufruct during the guilty party's life[57]. In practice, it often happened, and even in case of expressed *Fideicommissum*[58]. Fiscal authority could also subtract *trebellianica* and *legitima* from *Fideicommissum, ex persona condemnati*[59].

Local laws sometimes introduced new rules: in 1578, a Venitien statute law for the Mainland regions, derogating from common law, established that *Fideicommissa* could be confiscated[60]. From that moment, clauses excluding people who committed a crime punishable with confiscation from *Fideicommissum* started appearing in Wills[61].

These were called "penal clauses". Jurists did not think that these clauses were written trying to defraud the fiscal authority[62]: they simply considered that *prohibitio alienandi* and *voluntas testatoris* should prevail[63].

56 Alciato, *Responsa, op. cit.*, resp. 650, n. 2, ff. 429v.–430r.; Claro, *Volumen alias liber quintus, op. cit.*, § *Finalis*, q. 78, par. *Item quaero*; Pellegrini, *De iuribus et privilegiis fisci libri septem, op. cit.*,V, tit. I, n. 98 f.

57 Farinacci, *Praxis et theoricae criminalis, op. cit.*, p. I, tit. I, q. 25, n. 35 f.

58 The Senate of Savoy decided that the properties could be confiscated, but they had to be given back to the next heir, after the guilty party's death: Godefroy Denis, *Theorica criminalis*, Ultrajecti, Apud Wilhelmum Strick, 1646, n. 66–67, pp. 282–283.

59 Farinacci, *Praxis et theoricae criminalis,op. cit*, p. I, tit. I, q. 25, n. 45 f.

60 Priori Lorenzo, *Pratica criminale*, in Venetia, appresso Giacomo Zattoni, 1678, p. 63 f.

61 Povolo Claudio, *L'Intrigo dell'Onore. Poteri e istituzioni nella Repubblica di Venezia tra Cinque e Seicento*, Verona, Cierre, 1997, pp. 154–155, 242–243. On Lombard practice, Zorzoli Maria Carla, "Della famiglia e del suo patrimonio: riflessioni sull'uso del fedecommesso in Lombardia tra Cinque e Seicento", in Bonfield L. (ed.), *Marriage, Property and Succession*, Berlin, Duncker & Humblot, 1992, pp. 175–176; Maifreda, "Sant'Uffizio, confische e stime nel Cinquecento milanese", art. cit., p. 783.

62 De Luca Giovanni Battista, *Il dottor volgare ovvero il compendio di tutta la legge civile, canonica, feudale e municipale*, vol. IV, Firenze, coi tipi di V. Batelli e c., 1843, lib. X, cap. IX, n. 8–9. See also Longo Alfonso, "Osservazioni su i fedecommessi", in Francioni Gianni, Romagnoli Sergio (a cura di), *'Il Caffè' 1764–1766*, Torino, Bollati Boringhieri, 1993, pp. 125–126.

63 Farinacci, *Praxis et theoricae criminalis, op. cit.*, p. I, tit. I, q. 25, n. 23 s.: however, a Bull of Sisto V against bandits and lawless men stated that also *Fideicommissa* could be confiscated,

Qui confisque le corps, confisque les biens[64]

Following medieval local laws, Modern Age royal legislations often derogated from common law on confiscation. Therefore, jurists analysed the different provisions, by paying attention to the criteria for the implementation of this punishment.

In France, confiscation of property was a crown right and could be, by king's concession, a *droit de la haute-justice*. It was the punishment for the cruelest of crimes. It was used in different ways and especially in the regions of the customary law[65]. It was inflicted together with capital punishment and civil death (which followed as a consequence of condemnation to perpetual galley service, perpetual banishment, etc.). Moreover, confiscation was inflicted together with the damnation of the memory of the guilty party (for the crimes of divine and human lèse-majesté, duelling, homicide, etc.) or it followed a judgement by default[66].

Across the French Kingdom, there were also different rules regarding properties to be confiscated. An interesting example was the case law of the Parliament of Toulouse. This supreme court used confiscation – and it did so in a region of the written law – but, according to one of its *usages*, a third of the guilty party's properties, free of burdens, was destined to the widow and the

during the delinquent's life, in spite of any clause. See Padoa Schioppa Antonio, "Sul fedecommesso nella Lombardia teresiana", in De Maddalena Aldo, Rotelli Ettore, Barbarisi Gennaro (a cura di), *Economia, istituzioni, cultura in Lombardia nell'età di Maria Teresa*, Volume III, *Istituzioni e società*, Bologna, Il Mulino, 1982, III, pp. 819–821.

64 Loisel Antoine, *Institutes coustumières*, Paris, Chez Henry Le Gras, 1646, l. VI, tit. II, XIX, p. 152.

65 As an exception, in 1558 the Parliament of Rouen, *en robes rouges*, declared *abrogée par non usance* the custom which excluded the guilty parties' children from inheritance: Filhol R., Brunet M., "Autour de l'arrêt du "sang damné": l'abrogation de la coutume normande d'exclusion successorale des enfants des condamnés", in *Droit privé et institutions régionales: études historiques offertes à Jean Yver*, Paris, PUF, 1976, pp. 209–241.

66 *Ordonnance criminelle, St Germain en Laye, août 1670*, tit. XVII, art. 31–32. See de Ferrière Claude Joseph, *Dictionnaire de droit et de pratique*, Paris, Chez la Veuve Brunet, 1769, t. I, *Confiscation*, pp. 337–342; Soulatges Jean Antoine, *Traité des crimes*, t. III, Toulouse, Chez Antoine Birosse, 1762, p. 145 f.; Jousse Daniel, *Traité de la justice criminelle de France*, chez Debure Père, Paris, 1771, t. I, pp. 99–113.

children. This rule did not apply in case of lèse-majesté, when the children were also banned[67].

Generally, the Lord administrating high justice could do whatever he wanted with the confiscated properties. He only had to seize them within twenty years from the *arrêt* confirming the sentence. The King, instead, had to "rid himself of it"; he could not prejudice his feudal vassals. Therefore, he used to donate the confiscated properties, sometimes to the guilty party's children[68].

Moreover, in 1704, an *arrêt* rendered by the Parliament of Paris decided that the Lord should confiscate the estate as it was at the time of the verdict: in that specific case, the verdict of paying damages and interests to the plaintiff or victim was imposed on the estate[69]. This rule seemed to have been recognized in Modern Age France: compensation for damages claimed by the victim (or by the victim's children and heirs), as well as refund of trial costs had to prevail over confiscation[70].

Regarding the German States, the criminal law text of 1532, the *Constitutio criminalis Carolina*, tried to reorganise the use of confiscation in the imperial lands.

Confiscation was confirmed for a guilty man who confessed to a crime punishable with confiscation and then committed suicide fearing the punishment. In this case, confiscated properties had to go to the Lord holding jurisdictional rights (art. 135). Confiscation was abolished for the party accused of a crime who had failed to appear and answer to the charge: instead, an inventory of his properties and assets was mandatory and the judge administrated them in favour of his wife and children (art. 206); even when capital punishment was inflicted confiscation was generally forbidden, except in lèse-majesté cases (art. 218)[71].

67 Soulatges, *Traité des crimes*, *op. cit.*, pp. 157–159. See Carbasse Jean Marie, "Droit romain et droit royal: à propos du droit de confiscation à Millau à la fin du Moyen Age", in Hoareau-Dodinau Jacqueline et Texier Pascal (sous la dir. de), *Anthropologies juridiques: mélanges Pierre Braun*, Limoges, Pulim, 1998, pp. 115–134.

68 Soulatges, *Traité des crimes*, *op. cit.*, p. 170.

69 du Rousseaud de La Combe Guy, *Traité des matières criminelles*, Paris, Chez Theodore Le Gras, 1744, p. 10.

70 Claro, *Volumen alias liber quintus*, *op. cit.*, § *Finalis*, q. 78, par. *Vidi*; Jousse, *Traité*, *op. cit.*, t. I, p. I, tit. III, par. 11, n. 204, p. 109.

71 Ludovici Jakob Friedrich, *Caroli Quinti Romanorum Imperatoris Invictissimi Constitutiones criminales: vulgo Peinliche Halsgerichtsordnung … accessit Mater Carolinae, Ordinatio criminalis Bambergensis*, Halae Magdeburgicae, Apud Jo. Godofredum Rengerum, 1716.

Carpzov, one of the most prominent German authors, said that, following these rules, in imperial lands confiscation was no longer in use. Only in lèse-majesté cases did the fiscal authority take the guilty party's properties and only after paying the estate's debts. More specifically, in Saxony Electorate, a guilty party sentenced to death could even make his Will, which was not possible according to Roman law. It was, however, allowed by a general custom, in force almost everywhere[72].

Another example from the Iberian Peninsula was the *Leyes de Toro* of Castile, which, in 1505, authorised the guilty party sentenced to death to make his Will and to decide what to do with his properties, except with those which were confiscated (*ley* IV *de Toro*). Professor Antonio Gomez from Salamanca University said that this rule derogated from the common law of *Partidas*, which said that a man sentenced to natural or civil death was no longer a free man and was therefore unqualified to make his Will.

What meaning did a guilty man sentenced to confiscation being able to make his Will have? It meant that even if all of his *hacienda* was confiscated, he could still make his Will for other purposes, such as naming a tutor for his children. Moreover, he could establish a *mayorazgo*. He could do so with properties acquired after the verdict, which had not been confiscated. According to Gomez, following the royal laws, not only could a man sentenced to death inherit properties, but he was also free to negotiate contracts[73].

Turning our attention to the Italian Peninsula, and specifically to the Milan Duchy, we can see that the laws edited in 1541 inflicted confiscation for a very large number of crimes (lèse-majesté, poisoning, homicide, murder, rape, robbery, arson, forgery, duelling, etc.). But even in lèse-majesté

72 Carpzov Benedict, *Practica nova*, Wittebergae, Sumptibus haeredum D. Tobiae Mevii, 1652, pars III, q. 135 e pars I, q. 41, n. 99 s. See also Saur Abraham, *Fasciculus de poenis, vulgo, Straffbuch*, Franckfort am Mayn, Durch Nicolaum Bassaeum, 1596, pp. 506–507; von Böhmer Johann Samuel Friedrich, *Meditationes in Constitutionem criminalem Carolinam*, Goldbach, Keip, 1996, *passim*.

73 Gomez Antonio, *Ad Leges Tauri commentarium absolutissimum*, Matriti, Typis D. Gabrielis Ramirez, 1768, pp. 56–61; Nolasco de Llano Pedro, *Compendio de los Comentarios extendidos por el maestro Antonio Gomez, a las ochenta y tres Leyes de Toro*, Madrid, En la imprenta y libreria de D. Manuel Martin, 1777, pp. 36–38. See also Diaz de Luco Juan Bernardo, *Regularum iuris liber unus*, Lugduni, Apud Iacobum de Millis, 1550, reg. 165, p. 95 f.

cases, creditors' rights were safe, as well as those of the ascendants and descendants[74].

Here, it was the magistrate charged with the execution of all the judgements who proceeded to confiscation: an inventory of the estate was made, the properties were seized *a die commissi criminis*[75] and then proclamations were made[76]. This meant that the properties were to be sold through a public procedure. Town criers informed the people of it, following ancient rules[77]: anyone who had interests in the estate had to present themselves and the debtors of the estate had to pay their debts to the fiscal authority[78].

In the Milan Duchy, the rule was, and had been from the 14th century, that all the properties were first confiscated and only after the forfeiture could the children and wives of the guilty party, as well as the creditors of the estate claim their rights[79]. Frequently, there were judicial fights between the fiscal authority and these other parties pleading for their interests on the properties under confiscation[80].

74 *Constitutiones mediolanensis Dominii*, Mediolani, ex typ. J. Marelli, 1764, lib. IV, tit. *de crimine laesae maiestatis*, pp. 243–244; tit. *de iure et privilegio fisci*, pp. 293–295; Carpani Orazio, *In capitulum omnium Nov. Const. Tit. de Iure et privilegio fisci commentarii*, Mediolani, apud Iacobum Mariam Metium, 1583.

75 Maifreda, "Sant'Uffizio, confische e stime nel Cinquecento milanese", art. cit., pp. 801–803.

76 Cavallini Giovanni Battista, *Actuarium practicae criminalis*, Mediolani, apud heredes Matthei Besutij, 1587, p. 53 f.; Alciato, *Responsa*, *op. cit.*, resp. 522, f. 358r.

77 A decree issued by Filippo Maria Visconti, on april 29, 1444, reformed previous rules dating back to 1387: *Antiqua Ducum Mediolani decreta*, Mediolani, apud fratres Malatestas, 1654, *ad vocem*. All these laws were collected and ordered in the *Constitutiones mediolanensis Dominii*, *op. cit.*, lib. II, tit. *de bonis ad cridas ponendis*, p. 154 f. See Garoni, Commentaria in tit. de Iure et privil. Fisci art. 14 s., *op. cit.*, p. 61 f. On this procedure, Monti Annamaria, "Observations sur les transferts des droits de propriété: la perspective des juristes lombards à l'âge moderne", in *Histoire comparée des villes européennes*, Eauh 2008, Lyon, 2009, M01, *Around the property*.

78 Many acts relating to procedures of forfeiture are kept in Archivio di Stato, Milano, Finanze, Confische: Maifreda, "Sant'Uffizio, confische e stime nel Cinquecento milanese", art. cit.; Salvi Stefania, "La confisca nella prassi lombarda del tardo antico regime", in *Rivista di Storia del diritto italiano*, LXXXIII (2010), p. 205 f.

79 Often, the Senate of Milan issued *dispensations* to the parties involved in those procedures in front of the *Magistrato dei redditi straordinari*: Biblioteca Ambrosiana, Milano, ms. I 90 s.ss., ff. 88r.–v., 98v., edited in Monti Annamaria, *I formulari del Senato di Milano (secoli XVI–XVIII)*, Milano, Giuffrè, 2001, p. 354 and 365.

80 Claro, *Volumen alias liber quintus*, *op. cit.*, § *Finalis*, q. 78, par. *Quaeri*. See Maifreda, "Sant'Uffizio, confische e stime nel Cinquecento milanese", art. cit., p. 783 f.

Towards Abolition of Confiscation?

The first Codes, at the end of the 18th century, made an effort to simplify the penal law system. New principles came to the fore: the punishments had to impact only the party responsible for the criminal offence and they had to be proportionate to the crimes[81]. In the meantime, European society was going through a deep change, because the idea of different rules for each single social order was gradually abandoned, as well as the privileges granted to specific classes or corporations. This path led to the recognition of the equality of rights under the law, which was the real novelty of the modern European Codes[82], issued from enlightened absolutism, or from liberal revolutionary impetus[83].

Concerning legal doctrine, the 18th century novelty was that authors started to debate confiscation. By abandoning the typical attitude of accepting confiscation as part of the legal system, they started to question its legitimacy (instead of simply thinking of its limitations, as had been done until then).

In 1778, in his *Plan de législation criminelle* sent to a Swiss Society[84], Jean Paul Marat suggested that the fact that some penalties such as monetary sanctions and confiscations also impacted the guilty party's family members was an atrocity. However, he would not hear of abolishing them. In his opinion, what should have been done was prevention of abuse and the direction of the revenues to humanitarian aims[85].

Even Gaetano Filangieri wrote in favour of confiscation, as if it were just and useful, provided that abuse was prevented[86]. On the contrary, Beccaria

81 Alessandri Alberto, "Art. 27 I comma", in *Rapporti civili, art. 27–28, Commentario della Costituzione fondato da G. Branca*, Bologna, Zanichelli – Roma, Società editrice del foro italiano, 1991, p. 66 f.

82 Tarello Giovanni, *Storia della cultura giuridica moderna. Assolutismo e codificazione del diritto*, Bologna, Il Mulino, 1976, p. 28 f.

83 Cavanna Adriano, *La codificazione penale in Italia: le origini lombarde*, Milano, Giuffrè, 1975.

84 Marat Jean Paul, *Plan de législation criminelle*, Paris, Chez Rochette, 1790, *Notice de l'éditeur*, p. 5. See Cavanna, *La codificazione penale in Italia*, *op. cit.*, p. 43.

85 *Ibid.*, pp. 36–38.

86 Filangieri Gaetano, *La Scienza della Legislazione*, Napoli, Grimaldi & C., 2003, lib. III, capo XLVI, pp. 244–245. According to Burlamaqui Jean Jacques, *Principii del diritto politico*, In Venezia, presso Pietro q. Gio. Battista Pasquali, 1797, III, c. 4, 42, p. 201, confiscation was not unfair and its consequences were an inconvenience tied to human matters.

(previously mentioned) was against confiscation: as criminal liability was personal, punishments should have impacted the guilty party only. Family members hit by confiscation were ruined and they, in turn, could have been forced to commit crimes to survive[87].

Late 18th century reforms carried out by the Austrian sovereigns did not recognise confiscation as a rationally useful punishment and not only for humanitarian or ethic problems[88]. So, while the Tuscan Criminal Reform of 1786, the *Leopoldina*, abolished confiscation[89], the Joseph II Penal Code of 1787 inflicted it only in lèse-majesté cases[90].

In France, the confiscation of the estate was abolished in 1790; the Penal Code of 1791 did not recognise it, but it was reintroduced in 1793 and, then, by the Napoleon Penal Code of 1810. It was definitively abolished by the Constitution of 1814[91].

When the French National Assembly abolished confiscation, Pastoret, who shared Enlightenment ideas, said that he did not agree with Filangieri's opinion, but he thought that the respect owed to children and property should not have led to forgetting the respect also owed to citizens suffering from a crime. That is why he was not against confiscation of part of the properties, destined to refund innocent victims of judicial errors, as it could have been put to good public use. Furthermore, he said that confiscation was necessary to punish certain fiscal crimes, such as extortions where properties were acquired at the expense of the State: was it not immoral and impolitic to let the children enjoy the revenues of the father's crime, when the father was condemned for committing similar offences?[92].

87 Beccaria, *Dei delitti e delle pene*, *op. cit.*, par. XXV, pp. 79–80.

88 Alessandri, "Art. 27 I comma", art. cit., p. 67.

89 Zuliani Dario, *La riforma penale di Pietro Leopoldo*, Milano, Giuffrè, 1995, vol. 2, art. XLV.

90 *Codice generale sopra i delitti e le pene*, [S.l.: s.n.], 1787, par. 16, 42, 46, 53.

91 Schnapper Bernard, "Les systèmes répressifs français de 1789 à 1815", in Rousseaux Xavier, Dupont-Bouchat Marie-Sylvie, Vael Claude (sous la dir. de), *Révolutions et justice pénale en Europe: modèles français et traditions nationales, 1780–1830*, Paris, L'Harmattan, 1999, p. 22 s. See also Monti Annamaria, "La confiscation des biens dans les codes pénaux européens, XIXe–XXe s." in *Le Code pénal (1810–2010): les métamorphoses d'un modèle*, Actes du Colloque de Lille – Gand, 16–18 décembre 2010, forthcoming.

92 de Pastoret Claude Emmanuel Joseph Pierre, *De loix pénales*, Tome I, Paris, Chez Buisson, 1790, pp. 145–147.

Late 18th and early 19th century Penal Codes reflected the doctrinal hesitations on the legitimacy of confiscation. This was a complex punishment: it was connected to property rights and to being part of a society; it affected inheritance rights of children and spouses, as well as fiscal interests. Not uncommonly, legislators thought that they could not abandon confiscation, in spite of all the declarations of principle against it.

In fact, confiscation of the estate seemed to never completely disappear. It has been outlined that it would return, when liberal political systems were in crisis: for example, this was the Italian experience under Fascism. Instead, in war times, no matter what the political system was, it was largely used against traitors and deserters. In recent Italian history, we can mention the "symbolic" confiscation of properties belonging to fascists, in 1944–1946[93].

All of this has been stated apart from the current use of another type of confiscation, not to be confused with the confiscation of the estate, i.e. the confiscation of specific property. Specific property refers to properties connected to the execution of a crime[94], being the instrument, the product or the profit of the crime itself. Nowadays, confiscation of specific property is mainly used to fight criminal organisations and economic crime[95].

93 Vassalli Giuliano, *La confisca dei beni. Storia recente e profili dommatici*, Padova, Cedam, 1951; Foligno Dario Agostino, *Confisca dei beni e avocazione dei profitti di regime nella legislazione sulle sanzioni contro il fascismo*, Milano, Giuffrè, 1945.

94 Claro *Volumen alias liber quintus*, *op. cit.*, § *Finalis*, q. 79; Cavallini *Actuarium practicae criminalis*, *op. cit.*, p. 54.

95 *Civil forfeiture of criminal property. Legal measures for Targeting the Proceeds of Crime*, edited by Simon N.M. Young, Cheltenham UK – Northampton MA, Edward Elgar, 2009. Italian Penal Code of 1930 recognizes confiscation of specific property as a safety measure: Alessandri, "Art. 27 I comma", art. cit., p. 134 f.; Alessandri, "Confisca nel diritto penale", art. cit., p. 43 f. On the history of this rule, Civoli, "Confisca (Diritto penale)", art. cit., p. 899 f.

The "Negotiations for the Palazzo that Belonged to the Deceased Tomaso Marino".

Palazzo Marino and its Real Estate Evaluations and Use from the Sixteenth to the Eighteenth Centuries

Marica Forni

Between the sixteenth and the eighteenth centuries, the fortunes of Palazzo Marino in Milan[1] were determined in large part by the private and public juridical status of its owners and by the asynchronous oscillation between the various kinds of uses to which the building was put. The period was punctuated by two confiscations, in 1577 and 1706, that sanctioned violations committed by the respective contemporary owners of the palazzo, namely the banker Tommaso Marino, Duke of Terranova[2] (1475–1572) and then Carlo Homodei, Marquis of Castelrodrigo[3] (1655–ca. 1725).

1 Fundamental for subsequent study is the review of bibliographical and archival sources published by Casati Carlo, "Nuove notizie intorno a Tomaso De Marini tratte da documenti inediti", in *Archivio Storico Lombardo*, (1886), pp. 584–680, amplified and integrated by Baroni Costantino, *Documenti per la storia dell'architettura italiana*, Roma, Accademia dei Lincei, 1968, vol. II, pp. 398–418. These sources were used for the only monograph dedicated to this building by Bologna Giulia, *Palazzo Marino in Milano*, Milano, Comune di Milano, 1999. On the figure of Galeazzo Alessi, see Scotti Aurora, "I disegni alessiani nelle collezioni milanesi", in *Galeazzo Alessi e l'architettura del Cinquecento*, Genova, Sagep, 1975, pp. 470–473; Ead., "Per un profilo dell'architettura milanese (1535–1565)", in *Omaggio a Tiziano. La cultura artistica milanese nell'età di Carlo V*, Milano, Electa, 1977 (catalogo della mostra Milano, Palazzo Reale, 27 aprile–20 luglio 1977), pp. 103–105, 114–116; Houghton Brown N. A., *The Milanese Architecture of Galeazzo Alessi*, New York, Columbia University, 1978, pp. 202–254. I would like to take this opportunity to thank Starleen K. Meyer for her competent and acute English translation of my original Italian text, including the document citations. The citations in the original language are reproduced in the footnotes; in the case of multiple excerpts pertaining to a single footnote, the original citations are reproduced in the order in which they appear in the text.

2 For the political and institutional context of the credit activity of the banker, an indispensable source is Chabod Federico, *Storia di Milano nell'epoca di Carlo V*, Torino, Einaudi, 1971, passim.

This singular web of circumstances demanded a series of estimates of the structure, which were entrusted to government engineers (Ingegneri Camerali). These engineers worked in the government's technical bureaucracy and benefited from an accumulation of wide-ranging competences focused on the management and maintenance of public buildings. From the end of the sixteenth century, with only rare exceptions, their professional formation followed the course imposed in 1563 by the University of Engineers, Architects and Land Surveyors of Milan (Collogio degli Ingegneri, Architetti e Agrimensori di Milano), hereafter referred to as the College. This institution, structured on a guild-like matrix, controlled access to these professions, and adopted rigid mechanisms of co-option expressed as norms deduced from those in use by the Noble Colleges (Collegi Nobili), including the frequent dispensations that permitted circumvention of the norms.

With the goal of ascertaining the value of the structure and measuring the revenue it generated, technicians analysed the quantity and quality of the components characterizing the building in its technical and constructional aspects, in terms of its functional efficiency and its consequent suitability for various uses, including those uses originally planned, those trialled and implemented, and others which were only occasionally employed. The documentation of these technicians' work on the Palazzo Marino reveals a great deal about how they operated and about how they acquired and transferred knowledge. They constantly updated both their practical and theoretical know-how and skills through reference to the manuals that, from the middle of the sixteenth century, laid out the procedures and methodology to be employed in evaluating major buildings. Significant to this end was the work of the jurisconsult from Modena, Nicola Festasio[4], who opened a cycle of theoretical and practical

3 For information on the role of the family in Milanese society, see Signorotto Gianvittorio, *Milano spagnola. Guerra istituzioni, uomini di governo (1635–1660)*, Milano, Sansoni Editore, 1996, passim. Regarding the sale of the feud of Piovera to the Balbi, see Grendi Edoardo, *I Balbi. Una famiglia fra Spagna e Impero*, Torino, Einaudi, 1997, passim.

4 Nicolaus Festasio, *Tractatus de aestimo, et collectis*, Mutina, Paulum Gadaldium et Fratres, 1569, followed by the editions of Venice in 1571 and 1584. See also Gabba Alberto, *L'opera di stima nella formazione e nel rinnovo della città in età moderna*, Pavia, Tipografia del Libro, 1984, p. 15, and especially Id., "Un antico trattato di estimo nella Biblioteca Universitaria di Pavia", in *Bollettino della Società Pavese di Storia Patria*, CIV (2004) pp. 265–274. I would like to express my most heartfelt thanks to Prof. Alberto Gabba, with his vast competence

reflection about making evaluations. Another equally important contribution was that of the Milanese, Giulio Cesare Glusiano, in 1616[5].

The copious series of estimates, controls and official reports about the maintenance work and the reconstruction of the mansion – all paid for in order to accommodate the needs of the different uses of the building, which were sometimes difficult to reconcile with the structure's original uses – constitutes a fundamental reference point for understanding the actions that modified the value of the building and provides the basis of the interpretation put forward here. A full discussion of the issues raised by this source and other unpublished sources is beyond the scope of this paper but it is still possible to shed new light on one of the icons of the history of Milanese restoration. The vicissitudes of the nineteenth century conferred this role on Palazzo Marino. After having served as the seat of the provisional Lombard government in 1848, it was obtained by Milan's civic government in 1859 in exchange for the previous headquarters, the Broletto Nuovissimo, and used to house the city's administrative offices two years later. Restored in 1872 by Angelo Colla, then by Luca Beltrami, winner of the 1888 competition for the construction of the building's new façade (completed in 1892) on Piazza della Scala, it later was partially reconstructed and restored after the heavy damage inflicted by the bombing in 1943[6].

in this area, for his willingness to direct the in-depth research of these fundamental aspects, and to discuss their application to the case in question.

5 Iulio Caesare Glusiano, *Tractatus de precio et estimatione secundum ius civile*, Mediolani, Hyeronimum Bordonum, 1615.

6 For the Post-Unification period see Houghton Brown, *The Milanese Architecture*, *op. cit.*, pp. 236–243; Bologna, *Palazzo Marino in Milano*, *op. cit.*, pp. 72–92; in particular, on the works dedicated to Beltrami for his restoration work, see Bellini Amedeo, *La figura di Luca Beltrami nell'architettura lombarda del secondo Ottocento*, Milano, Civica Biblioteca d'Arte del Castello Sforzesco di Milano, 2000, pp. 4–5; regarding the war damage, see A. T. (Andrea Thum), "Palazzo Marino", in Marrucci Auletta Rosa, Negri Massimo, Rastelli Achille, Romanello Lucia (a cura di), *Bombe sulla città. Milano in guerra 1942–1944*, Milano, Skira, 2004, pp. 217–219.

"The value of said mansion is uncertain" The First Economic Evaluations of the Residence of Tommaso Marino

Four years after the death of Tommaso Marino, who had been condemned for insolvency, and in a city marked by famine and depopulation (the plague between August of 1576 and May of 1577 had reduced its population by one third), the bureaucratic machinery of the state again began to move to confiscate the patrimony that had been inherited in the meantime by his two daughters, Virginia De Leyva and Clara Tornielli. In the spring of 1576, the two sisters, "assailed by many, who pretended to be creditors of said inheritance of a significant amount of money", including the royal finance department (Regio Fisco), which claimed a credit of 20,000 scudi, agreed with the governor, the Marquis de Ayamonte, to put the family home up for sale. This was the only patrimony convertible into money since "nothing remained of the inheritance that hadn't been hocked". Both of the women had come to the conclusion that it was better "if not to get out most of what had been spent in that mansion, at least not to throw it away for nothing, as would happen, if left up to the creditors, who surely will come calling"[7].

The complete lack of bidders in the public auction having precluded *de facto* this possibility, on the 30th of October, 1577, the two heirs were condemned to the payment of the debt, and forced to cede the mansion to the government finance office for the price of 33,333 scudi, a sum that was equal, according to the norms of the New Constitutions (Nuove Costituzioni), to two-thirds of the estimated value of 50,000 scudi, as we will see[8].

Although the building was unfinished, Marino's home still represented the materialization of the fabled riches of its patron in the eyes of contemporaries, the symbol of his megalomaniac aspirations projected onto the weave of

7 The citations in this paragraph are taken from the petition (supplica) dated 17 May 1576 (Archivio di Stato Milano [afterwards ASMi], Fondi Camerali, 213): "travagliate da molti che pretendono essere creditori di detta heredità di rilevata quantità de denari"; "non essendo restata cosa alcuna spettante a detta heredità che non si è imbarazzata"; "cavar se non quanto principalmente si è speso in esso pallazzo, almeno non gettarlo via per niente come si saria, a discretione de creditori al sicuro seguito".

8 Fede di Cesare Croce Cancelliere del Magistrato (Archivio Ospedale Maggiore Milano, Archivio Litta Visconti Borromei, [afterwards: AOMMi, Litta], 412).

urban space. It followed the contours of his ambitious organizational plan – which had remained on paper – to connect the most important public places. With an act of hubris regarding the values of *civitas*, his immense fortunes were exhibited through reference, as only a few were able to understand, to the uncommon communicative force of the modern architectural language brought to Milan by Galeazzo Alessi (1512–1572). The choice of location in the parish of Santo Stefano in Nosigia in the institutional and commercial heart of the city, in addition to favoring the owner through highlighting his business as a creditor[9], also put this singular residence in close physical proximity to the new church of the Jesuits and the house of the sculptor, Leone Leoni. All three were manifestations of a search for modernity conducted through experimentation with different languages, and all were clearly not continuous with local tradition, if not in open contrast to it. The life style model and the distribution of spaces explain the firmly rooted – so as not to say "obvious" – ties with Genovese culture. It was not by chance that they were consistent with the kind of stylization that Peter Paul Rubens would employ for northern patrons: "It will be called by us *palazzo*, or private house, as grand and beautiful as is usual, that which will have the form of a solid cube with a salon in the middle, in other words, divided into contiguous rooms without an opening between them, as are most of the Genovese mansions"[10].

These fundamental critical facts, commonly accepted in the literature that has fixed the principle points of attribution and chronology of the mansion, are possible to trace in the few pieces making up the corpus of graphic works – which are not easy to interpret – related to this building, as well as in the fragmentary documentation. Nevertheless, a more ample foray into the large amount of notary-of-public records regarding the construction site might help in solving outstanding mysteries.

9 In the adjacent parishes of San Pietro Cornaredo, San Pietro all'Orto, San Paolo in Compito were to be found many residences of bankers, including Leonardo Spinola, first a partner then perhaps a rival of Marino; Dario Crivelli; Tommaso D'Adda; see D'Amico Stefano, *Le contrade e la città: sistema produttivo e spazio urbano a Milano fra Cinque e Seicento*, Milano, Franco Angeli, 1994, p. 73.

10 The citation is found in Poleggi Ennio, "I palazzi scelti da Rubens", in Id. (a cura di), *L'invenzione dei rolli. Genova città di palazzi*, Milano, Skira, p. 150, with bibliography: "Sarà detto da noi Palazzo o casa privata, pur grande e bella ch'ella si usa, quella che haverà la forma di un cubo solido col salone in mezzo, ò vero ripartito in appartamenti contigui senza luce fra mezzo, come sono la maggior parte tutti li palazzi genovesi".

Between the beginning of construction work in 1557 and the interruption of work after 1563[11] at the first rumors of the financial crisis that would befall the patron, the organization of the internal spaces and the decoration of the public rooms of the mansion were not realized in a way conducive to family life. In fact, when Tommaso died, he was living not in the semi-finished palazzo, but in a house near the mansion[12]. At that time, only two of the four façades of the mansion had been finished as planned in a sandstone conglomerate coming from the river Adda and fashioned in an exuberant apparatus of ornate decoration: the principal façade on Via Marino (*contrada*) and the contiguous one on the Piazza of San Fedele. The other two façades in tighter spaces – on the quarter of San Giovanni alle Case Rotte and in the narrow thoroughfare (*strecchione*) where most of the building's material remained in sight with areas in the rough ready for the continuation of work – remained unfinished (Figure 1).

Aside from the economic circumstances, from the very beginning these and other peculiarities made the work of evaluation and the decision on the eventual use of the building both complex and controversial. These difficulties

11 A contract for the supply of sandstone is dated 9 December 1562, but in 1568 Alessi's presence in Milan "for some services for Signor Tommaso" is noted; see Baroni, *Documenti per la storia dell'architettura italiana*, *op. cit.*, pp. 416–417.

12 See the unedited *post mortem* inventory that, among his goods, describes the mansion: "il pallazzo con le sue pertinentie posto nella città di Milano in porta Nova in parochia di Santo Fidele confina da tre bande la strada pubblica. Le ragioni et pretensioni della parte che se ha nella casa dove detto S.re habitava et stava al tempo della morte sua con tutti li miglioramenti fatti per detto S.re in detta casa la quale è posta discontro al soprascritto pallazzo diverso mezzo giorno mediante la strada pubblica la qual è posta in detta porta et parochia de Santo Fedele alla qual confina da settentrione detto pallazzo mediante strada da mezo giorno le suor di Santa Margherita da levante il S.r Ludovico Visconte da ponente il S.r Antonio Panzano" (The mansion with its appurtenances located in the city of Milan in Porta Nuova in the parish of San Fedele borders public streets on three sides. The reasons and pretensions of the part of the house in which the aforesaid sir lived and stayed at the time of his death with all the improvements made for the aforesaid sir in the aforementioned house, which is situated opposite the aforementioned mansion towards the south by way of the public street which is located in that quarter and in the parish of San Fedele to which the aforementioned mansion borders on the north by way of the street from the south the nuns of Santa Margherita, on the east Sir Ludovico Visconti, on the west Sir Antonio Panzano) Biblioteca Ambrosiana Milano [BAMi], Falcò Pio di Savoia, 197.

Figure 1. Drawing of the Palazzo Marino (End of the 16th Century)

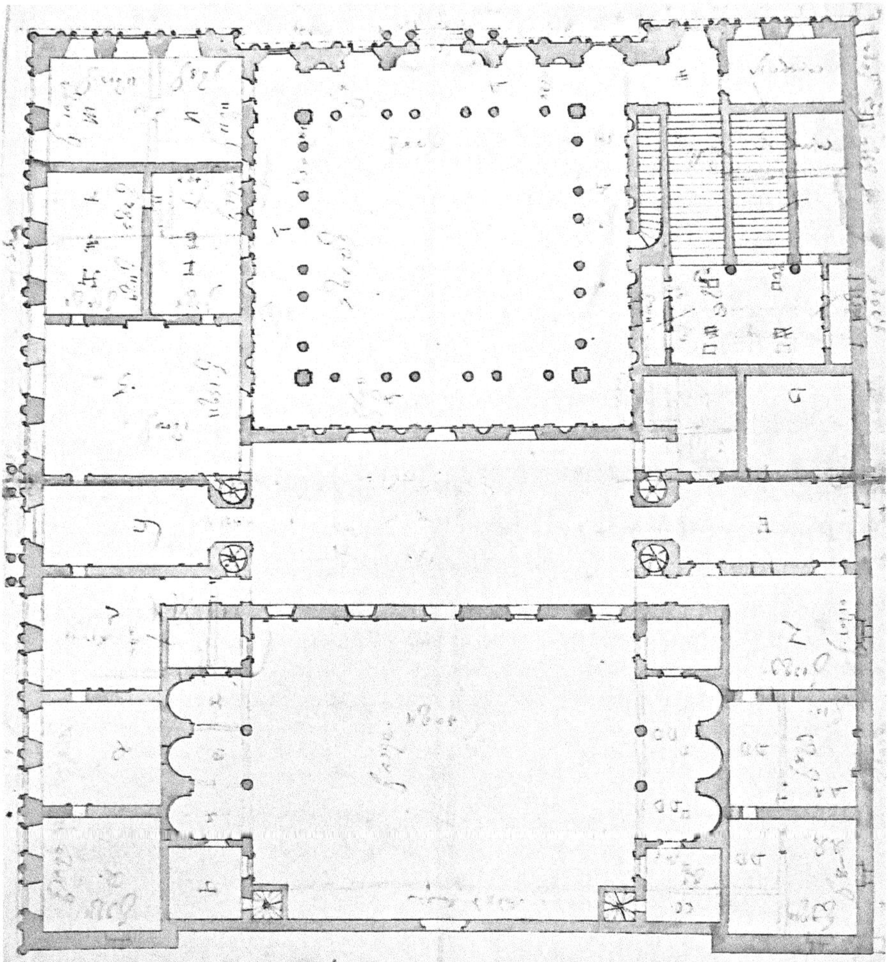

Source: Archivio Storico Civico Milano, Raccolta Bianconi, I-23, copyright © Comune di Milano – all rights reserved (ref. n. 124/13A/2012)

were explained by the government engineer, Giovan Battista Cairati[13] (Milan 1520/30 – Goa 1596) in the course of two estimates, which focus on some fundamental economic facts later used by all the technical consultants. The goal of the first estimate, consigned on July 27, 1576, was to determine the value of the building in light of the failed auction. The second, dated July 8, 1578, integrated the previous estimate, and proposed to define the rental fee[14]. His judgment, true to the canons of his discipline, is expressed with accuracy regarding the goal, while intending not to harm the interests of those involved, and, at the same time, to reach a fair price expressed in measured terms, giving proof of the stringent consequentiality contained in the then contemporary distinction between *Aestimo* and *Existimo*[15].

Cairati lingered over the intrinsic characteristics of the residence that would condition the subsequent ways of using it, and explained its defects, hinting at its foreignness to Milanese construction tradition and even more so to the lifestyle habits of the noble citizens with which other contemporary ambitious projects came to terms, adopted a middle way, or sought consonance[16]. Cairati's interpretation gathered, in fact, the double challenge launched to the *genius loci* by the will of the patron, which marked the destiny of the edifice.

> Palazzo Marino is a grand structure both for its height as well as for its ornament, a colossal work. Very flashy and highly visible, as Your Highness knows, but it has, however, few virtues, if usefulness is considered regarding the big shell, there are but a few rooms to enjoy because loggias, porticoes, hall-like salons, large stairways and other pomp occupy most of it, and leave little space in which to live, and this little is so inconvenient that one doesn't

13 See Viganò Marino, "Cairate Giovanni Battista", in Bossi Paolo, Langé Santino, Repishti Francesco (a cura di), *Ingegneri Ducali e Camerali nel Ducato e nello Stato di Milano (1450–1706)*, Firenze, Edifir, 2004, pp. 53–54.

14 The first appraisal was cited only by Casati, "Nuove notizie intorno a Tomaso De Marini", art. cit., p. 634, while the second has been cited at various, times beginning with Casati, "Nuove notizie intorno a Tomaso De Marini", *art. cit.*, p. 635. Both accompanied the report sent to the magistrate (Magistrato) by the quaestor (Questore) Alfonso Lopez Taboada, to which reference is made also in the subsequent citations. (ASMi, Finanza Apprensioni, 348, also available in AOMMi, Litta, 412-18).

15 For the accepted meanings of these two terms, see the thoughts of Gabba, "Un antico trattato", *art. cit.*, p. 267.

16 For a synthesis, see Della Torre Stefano, "Milano: le due città", in Conforti Claudia Tuttle Richard (a cura di), *Storia dell'architettura italiana. Il secondo Cinquecento*, Milano, Electa, 2001, pp. 375–378.

> know practically for what kind of person it might be adapted. For the prince, it is not big enough. For the knight, if his family is numerous, it will be difficult to house all of them and be served, and if the family members are few, they will get lost in lots of meandering nooks, so they will miss being notified[17].

If *venustas* and *utilitas* raise conditioned reservations, so, too, the *firmitas* seemed unexpected, and on this Vitruvian category was concentrated the attention of the Milanese engineer, who foresaw the need not only to finish the building, but also to remedy the most severe manifestations of ruin – consequences of inopportune choices – in a timely manner:

> The building, as much as it might be new, deteriorates nevertheless, because left unfinished and that which was finished is almost completely ruined in the parts above because the freezing weather of Milan, for its vehemence, does not allow hanging gardens, and unroofed galleries have disordered everything, so that the roof leaks badly, and is treated by the rain very badly, and if this is not remedied, [the building] will last only a little while, and to fix it will not be possible except that it be costly[18].

Ten years after the interruption of the construction work and in dramatic economic circumstances effected by the 1569–1570 famine, in 1576 Cairati had estimated the cost of construction to be between 50,000 and 60,000 scudi, even while declaring that he had not taken into account one important fact: the recent rise in the price of materials. This is an astronomical sum, certainly swollen both by the gigantic proportions of the work and the huge amounts

17 "Il palazzo del Marino si è un corpo grande per altezza et per ornamenti, opera colossale. Molto appariscente e di gran vista come V.S. Ill.ma sa però in effetto contiene poca virtù, se l'utile si considera rispetto al guscio grande, non ci sono se non poche stanze da godere, poiché logge, portici, saloni anditi, scale prodighe et altre pompe occupano il più et lasciano poco da loggiare, et questo poco riesce così incomodo che non si sa quasi a che qualità di persone si possa adattare. Per il principe non è capace, per cavagliero se la famiglia sarà numerosa si haverà difficoltà in alloggiarla et esserne serviti, se sarà di poche persone queste si perderanno per tanti ricetti sbandati et così lasciando essi bisognosi che si avisi". (ASMi, Finanza Apprensioni, 348 and in copy, in AOMMi, Litta, 412-18).

18 "[...] la fabrica poi quantanche sia nova, declina nondimeno, conciosiaché fu lasciata non finita et quel che se ne finì va quasi tutto a rovina nella parte di sopra essendo che i geli di Milano per la vehementia loro, non consentendo a quei giardini pensili et galerie di cima scoperte habbiano disordinato ogni cosa, onde la casa ne trapiove, et dalle pioggie viene malissimo trattata et se a questo non se vi rimedia durerà pochissimo et il rimediare non pol essere se non con buon costo". (ASMi, Finanza Apprensioni, 348 and in copy, in AOMMi, Litta, 412-18).

of capital invested in the acquisition of the adjacent properties[19], having taken advantage of the powerful leverage offered by the New Constitutions regarding *laute aedificare*, which, as is known, provided for an additional cost of one quarter of the value of the buildings.

Having examined and weighed all these factors with the conviction that "freehold patrimonies, not considering a particular appetite, desire, or passion, are worth the revenue that they are able to generate", the civic engineer invoked the cautious request of the circumstances, and concluded, "if one wants to consider the cost of this building, it ought to generate between two and three thousand scudi a year, except that it is neither to say, nor to think, if I say that from two hundred to three hundred scudi I see that with the demolition and sale of the material, it might be possible to get back more". This extreme and drastic option was not taken into consideration. Nonetheless, during the various building transformations, the unused stone was taken apart and sold at auction[20].

Conditioned in a practical way by the contemporary crisis of the real estate market, Cairati's economic estimate took into consideration the reduction in demand for noble houses, and noted that other "much more comfortable and well planned" homes[21], for example those of the Trivulzio, the Carcano and the Tolentini, were empty. To further underscore the exceptional nature of the contingencies and in order not to diminish completely the qualities of the building due to become part of the civic patrimony, Cairati underlines a deeply rooted fact: "if the house were in Rome, it would be worth much due to the demand of the principal prelates[22]". It was understood that the absence

19 Casati, "Nuove notizie intorno a Tomaso De Marini", *art. cit.*, p. 622 and 624; Baroni, *Documenti per la storia dell'architettura italiana*, *op. cit.*, pp. 401–402 and 405–406; Houghton Brown, *The Milanese Architecture*, *op. cit.*, pp. 205–206.

20 Among the documentary references, I will cite here only the information dated 23 February 1585 regarding the sale at public auction of twelve columns of marble coming from a window of the modernized court (as n. xiv): "i beni allodiali, non considerando particolare appetito, desiderio, o passione, vagliono secondo sono habili a dare rendita"; "se si volesse haver risguardo al costo di questa machina doverà frutare da due o tre mila scudi l'anno, eccesso che non è da dire ne da pensare, se io dico duecento in trecento scudi veggo che con la demolizione et vendita de materiali se ne potrà forsi far più ritratto".

21 "[...] ben più comode e ben distribuite". (ASMi, Finanza Apprensioni, 348 and in copy, in AOMMi, Litta, 412-18.

22 "[...] fosse in Roma valerebbe molto più per il concorso de prelati principali". (ASMi, Finanza Apprensioni, 348, also available in AOMMi, Litta, 412-18).

of the court at Milan reduced the need for public appearances of the nobles coming from other cities of the country, and limited the need to have adequate residences available, whether rented, or owned. This impasse made renting out the mansion the only practical choice to preserve intact the economic value of the patrimony, while attributing part of the maintenance costs to the renter, who then could have deducted the sums spent from the rent.

The Mansion and Marino's Heirs

In the following decade and owing to claims different in appearance, but analogous in substance, the daughters of Tommaso Marino, or indirectly their heirs, succeeded in contracting with the governmental administrative offices (Regia Camera) for various rights to use the mansion, favored perhaps as a partial reimbursement for the unjust sanctions of which they had been victims. In 1578, Manfredo Tornielli, husband of Chiara Marino, obtained from these same administrative offices the concession of the rental of the mansion in compensation for credit due him for services he had provided. Chiara, therefore, was able to live here, surrounded by sumptuous furnishings, alternating her residence between Milan and Novara, even after the death of her husband in 1584[23]. The objective declared by the administration to contribute rental income to the state coffers appeared completely unrealistic, considering that the fee remained constant, and, in fact, was not received at all due to the deduction of the maintenance costs. Two facts were at play which favoured the renter: the "quality of the person"[24] and the sums that were due him as "captain of armed forces".[25] On the other hand, in 1582 the conviction matured that "it would be better if that mansion were rented out to someone else, who took care of it, and who repaired it as occasion warranted, and didn't let it go to ruin, so much so that we are given to understand that it leaks very badly in many

23 See the two petitions (suppliche) dated 8 June 1578 and 28 September 1584. (ASMi, Finanza Apprensioni, 348, also available in AOMMi, Litta, 412-18). An extract of the inventory of the furnishings of Virginia's exclusive property is preserved in Milan, and is repeated in the dowry document dated 14 July 1579 of her daughter, Barbara (Archivio Storico Diocesano Novara, Archivio del Capitolo di Santa Maria, Opera pia Tornielli, teca D, n. 85).

24 "[...] qualità della persona [...]". (ASMi, Finanza Apprensioni, 348).

25 *Ibid.*: "[...] capitano de gente d'arme [...]".

places, and that that Sir Count doesn't do any repairs; we understand that the price of 150 scudi is rather little, and even if it were possible to find a lot more, we would still be in the red"[26].

Claims to maternal dowry credits inherited by the daughter of Virginia Marino, Marianna De Leyva (better known as the inspiration for the character of the nun of Monza in Manzoni's *Promessi Sposi*), are instead at the origin of the request presented to the administration by her father, Martino De Leyva. In 1589, the influential grandson of the first Spanish governor of the State of Milan saw recognized his right to receive 6,756 scudi when acquiring the property rights of an equivalent portion of Palazzo Marino. The sale was ratified in 1592 with the agreed clause to return the property, when the time came, "with as little bother as possible to the administration"[27]. In the subdivision of the mansion, the balance between disadvantages and benefits was carefully considered by the engineer, Giovanni Battista Clarici[28] (1542–1602), with an analytical approach of the ways of use. He focused on safeguarding the primary requisite of reciprocal independence of the two residences into which the building was to be split, beginning with the consideration of a multiplicity of conditions, among which figured the accessibility to the first – or "noble" – floor and the use of the service areas. Of the building's surface (including the little street) calculated in 9,553 little squares, the part assigned to De Leyva occupied an area of 1290 and 9 on the corner between Piazza San Fedele (with an entrance) and Via San Giovanni alle Case Rotte. The consideration that "it's of no account that the rest of the building can't do without it, and with less difficulty for the administration offices"[29] motivated the decision to isolate a

26 *Ibid.* 25 August 1582: "[...] saria se non bene che quel palazzo fosse affittato ad altra persona che ne tenesse conto et reparasse conforme alle occasioni affine che non vada in ultima rovina, tanto più che intendiamo che strapiove in molti luochi, et esso Signor Conte non gli fa alcuni ripari, si intendiamo che il prezzo di scudi 150 è assai poco et si ne trovasse assai più si rimettiamo nondimeno".

27 For this and subsequent citations, drawn from the estimate of G. B. Clarici, see the document of Cesare Regaino and Francesco Brambilla dated 2 September 1572 cited by Casati, "Nuove notizie intorno a Tommaso De Marini [...]", *art. cit.*, p. 8 and subsequent studies (ASMi, Finanza Apprensioni, 348 ; ASMi, Rogiti Camerali, 1596).

28 Viganò, "Cairate Giovanni Battista", *art. cit.*, pp. 62–63.

29 "[...] non interviene cosa niuna che il restante della fabrica non posse fare senza et con manco scomodo della Regia Camera [...]". (ASMi, Finanza Apprensioni, 348; ASMi, Rogiti Camerali, 1596).

small gallery, three rooms, a little portico (where two toilets were installed), the basement, a well and a little garden with two circular stairways that led to the upper living quarters. The administration offices would have kept full property rights of the patrimony with complementary value, that is to say, the nobler and larger portion of the mansion, distributed around the interior courtyard and with the entrance on Via Marina. The distribution of the spaces was described by the civic engineer:

> On the floor above there is a salon and three rooms with three smaller rooms and upper areas, it has a vaulted salon painted in a costly manner, which is as large as all three rooms and small rooms below, this suite has for its use the door that gives onto Via Marino, and it has the interior courtyard with twenty-four beautifully formed columns of granite of the Doric order, and the portico with its various bays divided by the same order, and the façades of the courtyard decorated with stucco, at the head of this courtyard in front of the door is the lower salon decorated with stucco and with a painted vault and various ornaments, and the principal stairs are for going to the upper areas of this suite, which I judge to be the most noble part and of greater value and it has basements and underground vaulted areas [...][30].

Quite quickly, the De Leyva family complained to the administration that they had acquired "something that generates such little revenue"[31]. They asked for additional funds from the generated rental fees beginning in 1594, to rise until it reached the equivalent of 8% of the capital of 6,756 scudi, which corresponded to the dowry credit. The request was denied since it was a great deal higher than the rental income for the entire mansion, of which only one-seventh was due to the De Leyvas, and which also entailed the responsibility – unfulfilled – of participating in the expenses of maintenance.

30 "[...] al piano vi sono sala et tre camere con tre camerini et luoghi superiori, ha un salone in volta dipinto con pitture di prezzo, il qual salone piglia tutte tre le camere et camerini da basso, questo appartamento ha per suo servitio la porta posta su la contrada del Marino et ha la corte con ventiquattro colone di sarizzo di bella forma, con ordini dorico et il portico con diversi resalti ripartiti con il medesimo ordine, et facciate della corte ornata di stucco, in testa d'essa corte in faccia della porta resta il sallone da basso con ripartimento di stucco et il volto dipinto et vari ornamenti et le scale principali servono per andare alli luoghi superiori di questo appartamento, il quale giudico che questa sia la parte più nobile et di maggior valore et ha le sue cantine et luoghi sotterranei in volta [...]". (ASMi, Finanza Apprensioni, 348; ASMi, Rogiti Camerali, 1596).

31 See the petition from the De Leyvas directed to the Regia Camera in the subsequent decade: "[...] cosa di poco reddito [...]". (ASMi, Finanza Apprensioni, 348, also available in AOMMi, Litta, 412-18).

"… there is such little income renting it because of the many imperfections that it has". The Search for a More Productive Use

In 1593, the quaestors (Questori), Giulio Dardanone and Alessandro Serbelloni, were charged by the Magistrate Chamber (Magistrato Camerale) to present a budget for the management of Palazzo Marino, in order to evaluate how it might be used more productively. Among the various options proposed were the transfer of public offices and selling or renting of the Palazzo to private individuals for living quarters. None of these options was definitively abandoned in the subsequent decades. The only proposal to be discarded immediately in 1594 was the less realistic idea of conceding its use to the Jesuit fathers of San Fedele, who, writing directly to the king, had requested it free-of-charge.

During the fact-gathering stage of this inquiry, the engineers Giovanni Battista Clarici and Giovanni Francesco Sitoni collaborated on the structure with their highly detail-minded technical competence. Later, in 1596, they would be given the responsibility to estimate all the maintenance work necessary to assign the contracts. Among the many critical aspects, two seemed to weigh most heavily in the decision-making process: the rent to the Tornielli family, whose subleasing of their premises to Count Agostino Somaglia[32] from 1586 did not produce any income for the government's coffers, as well as the generally ruinous state of the roofs, which made further costs and increased debt inevitable. The conclusion was immediate and drastic: "[…] there is such little income renting it because of the many imperfections that it has"[33].

Thus, the alternative of public offices was evaluated by Clarici, who was to visit the mansion and write up an overarching plan to transfer the mint to the Palazzo, as well as the post office and the offices of the merchant taxes, the salt taxes, the retail wine taxes and customs. The drawing published by Giacomo Bascapé, and identified as one of the two drawings that the engineer

32 Somaglia had rented the De Leyva portion only in 1594 thanks to an offer made in a public auction presented by a De Leyva representative (Memoriale De Leyva, 18 June 1697, ASMi, as in n. xiv).

33 See the Memoria dated 22 June 1596 (ASMi, Fondi Camerali p.a., 213; AOMMi, Litta, 412-20): "[…] si ricava poco utile volendo affittare per le molte imperfetioni che in esso vi sono".

attached to his evaluation of 1593, can be related to this circumstance[34]. Clarici's analysis was based on a valuation of the building equal to 117,000 lire to which was added the rent of the rooms occupied by various offices – based on a rate of 5% – and from which was deducted the cost of the repairs "because the said mansion is in a too ruinous state and is badly preserved"[35]. The basic value was "realistically"[36] approximated at 27,680 lire, with a net value of 89,320 lire. The foreseen expenses would be amortized in part by the income of the sale of the old mint at around 22,000 lire, reducing the effective cost to 1,000 scudi. The construction work he foresaw for the adaption of the building to new uses, excluding any restoration, generally increased the volumes of the building, but in unequal ways. The closure of three sides of the portico would have allowed the integration of the bays into the seat for the money-printing activities of the mint. The insertion of the foundry alone would have required extensive demolition and complex structural work. In the lower garden towards San Giovanni alle Case Rotte, there would have been twelve shops constructed to be let, reserving a small transit courtyard for the stalls for the post master, which were to be have been created out of the kitchen space under the salon.

The proposal to sell the residence was considered by the magistrates, who were attracted by the advantage of an immediate income for the coffers: "since this government treasury (Real Camera) is very exhausted and it finds itself with many and significant debts".[37] In their eyes, it must have seemed an encouraging sign when the wait for potential buyers resulted in the offer of 14,000 scudi presented in 1594 by the inhabitant, Count Antonio della Somaglia, which was superseded in 1606 by the offer of 18,500 scudi made by the Marquis Sforza

34 Of the "two drawings, one marked A, the other marked B" cited in the estimate (ASMi, Finanza Apprensioni, 348; ASMi, Rogiti Camerali, 1596) the first is identifiable with the published one (Bascapé Giacomo, "Il palazzo Marino due secoli e mezzo fa", in *Città di Milano*, LXVIII (1951), p. 23) and referred to the estimate (Scotti, *op. cit.*, p. 477, n. 34), but to this day is not to be found in the archive of the Ospedale Maggiore of Milan.

35 "per essere il detto palazzo troppo in ruina e mal redutto [...]". (ASMi, Finanza Apprensioni, 348; ASMi, Rogiti Camerali, 1596).

36 "per la verosimile[...]". (ASMi, Finanza Apprensioni, 348; ASMi, Rogiti Camerali, 1596).

37 "atteso che questa Real Camera è molto esausta et che si trova con molti e notabili debiti [...]". (ASMi, Finanza apprensioni, 348; AOMMi, Litta, 412-20).

of Caravaggio[38]. The dates seem to confirm the renewed interest in investing in real estate, concomitant with the cyclical dip in monetary and credit availability, which manifested itself from 1593–1597, 1607–1610 and again in 1619 as the resultant effect of ill-advised deflationary manoeuvres and of the growing drain induced by the financing of war operations[39].

Under these circumstances, it was the congruity between the market value of the building and the offers of the potential buyers that constituted the object of reflection on the part of the civic engineer, Pietro Antonio Barca, who was charged with doing the estimate. His estimate of the value of the mansion was decidedly superior at between 20,000 and 25,000 scudi, but prudent: "the reason is because in Milan there are no princes, who will buy it and finish it, there are only knights, gentlemen and merchants, who, with twenty thousand scudi, can find quite honourable homes in Milan, suited to their needs, and with a garden and they don't care about having so much cut live stone and ornaments"[40]. In a manner not dissimilar to that of his predecessors, the technician grasped "that unsuitability for inhabitation that other times has been noted, and which it is not possible to remedy without new and great expense"[41]. Nevertheless, his method of looking at the building participated in a changed climate, coherent with the dynamics of the capital of the State of Milan, where there was widespread wealth, but where the number of those who were willing to invest to acquire a home was not high. One senses between the lines the acknowledgement of previously unrecognised resources for the capital of the state when, estimating the cost of the restoration of the stuccoes, paintings and other decorations, he warned that "if they are not repaired every day, they go to ruin and decline, from which it follows not only some lessening in the value

38 ASMi, Finanza apprensioni, 348; AOMMi, Litta, 412-20.

39 See De Luca Giuseppe, "Mercanti imprenditori, élite artigiane e organizzazioni produttive: la definizione del sistema corporativo milanese (1568–1627)", in Guenzi Alberto, Massa Paola, Moioli Angelo (a cura di), *Corporazioni e gruppi professionali nell'Italia moderna*, Milano, Franco Angeli, 1999, p. 93.

40 "[...] la causa è che in Milano non vi è occasione di Principe che lo compri et farlo finire, solo vi sono cavaglieri, gentilhuomeni et mercanti li quali con scudi vinti mille troveranno casa in Milano honorevolissima al suo bisogno et con giardino et non si curano di haver tanti intagli di pietra viva et ornamenti". (ASMi, Finanza Apprensioni, 348).

41 "[...]quella incomodità al habitare che altre volte è stata avvirtita, et alla quale non si potrà rimediare senza nuova et grande spesa[...]". (ASMi, Finanza Apprensioni, 348).

of the mansion, but also the loss of notable ornament and decorum of this city"[42]. This sensibility, unusual for a material witness of the *civitas*, allowed him to distance himself from the pragmatism of Cairati, and he concluded, "Leaving aside the possibility of destroying it in order to sell its materials, which is expressly prohibited by law. We come to the opinion that the offer of the Marquis of Caravaggio ought to be accepted, provided that he raise it to the sum of 25,000"[43].

The negotiations with these potential buyers remained without a concrete outcome, however. By the end of the first decade of the seventeenth century, even the premise of turning it into public offices went up in smoke, leaving as the only option the reconfirming the preceding use sanctioned in 1603 for the renewal of the contract made with the heirs of Somaglia. Somaglia was succeeded by Sancho de Salinas (1614–1617); the field master and then governor Gonzalo de Cordova (1622–1628); don Filippo Spinola, Marquis of Los Balbases (1629–1631)[44]; the grand chancellor Ronquillo (1634–1645)[45] and, finally, Agostino Homodei, Marquis of Piovera, and his descendents (1645–1662). As is evident, the profile of the inhabitants changed, and they seem to have shared lifestyle habits more centered around appearances: the mansion of Tommaso Marini found its most consonant use in its singular characteristics as a temporary place to stay for exponents of the political and financial *coté* that gravitated around the crown, dedicated to activities in which the discrimination between public and private interests seemed uncertain, all having in common the need to reside in a recognizable residence, near to the seats of the institutions of the government of the state and the city, and all concentrated near the Broletto and the old ducal palace functioning as the seat of the senate.

42 "[...] se non si riparano ogni giorno vanno rovinando et declinando, dal che segue non solamente qualche diminuzione del valore del palazzo, ma si perde notabile ornamento, et decoro di questa città". (ASMi, Finanza Apprensioni, 348).

43 "Lasciando da parte il trattare di distruggerlo per vendere le materie, come cosa espressamente prohibita dalla legge. Veniamo in parere che si accetti l'oblatione del marchese di Caravaggio accrescendola però egli almeno fino alla somma di 25,000". (ASMi, Finanza Apprensioni, 348).

44 Fragmentary documentation in ASMi, Finanza Apprensioni, 349.

45 ASMi, Rogiti Camerali p.a. 151 F. Brambilla.

The Residence of the Bankers Homodei and the Undertaking of the Useless Mansion

Considerations from a fresh interpretative perspective are necessary given that research to this point has been based largely on fragments of estimate documents. Now the contribution will proceed through an analysis of contemporary unedited sources in order to widen the inquiry to include public and private archive material.

In 1645, Palazzo Marino was rented to Agostino Homodei (1605–1657), Marquis of Piovera, holder of an important governmental position ("Decurione"), an *hombre de negocios* among the most rich and enterprising, brother-in-law of the powerful president of the senate, Bartolomeo Arese, and brother to Giovan Battista Homodei, quaestor of the Ordinary Magistrate (Magistrato Ordinario). The constellation of his family and hangers-on, only briefly listed here, was so extended and so powerful that the administration offices accepted for three parts of Palazzo Marino a rent of 500 scudi a year, the equivalent of 2,750 lire, in order to anticipate the interest on a credit of 150,000 scudi, which his ancestor Giovanni Giacomo had lent to Philip IV, thereby renouncing the pursuit of a greater profit. The humble origins of this house, descended as it was from a "vulgar tax collector"[46], had already been rehabilitated by the fabulous fortune of their "very very rich"[47] uncle Emilio. This was an advantage above all to the generation of Agostino, who wove privileged relationships with the pontifical curia and the royal court, without excluding, as has been noted, the Milanese patricians with which he established opportune matrimonial alliances. The subsidies directed to the sovereign and the exercise of unscrupulous financial activity between Madrid and Milan contributed to the acquisition of funds and conspicuous income, such as those deriving from the contracting out of the tax collecting on lime[48] and that on the mill of the state of Milan.

46 "postaro di grasso"; Benaglia G., *La verità smascherata o sieno osservazini sopra la nobiltà di Milano*, Milano, 1714 (BAMi, P 260 sup.).

47 Signorotto, *Milano spagnola*, *op. cit.*, p. 152, passim: "valde pecunioso".

48 The activity of the family in this specific sector has been investigated by Fieni Laura, *Calci lombarde produzione e mercati dal 1641 al 1805*, Firenze, Insegna del Giglio, 2000, p. 42 passim.

The description of the state of Palazzo Marino in a formal document of the consignment to the new renter, put off until 1653, reveals traces of transformations in the building that satisfied the new needs, which had cropped up over the years, and which were evidenced, for example, in the sequence of four rooms comprising the "modern suite" on the first – noble – floor to the right of the salon. They were also seen in the wear of the finishing and in the ruin of the roofs, worsened by the static instability of the many trusses "shored up because they were detached from the walls"[49].

Starting in the last decades of the seventeenth century, the interests of the family gravitated ever more closely around the court. Carlo Homodei, son of Agostino, nominated Viceroy of Valencia, transferred his own residence to Madrid and in 1670 subleased Palazzo Marino to the Grand Chancellor Raffaele de Villosa, followed in 1692 by Pirro Visconti Borromei[50]. Status and privileges made it possible for Carlo to have advance knowledge of Spanish politics in Milan, and to take advantage of support from those very high up in local institutions, in order to realize investment opportunities relating to the most economical governmental patrimony available in the market. After a year spent assuring himself of the approval of the court, in 1682 he proposed to the administration offices that he acquire three quarters of Palazzo Marino for 70,000 ducats (919,442 lire) as payment in full for an old loan[51]. Shortly thereafter, he completed the real estate investment by buying from Giuseppe De Leyva the remaining fourth part facing towards San Fedele[52]. These choices reveal a long term plan intended to get income from rent in the short term, while at the same time investing capital in order to extend the nucleus of property, which he integrated in 1696 with the house, formerly belonging to Giacomo Crivelli, that faced onto the small street on the west of the mansion[53]. This building was of complementary value, and was destined to house

49 "[...] l'appartamento alla moderna [...]"; "[...] pontelate per esser fuori dal muro[...]". 12 March 1653. (AOMMi, Litta, 412).

50 The consignment of the building on 3 September 1670 was drawn up by the engineer Robiati G. B. On 1 October 1692, a private agreement was drawn up for the rental of the dwelling to the Visconti Borromei (Ivi).

51 ASMi, Rogiti Camerali p.a. 151 F. Brambilla.

52 24 September 1682, A. Ciprandi. (AOMMi, Litta, 412-18).

53 27 February 1696, Matteo Macchio. (AOMMi, Litta, 412).

service areas, alleviating the lack of space seen by then as an effective limit of the residence.

With the entrance into Milan of Eugene of Savoy in 1706, the political turn-of-events destabilized the fortunes of the family. Carlo Homodei, Marquis of Castelrodrigo, aligned himself with Filippo di Borbone during the war of Spanish succession, and so was labeled an "enemy of the Very Esteemed House", and was forced to take exile in Spain, while his goods, including properties and real estate rental income, were sequestered[54]. Exemplary and hard sanctions were counteracted by an immediate reaction: the launching of a complex strategy of patrimony governance entrusted to Giovanni Battista Scotti, the representative of the interests of the Homodei family in the State of Milan. The actions of this procurator were agreed with the potential heirs accredited in a secondary line of the family, which, because of the lack of direct heirs, involved influential families and created a sense of solidarity among them: the Pio, the Archinto, the Visconti Borromeo and their cousins, the Borromeo Arese, who were in favor of the Austrians, and who were not lacking power and the ability to influence those at the pinnacle of the institutions. Thanks to this teamwork, when Carlo died in 1725, even Palazzo Marino, free of entailments, was included in the inheritance. Each rightful heir was assigned three quotas of the undivided property[55].

In the period between 1711 and 1717, the government engineers Giuseppe Maria Robecco and Bernardo Maria Quarantini were charged by the administration offices to describe the distribution of the spaces in the mansion in relation to how they were used in order to establish objective parameters for the revision of the rental fees for the living quarters occupied by Catalan and Spanish families. They were to be classified as good, mediocre or infirm based on the collocation and quality of the spaces (Figure 2)[56]. Except for the spaces on the ground floor, which were reserved for the royal post offices, the rent available for the treasury was only 1,800 lire. More significant were the incomes obtained

54 "[...] nemico dell'Augustissima Casa". (ASMi, Finanza, Apprensioni, 400).

55 See the opening of the will – consigned in Madrid on 5 October 1723 – on 16 January 1725, as well as the description of the inheritance compiled the following year. (BAMi, Falcò Pio di Savoia, v.n. 208).

56 Unless otherwise specified, references are to this folder of unedited documents, among which are some elaborate drawings (ASMi, Finanza Apprensioni, 404).

Figure 2. Giuseppe Maria Robecco, Floor Plan of the Palazzo Omodeo, 1717–1718

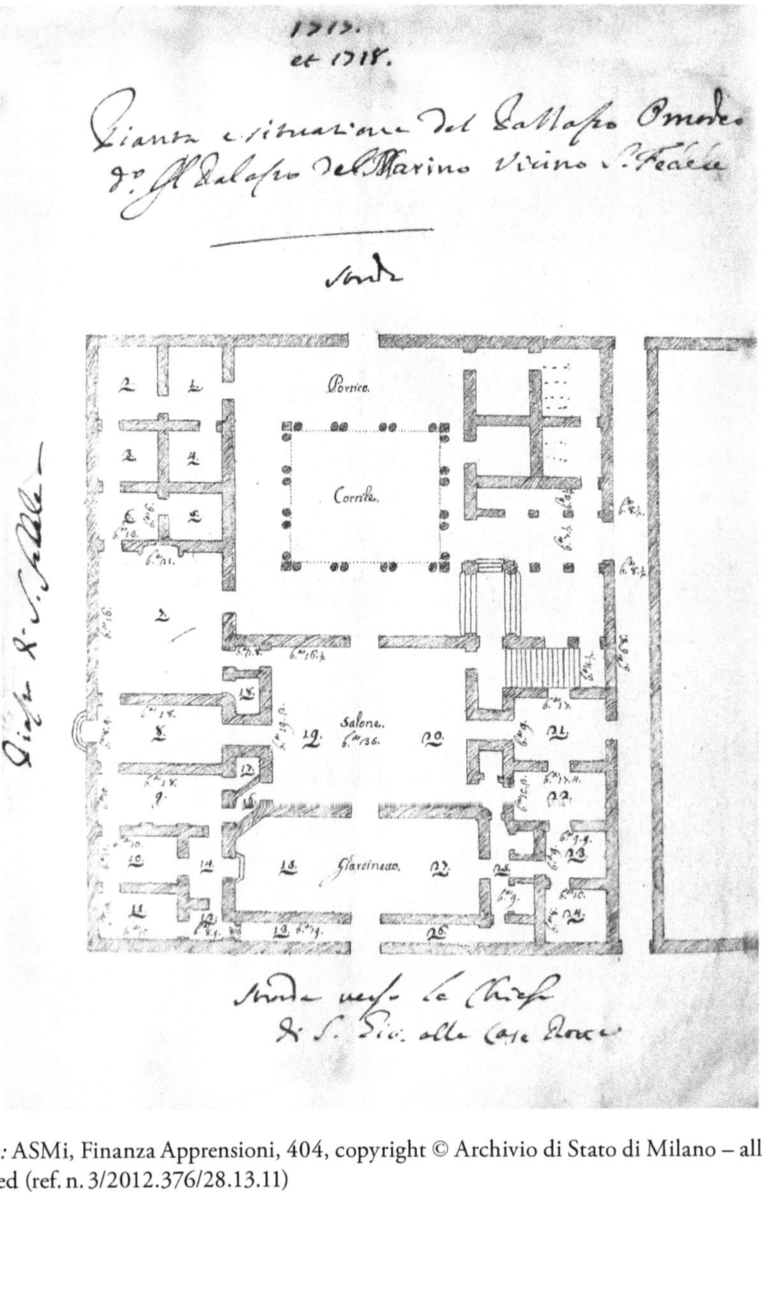

Source: ASMi, Finanza Apprensioni, 404, copyright © Archivio di Stato di Milano – all rights reserved (ref. n. 3/2012.376/28.13.11)

by the Homodei heirs from 1725 to 1774: from 2,500 lire (1725–1728) they fell and stabilized until the middle of the century at 2,400 lire (1728–1753), when they experienced a sharp rise to 4,000 lire (1753–1759) and then again to 4,500 lire (1760–1774), a sum that, when considering the hypothetical payments to the state, may have been higher.

At the beginning of the eighteenth century, the ancient sixteenth century abode was subdivided into an agglomerate of principle and secondary suites and modest abodes in the mezzanines, all connected to a complex system of service rooms, services, and public rooms – the grand salons – available for all to use. The criteria used to assign space tended to interpret the lifestyle needs in relation to the social status and effective number of people in the nuclear family, a practice that was no different from that adopted for the subdivision of noble residences, defined appropriately as "noble condominiums"[57] in the case of co-habitation.

The nature of the mansion, with the adjunct of the house on the narrow thoroughfare, was one of an *insula* dedicated to public functions understood in the broadest of ways, not excluding residences for bureaucrats on the first – noble – floor. It prefigured an experimental answer to those logistical and public needs to which the state's apparatus would respond once it had been modernised by the Hapsburg government. The state's interest in the palazzo Homodei followed, therefore, a kind of general test, but became a decisive theme for the launching of the definitive mutation of the building into one solely dedicated to public use at the end of 1771, when the prospect of purchase, or perpetual rent, was planned between Milan and Vienna[58].

57 "nobili condomini": an expression in common use at that time.

58 The governor, Count Karl von Firmian, expressed an opinion in favor of just such a move, asking for approval from the Chancellor of State, Prince Wenzel Anton Kaunitz von Rietberg: "Ancor io ne vedo la congruenza, e l'utilità. Oggi giorno si pagano £. 4,500 di affitto ai proprietari e se ne ritraggono £. 2,987.10 dai magazzeni accordati ai rispettivi mercanti. Deducendosi dal rimanente gl'aggravi di tasse, e di riparazioni incombenti ai padroni si potrà con meno di cento zecchini l'anno di spesa collocare stabilmente due dicasteri e insieme il Dazio grande. Ammettendone ora la trattazione ove essa sarebbe anche gradita ai compatroni per finire la divisione dell'eredità Omodea, si potrebbe non incontrare la stessa facilità in altro tempo". (I still see in it the congruence and the usefulness. Today one pays £4,500 for rent to the owners and one earns £2,987.10 from the store rooms granted to the respective merchants. Subtracting from what remains the taxes due and [the costs of] the necessary repairs to the owners, one could with less than one hundred "zecchini" a year of

"To calculate according to his skill following the rules of art and actual practice". Estimation Methodology and Public Utility

In 1778, negotiations for ceding the mansion were still being held. They ended only in 1781, when Pietro Verri, as president of the body of magistrates, completed the acquisition for a total of 250,000 lire[59]. In reality, circumstances had for some time excluded the building from the market, and from 1771 rendered it exclusively of state interest for its solidity, ampleness and location. In short, it was the ideal seat for public offices. Here, after adaptations (Figures 3–4) that had cost a great deal of time and money[60], there were the first offices of the finance department, then, beginning in 1772, of the department of accounts, the magistrate body, the two treasuries and the chief of import taxes.

In the estimate presented to Verri in 1780, the government engineer Dionigi Maria Ferrario proposed to "calculate according to his skill – following the rules of the art and actual practice – the capital equity of this mansion and the contiguous house[61]". The document, exemplary for its transparency and methodological rigor, takes up and shares the essential passages of preceding ones: the uniqueness of the object directly related to the category of those "grand houses for the use of noble families, and particularly mansions of like nature built with such expense so blatantly in evidence on the exterior", and the inevitable disparity between the original cost that would have required "obtaining

expenses house two ministries there on a permanent basis, and together [with them] the big tax office. Granting the negotiations, now, in which the presence of the co-owners would also be desirable, to finish the division of the Omodei inheritance, it could very well be that the same facility would not be encountered at another time) Lettera del 30 Novembre 1771, ASMi, Fondi Camerali p.a., 211.

59 14 July 1781, G. Francia (AOMMi, Litta, 412-31; ASMi, Fondi camerali p.a., 213). Generic indications, without a precise citing of sources, are to be found in Houghton Brown, *op. cit.*, p. 236; Bologna, *Palazzo Marino in Milano*, *op. cit.*, p. 134.

60 In the estimate of expenses dated 6 May 1772, the engineer Cesare Carcano determined a cost of 3466 lire (see note 58). For an analysis of the costs in the context of investments for public works, see Mocarelli Luca, *Costruire la città. Edilizia e vita economica nella Milano del secondo Settecento*, Bologna, Il Mulino, 2008, p. 91.

61 See the report of Ferrario following his inspection effected with the assistance of the master mason, Crippa, on 19 February 1780. (ASMi, Fondi camerali p.a., 213): "[...] calcolare a norma della mia perizia sulle regole dell'arte e della pratica attuale il capital valore di questo palazzo e della casa contigua".

Figure 3. Study for the Adaptation of the Ground Floor of the Palazzo Omodei and the Connected House into Governmental Offices, 1780

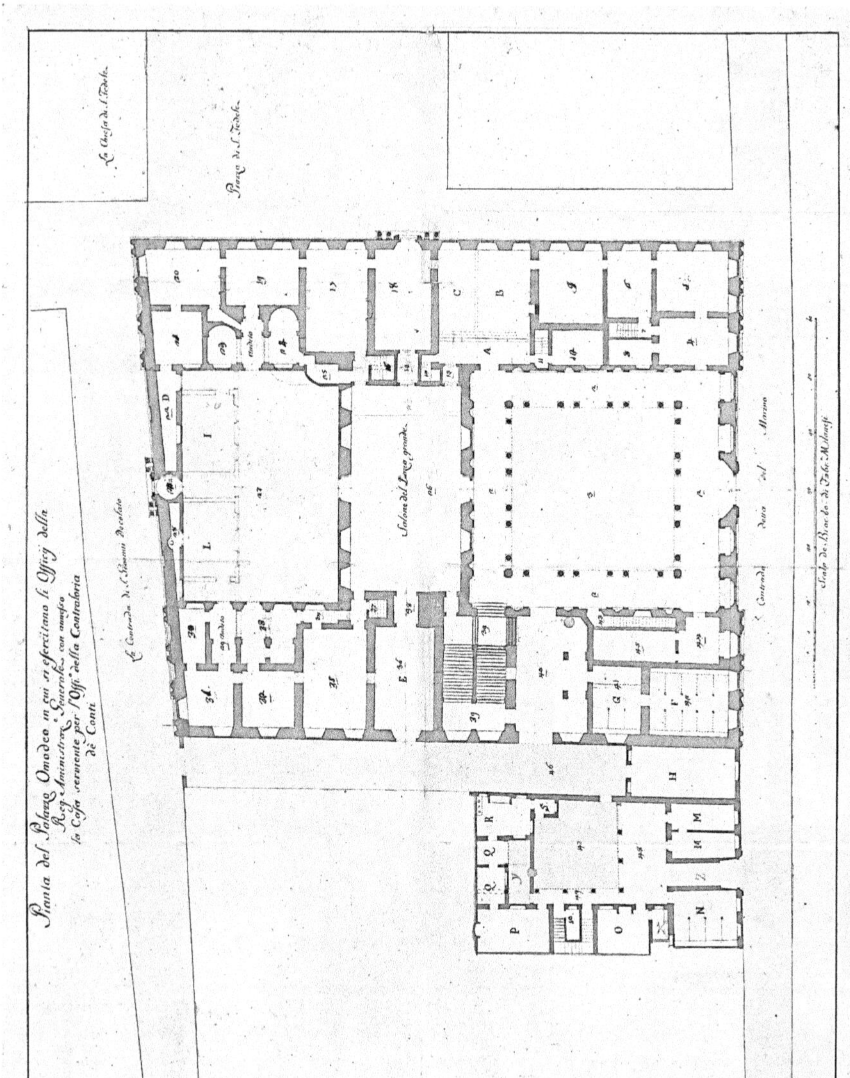

Source: ASMi, Fondi Camerali p.a., 213, copyright © Archivio di Stato di Milano – all rights reserved (ref. n. 3/2012.376/28.13.11)

Figure 4. Study for the Adaptation of the First Floor of the Palazzo Omodei into Governmental Offices,1780

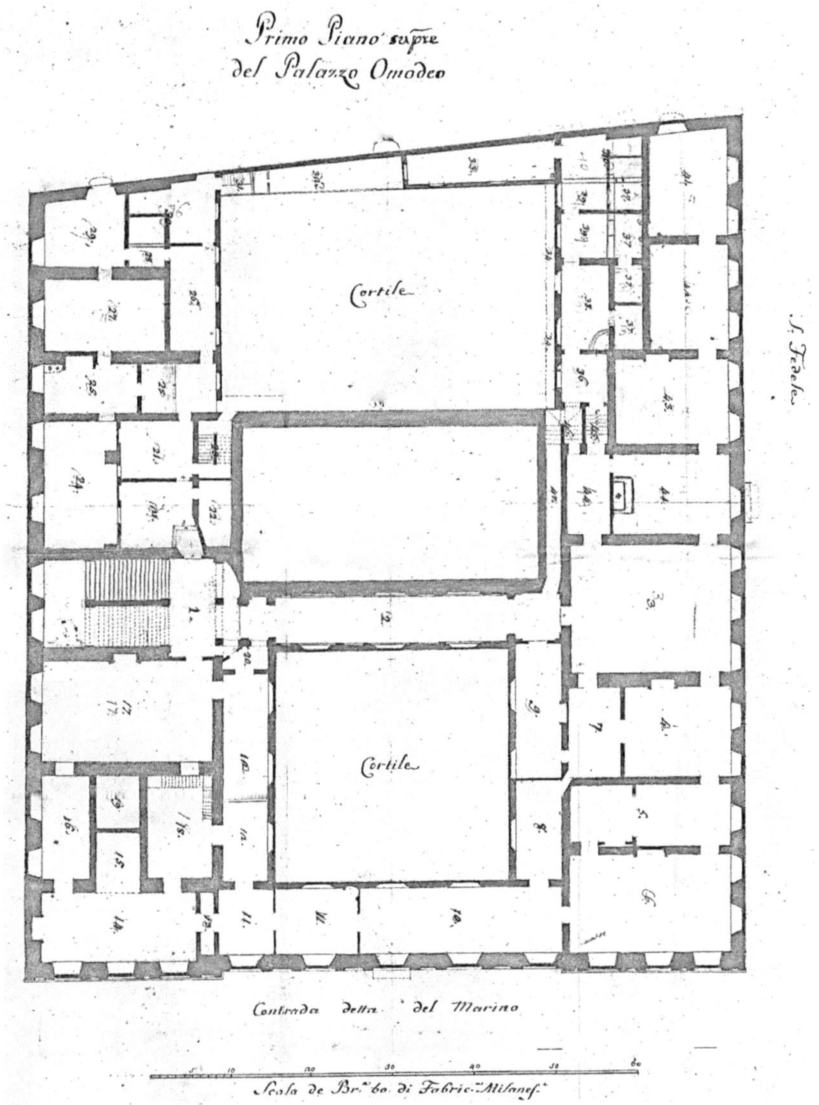

Source: ASMi, Fondi Camerali p.a., 213, copyright © Archivio di Stato di Milano – all rights reserved (ref. n. 3/2012.376/28.13.11)

an equal value" mediating between the "intrinsic value of the material and the site of the ancient structure" and the value calculated "based on that yearly yield, which today the noble owners there usually receive".[62]

He first arrived at 338,604 lire, after having considered technical data "both inside and outside, such as the quality of the pavements, the walls, the vaulted ceilings, the ceilings, the roofs, essential aspects of all kinds, ironwork and every other thing".[63] He took as his point-of-reference a new parameter: the land tax census of 3,332 scudi deduced from the recently introduced land registry. His second estimate, equal to 231,692 lire, was determined in part by the then current standardized rent of 5,000 lire minus the expenses of the taxes, of the annual repairs (305 lire) and ad hoc repairs (3,158 lire), regulating the investment at two per cent considering the quality of the structure. At the end of his described estimate process, the engineer attributed to the mansion a value of 285,148 lire and 31,445 lire to the house once belonging to the Crivelli on the little street, then rented to the administrative offices. With subtle acumen, he further excluded many adaptations imposed by the use of the building for public offices, recently financed by the state coffers, that might have raised the value of the property, and did not enter them under the category of improvements because they did not benefit the property directly, nor would they have been able to contribute in the future to increasing the rental income. This consideration effectively precluded the Homodei heirs from the possibility of benefiting indirectly from the increase in the value of the building through acting artfully on the parameter of the rental income, as the prince of Kaunitz had intuited, as can be seen from his comment on their request: "And then, the price of 6,466 lire is rather a lot for renting a house in Milan that has only one noble floor, and for which only with difficulty is one able to find someone able, or willing, to live in it at such a great price"[64]. With a final consideration,

62 *Ibid.* "[...] case grandi ad uso di famiglie nobili, e particolarmente di palazzi di tal natura fabbricati con tanto dispendio segnatamente nel giro esteriore [...]"; "[...] rilevare un valore equitativo[...]"; "[...] valore intrinseco di materiale e sito di fabbrica antica [...]"; "[...] in ragione di quell'annual cavata che sogliono al presente conseguire li nobili proprietari[...]".

63 *Ibid.* "[...] si nell'interno che nell'esterno la qualità de pavimenti, muri, volte, soffitte, tetti, vivi di qualunque genere, ferramenti ed ogni altro[...]".

64 "E poi in se assai riguardevole la somma di lire 6,466 per l'affitto d'una casa in Milano che ha un solo piano nobile e difficilmente troverebbe chi potesse o volesse abitarla a si gran prezzo". (ASMi, Fondi camerali p.a., 213).

Ferrario definitively destroyed the foolish aspirations of the sellers: since most of the work on the building had been geared to its conversion for public use, there would have been no advantage for eventual new renters, who could have asked for the structure to be returned to its untouched state. The building appeared, by then, inadequate as a residence because

> […] the uses for private homes are so changed, in today's system there are no more stalls, sheds for the carriages, kitchens, sinks, the noblemen's quarters have all been changed, various basements have been filled with earth in order to better protect the treasuries, in the end, all is well adapted for uses today by the administrative offices, but nothing, or very little, can be used for rental to private people because of all these adaptations, which, not being useful to the property, may not be calculated at all[65].

In this happy juncture, which was not just economic, but also political and social, the real estate market was characterized by the influence of public interest on the mechanism of demand[66]. The transformation of the Palazzo of the Marino family into a headquarters for public functions was complete and irreversible: the nature of the relationship between the property and its public uses only seemed open to debate with difficulty, however, whether from the reductionist point-of-view, or from the perspective of a more general utility, which understood the actions of the private sector.

65 "[…] gli usi per le private abitazioni sono del tutto variati, nel odierno sistema mancano tutte le scuderie, le rimesse per carrozze, mancano le cucine, lavandini, variati tutti i quarti nobili, terrapienate varie cantine per maggior cautela delle tesorerie, insomma tutto è ben inteso per gli usi odierni della Regia Camera, ma niente o ben poco può essere servibile per li privati affitti per conseguenza di tutti questi adattamenti, siccome non sono utili al fondo, non può calcolarsi alcun valore". (ASMi, Fondi camerali p.a., 213).

66 See Mocarelli, *Costruire la città*, *op. cit.* (especially Chap. IV, *Edilizia e vita economica*).

Les confiscations militaires au sein des exploitations agricoles du Hainaut français au cours des guerres de la fin du règne de Louis XIV

Fulgence Delleaux

À la fin du XVIIe et au début du XVIIIe siècle, les campagnes des anciens Pays-Bas méridionaux et plus spécialement celles de la province du Hainaut français sont marquées durement par deux guerres: celles de la Ligue d'Augsbourg (1688-1697) et de Succession d'Espagne (1702-1713)[1]. Sans surprise, les biens des paysans sont touchés. Au cours de leurs déplacements et de leurs campements, les armées ennemies et amies n'hésitent pas à confisquer bétail, grains et matériels agricoles des environs, afin de subvenir à leurs besoins en nourriture et en équipement.

Ces faits sont largement connus dans nos provinces par le biais de chroniques de curés de campagne ou de bourgeois urbains à l'image des journaux d'Alexandre Dubois ou d'André Gossiaux[2]. Il en va de même pour leurs premières répercussions: hausse des prix des denrées alimentaires à cause de leur rareté et endettement, parfois irréversible, des paysans. *A contrario*, la conséquence ultime de ces confiscations est beaucoup moins manifeste; en

1 Pour une vue synthétique des guerres dans cette région, se reporter à Lottin Alain et Guignet Philippe, *Histoire des provinces françaises du Nord. De Charles Quint à la Révolution française (1500-1789)*, Arras, Artois Presses Université, 2005, pp. 179-257.

2 Platelle Henri, *Journal d'un curé de campagne au XVIIe siècle*, Villeneuve d'Ascq, Septentrion, réed. 1997. Gossiaux André, *Livre des choses plus mémorables arrivées depuis l'an 1650 jusqu'à l'an présent (1716)*, édité par Edouard Leclair dans le *Bulletin de la Société d'études de la province de Cambrai*, t. XX, (1920), pp. 76-79. A titre de comparaison avec d'autres régions des anciens Pays-Bas méridionaux, sans multiplier les références: Servais Paul, « Le poids économique d'une occupation militaire (fin XVIIe-début XVIIIe siècle) », in *Annales de la Fédération des Cercles d'Archéologie et d'Histoire de Belgique*, (1975), pp. 433-435. Philippart Christian, « Conséquences socio-économiques des guerres de courses dans l'Hinterland namurois », in Jacquet Philippe et Jacquet-Ladrier Françoise (sous la dir de), *Assiégeants et assiégés au cœur de l'Europe. Namur 1688-1697*, Bruxelles, Crédit communal, 1992, pp. 249-275.

l'occurrence une restructuration des terroirs. Tout du moins, on connaît, sans réellement le savoir, l'achèvement de cette restructuration près d'un siècle plus tard. En effet, lorsque Georges Lefebvre observe la concentration des terres et la présence de grandes parcelles foncières au bénéfice des grands fermiers dans le nord du Hainaut français en 1789 au sein de son étude sur *Les paysans du Nord pendant la Révolution française*[3], il décrit un système agraire dont les origines semblent justement remonter à nos prélèvements militaires au sein des exploitations agricoles hennuyères lors des guerres de la fin du règne de Louis XIV. Il importe donc, dans les pages qui suivent, de retracer et clarifier le processus de cette importante mutation socio-économique.

La confiscation des biens des paysans

Invariablement le passage des régiments et des compagnies militaires dans les campagnes, où qu'elles soient, s'accompagne de multiples saisies en nature[4]. La première d'entre elles s'apparente à des « fourragements ». Ce terme regroupe aussi bien la paisson essentiellement des chevaux de l'armée sur les champs des paysans, que leur fauchage par les soldats ou encore le pillage par ces derniers des greniers à foin ou à grains. André Boulé, chanoine à Valenciennes, bon observateur, fournit témoignage sur ce point dans son livre de raison au moment de la guerre de Succession du roi d'Espagne Charles II:

> L'armée de France fourrage à Valenciennes et dans plusieurs villages. Le 31 juillet 1709, l'armée commandée par M. le chevalier de Luxembourg, campée à Saint-Saulve, [...] fourragea entièrement les villages d'Anzin, Beuvrages et Bruay et désola entièrement ces trois terroirs qu'il n'y resta autre chose que la terre [...] Le 1er juin 1711, les troupes françaises vinrent fourrager les terroirs d'Anzin, Saint-Waast-en-Haut et Beuvrages et coupèrent généralement les blés, les orges et les seigles, et, le 11 du même mois, elles vinrent derechef pour couper les blés depuis Beuvrages jusqu'à Raismes [...] Le 10 juillet 1712, l'armée de Hollande, campée à Denain, fit un fourrage sur le terroir de Beuvrages [...] Le 17 dudit

3 Lefebvre Georges, *Les Paysans du Nord pendant la Révolution française*, Paris, Armand Colin, 1924.

4 En Hainaut comme en Alsace: Boehler Jean-Michel, « La guerre au quotidien dans les villages du Saint Empire au XVIIe siècle », in Desplat Christian (sous la dir. de), *Les villageois face à la guerre (XIVe-XVIIIe siècle)*, Toulouse, Presses Universitaires du Mirail, 2002, pp. 65-88.

mois, l'armée de Hollande fit un fourrage sur les terroirs de Préseau, Saultain, Estreux, Saint-Saulve et Marly[5].

Non loin de là, Alexandre Dubois, le curé de Rumegies, relève à son tour des confiscations d'un genre identique subies par les paysans aux alentours de Saint-Amand en 1712:

> Le 27 août de cette année 1712, les Français firent un fourrage à Saint-Amand en blé. Ils prirent aux pauvres paysans une grande partie des blés qu'ils y avaient réfugiés. On en a été quitte pour 800 rasières dans la ville qu'on a prises le plus également qu'on a pu dans chaque grenier. Et l'abbaye en fut quitte pour 250, que le pauvre paysan a encore payées, y ayant réfugié son grain, et Messieurs les religieux ayant caché le leur. Ce ne fut point encore tout, car le 15 octobre toute la terre de Saint-Amand fut entièrement fourragée par l'armée d'observation de Bouchain. On a perdu généralement toutes les jarbées [gerbes] et une grande parties des [cultures de] mars, et cela deux jours avant que l'armée fusse décampée[6].

Plus au sud, au village de Dompierre, Etton Erraux, fermier d'une quarantaine d'hectares est quant à lui dépouillé de 1.040 bottes de foins. En 1709, sa grange a déjà été pillée, ainsi que ses terres. De plus, pendant 21 jours, les chevaux des troupes cantonnées au village ont pâturé sur ses terres[7]. Ceci n'a rien d'étonnant. Le secrétaire d'Etat à la guerre, Voysin, ancien intendant du Hainaut, signale la même année que «sur toutes les frontières, le soldat commence à marquer assez fortement par [...] des menaces de pillages»[8]. Des comportements qui s'expliquent par le non-paiement des soldats français et le manque de ravitaillement, car les caisses de l'Etat louis quatorzien finissant sont vides[9].

Pour autant, au cours de la guerre précédente, celle de la Ligue d'Augsbourg, les fourragements sont déjà monnaie courante. En août 1690, de nombreux paysans du nord du Hainaut sont touchés: à Condé, c'est plus de 45 hectares «quÿ ont estés galtés entièrement perdus et fourragés par les trouppeaux des

5 Boulé André, *Remarques et annotations de ce qui s'est passé et arrivé en la ville de Valenciennes de curieux depuis le 3ème de mai 1698 jusqu'à présent, (1698-1739)*, édité par l'Abbé Loridan, *Valenciennes au XVIIIe siècle. Tableaux historiques et journaux inédits*, Roubaix, 1913, pp. 322-342.

6 Platelle, *Journal d'un curé de campagne au XVIIe siècle*, *op. cit.*, p. 157.

7 Archives départementales du Nord (on notera dorénavant AD Nord), 9 H 2.464.

8 Cité par Defromont Arthur-Louis, *L'Avesnois au XVIIIe siècle. Contribution à l'étude des sociétés rurales*, Thèse de l'Université Lille III, 1972, p. 268.

9 Lachiver Marcel, *Les Années de misère. La famine au temps du Grand Roi*, Paris, Fayard, 1991, p. 358.

bœufs et moutons de l'armée de Monseigneur de Luxembourg»[10]. Au début du mois de juin 1694, 6 hectares de prés d'Etton Erraux sont croqués par «les chevaux des carabiniers du Roy»[11]. De l'autre côté de la frontière, près de Liège, en septembre, le fermier Nicolas Magnery note dans son livre de comptes que «les brandebourgeois ont enlevé tout [son] fourrage» entreposé dans son exploitation de Tillesse-en-Condroz[12].

Devant ces exactions, les exploitants préfèrent récolter leur blé encore vert afin d'éviter de tout perdre: en 1712, le fermier Montfort de l'abbaye de Crespin a «du faire faucher et battre ses grains à demi-mûrs, parce que deux partis de cavalerie se sont battus au milieu d'iceux»[13]. D'autres paysans essayent de se réfugier dans les enceintes fortifiées des abbayes ou en ville[14]. Ils y mettent à l'abri leurs récoltes, leurs matériels et leurs bestiaux. Ces derniers sont effectivement convoités par la soldatesque à des fins de nourriture ou de moyen de locomotion pour le transport en particulier des pièces de canons. Du bovin au cheval, en passant par le mouton, le cheptel des villages près de Valenciennes voit ses effectifs divisés au moins par deux entre 1686 et 1717 (Tableau 1).

Tableau 1. Cheptel (nombre de têtes) de 32 villages du Valenciennois victime des confiscations militaires

Année	Bovins	Ovins	Chevaux
1686	5.324	11.653	2.432
1717	2.470	4.375	1.728

Source: Bibliothèque de l'Institut de France, Ms 364 et Archives nationales, G/7/290.

10 AD Nord, C 11.172.

11 AD Nord, 9 H 2.464.

12 Rorive Jean-Pierre, *Les misères de la guerre sous le Roi Soleil. Les populations de Huy, de Hesbaye et du Condroz dans la tourmente du siècle de malheur*, Liège, Editions de l'Université de Liège, 2000, p. 377.

13 Cité par Trelcat Emile, *Histoire de l'abbaye de Crespin*, Paris, Arthur Savaete, 1923, p. 522.

14 Une immigration forcée de ruraux qui par ailleurs provoque dans la capitale hennuyère une poussée de natalité entre 1708 et 1711: Guignet Philippe, «Lille, Valenciennes et les autres au miroir des courbes paroissiales longues (1715-1789). ‹Temps des baisses› ou âge des croissances ralenties?», in *Revue du Nord*, LXXIX, (1997), p. 338.

Ces chiffres sont convergents avec les dires de l'intendant du Hainaut Dugué de Bagnols en 1698, à la fin de la guerre de la Ligue d'Augsbourg, au sujet de la région limitrophe de Bouchain: « le commerce de bestiaux pourra augmenter quand le pays sera un peu restablÿ des pertes qu'il a souffert pendant les dernières guerres »[15]. Effectivement, en 1699, on dénombre 3.886 bovins aux environs de Valenciennes contre 5.324 en 1686[16]. Malheureusement, les hostilités vont reprendre dès 1702. En 1717, on comptabilise ainsi une ponction de 1.416 têtes depuis le dernier recensement. Les causes de cette nouvelle chute, si on en doutait encore, se dégagent nettement à la lecture du *Journal* du noble valenciennois Charles-François Volckerick, après la bataille de Malplaquet du 11 septembre 1709:

> En effet, huit ou dix mille hommes, des fuyards de l'armée, s'estant retirés sur Valenciennes, se logèrent pendant la nuict dans les fossés, glacis et chemins couverts. De tous les troupeaux de moutons, bœufs, veaux, vaches et volailles que les paysans des villages circonvoisins avaient sauvé à Saint-Saulve, Marly et La Briquette, aussi bien que de ceux des habitants, il ne se trouva rien le lendemain qui ne fut tué, égorgé et en partie mangé[17].

Les moines de l'abbaye de Crespin affirment à leur tour que cette bataille « a causé une perte générale non point seulement des grains, des mars [blés de printemps] [...] mais encore les meubles perdus, ainsi que les chevaux, vaches, moutons »[18]. Après la signature du traité de paix d'Utrecht entre les grandes puissances européennes le 11 avril 1713, Charles Fiévet du village d'Iwuy déclare avoir « tout perdu ses grains, meubles, bestiaux et tout ce qu'il avoit d'effect par les troupes ennemis pendant le siège dudit Bouchain de l'année mil sept cent onze et mesme encore en 1712, de sorte qu'il ne luy reste qu'un mauvais cheval »[19]. On apprend en novembre 1713, que Roland Couplet est « réduit en pitoyable état de grande pauvreté, misère et mendicité ayant perdu deux chevaux de labour enlevés par les soldats ennemis de la place de Bouchain »[20].

15 Trénard Louis, *L'intendance de Flandre wallonne en 1698. Edition critique du mémoire « Pour l'instruction du duc de Bourgogne »*, Paris, CTHS, 1977, p. 150.

16 Bibliothèque municipale de Valenciennes, J 1. 11 (dénombrement de 1699).

17 *Journal* de Charles-François Volckerick, édité par l'Abbé Loridan, *Valenciennes au XVIIIe siècle*, *op. cit.*, pp. 163-164.

18 AD Nord, 4 H 193, pièce 132.

19 Cité par Bontemps A. et Dehaisnes O., « Histoire d'Iwuy jusqu'en 1789 », in *Bulletin de la Commission Historique du Département du Nord*, t. XVIII (1888), p. 212.

20 AD Nord, J 1.301/34.

Il faut souligner que la baisse des troupeaux n'est pas due uniquement et directement à des confiscations martiales. Outre d'éventuelles épizooties, dont les archives n'ont pas conservé la trace[21], le manque de foin et de blé suite aux fourragements et leurs prix par conséquent excessifs inclinent également à une diminution des effectifs. Alexandre Dubois le rappelle en 1711 à propos des chevaux:

> Il y a dans le village un tiers moins qu'auparavant parce qu'on n'a rien échappé pour les nourrir et que les foins et les jarbées [gerbes de céréales] sont d'une très grande cherté. Il les faut aller acheter et chercher par delà les bois vers Tournai, le foin à sept patars la petite ration et les jarbées à sept livres[22].

Flambée des prix et endettement: les premières conséquences des confiscations

La première séquelle de ces confiscations est la hausse du prix des vivres. On s'en tiendra ici aux céréales vendues à la halle de Saint Amand entre 1679 et 1710 (Tableau 2)[23]. La rasière de froment (mesure de capacité équivalant à 86,2 litres) entre 1679 et 1688 (période de paix) est en moyenne à 8 livres. Après le commencement de la guerre et jusqu'en 1692, son prix reste quasi-identique. Cela tient au fait que la région n'est pas touchée à ce moment directement par les combats à quelques exceptions près. Ceux-ci se déroulent en grande partie de l'autre côté de la frontière, aux Pays-Bas espagnols. Toutefois dès 1692, le Hainaut fait l'objet d'incursions d'armées ennemies accompagnées d'importants «prélèvements» de la part des soldats dans les réserves grainetières paysannes. Résultat: la rasière de froment passe à 24 livres et reste en moyenne à 19 livres jusqu'à la fin du conflit.

21 Contrairement à ce qu'établit Eric Shakeshaft, leur absence dans les documents d'archives ne signifie pas automatiquement leur absence sur le terrain: Shakeshaft Eric, *Epizooties chez les bêtes à cornes en Flandres, Hainaut et Cambrésis au XVIIIe siècle*, Thèse de l'Université Lille III, 2006, p. 740.

22 Platelle, *Journal d'un curé de campagne au XVIIe siècle*, *op. cit.*, pp. 153-154.

23 A titre de comparaison: Mestayer Monique, «Les prix du blé et de l'avoine de 1329 à 1793», *Revue du Nord*, t. XLV (1963), pp. 157-176 et Demoulin Bruno, *La principauté de Liège et l'Europe. Analyse du mouvement général des prix agricoles (1678-1728)*, Louvain, Centre Belge d'Histoire Rurale, 1982, pp. 5-30 Pour Saint-Amand, les chiffres s'arrêtent malheureusement en 1710.

Tableau 2. Premier impact des fourragements militaires: la hausse du prix du froment à Saint-Amand (1679-1710)

Année	Prix	Année	Prix	Année	Prix	Année	Prix
1679	11 l.	1687	4 l. 16 s.	1695	20 l. 10 s.	1703	9 l.
1680	8 l. 10 s.	1688	8 l.	1696	14 l.	1704	8 l.
1681	8 l.	1689	8 l. 10 s.	1697	16 l.	1705	8 l.
1682	9 l. 10 s.	1690	5 l. 10 s.	1698	24 l.	1706	7 l. 10 s.
1683	8 l.	1691	9 l.	1699	14 l.	1707	6 l.
1684	14 l.	1692	24 l.	1700	9 l.	1708	16 l.
1685	7 l.	1693	26 l.	1701	8 l.	1709	40 l.
1686	5 l.	1694	18 l.	1702	7 l. 4 s.	1710	18 l.

Source: AD Nord, 12 H 632; moyenne annuelle de la rasière.

On retrouve un schéma à peu près identique pour la guerre de Succession d'Espagne où les opérations se déroulent hors du Hainaut jusqu'en 1708. Néanmoins, la province sert de base arrière aux troupes françaises et les exploitants agricoles subissent des confiscations. Les religieux de Crespin rappellent qu'« en laditte année 1706 après la bataille de Ramillies [près de Namur], l'armée de France est venue camper et a fourragé en juin » dans leur village[24]. On n'observe pourtant pas de réelle élévation de la mercuriale amandinoise. En revanche, à partir de 1708 les combats se déroulent sur les terroirs hennuyers et le prix du froment s'en ressent cette fois de manière flagrante. Il convient de ne pas éluder dans cette affaire la conjoncture climatique parfois défavorable aux récoltes, au cours de notre période d'étude. On songe aux années très humides 1692-1693 et bien sûr au terrible hiver 1709 qui gèle les semences du froment plantées à l'automne 1708. Le prix de la rasière s'envole. Il atteint en moyenne les 40 livres en 1709. Malgré le retour de la paix au printemps 1713, le curé de Rumegies souligne que « toute l'année 1714, les grains furent encore d'un grand prix; mais l'année 1715, ils sont venus à un très vil prix »[25]. En fait, lors de la moisson de juillet 1713, les exploitations agricoles hennuyères sont loin d'avoir retrouvé

24 AD Nord, 4 H 193, pièce 132.
25 Platelle, *Journal d'un curé de campagne au XVIIe siècle*, *op. cit.*, p. 161.

leur niveau de production d'avant guerre. Leur remise en état de marche après les confiscations ne peut évidemment se faire du jour au lendemain: nettoyage des terres dont certaines sont retombées en friche et sont envahies par les épines et les ronces, achat de semences, de nouveaux chevaux pour la traction du matériel aratoire, de nouveaux bovins et ovins pour l'apport indispensable de fumier. Seuls les grands et moyens exploitants en fermage, appelés fermiers ou «censiers», possédant une ou plusieurs charrues, qui par définition peuvent détenir un surplus de production négociable, profitent de ces chertés, lorsqu'ils échappent par chance à des réquisitions militaires répétées. Alexandre Dubois le rappelle en 1696:

> Pour les censiers qui ont quantité de grain à vendre ou des chevaux qui n'ont plus de prix, ces sortes de gens peuvent appeler cette guerre heureuse; de connaissance d'homme, jamais ils ne furent plus riches. On vendait à Rumegies l'an 1686, 1687 et 1688 le seigle cinq patars le havot [équivaut au quart de la rasière, soit 21,55 litres], et, depuis ce temps qu'il est guerre, il a valu 20, 30, 40, 50, 60, 70, 80, 90 patars [...] Point seulement cette richesse des censiers provient de la cherté du grain, mais encore de la cherté des avoines, pois, fèves, des bestiaux [...] qui se vendent tous d'un prix excessif[26].

On saisit mieux maintenant comment un Grégoire Pierrart, puissant censier à Boucheneuil-lez-Bouchain, peut sortir de sa trésorerie, en plein cœur des combats, en juillet 1709, 10.000 livres pour la dot de sa fille, «Damoiselle Marie», qui convole en juste noce avec le fils d'un censier de Bapaume[27].

À l'inverse, pour les petits exploitants (journaliers, manouvriers, ménagers, laboureurs), l'endettement pour pallier les spoliations militaires devient vite une réalité. Les constitutions de rente et les ventes «pour s'assister à cause des grandes guerres qui ont régné et ruiné tout leur païs» encombrent les liasses de notaires, notamment celles du tabellion de Bouchain[28]. Ainsi en novembre 1710, Jean-Baptiste Buisset, ménager au village d'Ecaillon, «pour s'aider à vivre dans la calamité du temps qui règne présentement» vend au prix de 380 livres

26 Platelle, *Journal d'un curé de campagne au XVIIe siècle*, *op. cit.*, pp. 104-105.

27 AD Nord, J 1.301/25.

28 AD Nord, J 1.301/8 (avril 1698). Il n'est alors pas surprenant que dans la Flandre wallonne et le Cambrésis voisins, les ventes foncières au cours des années 1692-1694 soient multipliées par huit en quelques mois: Vigneron Sylvain, *La pierre et la terre. Le marché foncier et immobilier dans les dynamiques sociales du Nord de la France aux XVIIe et XVIIIe siècles*, Villeneuve d'Ascq, Septentrion, 2007.

une trentaine d'ares « de terres labourables en une piesse »[29]. Il en va de même pour Antoine Dufour, ménager à Marquette, six mois plutôt, pour plus de 326 livres[30]. Deux ans plus tard, Bernard Bullo, petit exploitant au même lieu est contraint également de faire une « vente de terres pour s'aider à vivre dans le temps de guerre où nous sommes »[31]. Il réitère l'opération en juillet 1713[32]. Enfin, Jacques Tellier, laboureur à Aubigny au Bac « avec quatre petits enfants à nourrir », réalise en mai 1711 une vente foncière au profit du curé Maximilien Boucher, « à cause de la chereté des vivres et du fourragement des troupes ennemies campées sur les voisinages »[33].

Une restructuration des terroirs: l'aboutissement des confiscations

Mais souvent les confiscations réitérées de la soldatesque, ajoutées aux hausses d'impôts, finissent par avoir raison de bon nombre de petits exploitants. Certains sont obligés de jeter l'éponge. Les faillites se multiplient. En 1693, le curé de Rumegies affirme que cette année « fut le tombeau de presque tous les ménagers [...] et fut l'enrichissement des gros censiers »[34]. Dès cette époque, plusieurs de ces petits exploitants relativement indépendants dits aussi « à part de charrue », qui en général cultivent 4-5 hectares et s'associent de fait avec un ou plusieurs confrères pour fonctionner, paraissent être ruinés par les guerres. Lorsqu'ils arrivent à résister à la dure conjoncture, de par leur assise terrienne, ce qui n'est pas toujours le cas[35], plusieurs grands et moyens exploitants vont tenter de tirer leur épingle du jeu. Les dénombrements des 32 villages du Valenciennois semblent le suggérer également (Tableau 3).

29 AD Nord, J 1.301/28.
30 AD Nord, J 1.301/27.
31 AD Nord, J 1.301/31: mai 1712.
32 AD Nord, J 1.301/33.
33 AD Nord, J 1.301/30.
34 Platelle, *Journal d'un curé de campagne au XVIIe siècle, op. cit.*, p. 86.
35 Delleaux Fulgence, « Les Années noires des fermiers du Hainaut. De l'endettement à la faillite (1650-1720) », in *Revue Belge de Philologie et d'Histoire*, t. LXXXV (2007), pp. 109-124.

Tableau 3. Concentration foncière autour de Valenciennes dès la fin du XVIIe siècle

Année	1686	1693	1699
Type d'exploitation			
«à part de charrue»	130	29	2
1 charrue	88	78	69
2 charrues	40	38	32
3 charrues	6	11	14
4 charrues	2	1	4
Total des exploitations	266	157	121

Source: Bibliothèque de l'Institut de France, Ms 364; Bibliothèque nationale de France, Ms 8526 et Bibliothèque municipale de Valenciennes, J 1. 11.

Entre 1686 et 1699, on passe de 130 exploitations « à part de charrue » à 2 seulement. En 1699, il ne subsiste qu'un Jean Gilleron et un Philippe Hautecoeur au village de Verchain, pour posséder chacun une demie charrue avec quatre chevaux. Six ans auparavant, il ne demeurait déjà plus que 29 exploitations de ce type. On distingue également un recul de 21,6 % des moyennes exploitations, les censes à une charrue. En 1699, elles dominent toujours l'ensemble avec 58 % du total contre 65 % en 1686. On peut présumer que pas mal de ces exploitations ont été fondues au sein d'unités plus vastes, à deux ou trois charrues. Plusieurs exemples corroborent ce type de fusion, par l'intermédiaire d'une augmentation significative du capital d'exploitation. Parmi eux, celui de la ferme de Pierre Vallet à Estreux, au sud de Valenciennes. En 1686, ce censier détient deux charrues et une cavalerie de huit chevaux. Sept ans plus tard, on recense chez lui trois charrues et quinze chevaux. La détention d'un train de culture supplémentaire ne peut être que le résultat patent d'une concentration foncière. Pierre Vallet n'est pas le seul à bénéficier d'une telle restructuration. En plus de dix années, on passe de 6 à 14 fermes à trois charrues.

Bien des exploitations à une ou deux charrues ont sans doute augmenté de manière non négligeable leur superficie sans modifier par ailleurs leur capital d'exploitation. Dans ce cas, les censiers ne préfèrent pas investir dans une deuxième ou troisième charrue qui nécessiterait des chevaux et un valet de charrue supplémentaires. En temps de guerre, nos grands exploitants cherchent à restreindre leurs charges. La capacité de la charrue apparaît être rentabilisée à son maximum, jusqu'à près de 50 hectares. Par exemple, Pierre Vallet ne dispose en 1700 que de trois charrues pour labourer ses 147,3 hectares. Ceci peut expliquer la faible hausse des exploitations à quatre charrues[36].

En 13 ans, 147 petites et moyennes exploitations agricoles ont disparu dans le Valenciennois. Ces unités de production ont donc été vraisemblablement absorbées dans de plus grands ensembles. Pour voir concrètement ce nouveau partage des terres au sein des terroirs, il convient de consulter les rôles fiscaux. Nous nous bornerons à ceux du village d'Estreux en 1700[37]. Les deux grandes fermes de Pierre et Godefroy Vallet monopolisent plus de 60 % de la superficie totale du terroir, soit 235,3 hectares. Si l'on rajoute les moyennes exploitations allant de 10 à 40 hectares, on atteint les 87 %. Le reste est occupé par de petits exploitants ne possédant bien souvent plus de train de labour. Ils sont toutefois majoritaires sur le plan numérique, puisqu'ils représentent 85,2 % de l'ensemble des exploitants[38].

Cette restructuration des terroirs s'effectue donc par un regroupement parcellaire et à certaines occasions par le cumul de deux corps de fermes entiers. À la mort de Louis XIV, Jeanne Blary, la veuve de Jacques Hautecoeur, est à la tête

36 On admet communément en Hainaut français que la charrue offre en moyenne une capacité culturale d'une trentaine d'hectares, à l'image de la Flandre maritime ou du Namurois. Cette assertion est confirmée par le rôle d'impôt du village d'Anzin de décembre 1695 où l'on apprend que « la veuve Christophe Moreau, censière occupe la labeur d'une charrue occupant 144 mencaudées », soit 32,7 hectares (AD Nord, C 13.859). Dans la région de Namur, la capacité de la charrue est évaluée à environ 26 ha d'après Recht Pierre, *Les biens communaux du Namurois et leur partage à la fin du XVIIIe siècle. Contribution à l'étude de l'histoire agraire et du droit rural de la Belgique accompagnée d'une description des classes rurales à la fin de l'Ancien Régime*, Bruxelles, Emile Bruylant, 1950, p. 239. *Idem* en Flandre maritime: Vandewalle Paul, « Stabilité et perfection d'un système agricole: la châtellenie de Furnes », in *Annales ESC*, 3 (1981), pp. 382-389.

37 AD Nord, E 1.120/6.

38 On rallie ici une caractéristique commune au Cambrésis du début du XVIIe siècle, où l'on assiste à une « polarisation aux deux extrêmes » suivant l'expression d'Hugues Neveux; pléthore de petites unités agricoles et ampleur de la surface occupée par une minorité de moyennes et grandes censes: Neveux Hugues, *Vie et déclin d'une structure économique: les grains du Cambrésis (fin du XIVe-début du XVIIIe siècle)*, Paris, EHESS, 1980, p. 237.

de pas moins de 120 hectares répartis en deux censes à Quérénaing[39]. En 1699, son défunt mari n'occupe encore que la grande cense du château à trois charrues du marquis de Nédoncelle, dont il est le receveur général[40]. Quelques années plus tard, Jacques Hautecoeur, conforté par la hausse des prix, n'hésite pas à briguer auprès du seigneur une seconde unité: la seconde cense seigneuriale à une charrue dite «le marché Jean Waxin», du nom du précédent locataire[41] avec «les chevaux et ustensiles de labour, vaches et meubles»[42]. En ces temps troublés, les deux parties en présence ont trouvé un intérêt commun à cette refonte.

Pour les seigneurs, principaux propriétaires en Hainaut, c'est l'occasion de mettre en œuvre une gestion plus rationnelle de leur réserve. N'est-il pas plus sécurisant et plus simple, pour eux, de louer un maximum de terres à seulement un ou deux grands exploitants aux reins solides qu'à une multitude de petits paysans «à parts de charrue» dont la situation est rendue très aléatoire par les fourragements et saisies de bestiaux et dont il sera peut-être difficile dans ces conditions d'obtenir chaque année le paiement de leur fermage et le versement de la redevance du terrage (8 % environ de la récolte)? Dans la mesure du possible, les seigneurs ont tout intérêt à concentrer leurs terres en un petit nombre d'exploitations confiées à des personnes capables de les entretenir et de les rendre productives et de s'assurer *in fine* un minimum de revenus. C'est sans doute pour cette raison qu'ils accordent régulièrement des ristournes de fermage ou revoient à la baisse le montant lors des guerres. Il en va ainsi de la cense de 103 hectares située au village de Cartignies et propriété de l'Abbé de Liessies. Celui-ci stipule en 1706 que Séverin Caniot, locataire des lieux, est «exempt de modération pour guerre et autres accidents [...] attendu que ledit marché a été accordé pour ce prix [1.112 livres pour toute la durée du bail et 150 livre chaque année] en considération de ces événements»[43]. Les grandes fermes ou censes revêtent alors le rôle de pièces maîtresses au sein du système

39 AD Nord, J 549/29.

40 Il est receveur de la réserve du seigneur de Quérénaing depuis au moins 1697: AD Nord, 4 G 454.

41 Bibliothèque municipale de Valenciennes, J 1. 11.

42 AD Nord, J 549/29.

43 AD Nord, 9 H 308.

Figure 1. Apparition de grandes parcelles de terres: l'exemple de la seigneurie de Rouvignies-Cantin en 1727

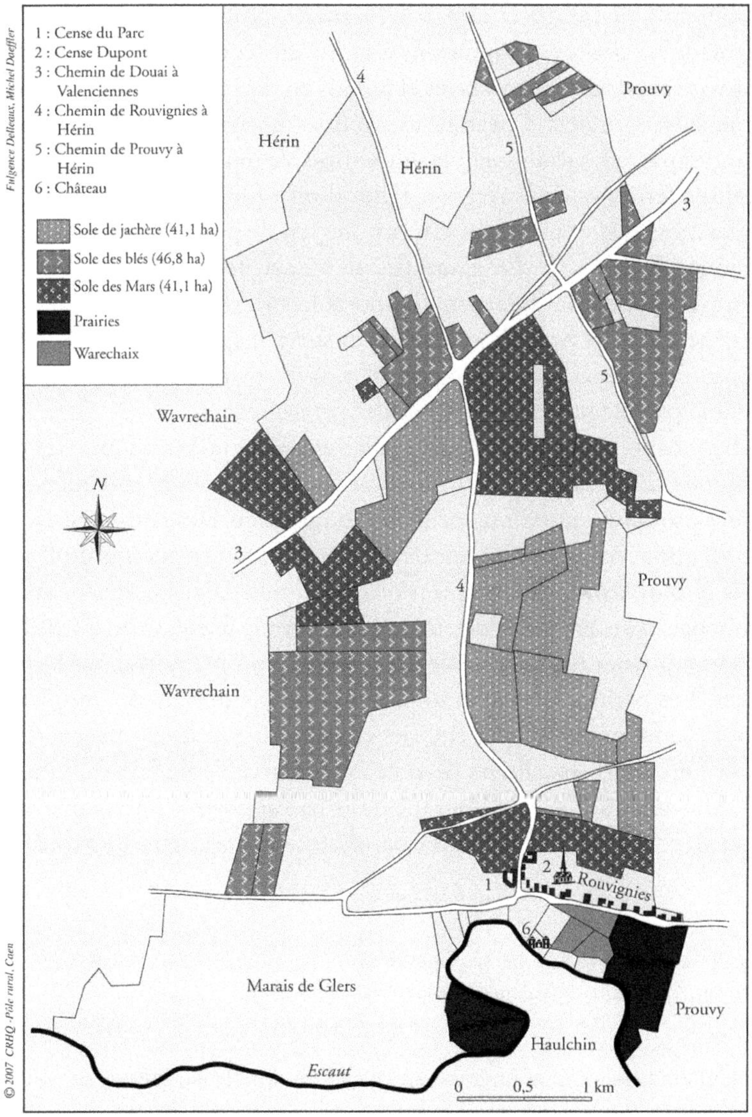

Source: Bibliothèque Municipale de Valenciennes, II 75.

économique de la seigneurie[44]. Désormais agrandies, elles occupent une place de choix dans la structure seigneuriale. Le cas de celle de Rouvignies-Cantin, sise au sud de Valenciennes, en 1727, est très significatif (Figure 1).

Le remembrement effectué par le seigneur, probablement à la suite de la dégringolade de petites exploitations à la fin du règne de Louis XIV, fait que les petites pièces de terres sont rares et jamais en dessous d'un demi-hectare. En moyenne, elles sont de 2,4 hectares. Certaines atteignent même les 9 hectares. Ces grandes parcelles soulignent la vraisemblable mutation morphologique des deux censes restantes de la réserve, celles dites « Dupont » et « du Parc ». Pour les censiers, ces rassemblements sont un moyen de prendre le contre-pied plus efficacement de la crise[45]. En agrandissant leur surface cultivable, ils se garantissent un chiffre d'affaire toujours honorable en cas de déprédation militaire sur plusieurs de leurs parcelles. Ils peuvent surtout spéculer sur ce capital agricole désormais plus considérable. En effet, il est susceptible de se transformer en véritable pactole lors de l'inflation des prix céréaliers.

Le diagnostic, que nous venons de réaliser, réclame sans doute des nuances en raison de la faiblesse de l'échantillon utilisé. Nonobstant, la tendance lourde reste: une profonde mutation socio-économique en Hainaut français à cause des confiscations militaires au temps des deux dernières guerres du Roi-Soleil. Celles-ci aboutissent à une suppression, au moins partielle, des petits exploitants indépendants au profit des moyens et grands fermiers ou « censiers » qui rassemblent dorénavant, avec l'aide des seigneurs-propriétaires, une large partie des terres. Les petits exploitants sont contraints désormais de compléter leurs revenus en se faisant employer chez les censiers. Cette situation sera dénoncée au grand jour dans les cahiers de doléance à la veille de la Révolution française[46]. Elle apparaît déjà en filigrane dans les rapports d'intendance au cours des années 1770: « Dans certaines paroisses, ce sont deux ou trois fermiers

44 Hug Stéphane, *La gestion des seigneuries dans l'espace wallon au XVIIIe siècle*, Thèse de Doctorat, Université de Valenciennes, 2006.

45 Cependant, cette stratégie n'est pas exempte de risque; voyez la faillite exemplaire de Nicolas Lasne, malgré le cumul de 230 hectares au village de Salesches à la fin du règne de Louis XIV: Delleaux, « Les Années noires des fermiers du Hainaut », *art. cit.*, pp. 332-336.

46 Rémy Francis, *Cahier de doléances de la Prévôté-le-Comte de Valenciennes. La région valenciennoise et les revendications des villageois vers 1789*, Mémoire de maîtrise de l'Université Lille III, 1973.

qui donnent la loi et qui par leur soin à augmenter l'étendue de leurs fermes, réduisent le surplus des habitants à la classe de simples ouvriers, manœuvres et valets de charrue»[47].

47 AD Nord, C6.690: lettre de l'intendant du Hainaut au Contrôleur Général (04-08-1774). Ce processus de concentration des terres et des exploitations continue tout au long du XVIIIe siècle en raison cette fois de l'importante croissance démographique que connaît le Hainaut à partir des années 1720-1730 et sur laquelle les moyens et grands exploitants souhaitent spéculer: Delleaux Fulgence, «Grands exploitants et mutations agricoles dans les campagnes du Hainaut français de Louis XIV à la Révolution», in *Actes du VIIIe Congrès de l'Association des Cercles francophones d'Histoire et d'Archéologie de Belgique*, Namur, Presses universitaires de Namur, 2011, pp. 276-278.

Jewish Assets in Italy: Attachment, Confiscation and Restitution (1938–1945 / 1943–2001)

Marino Viganò

The "Commission on Jewish Assets"

On 1 December 1998 the then president of the Council of Ministers of the Italian Republic, Massimo D'Alema, set up a *Commission for the reconstruction of the events characterising the activities of acquisition in Italy of the assets of Jewish citizens by public and private organisations,* more commonly known as the "Commission on Jewish Assets". The decrees confirmed the proposal originally issued in note 2.664, dated 30 March 1998, by Carlo Azeglio Ciampi, Minister of the Treasury in the first Prodi government. After the fall of that government on 9 October, Ciampi's note was acknowledged and carried into effect by the first D'Alema government, which was in power from 21 October.

Presided over by Tina Anselmi, deputy of the Christian Democrats from 1968 to 1992 and former president of the parliamentary commission of inquiry into the Masonic lodge "P2" from 1981 to 1985, the "Commission on Jewish Assets" included a dozen members who were high officials of the state, representatives of Bank and insurance associations, delegates of the Italian Union of Jewish communities, and archivists and historiographers nominated by the prime minister from universities, ministries or other relevant institues[1]. On

1 "Art. 2 § 1. The Commission is composed as follows: honourable Tina Anselmi, president; dott.ssa Paola Carucci, supervisor of State Central Archive, member; dott. Piero Cinti, private secretary of the Ministry of Industry, Commerce and Agriculture, member; avv. Luigi Desiderio, director of the Office for Juridical consulting and management of legal cases of the Institute for inspection on private and of common interest (ISVAP), member; dott. Antonio Farrace, retired prefect, member; avv. Enrico Granata, central director of Associazione bancaria italiana (ABI) (Italian Bank Association), member; prof. Luigi Lotti, president of Italian Historic Institute for modern and contemporary ages, member; cons. Domenico Marchetta, legislative head of Ministry of the Treasure, of the Balance and of the Economical planning, member; avv. Francesco Nanni, director of legislative area

26 March the Commission was invested, thanks to a decree of the general secretary of the Presidency of the Council, with responsibility for the historical Archive of the Banca d'Italia[2]. Assistants with specific research tasks would work along with the commissaries.

Officially installed in Palazzo Chigi on 17 December 1998 by the undersecretary of the Presidency, Marco Minniti, the Commission should have lasted 6 months; it was then extended for a further 12 months, up to June 2000[3], due to the huge amount of historically complex material gathered, and then again for another 9 months, until 31 March 2001[4]. The Commission concluded on 2 May 2001, on the eve of the political elections of 13 May, after 28 months of work, with the delivery to the press of a General Report containing data banks and lists[5]. The report included not only categorised segments, but also a guideline on how the Commission worked and how to approach the document. This proved to be more a more intricate process than initially envisaged.

of Associazione nazionale delle imprese di assicurazioni (ANIA) (National Association of Insurance Companies), member; dott. Michele Sarfatti, coordinator of the Foundation Contemporary Centre of Jewish documentation in Milan, member; avv. Dario Tedeschi, proxy of the Union of Italian Jewish communities, member; prof. Mario Toscano, researcher in 'contemporary history' – Università La Sapienza in Rome, member; dott. Marino Viganò, delegate for the researches in Italy of the independent Commission of experts 'Svizzera – seconda guerra mondiale' (Commissione Bergier), member": Decree of the President of the Council of Ministers 1 December 1998, *Institution of the Commission for the research on events characterizing the attachment activities of Jewish assets in Italy by public and private bodies*, Rome, 1 December 1998, signed "D'Alema".

2 "The above-mentioned Commission also includes dr. Sergio Cardarelli, responsible of the Historical Archive of the Banca d'Italia": Decree of the General Secretary of the Presidency of the Council of Ministers, 26 March 1999, signed "Paolo De Ioanna".

3 "The President of the Council of Ministers [...] *decrees* Art. 1 – The Commission, including all the added members, is confirmed in its mandate extended by one year starting from 17 June, in order to allow it to complete the requested tasks": Decree of the President of the Council of Ministers 21 May 1999, signed "Massimo D'Alema".

4 "The President of the Council of Ministers [...] *decrees* Art. 1 – The above-mentioned Commission is extended until 31 March 2001": Decree of the President of the Council of Ministers 18 April 2000, signed "Massimo D'Alema".

5 *Commissione per la ricostruzione delle vicende che hanno caratterizzato in Italia le attività di acquisizione dei beni dei cittadini ebrei da parte di organismi pubblici e privati. Rapporto generale*, Roma, Edizione Presidenza del Consiglio dei Ministri – Dipartimento per l'Informazione e l'Editoria, 2001, p. 540, attached CD Rom with data bank.

Context and Method

The *Commission for the reconstruction of the events characterising the activities of acquisition in Italy of the assets of Jewish citizens by public and private organisations* was established following the example of similar bodies established in five other European countries – in 1996 in Norway[6] and Switzerland[7], in 1997 in Sweden[8] and France[9], in 1998 in Austria[10]; as well as in Argentina in 1998[11]. The governments of these countries conducted research on the financial and patrimonial consequences of Fascist and Nazi dictatorships and of collaborationism with the Third Reich. They focussed on persecutions of Jews and other opponents, on cases of deportation for hard labour, and on the acquisition of goods by the Nazis in Hitler's Germany, by collaborationist governments in Europe, and also in the countries to which fascist and Nazi hierarches fled after the war.

This multifaceted historical process was carried out in a systematic way for the first time in Italy thanks to the unprecedented availability of sources

6 *Committee to investigate what happened to the property of Jews in Norway during World War II*, was nominated on 29 March 1996 by the Minister of Justice. It states that its tasks were completed on 23 June 1997 and submitted 2 reports to the Minister, one majority report signed by 5 members, and one dissenting report signed by "Reisel-Brulard".

7 *Unabhängige Expertenkommission Schweiz-Zweiter Weltkrieg – UEK*, established on 19 December 1996 following a decree of the Federal Council, ceased on 19 December 2001, after various intermediate reports it published its final report: *Die Schweiz, der Nationalsozialismus und der Zweite Weltkrieg. Schlussbericht*, Zürich, Pendo Verlag GmbH, 2002.

8 *Commission on Jewish Assets in Sweden at the time of the Second World War*, established on 13 February 1997 by the Minister for External Affairs, it completed its works on 1 March 1999 publishing: *Sweden and Jewish Assets. Final Report (Sverige och judarnas tillgangar).*

9 *Mission d'étude sur la spoliation des Juifs de France*, established by decree of the prime minister on 27 April 1997, extended on 6 October 1997, ceased on 17 April 2000 publishing a *Rapport général*, with various attachments.

10 *Historikerkommission der Republik Österreich für Restitutionsangelegenheiten*, established by the federal Government on 26 November 1998, ceased in 2003 with the publication of the report *Vermögensentzung*, München, R. Oldenbourg Verlag, 2003.

11 *Comisión para el Esclarecimiento de las Actividades del Nazismo en la República Argentina – CEANA*, established by decree of the President of the Republic on 6 May 1997, it began its work in July 1997, publishing various *Informe de Avance* of the work in 1998 and an *Informe final*, Buenos Aires, Ministerio de Relaciones Exteriores, 1999.

guaranteed by the breadth of the mandate of the Commission. According to paragraph 1 of article 1 of the decree of institution, the Commission was tasked with reconstructing the development of attachments and confiscations of Jewish assets from November 1938 to April 1945, as a consequence of the "racial laws" issued by the Fascist regime and in force in the national territory. Therefore, it considered not only the measures taken against the Italians qualified as "Jews", but also against foreign "Jewish" citizens living or travelling in Italy and, for obvious reasons, the rules and procedures of restitution concerning the assets already attached and/or confiscated before 1943. This latter mechanism was sometimes complicated by carelessness, bureaucratic hindrances and defaults which delayed and sometimes even blocked, the procedures.

In pursuit of these goals, following paragraph 2 of article 1 of the decree of institution, the Commission "which co-operates with similar organisations set up in foreign countries", had to consult "public archives and, upon previous agreement, the archives of private organisations", entrusting, if necessary, "to a single person specific inquiries of the general research, also in connection with the specific queries of the prime minister"; and "it can also order hearings of witnesses and propose the participation to its work of experts in this field". This right, as we will see below, was used from time to time in order to find sources, consult inaccessible archives, and go through monographic profiles of the events. It was even used to deal with some questions covering all the concerned subjects.

The First Tasks of the Commission

It is difficult to briefly summarize the complexity of the tasks of the Commission, the wide range of documents it unearthed, gathered and studied, the ordinary and exceptional cases it discovered: the object here is to elucidate its geographic and normative aspects. This research involved studying the areas where "racial laws" were in force, and considered whether the historical geography under review coincided with today's Italian state. Of course, the provinces established after the war are missing: some of them changed their names (Littoria is now Latina, Apuania is now Massa-Carrara); the provinces of Istria and Dalmatia are included as "possessions", the 14 islands of Dodecanese in the Aegean Sea, colonies in Africa, the Kingdom of Albania (from 1939), occupation zones in France (from 1940), the former Yugoslavia and Greece (from 1941), and also some departments of the former French "Free Zone" (from 1942).

It was then decided to separate the profiles of the spring 1938–summer 1943 period and the autumn 1943–spring 1945 period, with the turning point being the fall of the regime and the surrender of Italy to the Allies (25 July–3 September 1943). The criteria of historical geography are consistently applied and take into account the loss of the colonies in Africa (1941–1943) and of Albania (1944), the reduction of the territory subject to the Italian Social Republic (RSI) with the application of German administration inn Alto Adige and the Eastern provinces (1943–1945); and the advance of the Allies in the peninsula and retreat from France and Yugoslavia (1944–1945). The following actions were documented: "precautionary" sales and clearance sales for missing orders and credits to "Jewish" companies before the issuing of 1938's "racial laws"; sales and clearance sales which were not compulsory, breaches of orders and assignment of "surplus" real estates and of "not preservable" companies between 1938 and 1943; "legal" and "illegal" attachments and confiscations between 1943 and 1945; and then restitutions, reparations and refunds from 1944 onwards.

The activity of the Commission began with two forms of research into sources: gathering of material in known archives and investigation of forgotten warehouses which were usually untraced or inaccessible. In the first case the Archives of State and the Central office for archives were taken into account, along with the records of prefectures, police headquarters, and government commissary's offices of autonomous provinces. Moreover, other documents were secured in a variety of contexts: from the Ministry of the Treasury, of the Balance and of Economical planning; from General state advocacy; from the Ministry of Finances and General headquarters of Tax Police; from the managing director of INA (National Institute of Insurances); from Italian insurance companies; from Italian Post; from the general military prosecutor of the Republic's files on crimes committed by military forces of the Italian Social Republic and Third Reich against the assets of the "Jews"; and from the Union of the Italian Jewish communities.

Investigations and First Report

The Commission was supported by the representatives of the Italian Bank's Association (ABI) and the National Association of Insurance Companies (ANIA). Questionnaires were sent to Bank and insurance institutions to ascertain if they had documents on the matter. The inter-ministerial Commission for the collection of works of art was asked to communicate on mutual topics of research; the Central Office for archival goods invited its representatives to verify "the presence of documentary series" in connection with the investigations "with particular reference to those of towns and Banks which subscribed contracts with EGELI in order to locate the goods to be expropriated and manage them". Some institutions replied to the questionnaires that they had uncatalogued archives of unidentified material: general investigations followed and in the offices of prime minister on 16 November 1999 and 1 February 2000, representatives of the different bank and insurance institutions declared the existence and importance of the documents and their willingness to open the archives.

An important part was played by chambers of commerce and other institutions of commerce and handicraft. Following the periodical dispersion or destruction of documents in their archives, there were not many replies to the questionnaire of the Ministry for Industry, commerce and agriculture by entrepreneurial associations: Confindustria, Confcommercio, Confesercenti, Confai, Confederazione nazionale artigianato, Confederazione autonoma sindacati artigiani (CASA), Confartigianato. The same holds true for Unioncamere. From the qualitative point of view, the results were more encouraging, particularly when the data published in the "Official Gazette" regarding concerned companies is compared with the documents available in a variety of chambers of commerce.

The results pushed the Commission to edit statistical data in the *Prima relazione intermedia (First intermediate report)*. After the first six months 56 answers came from prefecture archives (41 negative, 12 interlocutory, 3 positive); 57 from the archives of the police headquarters (51 negative, 6 positive); 80 from state archives (55 positive, 25 negative); and some from the archives of the superintendents. More would come later. The answers revealed the existence of an underground and unexpectedly vast amount of exceptionally interesting documents. This convinced the Presidency of the Council to extend the Commission, as mentioned above. Huge volumes of files would be found in the Ministries of the Treasury, Foreign Affairs and Internal Affairs, as well as in the Chamber of Deputies, the Banca d'Italia, Jewish Communities, Tax Police offices, Military prosecutor's offices, technical fiscal and revenues offices, and in private hands.

Outlines of the Issue 1938–1943

Talking about racist persecutions in Italy is not the main topic of this text and it is enough to remember that in the main frame of "racial" discrimination promoted by the head of the Italian government, Benito Mussolini, and approved by the authorities of the fascist state, on 22 August 1938 the Ministry for Internal Affairs implemented its general directions on demography and race, "Demorazza", with the census of the "Jews" – following questionable criteria those qualified and defined as a "race", according to the largest estimations, numbered 58.412 individuals (among them 10,380 foreigners); the figure was 46.656 (among them 9,415 foreigners), when based upon the subscription to a Jewish community or a self-certification. The total Italian population was 45 million.

The direct consequences were measures aimed at distinguishing "Jews" from "Aryans" and to progressively limit the civil and economic rights of the former, pushing them to migrate and leave behind their assets. In September, foreign "Jews" were forbidden to live in Italy and in its possessions (Libya, the Aegean), and were forced to leave national territory within six months; their citizenship was revoked if obtained after 1919. Starting from 5 September 1938 people belonging to the "Jewish race" were no longer allowed to attend state schools, from 16 October teachers were "suspended from service"; only university students who were already matriculated could finish their studies and then only under specific conditions. On 6 October the Grand Council issued the "Declaration on race". Measures were taken "to protect the Italian race" by decree nr. 1.728, dated 17 November 1938, signed by King Vittorio Emanuele III and countersigned by Mussolini and his ministers of Foreign Affairs (Galeazzo Ciano), Justice (Arrigo Solmi), Finance (Paolo Thaon di

Revel) and Corporations (Ferruccio Lantini). "Jews" were excluded from positions in public administration and in the Fascist Party, from the possession of lands and real estates and companies of a certain size, and they could not be elected to public office.

The "Duce" then oversaw the issuing from various ministries (Internal Affairs, Finance, Public Works, Corporations, Exchanges and Currencies, Agriculture) of memoranda urging the increasingly stronger application of the rules that between 1939 and 1943 – particularly after the Italian entry into the war on 10 June 1940 – limited in an obsessive way the economic and social life of Italian and foreign "Jews", hindering this or that activity, licence or faculty. The goal was to force them to leave the country leaving behind all their assets which could not be exported. The Commission gathered, for this first period, the following topics connected with "racial" legislation: 11 laws and decrees in 1938, 17 in 1939, 9 in 1940, 2 in 1941 and 7 in 1942; 107 memoranda of a national level in 1938, 75 in 1939, 40 in 1940, 24 in 1941, 30 in 1942 and 14 in 1943 (until 13 September). The influence of other such documents which could not be found could nonetheless be estimated. Rights were drastically reduced. This situation became even worse when the borders were closed and more and more countries declared war on the Axis and refused to accept refugees. This situation lasted until the vote of the Grand Council against the "Duce" on 25 July 1943. This led to the fall of the fascist regime but also opened a new and even worse period.

Outlines of the Issue 1943–1945

The fall of the regime, the signature and the announcement of Italian surrender to the Americans (on 3 and 8 September 1943 respectively) did not immediately change the status of the "Jews". Only on 20 January 1944 did the first Badoglio government repeal the "racial" legislation in free Italy. In the rest of the country, still occupied by the Germans and governed by Mussolini and the fascists of the Italian Social Republic, the fiercest phase of persecution began and concerned other groups of people. The "Jews", bereft of any right, could still be deported. On 14 November 1943 the congress of the Fascist Party acknowledged a directive of the "Duce": "As far as the Jews are concerned", it stated, "the direction of the Party proposes that on this matter measures have to be adopted not to leave any doubt or misunderstanding and that clearly say that people belonging to the Jewish race are foreigners who, during this war, belong to the enemy nationality"[12]. The manifesto also announced, at point 7, that: "people belonging to the Jewish race are foreigners. During this war they belong to the enemy nationality". This definition seemed to be, as far as the choice of the words is concerned, aimed at a clearly identifed goal.

As they were "foreigners" and "enemies", and therefore subject to a specific and well established juridical regulation, as happened to these categories of citizens in all belligerent countries, following police order nr. 5 of the Ministry for Internal Affairs dated 30 November, the "Jews" had to be shut in a concentration camp. Their assets would be "immediately attached waiting to be confiscated", in order to refund the "victims of air raids of the enemies". Measures were implemented in Verona: "in these days we are taking care of attaching Jewish assets", read the ad. "Our goal is not to make any rhetoric, this is blood which was sucked from the Italian people: It is right that this blood is given back to the people: It seems to me that there is no better way, to give it back to the people, than to take care of the needs of the victims of bombings, of those who were touched by the war, the responsibility of which has to be given to the Jews", it was stated. "We can evaluate, thanks to the calculations we carried out, that the first sum we can place at their disposal for this goal is 1 billion lira"[13]. The Commission highlighted the following laws linked with the "racial" legislation: 13 laws, decrees and bills in 1944, and 3 in 1945; as well as 11 documents and memoranda of national level in 1943 (from October), 115 in 1944 and another 14 in 1945 (until 20 April).

The legal attachment of assets began again thanks to memoranda which intensified the application of the laws. Illegally attachments were carried out by squadrons of German and Fascist "independent police", which proliferated in a country ruined by political and administrative chaos and torn to pieces by civil war. Such 'indpendent police' groups were the main perpetrators of thefts. In the case of Italian, foreign and stateless "Jews" – who now shared

12 Archivio Centrale dello Stato (afterwards: ACS), Roma, Repubblica Sociale Italiana, Segreteria Particolare del Duce, carteggio riservato, box 61, entry 630, n. 12. *Prima Assemblea Nazionale del Partito Fascista Repubblicano*, [14 November 1943].

13 *Ibidem*.

the same destiny – they preceded, accompanied and followed deportation of those who could not quickly find a refuge. The huge quantity of assets taken from Italian and foreign "Jews" by the regime, above all in the two years of RSI, was mostly confiscated by the state and managed by administrators with the help of accountants, bookkeepers and notaries. Therefore, there was a form or method of "bureaucratic anti-Semitism", of which little is known: professional men and state employees managed the assets; they were workers who were not anti-Semitic but who took part in the process of bookkeeping and management of assets and real estates. While they were not the instigators of persecution and not even "guilty" from a legal point of view, they had to be well aware of their role.

The Administration of Attached Assets

In order to coordinate acquisition, administration and sale of the "exceeding" assets of the "Jews", the fascist government established, on 9 February 1939, the Ente di gestione e liquidazione immobiliare (EGELI) (Board for the administration and sale of real estates). Statements made by its officials in May 1945 provide an account, albeit an account which is probably skewed, of its activities, from the eve of Second World War until Liberation. The "authorized" quota and the "exceeding" quota of "Jewish assets" was calculated by revenue technical offices "multiplying by eighty the lands valuation and by twenty buildings valuation"; this amount was paid by thirty-year bonds. The Ministry for Internal Affairs had to decide whether a limitation on assets was applicable or not; the revenue technical and local offices had to calculate the "authorized" or "exceeding" value; EGELI had to transfer to Revenue Offices the research results in order to issue expropriation decrees regarding "exceeding" assets. Following the analysis of the data by the Board in September 1943, the "Jews" were deprived of quotas of real estates valued at 726 million lira, which were transferred to EGELI for only 55 million and a half (7,6%) and recorded as a "transfer" of 265 firms. Re-sold estates valued 9,800,000 lira and unsold estates valued 46 million at the end of 1943.

In the five-year period, twelve institutes co-operated with EGELI as administrators of credit on land. There were eventually nineteen such institutes. The remit of EGELI was extended in order to cope with the multiple tasks specified by the decree of the "Duce" dated 4 January 1944, n. 2: "buying, administering, transforming and selling real estates along with the real estates fixtures, as well as industrial and commercial companies for the interest or upon charge of the state". This statute was approved on 31 March 1944 and published in the "Official Gazette" on 6 April. This is the point at which administrative entries became so complicated that they were sometimes impossible to manage. As prefectures had then to evaluate the assets to be attached, they often entrusted them to commissary's offices for internal "Jewish affairs", if not to professionals or administrators who were linked with the trade union or nominated by EGELI; the result was that attachment decrees were not issued and assets did not arrive. Sometimes, even after the issuing of decrees, the administration of assets was entrusted to or retained by administrators nominated by the head of the province (the prefect).

There were many irregularities in a system of management which was fairly confused. The interference of the occupying Germans was an additional complicating factor: they carried out attachments and confiscations in Italian provinces by themselves, in an "official" form or with criminal methods, taking "Jewish" assets from the administration of the RSI. Resulting negotiations between Fascists and Nazis did little to clarify matters. In the provinces under German administration and governed by *Gauleiter* of the Reich on the "Adriatic Coast" (Fiume, Gorizia, Pola, Trieste, Udine) and in the "Prealps" (Belluno, Bolzano, Trento), Nazi legislation was directly enforced. The numerous unrecorded "Illegal" acts carried out by German forces in the Italian territory and in those governed by the *Gauleiter*, besides not being a part of the "racial" legislation, were mostly ignored as they were just criminal dispossessions and not among the administrative cases. There were many doubts about how to classify the "special actions" – whether they were not direct consequences of "racial laws" of the RSI, or whether they were side effects of the occupation of the Italian territory; there were also doubts about how to evaluate the quantity and quality of the assets taken *manu militari* by the representatives of the Reich.

The Reduction of Property Rights

The papers of the RSI point to attachments which became confiscation, of houses, companies, shops, works of art, lands, insurance policies, bank and post savings books, jewels, money, safe-deposit boxes, and objects of significant as well as of little or no value, such as: underwear, used clothes, everyday objects, and toys. Moreover, there was evidence of thefts, robberies, destructions, and ransom or bribery payments to corrupt officials to arrange an escape form the hunt or smuggling across the border. As a result, the "Jews" in the camps, those who lived underground or were fugitives, lost much of what they owned if not everything. While the Fascist government – which continuously issued decrees and memoranda against property of "Jewish origin" – called in, at the most dramatic moment of a lost war, the bureaucratic and white-collar resources to administer the attached assets, the commissary declared that, up to April 1945, 7,847 prefect's decrees of confiscation were transmitted to EGELI. Conservative administration of real estates and personal properties was given to the administrator of EGELI, authorized banks or the heads of the provinces.

Savings and bonds were transferred to adminstrating institutes in Turin, Milan and Verona (namely Fondiario dell'Istituto San Paolo, Fondiario della Cassa di Risparmio delle province Lombarde and Fondiario di Verona). Exceptions were made in several provinces: in Mantua, "the prefecture entrusted the administration to the Banca Agricola Mantovana when the attachment prefect's decree was issued, that's to say before the confiscation", therefore EGELI gave the conservative administration "to the Bank itself after the confiscation"; in Ravenna there were no confiscations due to the lack of "Jewish" assets and the liberation of the province in the autumn of 1944 by the Allies; in various regions of central Italy – Tuscany, Umbria, Latium, Abruzzi, Marche – few confiscations were carried out for similar reasons. In the period after 8 September 1943 there were thirteen institutes entrusted with the administration of attached assets.

It is difficult to estimate the reduction of the property rights of "Jews" in Italy, in the colonies, in the possessions, in the occupation zones and in the areas annexed by the Reich from 1938 to 1945. Another difficulty is posed by "racial" legislation which had side effects on the property of the communities and individuals concerned. In 1938 memoranda stated that:

> Measures of economic kind which were adopted or have to be adopted in connection with the recent decrees in order to protect the race, Requests of information concerning funds in the name of Israelites, Cession of currency and export authorization for household goods owned by people belonging to the Jewish race, Buying out of Bank credits towards the Jews; in 1939: Limits of real estate property and industrial and commercial activities for the Italian citizens of Jewish race, Measures to protect the national artistic heritage owned by the Jews, Real estates owned by the Jews; in 1940: Firing the Jews from hotel propaganda companies, Economic activities are forbidden for the people belonging to the Jewish race; in 1941: Chemists of Jewish race, Exclusion of Jewish firms from import and export activities; in 1942: Summoning of Jews for work; in 1943: Jewish assets and revenues. Jewish entrance – Extraordinary war surtax; in 1944: Registration of goods belonging to people of Jewish race, Works of art of Jewish property, Jewish assets – Registration of the credits towards the Jews, Jewish assets – Life insurance policies, Jewish assets – Attached Agricultural Companies; in 1945: Confiscated Jewish assets – Pensions and life annuity […]

The limitations, major and minor, were too numerous to list.

The Reintegration into Property

The abolishment of "racial" legislation began in free Italy in January 1944. The process spread throughout the peninsula as the Allied forces moved northwards. Meanwhile, the first restitution acts were issued and they were aimed at abolishing fascist laws; later on they would also refund or compensate victims of economic or personal persecution. The measures, which were adopted and strongly supported by legislation during the '50s and '60s but less so thereafter, solved – as far as we know – a substantial proportion of the cases of attachments and confiscations made following "racial laws" (if that is the most appropriate term). They were less effective in the cases of employment terminations, robberies and thefts carried out by personnel or units of the RSI or German forces who operated outside of these "racial laws" themselves, and in other cases involving private citizens who took advantage of the situation for their own gain.

The Commission identified a wide range of laws connected with the abolishment of "racial" legislation and the restitution of civil and property rights: 14 laws and decrees in 1944, 7 in 1945, 8 in 1946, 15 in 1947, 5 in 1948, 1 in 1949, 6 in 1950, 3 in 1953, 2 in 1954, 4 in 1955, 3 in 1956, 6 in 1957, 1 in 1960, 5 in 1961, 1 in 1962, 2 in 1963, 1 in 1965, 2 in 1967, 6 in 1968, 1 in 1969, 1 in 1970, 3 in 1971, 1 in 1972, 2 in 1973, 6 in 1974, 2 in 1978, 2 in 1980, 1 in 1983, 1 in 1987, 1 in 1994, 2 in 1997, 1 in 1998, 2 in 1999, 2 in 2000, and 1 in 2001; moreover, 3 memoranda of national level in 1943, 10 in 1945, 8 in 1946, and 2 in 1947. The procedure was carried out over a long time span and realized in a legislative manner in the shape of general measures in favour of people who were deported for political and military reasons, including partisans.

The first balance of attachments and confiscations made up the final report of EGELI (which in turn was liquidated on 29 December 1997) dated May 1945. It registered an unchanged quantity of "Jewish" assets of 45 million owned by the Board at the end of the war. EGELI entrusted the administration of real estates and movables to credit institutes and declared that the assets did not undergo any "remarkable detriment", apart from war damages, as their sale did not take place; only movable properties – furniture, clothes, personal objects, goods, state and industrial bonds, savings and credits – were partly sold, diminished, or spoilt because of thefts and bombings. Bonds, savings and credits should not have experienced any remarkable change. Companies were managed in a proper way by EGELI itself; less clear were the workings of the management of assets entrusted to administrators nominated by prefectures. This was complicated by the thefts of commercial goods by the Germans. The boundaries between the various kinds of management, the participants concerned, the total and percentage amount of managed assets, the degree of restitution, and the quantity of attached or lost assets cannot be thoroughly traced.

A Rough Balance

In the fascist "racial" legislation of 1938–1945 property was not the focus. It was much more about persecutions, slaughters and deportations and this cannot be ignored. Seventy years later Italian historiography is concentrated on the reconstruction, beginning from the sources, of the legislative processes of "state" anti-Semitism in economic and property fields and their enforcement. The task of the "Commission on Jewish assets" of the Presidency of the Council is gathering, listing and analysing the laws and decrees aimed at limiting the rights, above all the property rights, of those whom the regime wanted to classify as "Jews".

It has to verify if cases really existed or not, or if restitutions and refund were not applied for because of deaths. It must contend with the difficulties of lost documents and the problems of tracing extra-EGELI administrators. It is impossible to summarize here the huge variety of cases considered by the Commission. Among many organisation challenges – finding and gathering sources – and interpretative challenges – examining tens of thousands of particular acts, as well as general events – the "Commission Anselmi" represented the first and only attempt to recall, if possible, the principles, procedures and consequences of the attachments and confiscations of the "Jewish" assets. It documented an abnormal violation of property rights for clear-cut "political" goals rather than utilitarian goals

The main characteristic of the reductions put into force by the "racial laws" of the Fascist regime in Italy and by the "racial" or other legislations of other countries at various points is, in fact, the ideological basis of attachments and confiscations. They were planned not for common welfare, whatever it might be, or for need but to exclude from society some categories of citizens, subjecting them to economic and other restrictions which became more and more widespread. The goal was to force them to migrate once they were deprived of jobs and assets. Concerning this matter, and it is almost a paradox, the programme of the RSI for attaching all "Jewish" assets and for "meeting the needs of the victims of bombings", seems to be more utilitarian and less ideological than that of the regime: taking away to discriminate. The violation of property rights based upon "political" reasons and carried out by Fascism can be considered, in the end, as a warning to evaluate those legislations which are not based on personal sanctions or attachments for a certain goal but which are aimed at affecting a community on the basis of ethnic and abstract criteria.

II

Models and Practices of Expropriation in the Modern Age

Modèles et pratiques de l'expropriation durant l'époque moderne

Expropriations (et confiscations) d'immeubles pour la construction des Offices

Claudia Conforti et Francesca Funis*

L'expropriation et le chantier

Le succès de la valeur politique et propagandiste de la *forma urbis* est le produit de l'absolutisme moderne. La beauté de la ville ne peut être qu'une beauté « réglée », qui reflète l'ordre, l'équité, l'abondance, la justice et la rigueur propres au pouvoir du Prince. La règle, l'utilité publique et l'ornement à Florence, à Mantoue, à Ferrare, ainsi qu'à Rome, contribuent à la prospérité des sujets pour la gloire des Princes. Pour atteindre ces objectifs, il a fallu adopter des restrictions très nettes – quoique partielles – du droit de propriété du sol et des immeubles; ceci même hors des urgences de la guerre, lorsque les nécessités de défense devancent le droit de propriété. On justifie ainsi la démolition de couvents et de faubourgs pouvant abriter les troupes ennemies. À partir de 1551, Cosme Ier de Médicis (1537-1574) – duc puis grand-duc (1569) de Florence – adopte des normes qui règlent l'expropriation et la configurent comme une vente forcée d'un bien dont la valeur marchande est essentiellement reconnue par une indemnisation[1]. Avant d'aborder les différents cas d'expropriation ainsi

* Le premier paragraphe de l'article a été rédigé par Claudia Conforti, alors que le deuxième a été rédigé par Francesca Funis.

1 Décret ducal du 28 janvier 1551 (*Legge di commodo di quelli che volessino edificare...*), in Cantini Lorenzo, *Legislazione toscana raccolta e illustrata da L. Cantini*, Firenze, 1800-1808, vol. II, 28 janvier 1550, pp. 194-197; Cascio Pratilli Giovanni, Zangheri Luigi, *La legislazione medicea sull'ambiente*, Volume 1, Florence, Leo S. Olschki, 1998; Romby Giuseppina Carla, *La costruzione dell'architettura nel Cinquecento. Leggi, regolamenti, modelli, realizzazioni*, Florence, Alinea, 1982, pp. 81-105. Pour des indications relatives au bâtiment réalisé après ce décret, voir Conforti Claudia, « Cosimo I e Firenze », in Conforti Claudia, Tuttle Richard J. (a cura di), *Storia dell'architettura italiana, Il secondo Cinquecento*, Milano, Electa, 2001, pp. 130-165; Belluzzi Amedeo, « Residenze di Mercanti fiorentini nel Cinquecento », in Calabi Donatella, Beltramo Silvia (a cura di), *Il mercante patrizio. Palazzi e botteghe nell'Europa del Rinascimento*, Milano, Bruno Mondadori, 2008, pp. 117-130.

que les confiscations – justifiées par d'urgentes raisons d'ordre politique – nécessaires pour construire les Offices (1559-1581), il faut évoquer quelques aspects concernant la structure et la fiscalité des biens fonciers et immobiliers de la ville au début de la principauté des Médicis.

Dès 1532, toute propriété des citoyens de Florence était enregistrée dans un cahier – la *Decima Granducale* – de même que tout changement de situation patrimoniale. L'aliénation volontaire d'un bien et l'expropriation, ainsi que tout passage de propriété et toute démolition de bâtiments privés sont régulièrement signalés dans les volumes de la *Decima Granducale* qui – même si cela n'arrive pas toujours immédiatement – signale la suppression de la taxe immobilière en question. Les *Filze di Partiti* (tomes 175-189) et les *Libri di Partiti* (tomes 31-35) des Dîmes Grand-ducales enregistrent, pour chaque propriétaire, la description du bien possédé, la raison de l'éventuel effacement et une garantie de l'annulation soussignée par des personnes de confiance et au courant du fait.

Dans ce fonds, conservé aux Archives d'État de Florence, sont recensés tous les propriétaires expropriés suite à la construction des Offices: l'attestation de garantie est à chaque fois rédigée et signée par le Chancelier de la *Fabbrica dei XIII Magistrati* (soit les Offices), Giuliano Speziali da Terranova. Lorsque l'effacement de la Dîme s'avérait particulièrement compliquée du fait qu'il s'agissait d'immeubles composés de plusieurs parcelles, la garantie du Chancelier était accompagnée d'une autre attestation souscrite par Bernardo Puccini, inspecteur de la *Fabbrica dei XIII Magistrati*, ingénieur militaire très réputé à l'époque et disciple du célèbre Bellucci, dit *Il Sanmarino*.

Dans les registres de la *Decima Granducale* figurent aussi les dates d'effacement de la dîme qui fixent le début du calcul des intérêts à 5 % sur le capital à verser au propriétaire exproprié. Il importe de préciser que dans le cas des expropriations pour les Offices, les ventes forcées ont été conclues sans aucune transaction monétaire. Durant les dix premières années qui suivaient la vente du bien, les propriétaires étaient indemnisés avec des titres de crédit déposés au *Monte di Pietà* dont la valeur – égale à l'estimation du capital – ne pouvait être touchée, seuls les intérêts – dont le taux fut fixé, selon la coutume, à 5 % par an – étant versés aux expropriés[2].

2 Cosme Ier avait l'habitude d'utiliser pour toute nécessité d'ordre étatique ou familial et pour tout chantier public ou privé les fonds accordés par les lieux pieux florentins, parmi lesquels le Mont de Piété, l'Hôpital des Innocents et celui de Santa Maria Novella, qu'il utilisait

Ces titres de crédit pouvaient être échangés, vendus et légués par testament, à travers un acte notarié; par ce biais, ils continuaient à circuler, même longtemps après la démolition de l'immeuble objet du titre de crédit[3].

Nonobstant la méticulosité de la bureaucratie du gouvernement de Cosme Ier, dans les registres des dîmes grand-ducales on ne trouve aucune information concernant les bâtiments à exproprier (et à abattre) pendant la construction des deux premiers *Uffici dell'ala Lunga di Levante*, à côté de l'église de San Pier Scheraggio, près du Palazzo Vecchio.

Cette curieuse absence s'explique probablement par l'existence, sur le terrain en question, d'une agglomération de propriétés ecclésiastiques liées à l'ancienne église paroissiale. Les biens religieux jouissant d'une exemption fiscale, ils ne figuraient pas dans les cahiers des dîmes.

Dans ces registres fiscaux, on précise par contre explicitement si la date de l'expropriation (et du calcul des intérêts) coïncide avec celle de la démolition du bâtiment, ce qui constitue une donnée fondamentale pour notre recherche. On y indique aussi lequel des treize futurs offices de la *Fabbrica* affecte les fonds pour l'expropriation de la propriété. Des siècles après, cette information permet encore de localiser ces lots à l'intérieur du périmètre de la nouvelle construction. La comparaison et le collationnement de toutes ces informations a permis de faire une récapitulation topographique schématique des offices et des unités immobilières préexistants. Elle représente un instrument très utile pour l'évaluation rapide des procédures d'estimation qui précèdent l'expropriation (Figure 1).

À l'instar de l'ordre ducal du 26 juin 1560[4], les sept *Arti e Magistrature* transférés dans les sept sièges de *Levante* étaient auparavant situés à San Piero all'Arno; il s'agit des *Nove Conservatori del Dominio*, *Mercatanti* ou *Calimala*, *Cambio*, *Seta*, *Medici e Speziali*, *Fabbricanti* et *Mercanzia*. Dans les *Uffizi di*

comme trésorerie. Sur l'importance de l'expropriation pour la construction des Offices, voir Conforti Claudia, *Giorgio Vasari architetto*, Milano, Electa, 1993, p. 162 et Gavitt Philip, *Charity and children in renaissance Florence: the ospedale degli Innocenti, 1410-1536*, Ann Arbor, University of Michigan Press, [s.e.], 1990.

3 Voir l'acte notarié pour le recouvrement du crédit de Piero et Alamanno Gherardini. Archives d'État de Florence (désormais ASFi), *Notarile Antecosimiano 19.421*, Protocolli di Speziali, cc. 233r-v) et la demande pour le paiement d'un crédit à Suor Orsina (ASFi, Magistrato Supremo 1.330, n. 292).

4 ASFi, Magistrato Supremo 4.310 (Libro IV di Deliberazioni Pubbliche), cc. 42r-45r. Cantini, *La Legislazione Toscana*, IV (1802), p. 43; Lessmann Johanna, *Studien zu einer Baumonographie der Uffizien Giorgio Vasaris in Florenz*, Bonn, 1975 (Diss. dactyl.), doc. 6, pp. 232-234.

Figure 1. Giuseppe Ruggieri, *Pianta del Piano Terreno degl'Ufizi ed altri quartieri, sotto i quali vi è la scuderia,* 1742.
Disegno a penna e acquerello su carta; cm 52 x 74;
libro aperto cm 51 x 150 circa.

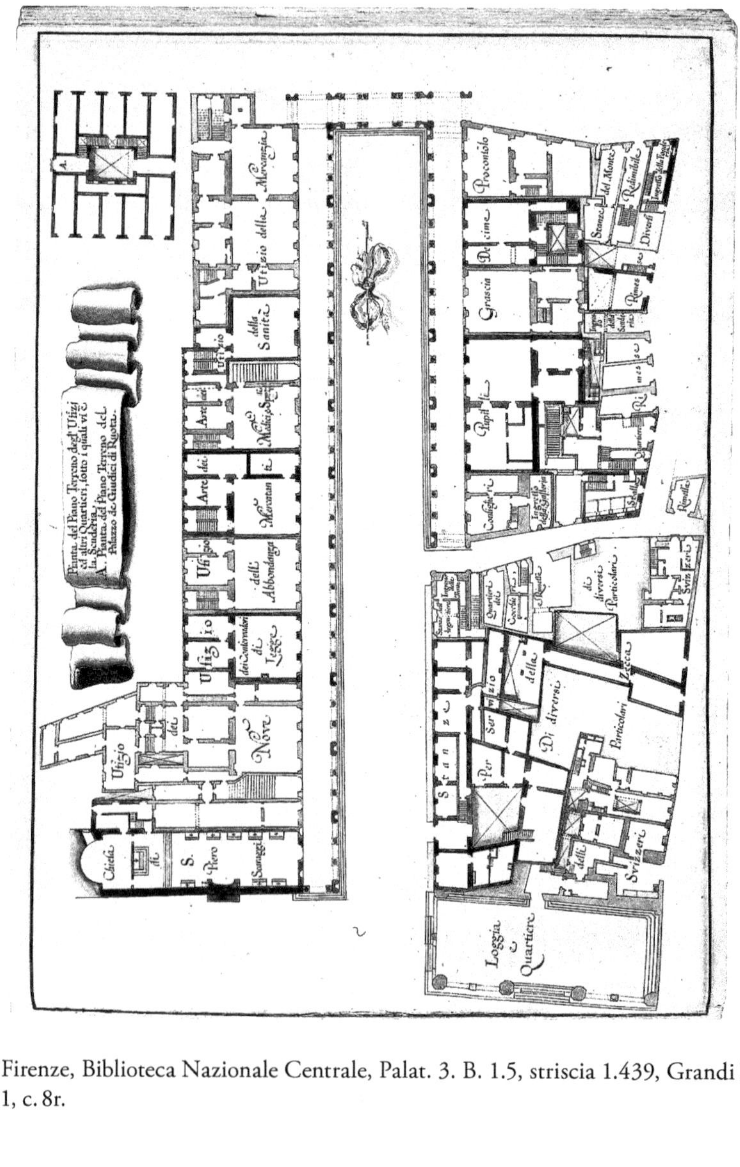

Source: Firenze, Biblioteca Nazionale Centrale, Palat. 3. B. 1.5, striscia 1.439, Grandi Formati 181, c. 8r.

Ponente, depuis la partie postérieure de la loge des Lanzi où se trouve l'ancien Hôtel de la Monnaie, s'alignent en direction de l'Arno les *Pupilli*, les *Conservatori delle Leggi*, les *Commissari delle Bande*, la *Grascia*, les *Decime e Vendite* e l'*Onestà*. La phase préliminaire de la construction du bâtiment concernant les premières expropriations et démolitions – ainsi que la fouille et le coulage des fondations, le triage et l'accumulation systématique des matériaux de démolition destinés au réemploi – n'était ni gérée par la *Fabbrica* ni par les ministres chargés de l'édification, mais par chaque *Arte e Magistratura*, à savoir les institutions mêmes qui seront accueillies dans les nouveaux espaces administratifs. Ce résultat inattendu est le fruit des comparaisons réalisées sur des sources différentes et hétérogènes[5]. Depuis le commencement des travaux (début du mois d'août 1560) jusqu'à la nomination de Bernardo di Francesco Puccini en qualité d'Inspecteur Général (juin 1561), chaque corporation gère directement la première phase des expropriations et la démolition des immeubles qui se trouvent sur la parcelle où sera édifié son propre office. Elle gère aussi directement – chacune par rapport à la parcelle (ou les parcelles) de sa pertinence – le stockage des matériaux de réemploi, les fouilles et le coulage du *primo* (juillet-novembre 1560) et du *secondo* (février-mai 1561) *fondamento* de la loge.

Au moment même où l'on jette les fondations des arcades – composées de treize sections autonomes, indépendantes et asynchrones – les inspecteurs des magistratures procèdent au déménagement des maisons situées à proximité. Ils informent les « habitatori de' siti vicini ai primi fondamenti che infra octo dì ce le relascino perché non si può fare doppo il primo, il secondo fondamento senza haver il possesso ». Autrement dit, les responsables du chantier sollicitent les habitants du voisinage immédiat aux premières fondations à déménager dans les huit jours, car on ne peut creuser les secondes fondations sans la possession totale du sol; il est donc nécessaire de *scasarli*, c'est-à-dire de les déloger[6].

5 Nous avons comparé les données trouvées dans le *Memoriale*. Cf. ASFi, Nove Conservatori della Giurisdizione e del dominio fiorentino 3.710; la transcription intégrale du manuscript est publiée dans Conforti Claudia, Funis Francesca (a cura di), *Deliberazioni di Partiti della Fabbrica de' 13 Magistrati*, Ministero per i beni e le attività culturali, Direzione generale per i beni architettonici e paesaggistici, Roma, Gangemi, 2007, « Filze di Partiti » (ASFi, *Decima Granducale*, vol. 175-189), dans les Dîmes avec les « Libri di Partiti » (ASFi, *Decima Granducale*, vol. 31-35) et Arroti, dans les deux cahiers du *Cambio* (ASFi, Arte del Cambio 115) et de la *Grascia* (ASFi, Nove Conservatori della Giurisdizione e del dominio fiorentino 3.726) et dans les *Notarili*.

6 Deliberazioni di Partiti 2007, *op. cit.*, c. 4v.

Les documents attestent que parmi les treize magistratures, au moins huit confient ces tâches à un maître maçon jouissant de leur confiance et œuvrant sur deux modules. Il s'agit de Bernardo di Monna Mattea pour les *Mercatanti*, de Tommaso di Giuliano del Mugello pour le *Cambio*, de Domenico di Zanobi pour les *Pupilli* et la *Seta*, de Noferi Salta pour la *Mercanzia*, de Baccio Lottini pour l'*Onestà*, de Giovanni di Valdimarina pour les *Decime e Vendite* et enfin de Battista Battaglioni pour les *Conservatori di Legge* et les *Bande*. Une fois les secondes fondations achevées, les *Arti* renvoient les maçons, tout en gardant les *scalpellini e cazzuole* (à savoir les tailleurs de pierre et plâtriers). À compter du 23 mars 1561, restent sur le chantier trois équipes d'ouvriers maçons, chacune sous un maître d'œuvre choisi parmi ceux qui avaient été appelés précédemment: Giovanni di Valdimarina, Baccio Lottini et Bernardo di Monna Mattea. Les trois équipes travaillent simultanément, chacune sur un tiers du chantier.

Les premières fondations (juillet-novembre 1560) d'où s'élèvent les colonnes et les piliers de la loge, s'étendent le long d'une tranchée continue d'une largeur de 3,6 brasses et d'une profondeur comprise entre 9,75 et 13,5 brasses; elles délimitent aussi le périmètre en U de la place (240 brasses pour les *Uffizi lunghi*, 32,6 pour la tête et 132,6 pour les *Uffizi corti*). Les arcades définissent les contours de la « route-place », qui est tracée dès 1546, lorsque Cosme Ier entame la première phase des expropriations et démolitions. Les deuxièmes fondations (février-mai 1561) d'où se dressent les murs des façades intérieures de la loge, sont jetées sur les ruines d'un vaste ensemble d'immeubles occupés par la *Fabbrica*, en août 1560, suivant une tranchée continue et parallèle à la précédente mais plus longue (254,5 brasses pour les Offices longs, 56,5 pour la tête et 147 pour les Offices courts) et plus large (4 brasses), bien qu'aussi profonde. Derrière les deux fondations, les démolitions se poursuivent jusqu'en 1566. Ainsi, l'aile ouest de l'*Ufficio dei Pupilli*[7] – dont l'édification s'étale sur plusieurs années – englobe plusieurs bâtiments: en 1560, en 1561 et en 1566. À droite, les *Fabbricanti*, le deuxième Office depuis l'Arno incorpore des immeubles en 1560, en 1561 et en 1563[8].

7 ASFi, *Decima Granducale 184*, « Filza di Partiti », c. 219r-v; *Deliberazioni di Partiti* 2007, *op. cit.*, cc. 64v, 90r, 109r, 111v; ASFi, *Decima Granducale 187*, « Filza di Partiti », c. 785r; ASFi, *Decima Granducale 34*, « Libro dei Partiti », c. 95r.

8 *Deliberazioni di Partiti* 2007, *op. cit.*, cc. 64r, 88r, 92r.

Déménagements et expropriations

Les trente-sept cas d'expropriation pour la construction des Offices ont des caractéristiques communes, propres d'ailleurs à toutes les procédures d'expropriation destinées à l'édification, à Florence, de bâtiments et mises en œuvre par le décret ducal du 28 janvier 1551, à savoir la *Legge di commodo di quelli che volessino edificare ...*[9]

Lors de précédentes études, nous avons déjà examiné trois cas, dont deux se distinguent par leur caractère exceptionnel[10]. Le premier concerne l'achat par le Grand-duc du palais des Castellani[11], qui se trouve pratiquement adossé à la *Fabbrica*, mais en dehors du périmètre du projet. Le deuxième se réfère aux *Mannelli*, un cas tout à fait inhabituel puisqu'il s'agit d'une expropriation manquée pour la réalisation d'un couloir reliant le Palazzo Vecchio au Palais Pitti. Ci-dessous nous présentons une série d'*exempla* qui illustrent les pratiques d'expropriation les plus fréquentes – et donc les plus éclairantes – effectuées à Florence au cours du XVIe siècle.

L'évaluation du bien constitue l'acte préliminaire de chaque expropriation: dans ce but, dès mars 1560 (l'achèvement de la maquette en bois du nouveau bâtiment date de la fin de l'an 1559[12]), l'inspecteur Antonio de' Nobili est adjoint à Giorgio Vasari (1511-1574), architecte ducal et auteur du projet des

9 Cf. note 1: Décret du 28 janvier 1551 (*Legge di commodo di quelli che volessino edificare...*), in Cantini, *Legislazione toscana, op. cit.*, Firenze, 1800-1808, vol. II, 28 janvier 1550, pp. 194-197.

10 Conforti Claudia, Funis Francesca (sous la dir), *Dalla Pubblica Comodità alla Pubblica Utilità: un caso di esproprio nella Firenze del Cinquecento*, in «Urbanistica», CXLV (2011), pp. 77-81.

11 ASFi, *Decima Granducale* 2.280, Arroti dell'anno 1560, Santa Croce 3, c. 86; ASFi, *Magistrato dei Pupilli del Principato* 2.708, cc. 70r-73r; ASFi, *Notarile Antecosimiano* 8.739, Protocolli di Dell'Orafo, c. 164v; ASFi, *Magistrato dei pupilli del Principato* 14, c. 203r; ASFi, *Notarile Antecosimiano* 8.742, Protocolli di Dell'Orafo, c. 150v-156r; ASFi, *Magistrato dei pupilli del Principato* 14, c. 276r; ASFi, *Notarile Antecosimiano* 8.742, Protocolli di Dell'Orafo, cc. 240r-241r.

12 Lettre du duc Cosme Ier de Médicis à Giorgio Vasari du 24 octobre 1559; Arezzo, Musée de la Casa Vasari, Carte Vasari (AVA), Cod. 8, c. 21 (Archives de Rasponi Spinelli, Cod. XLII, n. 11); Frey Karl, *Il Carteggio di Giorgio Vasari, edito e accompagnato di commento critico dal Dott. Carlo Frey*, München, Georg Müller, 1923, CCLXXXIII, pp. 520-521; Lessmann, *Studien zu einer Baumonographie, op. cit.*, doc. 1, p. 229.

Offices[13]. Il est chargé de procéder aux estimations des maisons et des ateliers qui se trouvent à l'intérieur de l'aire où sera édifié la *Fabbrica* (le mot indique à la fois le chantier et le futur bâtiment) et qui sont destinés à la démolition[14].

Pour identifier sur le plan topographique les immeubles qui occupent l'espace de chaque magistrature et en donner une estimation quantitative, Vasari utilise un modèle[15] qui lui permet d'établir pour l'ensemble de l'aire les niveaux altimétriques, d'évaluer les dénivellations du terrain (caractérisé par une forte pente) et de déterminer les volumes éventuellement réutilisables[16].

Dès le départ, il est clair que la possibilité d'exploiter cette aire repose sur des expropriations systématiques, les propriétaires ne pouvant ni s'y opposer ni s'y soustraire. La preuve en est que le duc souscrit l'ensemble du projet bien avant la première rédaction de l'inventaire des estimations des immeubles à acquérir.

Les procédures d'évaluation des immeubles devant être expropriés sont clairement attestées: l'architecte et l'inspecteur désignent chaque parcelle à exproprier par un numéro leur permettant de l'identifier de façon univoque dans tout document de nature notariale, comptable ou fiscale (par exemple dans le Registre des Dîmes), mais aussi dans le *Memoriale*, qui recueille les prescriptions ducales réglant l'édification des Offices[17]. L'identification des parcelles par des numéros (écrits en chiffres romains) est confirmée par le seul dessin qui nous est parvenu. Contemporain du projet des Offices, il est attribué à Giorgio Vasari, du fait de la présence, au verso, d'un dessin portant sa signature[18]. L'analyse calligraphique de ces inscriptions semble désavouer cette attribution à l'architecte

13 En ce qui concerne la *Fabbrica*, son chantier et son contexte artistique par rapport à la cour de Cosme Ier de Médicis, voir Conforti Claudia, Funis Francesca, de Luca Francesca (a cura di), *Vasari, gli Uffizi e il Duca*, catalogo della mostra Firenze 2011, Firenze, Giunti 2011.

14 Lettre de Giorgio Vasari à Cosme Ier du 5 mars 1560, in: ASFi, *Mediceo del Principato* 483/A, c. 793r. Gaye III, p. 55; Milanesi VIII, XCIII; Karl Frey 1923, CCXCIV, pp. 533-534 ; Lessmann, *Studien zu einer Baumonographie*, *op. cit.*, doc. 3, p. 229-230.

15 ASFi, Mediceo del Principato 659/A, c. 156r; ASFi, Nove 3.710, cc. 1v, 43v.

16 Lettre de Giorgio Vasari à Cosme Ier du 5 mars 1560, cit.

17 Par exemple, une propriété de Iacopo del Rosso Pieri est identifiée par le numéro 36 dans ASFi, *Notarile Antecosimiano 19.420*, protocolli di Speziali, c. 24r-v; ASFi, *Decima Granducale184*, Filza di Partiti, c. 360r; *Deliberazioni di Partiti* 2007, *op. cit.*, c. 71v.

18 Ferri Pasquale Nerino, *Indice geografico-analitico dei disegni di architettura civile e militare esistenti nella R. Galleria degli Uffizi in Firenze*, Firenze, 1885, p. 4.

de Arezzo[19], qui n'a probablement tracé de sa main que le périmètre de la parcelle. Le dessin délimite le périmètre de l'Office de *Decima e Vendita* (Figure 2), la deuxième magistrature en partant de l'Arno située dans l'aile ouest: du point de vue géométrique, en dessous du plan de l'Office sont dessinés, comme en filigrane, les périmètres des parcelles cadastrales à exproprier.

Ces dernières sont orientées selon une trame oblique par rapport aux Offices – reflétant ainsi l'aménagement des tracés de bâtiments médiévaux – que la nouvelle construction de Cosme va bouleverser. Le dessin en question n'est évidemment pas le véritable projet: il s'agit simplement d'un relevé graphique de synthèse, esquissé pour des raisons cadastrales, pour évaluer le nombre et l'entité des expropriations par rapport à l'office en question. Les immeubles sont représentés graphiquement et identifiés par des numéros en chiffres romains et par le nom des propriétaires. Le relevé indique aussi la répartition des frais de démolition entre les différentes magistratures: les propriétés entièrement à la charge de l'Office de Dîme sont marquées d'une ligne continue, tandis que les parcelles qui ne relèvent que partiellement de sa compétence (« ce n'entra il terzo ») – ou pas du tout[20] – sont hachurées. Les données qu'on retrouve dans les Dîmes, dans les contrats et dans le Mémorial (voir annexe 1) prouvent que la numérotation des immeubles destinées à la démolition ne suit ni la séquence topographiques des sites, ni les temps de démolition des bâtiments: bien que la démolition ait été exécutée des années plus tard[21], cette liste a été rédigée selon l'ordre d'enregistrement des estimations dans la *Filza Prima* (qui a été égarée) des *Ufficiali della Fabbrica*.

À l'instar des normes fixées par le décret ducal du 28 janvier 1551 (*Legge di commodo di quelli che volessino edificare…*), les estimations seraient le résultat d'un examen opéré par les experts des deux parties (les vendeurs et les acquéreurs). Toutefois, les documents qui nous sont parvenus ne mentionnent que les noms des experts ducaux, à savoir Bernardo d'Antonio di Monna Mattea et Piero del Zucca[22], deux techniciens renommés du bâtiment florentin du XVIe siècle.

19 Fairbairn Lynda, *Italian Renaissance drawings from the collection of Sir John Soane's Museum*, London, Azimuth Editions, 1998, vol. 1-2, II, pp. 517, 520.

20 Gabinetto Disegni Stampe Uffizi, 236v A.

21 Cf. *Deliberazioni di Partiti* 2007, *op. cit.*, passim.

22 Pour une note bibliographique synthétique sur Bernardo d'Antonio, dit di Monna Mattea, voir Funis Francesca, « Scavalcando il fiume la costruzione del corridoio vasariano », in Conforti Claudia, Hopkins Andrew (a cura di), *Architettura e tecnologia. Acque, tecniche e cantieri nell'architettura rinascimentale e barocca*, Roma, Nuova Argos, 2002, p. 68, note 14.

Figure 2. Anonimo, *Pianta e topografia dell'Ufficio della Decima e Vendite* Marzo 1560; Penna e acquerello su tracce di matita su carta bianca; mm 350 x 194

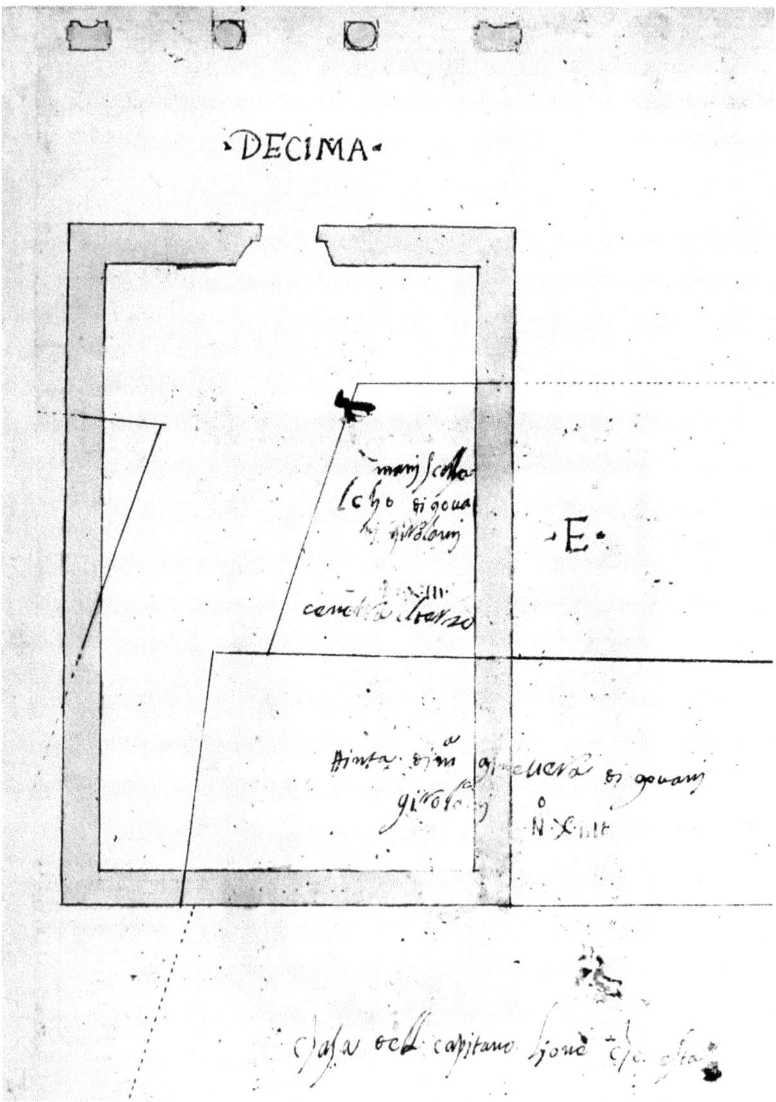

Source: Firenze, Gabinetto Disegni e Stampe degli Uffizi, 236Av.

L'analyse des documents suggère en premier lieu une discordance entre l'évaluation du nombre des immeubles et des propriétaires. Alors que les listes des matériaux de construction indiquent 234 estimations, les immeubles expropriés ne sont que 37 et concernent 43 noyaux d'habitation[23]. Cette donnée montre à la fois la forte densité d'habitation des immeubles en question et leur subdivision en plusieurs unités d'habitation de petite surface, louées à l'habitant.

En second lieu, on relève aussi l'hétérogénéité du tissu urbain précédant la construction des Offices dans les zones situées à l'ouest et à l'est de la route qui, depuis 1546, relie le Palazzo Vecchio au fleuve. Les treize propriétés situées dans l'aile occidentale, du côté où se dresse l'Hôtel de la Monnaie du XVe siècle et la Loge des Lanzi du XIVe siècle, sont relativement vastes et bien bâties. Par contre, du côté opposé, en direction de l'église de San Pietro Scheraggio, s'entassent des masures et des taudis que Vasari qualifie de « porcili, le più scomode abitationi et luoghi da non essere abitati se fussino altrove »[24].

Il s'agit de petits magasins, bistrots, ateliers de tisseurs, matelassiers et teinturiers ayant pour seule et unique valeur – soulignée par Vasari – leur contiguïté avec le palais Ducal et l'Arno. Le fleuve fournissait d'ailleurs l'énergie hydraulique aux diverses activités artisanales que ces ateliers abritaient, ce qui explique aussi les loyers très élevés, voire exorbitants, en dépit de leur état souvent déplorable[25]. « [...] luoghi da non essere abitati se fussino altrove » (« lieux qu'on n'habiterait jamais s'ils se trouvaient ailleurs »): cette remarque de Vasari anticipe le critère de la quantification des estimations des experts ducaux. Les

Maître maçon au parti guelfe, Piero del Zucca réalise de très nombreuses estimations pour le duc, notamment celle du palais des Castellani, effectuée en 1568 avec Battista Battaglioni pour la partie ducale et Filippo di Baccio di Agnolo et le menuisier Giovanni Moretti du côté des Castellani. ASFi, Magistrato dei pupilli del Principato 14, c. 203r.

23 D'après la lettre de Bartolomeo Concino à Vasari du 10 mars 1560, il y aurait « *quaranta tre [...] case* » (AVA, Cod. 13, c. 124; Karl Frey 1923, CCXCV, pp. 536-537; Lessmann, *Studien zu einer Baumonographie*, *op. cit.*, doc. 4, p. 231), alors que les numéros progressifs attribués aux immeubles à exproprier sont trente-sept (ASFi, *Nove Conservatori della Giurisdizione e del dominio fiorentino 3.710*, passim); pour les « *234 stime fatte dalli stimatori* » voir *Deliberazioni di Partiti* 2007, *op. cit.*, c. 47v.

24 Lettre de Giorgio Vasari à Cosme Ier du 5 mars 1560, *cit.*

25 Conforti, *Giorgio Vasari architetto*, *op. cit.*, p. 162; Conforti Claudia, « Gli Uffizi: progetto e cantiere della Fabbrica dei XIII Magistrati », in *Rassegna di Architettura e Urbanistica*, XXVIII, n. 84/85 (1994-1995), p. 38.

estimations des immeubles ne sont pas calculées en fonction de leur rente périodique (mensuelle ou annuelle) qui définit le prélèvement fiscal des Dîmes, mais d'après la qualité de l'immeuble: « non tanto quanto elle rendono oggi d'entrata per le pigioni loro, ma tanto quanto vale la quantità e la qualità delle mura » explique Vasari dans cette lettre à Cosme[26]. Il faut donc « luogo per luogo [a] misurare [...] la qualità de muri et de palchi[27].

Le critère d'estimation favorise évidemment les intérêts des promoteurs de l'expropriation qui dédommagent les propriétaires en estimant, d'après la dimension de l'immeuble, la quantité de matériaux de construction qu'ils peuvent tirer de sa démolition.

Par ces critères, favorables à ses intérêts, la *Fabbrica* peut réutiliser les pierres, les briques, le bois, le fer et profiter de leur vente. En ce sens, les experts ducaux évaluent les immeubles à démolir comme autant de matériaux de construction destinés au réemploi et dont la *Fabbrica* est l'unique bénéficiaire. Pour cette raison, ils attribuent une valeur supérieure aux murs les plus épais, aux planchers les plus solides (à savoir les greniers en bois convenablement bâtis), en privilégiant les bons matériaux par rapport aux mauvais[28].

Ceci dit, dans la casuistique des exemples que nous avons pris en compte, le choix de ce critère pour l'estimation des bâtiments à exproprier est assez singulier: il se justifie à la fois par la destination finale des immeubles expropriés – dans ces cas, il ne s'agit ni de restructuration ni d'agrandissement, mais d'une démolition complète – et par le principe sous-tendu aux expropriations de la *Publica Commoditas*, sur lequel repose le projet des Offices.

La profonde déchirure infligée dès le 26 juillet 1560 au tissu urbain de Florence fut appelée par les chroniques de l'époque la grande *« muraglia rovinata »*[29]; dans le projet ducal, au contraire, elle apparaît comme une sorte de carrière à ciel ouvert idéale, d'où extraire les matériaux de construction. D'après les prescriptions des Délibérations et des Partis des *Ufficiali della Fabbrica*[30], les treize Arts et Magistratures pouvaient puiser à cette carrière afin

26 Lettre de Giorgio Vasari à Cosme Ier du 5 mars 1560, cit. (« il ne s'agit pas d'estimer la rente actuelle de la location de ces immeubles mais leur valeur par rapport à la quantité et à la qualité des murs », note du traducteur).

27 « mesurer endroit par endroit la qualité des murs et des planchers en bois », note du traducteur.

28 Lettre de Giorgio Vasari à Cosme Ier du 5 mars 1560, cit.

29 ASFi, *Decima Granducale* 3.582, c.92 avere. (« muraille en ruine », note du traducteur).

30 *Deliberazioni di Partiti* 2007, *op. cit.*, c. 70r.

de réemployer les décombres des bâtiments ruinés ou de les vendre à des tiers. En fait, les éléments de petite taille tels que les pierres et les briques étaient affectés, d'après le projet de Vasari, à chaque Art et Magistrature pour la partie inclue dans le périmètre de l'office en cours de réalisation. Dans les caisses de la *Fabbrica* conflue aussi l'argent provenant de la vente des « coprimi, legnami, ferramenti et conci »[31].

Nous présentons ici quelques cas spécifiques que l'enquête a permis de mettre en lumière suite à l'examen des expropriations réalisées lors de la construction des offices et du couloir de Vasari reliant le Palazzo Vecchio au Palais Pitti.

En premier lieu, l'*osteria di Baldracca*: un bistrot avec débit de vin, fréquenté par des femmes de mauvaise réputation, conférant le nom à la ruelle et au quartier, connus sous le toponyme de *in Baldracca*. L'historien Benedetto Varchi le mentionne dans *L'Ercolano*, un dialogue littéraire publié en 1570, après sa mort. Dans ce texte, l'auteur dialogue avec le comte Ercolano au sujet du vulgaire toscan:

> Baldracca era, ed è un'osteria in Firenze vicina alla piazza del grano, ma starà ben poco a non esser più, perché l'Eccellenza del nostro Duca, essendo ella quasi dirimpetto al suo palazzo, la vuol fare spianare, e murare in tutti quei contorni, edifizii e casamenti, dove si ragunino i Magistrati[32].

Les documents révèlent néanmoins qu'entre 1546 et 1562 l'*osteria di Baldracca* fut par deux fois au moins démolie et par trois fois rouverte aux alentours du *Palazzo Vecchio* et de l'Arno. Malgré ces multiples démolitions et reconstructions, elle conserva son rôle d'auberge et de lieu de rencontre et de détente tant pour les ouvriers que pour les habitants. Son emplacement originaire est localisable grâce aux documents des inspections du 15 février 1546 pour la réalisation de la nouvelle route entre le Palais Ducal et le fleuve. Par ce dossier on apprend que « stanze dua terragnole di Girolamo et Giovanni Corbinelli alato [sic] alla cucina dell'hostaria di Baldracha di deti Corbinelli [è valutata]

31 Des tuiles, des bois, des quincailleries et des claveaux.

32 Varchi Benedetto, *L'Ercolano*, Firenze, Giunti, 1570; édition consultée: *L'Ercolano, dialogo di Benedetto Varchi dove si ragiona delle lingue e in particolare della Toscana e fiorentina…*, Firenze, Per L'Agenzia Libraria, 1846, pp. 438-440. (« Baldracca était et est un bistrot de Florence près de la piazza del grano, mais bientôt il ne sera plus car notre Duc, ayant son palais pratiquement en face, veut le faire raser pour y faire construire des édifices et des bâtisses où les Magistrats se réuniront. », note du traducteur).

compra et stimata per fiorini centotrenta, fiorini 130»[33]. L'*hostaria* se trouvait à proximité de Piazza del Fiorino et donnait sur une ruelle, *chiasso di Baldracca*, qui avait pris son nom. Après les démolitions de 1546, le bistrot fut déplacé de quelques brasses de son lieu d'origine. Il occupa alors l'une des masures donnant sur la cour autour de laquelle on construira les Offices, «pratiquement en face» du palais ducal, comme le note Benedetto Varchi[34]. Dans ce cas aussi, le nom du bistrot s'étend à la rue qui – poursuivant le tracé de via Lambertesca – croisait les loges des *Mercanti* et du *Cambio* qu'on allait construire. L'auberge, la taverne et la cuisine de propriété des Corbinelli confinaient avec la *Congregazione della Visitazione* et étaient probablement placées à l'intérieur du périmètre du futur *ufficio dei Mercatanti*, le deuxième office à partir de San Piero Scheraggio.

On a des nouvelles de cette deuxième *osteria di Baldracca* par l'évaluation faite en 1560 pour l'édification de la Fabrique des treize Magistrats: indiquée par le numéro 9, ses espaces furent occupés par le chantier dès le 1er septembre 1560. Les officiers de la *Fabbrica* établirent aussi le moment du passage de l'usage du bien à sa propriété: il décidèrent que le charcutier et le patron de Baldracca devaient payer le loyer du bistrot au propriétaire seulement jusqu'à la fin du mois d'août 1560, quand celui-ci deviendrait «creditore da quel Magistrato nel cui nuovo sito la viene o verrà comprehesa et occupata per la concorrente quantità della stima factane»[35].

D'après les deux recensements des maisons et des ateliers rédigés en 1561, lors des démolitions pour l'édification des offices, *l'osteria di Baldracca* avait déjà été abandonnée, le deuxième emplacement étant ainsi l'un des premiers bâtiments à disparaître. Le bistrot avait été rouvert en dehors du périmètre de la *Fabbrica dei Magistrati* en phase d'élaboration, dans le lot situé entre la ruelle qui délimitait le côté postérieur oriental des offices – qui dès lors fut nommé

33 ASFi, Magistrato Supremo 4.307, Libro I di Deliberazioni Pubbliche, c. 20r; ASFi, Pratica Segreta 158, c. 102r; ASFi, Scrittoio delle Fortezze e Fabbriche, Fabbriche Medicee 17, c. 14 dare e avere («il s'agit de deux pièces, de propriété de Girolamo et Giovanni Corbinelli, situées au rez-de-chaussée, à côté de la cuisine de l'*hostaria de Baldracha* de Corbinelli, qui ont été évaluées et achetées pour 130 florins», note du traducteur).

34 Varchi Benedetto, *L'Ercolano*, *op. cit.*

35 *Deliberazioni di Partiti* 2007, *op. cit.*, cc. 43v-44r («créancier du Magistrat qui a pris ou prendra la place du bistrot et percevra une somme d'argent correspondante à l'estimation», note du traducteur).

chiasso di Baldracca – et Piazza del Vino, qui correspondait au tracé actuel de la rue des Castellani. L'« hosteria detta l'hosteria di Baldracca nuova », gérée par un nouveau patron – Giovanni Antonio Mannucci, – avait deux accès: l'un par Piazza del Vino, juste à l'endroit surnommé *canto del segno del vino*[36] et l'autre par *chiasso di Baldracca*, une ruelle qui un peu plus loin prenait le nom de *via dell'Oro* (rue de l'Or).

Le deuxième cas considéré concerne l'expropriation de biens appartenant à Bernardo di Raffaello Girolami. Républicaine et adversaire des Médicis depuis toujours, la famille Girolami avait recouvert d'importantes charges pendant la République. Raffaello Girolami (1472-1532) avait pris part activement à la vie politique de la République florentine comme Prieur. De plus, il avait été l'un des Douze Bonshommes, ainsi que Gonfalonier de justice (1529-1530). Lorsque les Médicis prirent à nouveau le pouvoir après la victoire des forces impériales et papales, Raffaello fut destitué et emprisonné, d'abord au Bargello, puis dans les prisons de Pise où il décéda en 1532. Son fil Bernardo (né en 1521), également hostile au gouvernement des Médicis, dut abandonner la ville et s'exiler en France. En 1554, il fut déclaré rebelle par Cosme Ier et dépossédé de tous ses biens[37]. Parmi les biens confisqués il y avait deux petites maisons, faisant partie d'une plus ample demeure d'une valeur considérable, estimée à de 1.350 écus. Elle avait son accès principal depuis le Lungarno et le côté postérieur sous les voûtes des Girolami et des Castellani, eux-aussi expropriées pour l'édification des Offices. De l'attestation sur l'effacement de la dîme, souscrite par l'inspecteur de la *Fabbrica* Bernardo Puccini, on apprend que la confiscation des biens fut décrétée comme peine pour la rébellion de Bernardo et que le duc en fit cadeau à son fidèle *condottiere*, le capitaine Leone de' Santi da Carpi[38].

Les *Provveditori della Fabbrica* assignèrent à l'immeuble du capitaine Leone[39] le numéro 28 et décidèrent de ne pas le démolir, mais de l'unifier à l'office des *Decime e Vendite*. Le bâtiment confisqué confinait avec une autre propriété des Girolami, à savoir l'atelier de maréchal-ferrant de Giovanni Girolami, et

36 ASFi, *Decima Granducale* 3.781, ricerca delle case di Firenze, Quartiere di Santa Croce, 1561, c. 90r-v; ASFi, *Decima Granducale* 3.784, c. 70r.

37 Arrighi Vanna, ‹Girolami, Raffaello› in *Dizionario Biografico degli Italiani*. XVIII, Rome, Istituto della Enciclopedia Italiana, 1975; Calonaci Stefano, ‹Girolami, Bernardo›, *ibid.*

38 ASFi, Decima Granducale 187 (Filza di Partiti), cc. 55r-56r.

39 *Deliberazioni di Partiti* 2007, *op. cit.*, cc. 9v, 10r, 10v, 11r, 15r, 15v, 16r, 16v, 17r, 25v, 26r, 52r, 53r, 54r, 55v, 58v, 62v, 63v, 65r, 99v.

l'atelier de teinturier – incluant aussi la tour médiévale – propriété de Costanza Antinori, épouse de Giovanni Girolami. Les deux immeubles, identifiés par les chiffres romains XIII et XIV[40], étaient destinés à la démolition. D'après le plan du GDSU 236/A, derrière l'office des *Decime e Vendite* se situait la propriété du capitaine Leoni de' Santi où on avait écrit *« che resta »* (« qu'elle reste »). Comme nous l'avons déjà relevé, cet édifice aurait dû être rattaché à la nouvelle *Fabbrica*. En réalité, il sera accidentellement détruit par l'écroulement de la maison-tour des Girolami se trouvant à ses côtés[41]. L'effondrement de la tour et d'une partie du bâtiment du Capitaine ouvre de nouveaux scénarios et provoque des expropriations supplémentaires. Pourtant, d'après les techniciens, la maison aurait pu être habitée; il suffisait de construire un passage aérien permettant de la raccorder aux autres pièces – au-delà de la ruelle – faisant partie de la propriété des Gherardini, qui était déjà « compresa nelle stime fatte et che avanzano a questa muraglia » (« comprise dans les estimations faites »)[42].
L'édit ducal du 29 avril 1561 « facciasi per hora in questo modo » trancha la question[43]: l'architecte de la *Fabbrica* Giorgio Vasari s'engagea à construire ce passage, tout en cherchant à rassurer le Capitaine Leoni – « non mi bastava l'animo quietarlo », écrit-il au duc[44] – et à le convaincre de l'habitabilité et du décorum de l'immeuble qui avait été réintégré avec tant de difficultés[45].

Le dernier cas examiné illustre une forme d'expropriation forcée commune aux 37 immeubles situés à l'intérieur du périmètre de la *Fabbrica*. Antonio Castellani possédait la moitié du palais Castellani – celle de moindre valeur

40 Les deux propriétés sont indiquées par les numéros XIII et XIV dans ASFi, *Decima granducale* 184, « Filza di Partiti », c. 98r-v; *Deliberazioni di Partiti* 2007, *op. cit.*, c. 64r et dans le dessin Gabinetto Disegni Stampe Uffizi, 236v A; par contre, dans le contrat notarié l'indication de la parcelle est omise: ASFi, *Notarile Antecosimiano 19.421*, Protocolli di Speziali, cc. 365r-367v.

41 AVA Cod. 13, c. 26 (antico ARS, Cod. XLVII, N° 13); ASFi, *Mediceo del Principato* 604, Inserto 9, cc. 450v-451r; *Deliberazioni di Partiti* 2007, *op. cit.*, cc. 9v, 10r, 10v, 11r, 15r, 15v, 16r, 16v, 17r, 19r, 52r, 54r, 55v, 58v.

42 *Ivi*, cit., c. 10r. (la propriété des Gherardini étant déjà considérée dans les estimations, elle n'avait pas subi d'expropriation, note du traducteur).

43 *Ivi*, cc. 9v, 10r, 10v, 11r, 15r, 15v, 16r, 16v, 17r, 25v, 26r, 52r, 53r, 54r, 55v, 58v, 62v, 63v, 65r, 99v.

44 AVA Cod. 13, c. 26 (antico ARS, Cod. XLVII, N° 13); Karl Frey 1923, CCCXLI, pp. 619-621; Lessmann, *Studien zu einer Baumonographie*, *op. cit.*, doc. 54, pp. 264-265.

45 *Deliberazioni di Partiti* 2007, *op. cit.*, c. 10r.

puisqu'elle donnait sur Chiasso d'Oro et non sur la place homonyme – ainsi que quelques masures dans la même ruelle. La proximité du fleuve en faisait une zone très intéressante pour les tisseurs de brocart[46] et les teinturiers, qui utilisaient une herbe médicinale – la guède – pour colorer les étoffes en bleu. La proximité du Palais Ducal justifie aussi la présence d'ateliers de bridiers, de selliers, de maréchaux-ferrants. Par son inspecteur, Luca Mini, en charge jusqu'à la fin du mois de mai de 1561, la *Fabbrica* acquit le 1er août 1560 l'immeuble de Chiasso d'Oro. On ne procéda pas immédiatement à sa démolition; en revanche, le 29 avril 1561, Luca Mini loua la maison à Pietro di Antonio, un bridier de Borgo San Jacopo. Dans la marge gauche du document, le chancelier précise que cette maison est la « n. 37 »[47], attestant ainsi sa correspondance avec le numéro d'expropriation que Giorgio Vasari et Antonio de' Nobili avaient attribué à cette propriété. À l'échéance du contrat de location, la maison aurait dû être démolie.

Ces procédures, qu'on peut d'ailleurs relever dans d'autres cas, font ressortir deux éléments distincts: tout d'abord, elles laissent entrevoir une timide volonté de sauvegarde de l'activité productive du propriétaire. Ce dernier, en effet, peut immédiatement toucher l'intérêt de 5 % sur la valeur des biens expropriés sans devoir faire face à des incertitudes quant à la date fixée pour sa démolition. Il peut ainsi louer dans la même zone une autre maison non intéressée par le chantier. Ensuite ce cas – comme les deux autres illustrés précédemment – met en évidence le fait que nonobstant la présence du chantier de la *Fabbrica*, la demande à l'égard des masures situées à proximité restait intacte. Elles continuaient d'ailleurs à être exploitées jusqu'au moment de leur démolition. En d'autres termes, les masures conservaient leur valeur d'usage en dépit de leur contiguïté avec le fleuve et le Palais Ducal. Le calendrier des appropriations des vieux bâtiments par la nouvelle *Fabbrica* explique le développement chronologique du périmètre du chantier. De même, le cadre des incorporations des vieux bâtiments montre que les changements continus des limites de la *Fabbrica* étaient constamment signalés dans les documents notariaux, dans

46 La propriété « n. 35 » appartient aux Pacini, tisseurs de brocart. ASFi, *Notarile Antecosimiano* 19.421 (Protocolli Speziali), cc. 147r-v; ASFi, *Notarile Antecosimiano* 6.669 (Protocolli di Fabbroni), c. 349r; ASFi, *Decima Granducale* 3.667 (Campione a parte anno 1549), c. 32 dare-avere.

47 ASFi, Notarile Antecosimiano 19.420 (Protocolli di Speziali), c. 26r-v.

les Dîmes, ainsi que dans les deux recensements des maisons et des ateliers rédigés en 1561[48]. En l'espace de quelques mois, des maisons, des teintureries et des bistrots attenants à la Fabrique se retrouvent à l'intérieur du périmètre du chantier, exploités comme dépôts pour les outils du chantier, puis démolis. La démarcation entre les immeubles gardant leurs fonctions productives et d'habitation et la zone des démolitions est tracée, au fur et à mesure qu'on construit, par des lignes concentriques qui s'élargissent à partir du périmètre des premières fondations et s'étendent en profondeur jusqu'aux offices derrière la galerie. Elles jouent ainsi un rôle de premier plan au cœur de la nouvelle capitale des Médicis.

Annexe 1. Schéma des immeubles expropriés

Office	Numéro attribué	Date	Propriétaire	Rue
1 Nove				
	XII	01/08/1560	San Piero Scheraggio – sito et cortile, pozzo, tecti et volta et stanza sopra detta volta e casa dove abitava il Franzese	
	XII	01/08/1560	Cristofono di Girolamo di Bartolomeo Vannelli texitor di panni lani	
2 Mercatanti				
	VIII	fine 08/1560	Congregazione della Visitazione e sua cucina compresa nell'osteria dei Corbinelli	Via Baldracca
	IX	01/09/1560	Girolamo di Carlo pizzicagnolo et hoste di Baldracca et Giovanni di Lorenzo di Girolamo Corbinelli, Osteria taverna e cucina detta di Baldracca	Via Baldracca

48 *Ivi*, c. 24r.

Office	Numéro attribué	Date	Propriétaire	Rue
3 Cambio	V	01/08/1560	Alexandro di Bardo fa albergo nella casa di Iacopo d'Antonio del Rosso Pieri (Osteria o albergo detto la Bruna)	Chiasso di Baldracca
	VI	03/06/1564?	Simone di Bartolomeo Isolani tavolaccino	
	?	01/05/1564	Monna Lisabetta vedova donna fu di Pagolo di Iacopo Mangieri	
4 Seta	XV	01/11/1563	Gherardo Gherardini	
5 Medici e speziali	VII	01/11/1563	Cappella di San Salvestro di San Piero Scheraggio – quattro casette	
	XVII	01/08/1562	Giovanni di Roberto della Foresta – Tinta	Chiasso d'oro
	XVI	16/08/1560	Guasparri d'Antonio Fetti tintore	
6 Fabbricanti	XVIII	01/11/1561	Francesco di Giovan Baptista del Gabburra	Chiasso d'oro
	XIX	01/11/1563	Antonio di Bartolomeo Castellani	Chiasso d'oro Ch. Baldracca
	XX	01/09/1560	Ridolfo di Francesco Lotti	Baldracca
	XXII	01/11/1563	Jacopo di Vittorio del Rosso Pieri	Chiasso d'oro
7 Mercanzia	XXXII	01/08/1560	Battista di Bartolomeo di Corso tavolaccino detto Mazzaferri	Piazza d'Arno rovinata
	XXXIII	01/08/1560	Monna Paula di Donato d'Arezzo e Tommaso di Michele Miransù	Angolo tra Lungarno Castellani
	XXXIV	01/11/1562	Monna Margherita vedova figliola fu di Ser Antonio di Marcho Lippi e donna fu di Ser Francesco Peri	Via Castellani

Office	Numéro attribué	Date	Propriétaire	Rue
	XXXV	01/08/1560	Giovanmaria Pacini e Monna Lisabetta vedova donna fu di Lorenzo di Pacino di Francesco.	Da' Castellani
	XXXVI	03/12/1560	Iacopo di Vittorio del Rosso tintore appigionata a Girolamo d'Antonio tintor di guado et Davit di Giovanni battilano (istruendo vallato)	Da' Castellani Chiasso Baldracca
	XXXVII	29/04/1561	Pietro di Antonio di Pietro brigliaio	Chiasso d'Oro
	XXXVII½ XXXVII½	01/08/1560 10/11/1560	Antonio di Bartolomeo Castellani	
8 Pupilli	XXIV	01/08/1560	Suor Orsina – San Matteo Arcetri – una casa e un magazzino sotto la camera di detta casa – «a piè della Zecca»	Chiasso di Baldracca
	XXV	01/11/1561	Francesco di Giovanni di Nerlo altrimenti del Coreggiaio (merciaio)	Via de' Pulci
	XXVI	01/05/1566	Lorenzo di Lorenzo di Piero Galli	
	XXVII	01/11/1566	Niccolò di Giovanfrancesco Baroncelli	
9 Cons legge	X	01/11/1566	Iacopo d'Agnolo Giacomini	
10 Bande	XXIX	01/06/1561	Piero e Alamanno di Antonio Gherardini	
	XXX	01/08/1560	Piero di Bartolomeo Castellani	
11 Grascia	XXVIII	17/12/1560	Girolamo di Bernardo di Zanobi Guidotti Casa dei Girolami	
	XXXI	26/07/1560	Matteo Quercetani	

Office	Numéro attribué	Date	Propriétaire	Rue
12 Decime e Vendite	XIII	01/08/1560	Ginevra Antinori nei Girolami – Casa a uso di maniscalco	
	XIV	01/08/1560	Ginevra Antinori nei Girolami– Tinta	
	XXVIII	06/08/1560	Giuliano di Raffaello di Francesco Girolami data al capitano Leone	via di Lungarno volta de' Castellani
13 Onestà	XIII, XIV		Case di Ginevra Girolami	
		01/05/1565	Aschanio di Messer Bastiano di Francesco da Ripa– Corridoio Vasariano	

Expropriation, Forced Sale, and Compensation: Legal Institutions and Professional Practice in Rome during the Pontificate of Alexander VII Chigi (1655–1667)

MARIA GRAZIA D'AMELIO*

Richard Krautheimer, in his still unsurpassed volume *The Rome of Alexander VII* (Rome 1987), reconstructed the building activity undertaken by Pope Alexander VII (Fabio Chigi, 1599–1667) to bring Rome back to its former glory[1]. When he became pope in 1655, only a few piazzas of the city had been regularized, and only the urban areas developed in the sixteenth century – along the edges of the Campo Marzio, Colonna and Monti quarters – were innervated by streets that were relatively wide and straight. The contrast between monumental edifices and simple housing (*domestica*) on medieval lots of land was glaring. It is interesting to read the comments of an English traveller, who was shocked by the discrepancy: "There is no other city where the churches, convents and palaces look so noble [...] and the other buildings look so poor"[2].

Comfortable and *convenient, ornament* and *embellishment* are terms used repeatedly in documents concerning Chigi building sites. They were used to justify works that redesigned and modernized buildings, straightened and broadened roads, and expanded and regularized piazzas. Significantly, these squares were called *hippodromum, theatrum, machina heroica*[3].

* Dedicated to Vera Comoli, whose words are in my heart. I thank Iris Jones for her invaluable help.

1 Krautheimer Richard, *The Rome of Alexander VII, 1655–1667*, Princeton/N.J, Princeton University Press, 1985, trad. it. *Roma di Alessandro VII: 1655–1667*, Roma, Edizioni dell'Elefante, 1987. See the fundamental Connors Joseph, "Alliance and Enmity in Roman baroque urbanism", in *Römisches Jahrbuch der Bibliotheca Hertziana* 25 (1989), pp. 207–294; Connors Joseph, *Alleanze e inimicizie. L'urbanistica di Roma barocca*, Roma, Laterza, 2005.

2 Krautheimer, *The Rome of Alexander VII*, *op. cit.*, p. 135.

Plate 1. G.B. Falda, *Disegno delle fabriche prospettive e piazze fatte nuovamente in Roma d'ordine della S.ta di N.S. Papa Alexandro VII*, Giovanni Giacomo de Rossi, Rome 1662.

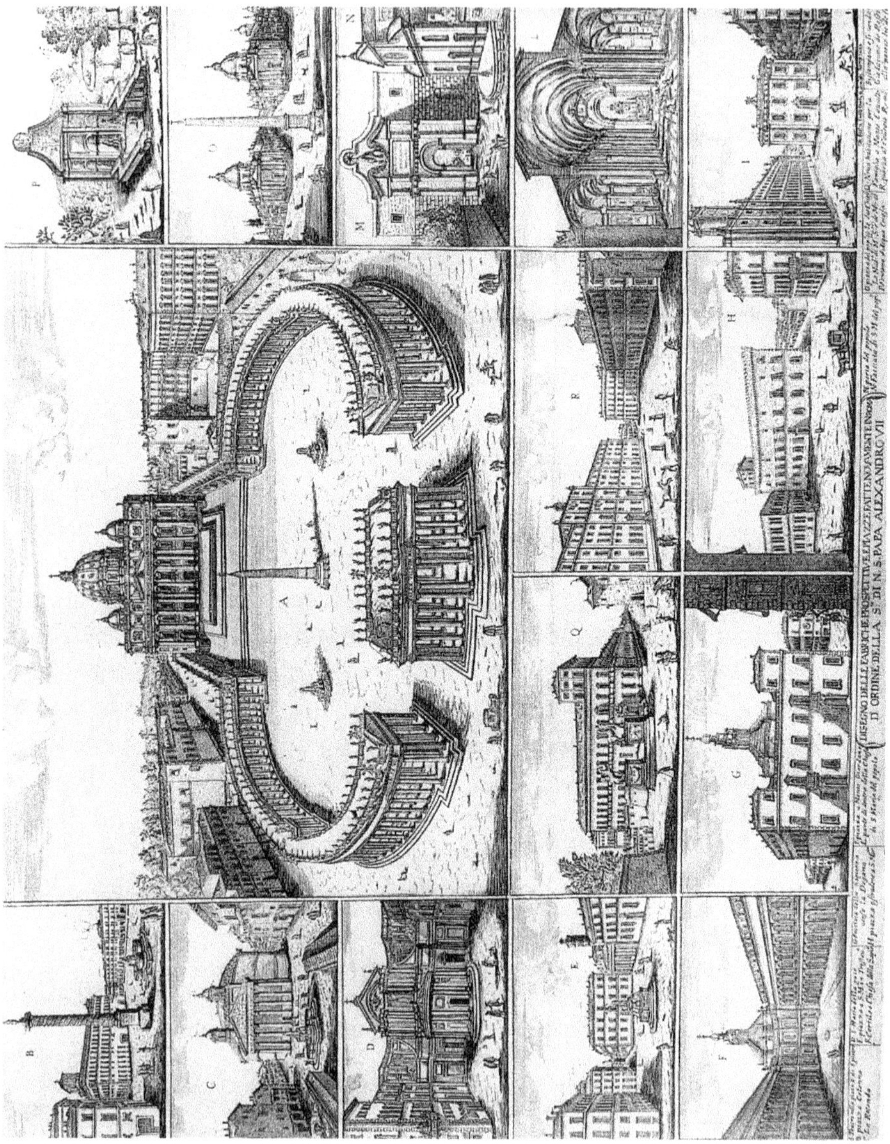

The Chigi pope's first, ambitious goal was to superimpose *Alexandrian Rome* on other images of Rome: the most glorious city of antiquity and the centre of the Church, which had been the city's role since the age of the apostles. This *Alexandrian Rome* would be characterized by large squares, broad, straight roads, opulent churches and splendid palaces. It was an eloquent response to post-Westphalian Europe[4]. Alexander's second objective was to use architecture as a driving force to re-establish Rome's economy, after the devastating epidemic of oriental bubonic plague, which spread from Naples to Rome in 1656[5].

Apart from the buildings and infrastructures immortalized in Giovanni Battista Falda's engravings, how much of Alexander VII's *Modern Rome* was realized? Why was the Pope unable, in spite of his aspirations, to open any large, new roads, and instead simply implemented tiny, microsurgical operations in the dense city fabric, straightening, flattening and removing projections from existing roads?

Although further research is needed to answer the first question, one of the reasons that projects were not realized during his pontificate was certainly that buying land and buildings that could be demolished was very expensive, too expensive even for the Holy See. Another, equally important reason, was that in the seventeenth century there were no specific norms on the procedures of expropriation and compensation, in spite of the fact that almost two centuries had passed since Pope Sixtus IV's bull *Et si cunctarum civitarum* was

3 Falda Giovanni Battista, *Nuovo Teatro delle Fabriche et edificij in prospettiva di Roma moderna sotto il felice pontificato di N.S. Papa Alessandro VII*, Giovanni Giacomo de Rossi, Roma 1665 and 1667.

4 Not surprisingly, Giovan Battista Falda's dedication of the "piccola pianta" (1667) to Alexander VII is supported (left) by Faith crushing Heresy and (right) from Architecture stepping on Time to give the Pope's name enduring fame.

5 "Havendo la Santità Vs. resoluto […] dar occasione di tener occupata tanta quantità di artisti", Biblioteca Apostolica Vaticano (from now on BAV), *Codice Chigi*, H I 22, fols.102–103. The same reasons "pro sovventione pauperum aliorum indigentium familiarum Urbis" are used in the minutes of the *Congregazione* held on August 19,1656, Archivio Fabbrica San Pietro (from now on AFSP), Arm. 16, Rip. A, Vol. 163, ff. 89 r e v, see D'Amelio Maria Grazia, "Il proprio, il bello, il necessario nel Colonnato di San Pietro a Roma: architettura, economia, cantiere", in Chauvard Jean François, Mocarelli Luca (a cura di), *L'économie de la costruction dans l'Italie moderne*, MEFRIM 119-2 (2007), Rome, École Française de Rome, 2008, pp. 375–388.

Plate 2. C. Fontana, Prospect of the Façade of S. Andrea della Valle

Source: BAV, Codice Chigi, P VII 9, c. 90r.

Plate 3. C. Fontana, Survey of the Area between S. Andrea della Valle and Sant'Apollinare

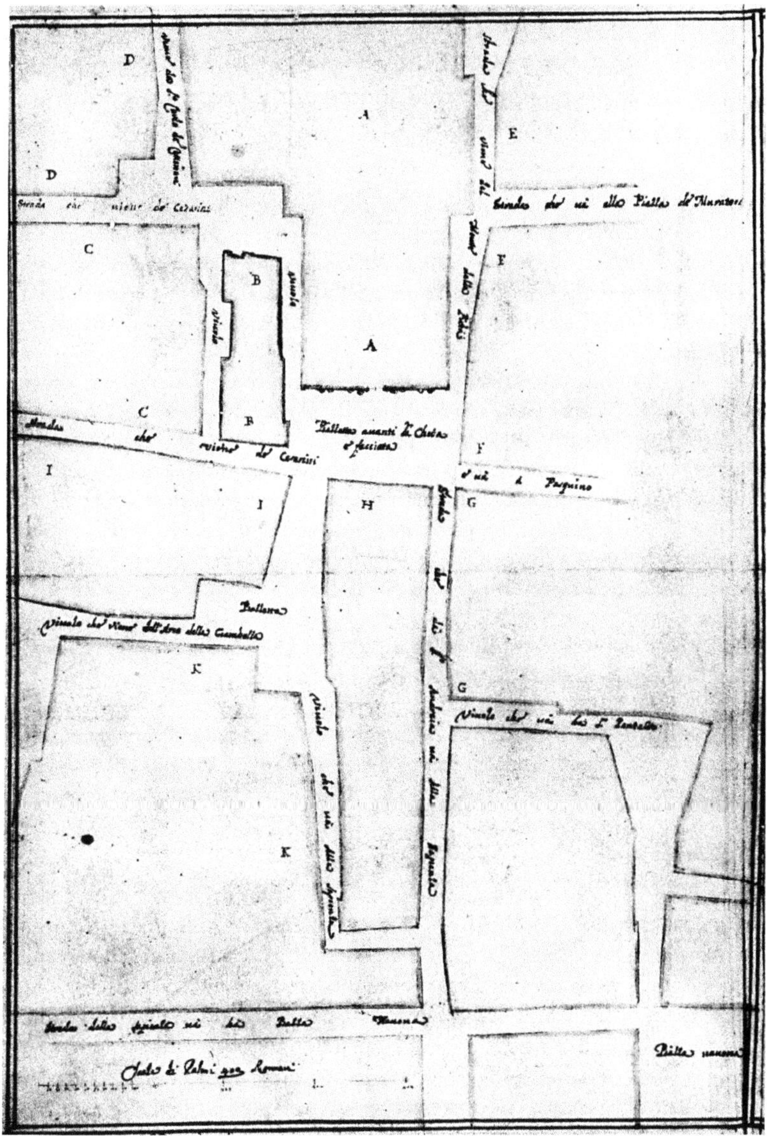

Source: BAV, Codice Chigi, P VII 9, c. 90v.

promulgated in 1480[6]. The Bull was followed by the provisions (called *constitutions*) of Alexander VI (1500), Leo X (1516), Pius IV (1565), and Gregory XIII (1574). These all had the intent of encouraging the expansion of inhabited areas in Rome along specific roads, facilitating construction inside the city walls and favouring the amalgamation of town houses with the magnificent palaces *ad majorem Urbis ornamentum*, that so powerfully represented a triumphant aristocracy and clergy[7].

6 *Ampliatio Jurisdictionis Sanctae Romanae Ecclesiae Camerarij, et Magistrorum viarum Urbis circa aedificia ad ejus ornatum construenda, una cum privilegiis ejusmodi aedificia construentium, vel amplientium*, 30 giugno 1480, in *Bullarum privilegiorum ac diplomatum Romanorum Pontificium amplissima collectio* (from now Boll. Coll.), t. III, parte III, pp. 179–182, par. I. See Guidoni Enrico, *La città dal Medioevo al Rinascimento*, Roma, Electa, 1981, pp. 223–224.
For the norms on expropriation between the fifteenth and seventeenth centuries, see Delumeau Jean, *Vie économique et sociale de Rome dans la seconde moitié du XVIe siècle*, vol. 1, Paris, De Boccard, 1957–1959, pp. 230–246; Scavizzi C. Paola, "Considerazioni sull'attività edilizia a Roma nella prima metà del Seicento", in *Studi storici*, IX (1968), pp. 171–192; Scavizzi C. Paola, "Le condizioni per lo sviluppo dell'attività edilizia a Roma nel sec XVII: la legislazione", in *Studi Romani*, 17 (1969), pp. 160–171; Lefevre Renato, "La costituzione edilizia romana del 1574: contenuto, valore e applicazione", in *Economia e Storia*, XIX, 1 (1972), pp. 20–39; Fregna Roberto, "Edilizia a Roma tra XVI e XVII secolo", in *Controspazio*, V, 5 (1973), pp. 48–61; Solidoro Maruotti Laura, "L'antica disciplina dei casi di esproprio per pubblica utilità", in *Index*, 23 (1995), pp. 522–535; Verdi Orietta, "Maestri di edifici e di strade a Roma nel secolo XV. Fonti e problemi", in *Roma nel Rinascimento*, Roma, Roma nel Rinascimento, 1997; Vaquero Piñeiro Manuel, *La renta y la casas: el patrimonio immobiliario de Santiago de los Españoles de Rome entre los siglos XV y XVII*, Roma, L'Erma di Bretschneider, 1999, pp. 75–80; Gualandi Maria Luisa, "Roma resurgens. Fervore edilizio, trasformazioni urbanistiche e realizzazioni monumentali da Martino V Colonna a Paolo V Borghese", in Pinelli Antonio (a cura di), *Roma nel Rinascimento*, Roma-Bari, Laterza, 2002, pp. 123–150.
For the nineteeth century, see Jamonte Francesco, "Annotazioni per una storia dell'ornato edilizio urbano a Roma tra XVIII e XIX secolo", in Morelli Roberta, Sonnino Eugenio, Travaglini Carlo M. (a cura di), *I territori di Roma: Storie, popolazioni, geografie*, Roma, Università Roma La Sapienza-CISR, Università Roma Tor Vergata-Dipartimento di Storia Università Roma Tre-CROMA, 2002, pp. 107–136.

7 *Privilegia aedificantium in via Alexandrina nuper in Urbe directa, a Castro Sancti Angeli ad Plateam S. Petri Principis Apostolorum*, 1500, Boll. Coll., t. III, parte III, p. 244; *Confirmatio et extensio jurisdictionis S.R.E. Camerarii et Magistrorum Viarum Almae Urbis*, 1516, Boll. Coll., t. III, parte III, pp. 427–429; *Erectio Civitatis Piae, prope Arcem S. Angeli de Urbe, et privilegia in ea aedificantium, ac ad eamdem translatio Conventus et Ecclesiae S. Mariae Transpontinae nuncupate*, 1565, Boll. Coll., t. IV, parte II, pp. 244–247; *De Aedificiis,*

This legal *corpus* was designed to stimulate private investments in the adornment of Rome, playing on the inevitable conflict between *publice utilia* and the advantages it gave to a few greedy people.

However, the lax definitions that often affect the general principles of personal rights became a breeding ground for non-compliance, abuse and fraudulent activities. These were curbed by repeated decrees and edicts, such as those issued by Pius IV (1571), Paul V (1611), Urban VIII (1628), and Alexander VII (1658). The *maestri delle strade* Domenico Jacovacci and Giacinto del Bufalo also checked illegal activities (1660)[8].

From this point-of-view, in these papal provisions individual property – which is or should be an absolute right in the relations between individuals – becomes a simple, conditional right both for the community and for private citizens[9]. This led to forced selling of property, where the will of the owner was replaced by the will of the state (the Papal States in our case), with the aim of adorning the city, to the benefit of other private citizens.

However, when owners were deprived of the right to enjoy and dispose fully and exclusively of their property, they had to be paid an indemnity. The guiding principle for calculating this indemnity was that the financial damage of the transaction should impact as little as possible on the patrimony of persons affected by the forced sale, and as much as possible on the individual or the community who benefitted from it.

It is not possible in this instance to examine in detail all the papal provisions implemented to protect the decorum of Rome. They were activated through a series of mechanisms that involved buying properties with the aim of modifying and beautifying the city's *facies*, as well as increasing security and improving

---

et Iure congrui, ac jurisdictione, et facultatibus S.R.E. Camerarii, et Magistrorum Viarum Urbis, 1574, Boll. Coll., t. IV, parte III, pp. 282–287. See the (incomplete) transcription in Guidoni Enrico, Petrucci Giulia, *Urbanistica per i Giubilei: Roma, Via Alessandrina*, Roma, Kappa, 1997, pp. 96–98 and 104–105. Gregory XIII's provisions remaine valid, at least formally, until 1865, Borgnana Carlo, *Degli edifici e delle vie di Roma al cadere del secolo XVI e della Costituzione* "Quae publice Utilia", Roma, Stab. tip. Aureli, 1860.

8 *Reductio ad terminos juris communis, Constitutionum a Sisto V, Leone X, et Pio IV, ac aliis Pontificibus editarum super Jure congrui, et super novis (exceptis tamen Sacris aut publicis) aedificiis construendis, aut ampliandis in Urbe*, 1571, Boll. Coll., t. IV, part III, pp. 162–163.

9 Zamboni Giuseppe, "Espropriazione", in *Enciclopedia Italiana Treccani*, vol. XIV, Roma, Istituto Enciclopedia Treccani, 1932, pp. 369–372.

public hygiene. And I do not intend to study the legal principles and building practices of the time, which are still in use today, such as the preference to be given to neighbours when property was sold (incurring the cancellation of the sale to third parties) or the concession of demolition material as partial payment to builders[10].

My aim is to study the social, economic and technical implications, and to trace the development of methods used to calculate fair compensation, both when the property was expropriated for public use (such as the creation of piazza San Pietro, del Popolo or della Pace) and when private citizens bought properties in order to make space for luxurious buildings. A good example of the latter is Palazzo Chigi in Piazza Colonna. I will also focus on situations when the advantage of the transaction is ambiguously shared by the community and a private citizen (for example the Piazza di Corte of Ariccia, a Chigi fief).

Determining the value of the properties that were about to be expropriated was, in fact, a critical aspect of the operation. It was easy to challenge the numerical data in a legal context, which then became fertile ground for conflict between the experts called in by the contenders.

As a result of this, the criteria applied to compensation changed repeatedly over the years, and in the mid-seventeenth century the rules to be followed for *misure* and *stime* were still being debated. An attempt was made to draw up a protocol, which was to be shared only with carefully selected technicians, "because it would be good if the Magistrate of the *Maestri delle Strade* made sure that the practice was equal, and well regulated, and that not everyone could make estimates, but only those people who were well educated in the profession"[11]. Exchanging goods of virtually equal value as compensation for a

10 The contractor only kept the most expensive materials (metal, cut stone and timber) to reuse, D'Amelio Maria Grazia, "*Ruzza e ferraccio*, ferramenta e strumenti della reverenda Fabbrica di San Pietro per le rchitetture della Roma moderna", in Bernard Jean-François, Bernardi Philippe, Esposito Daniela (a cura di), *Il reimpiego in achitettura: recupero, trasformazione, uso*, Roma, École Française de Rome, 2008, pp. 395–406.

11 At that time, the architect was supposed to make the estimate, as well as drawing up the project and supervising the construction site. The architect had to "measure and describe the site [...], assist the demolition, sort the materials, and hand over the tools to the *chiavaro*", see the bill (*parcella)* of Nicola Forti (July 1773), Archivio di Stato Roma (from now on ASR), *Ospedale di S. Rocco*, reg. 728, cc. nn., in Scavizzi C. Paola, *Edilizia nei secoli XVII*

property only happened on rare occasions. An example of this kind of transaction occurred when the Font of Acqua Acetosa near Ponte Milvio was restored in 1661–1662. The plans by Domenico Legendre (1621?–1687) include the text of Pope Alexander VII's *motu proprio* for the expropriation[12].

The drawings show a straight avenue, lined with mulberry and elm trees, that leads up to the Font (now no longer existing). It was only possible to build this because a vineyard measuring 185 square meters was expropriated from the Abbey of S.Lorenzo fuori le Mura (or rather by the Abbot, Archbishop Francesco Boncompagni, who was Alexander VII's majordomo). In compensation, the Abbey was assigned a nearby public area of 230 square meters, which was more valuable and therefore adequately recompensed the infringed right.

More often, it was necessary to make an estimate of how much the property was worth in order to determine compensation. At first glance, the procedure seems completely objective. Basically, according to the *Minuta del modo per stimare le case vecchie* [...] *se si vende in vigore della Bolla Gregoriana,* several elements determined the price of the property[13]:

- the value of the land on which the building stands;
- the value of the building elements (*bonitas intrinseca domorum*);
- and any capitalization of the annual rent (only when documented by a registered notary's contract).

---

e XVIII a Roma. Ricerca per una storia delle tecniche, Roma, Ministero per i Beni Culturali e Ambientali, 1983, p. 121.

See also Eimer Gerhard, *La fabbrica di S. Agnese in Navona*, Stockholm, 1970, vol. I, p. 212, note 6. For the professional practice of architects see Curcio Giovanna, "La città degli architetti", in Contardi Bruno, Curcio Giovanna (a cura di), *In Urbe Architectus. Modelli Disegni Misure. La professione dell'architetto Roma 1680–1750*, Roma, Argos, 1991, pp. 143–153; Curcio Giovanna, "Il commitente e l'architetto: cantieri e fabbriche nella Roma del Seicento", in Scotti Tosini Aurora (a cura di), *Storia dell'Architettura Italiana. Il Seicento*, vol. 1, Milano, Electa, 2003, pp. 278–313.

12 D'Amelio Maria Grazia, "La sorgente dell'Acqua Acetosa fuori Porta del Popolo a Roma: medicina, architettura e architettura del paesaggio (XVI–XVII secc.)", in *Roma Moderna e Contemporanea*, XVII, 1–2 (2009), pp. 167–183; Fagiolo Marcello, "Genius loci: la sacralità della fonte e degli alberi", in Cardilli Luisa, Fagiolo Marcello (a cura di), *La fontana dell'Acqua Acetosa a Roma. La storia, il restauro e il nuovo parco*, Milano, Silvana Editoriale, 2010, pp. 40–51.

13 ASR, Ospedali, *Ospedale di S. Spirito*, vol. 48, ff. 81–86.

Plate 4. D. Legendre, *Progetto per la sistemazione dell'area intorno alla fontana dell'acqua Acetosa*, 1662

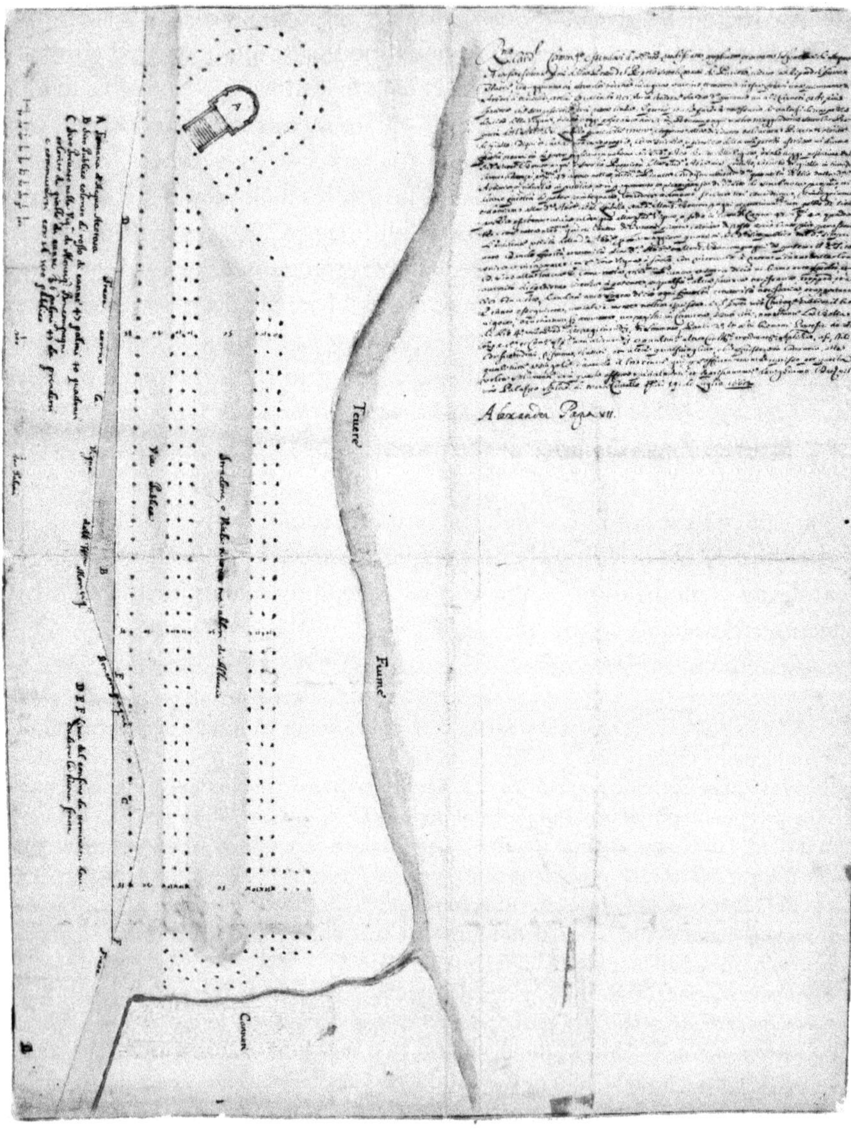

Source: ASR, Collezione di piante, mappe e disegni, cart. 78, n. 212, c. 381.

However, according to the documents I consulted for this study, the apparent objectivity of the estimate was actually very much at the discretion of the surveyors, who were not controlled by any well-regulated procedures.

For example, one of the problems addressed by the experts was how to divide the land value of a multi-storey building between several owners. At that time, it seemed unsolvable. The cumbersome formulas of an anonymous surveyor who worked on the properties of the Ospedale di Santo Spirito outline one solution: allocating decreasing quotas from the ground floor up to the top floors[14].

Land estimates, on the other hand, applied much the same criteria we use today. Land was valued according to location (which could be "more noble or less noble"), the degree of urbanization and how healthy the area was. Other factors considered in the appraisal of buildings destined for expropriation were its topology and the façade. The length of the façade and how it aligned with the road were important factors, and corner locations were more valuable. Any servitudes on the property impacted on its value and so did the building's exposure.

Along with estimating the value of the land (*sito*) the surveyors also appraised the construction materials of the building: the walls and *cimenti* (i.e. the foundations and *tevolozza*, the pavement, glues and plaster, floors and roofs). They measured the property as well, and their estimate of price per metre was very close to that of a new building[15]. This reveals an important principle of the time: the deterioration of a building only affected its value slightly[16]. The standard

14 *Modo come si misurano i siti*, XVII secolo, ASR, *Ospedale di S. Spirito*, vol. 48, ff. 96–97, in Scavizzi, *Edilizia nei secoli XVII e XVIII a Roma*, *op. cit.*, 1983, p. 101.

15 Ehrle Francesco, *Dalle carte e dai disegni di Virgilio Spada (codd. Vaticani Lat. 11257 e 11258)*, Roma, Tip. Poliglotta Vaticana, 1927, p. 62; he mistakenly believed that the estimate of building materials was made to establish their value if they were sold.

16 The estimate of construction materials was not affected by the building's location. This fact is not particularly obvious in archival documents, see October 16, 1662, *Relazione di Congregazione sopra le stime delle case mandata a Sua Santità* (Alessandro VII) and *October 16,1662 Relazione di Giovan Antonio de Rossi sopra il modo di stimare*, in Güthlein Klaus, "Quellen aus dem Familienarchiv Spada zum Römischen Barock (2. Folge)", in *Römisches Jahrbuch für Kunstgeschichte*, 19 (1981), pp. 240–243.
Prezzi ordinari di muri mattonati, siti et altro conforme ala stima comune, AFSP, Arm. 7, Rip. F, Vol. 467, f. 77.

criterion was compensating the owner with a sufficiently large sum to enable him to rebuild the property. In this context, applying *ex novo* tariffs when assessing a building, without considering in any way its true state of preservation, is fully justified.

One the one hand, a price applied "if you sell on the basis of the Gregorian Bull" was commonly accepted. But disputes arose when it came to estimating artefacts, especially in parts of the buildings where approximation for certain types of jobs was inevitable (foundations, excavation, etc.). Considerable variation of land values in city neighbourhoods (sometimes even within the same block) were also a source of contention[17].

As a result, the methodology for assessing property was completely inconsistent. Properties could possess a wide range of characteristics that justified, in an alchemic equation, a re-evaluation of the capital (i.e. capitalization of the income). The underlying principle was this: a property that produced an income was worth the same amount as capital that would produce an equivalent income, if put to good use.

In fact, the evaluation of the land and building (site and materials) was added to the capitalization of the annual rent, which ranged in relation to the quality of the area and the nature of the building[18]. For example, "ordinary

---

Li muri sogliono valutarsi scudi 2,0 almeno 1,90 la canna
Le colle la canna (baiocchi) 20
Il mattonato vecchio almeno la canna scudi 1
Li tetti vecchi almeno scudi 3
Li solari d'Abeto vecchi scudi 3.30 le terre di cantina la canna 3
Il sito scudi 7
De Rossi states in his *Relazione* that, in assessing the value of each part of the building, the parts that appear to be in good condition "are valued as good, and those in bad condition are considered bad". It is interesting to compare this information with the prices of new construction work published by Scavizzi, *Edilizia nei secoli XVII e XVIII a Roma*, op. cit., 1983, p. 93.

17 For example, see the debate between the Fabric of St. Peter and Innocenzo Cibo. The latter was not satisfied with the compensation he received for his palace, which was partially destroyed to make space for the work on St. Peter's Square. He asked Francesco Contini to do a new estimate, but still did not get the amount he wanted, and therefore in 1668 (10 years after construction had ended), he petitioned Clement IX Rospigliosi to appoint a third surveyor, AFSP, Arm. 1, Rip. A, Vol. 9, f. 247.

18 Nella Congregazione sopra le stime delle Case fatta li 16 Ottobre 1662.
A. Al primo punto quanto si debbano valutare le piggioni.

houses in good locations are assessed at 4 percent". This is the category of buildings expropriated for constructing St. Peter's Square, for which it was estimated that compensation should be made based on an income of 4% per annum, i.e. these houses were worth the equivalent of a sum which, put to good use at 4% per year, would give an annuity equal to the rent of the property. It is interesting to note, however, that nearby housing "in an abandoned place without much good air, for example in the quarters around the Castel walls, and similar places" made the market value of the buildings collapse. The value of property that had been split up and leased to multiple tenants was also far less, sometimes half the value of other properties, because the risk of not being paid rent was higher. Therefore, the fair price for recompensing expropriation was equal to half the value of the property, estimated as the sum value of land, building and annuities. The sum was also affected by the location and type of property involved.

Since the sophisticated tools used for financial mathematics, which were developed in the nineteenth century by Giuseppe Borio, were not at that time available, the capitalization rate was fixed. *Unlimited constant annual income* (V) was calculated using the formula $V = R / i$, where R stood for the annual income from rent and i was the interest rate (in documents this varies from 2,5 to 12 percent).

An important distinction was made to prevent losses being incurred by the dispossessed owner: the capitalization of the annual rent was only added if it was higher than the sum of the land and building values[19]. This calculation

---

1. Dui Architetti chiamati dissero, che si valutano à 4,6, et 8 secondo i siti delle case, ò numero de piggionanti.
Giunse tal pratica nuova à molti, tuttavia parve fondata, perché dove le case non stanno mai spiggionate, la pigione si considera al minor segno, dove poi è difficile appigionarle, ò difficilmente si riscuote per il gran numero de pigionanti nella medesima casa, si considera al magior segno, e chi calculerà l'esatto in 25 anni, trovarà, che tanto hà riscosso il primo à 5 per 100, quanto il 2° à 7", in Güthlein, "Quellen aus dem Familienarchiv Spada", *art. cit.*, p. 240.

19 "Per dimostrazione vi sia una una casa di Pigione annua di scudi 160, stimandosi si trova, che il valore del capitale delli muri, cimento e sito importa scudi 3000, e poi valutata la Pigione delli scudi 160 à scudi 4 per Cento rende un capitale di scudi 4000. Si uniscono insieme, e fanno la somma di scudi 7000 quali divisi per metà sono scudi 3500 et questa somma da periti si termina per il giusto prezzo del valore della Casa. Succedendo poi ne sia una Casa di Pigione annua di scudi 100 stimandosi si trovi che il valore del capitale delli

was of paramount importance, because it was the only possibility the owner had of materially increasing the property's value[20].

This rule is clarified in the *Relazione sopra il modo di stimare gli immobili sia in città sia in periferia*. This report was written by Giovanni Antonio De Rossi (1616–1695), and presented at a meeting of the Congregazione della Fabbrica di San Pietro (October 16, 1662), attended by Gian Lorenzo Bernini (1598–1680) and Angelo Pichetti (1595–1668). The purpose of the meeting was to start the expropriation campaign for building the southern branch of St. Peter's Colonnade[21].

De Rossi used two extreme cases to explain the method: for example, in the assessment of an area used as a slaughterhouse, which was typically without

---

muri, cimenti e sito importa scudi 3000, e poi valutata la pigione delli scudi 100 come sopra à scudi 4 per Cento rende un capitale di scudi 2500 dove restando detto capitale di pigione inferiore al capitale delli muri, cimenti e sito si tralascia non tenendosi conto, e si termina da periti, che il giusto prezzo del valore di detta casa siano li sodetti scudi 3000". See de Rossi's *Relazione* in Güthlein, "Quellen aus dem Familienarchiv Spada" *art. cit.*, pp. 241–242. The formula is: Land + Building + revalued income or capitalization of income (but the re-evaluated annuity is added only if it is greater than the sum of the Land + Building and in this case everything is divided by 2, otherwise the building would be appraised twice). Basically, an average is applied only when capitalization of the income is greater than the estimated value of the land added to the building.

First example

L + B = 3000 scudi

Revalued income = 160 / 4 × 100 = 4000 scudi (more than 3000)

3000 is added to 4000, and the result is divided by 2 = 3500 scudi

Second example:

L + B = 3000 scudi

Revalued income = 100 / 4 × 100 = 2500 scudi (less than 3000)

The indemnity is 3000 scudi (not divided by 2).

20 Compare the methods of evaluation in Trinci Cosimo, *Il Trattato delle stime de' beni stabili*, Firenze, 1755.

21 D'Amelio Maria Grazia, "Gli espropri per la costruzione del Colonnato di San Pietro a Roma", in *Città e Storia*, supplement to issue 1 of *Roma Moderna e Contemporanea*, new series, I, 0 (2004), pp. 159–167. See Alexander VII's chirographs regarding the demolitionof building sto create St.Peter's Square (23.11.1656) Archivio Segreto Vaticano, Avvisi, 103, c. 272 and regarding the acquisition of houses that were to be demolished (23.12.1656) in L. von Pastor, *Storia dei papi*, XIV, I, Roma, Desclée, 1961, p. 523, n. 2. Also see *Restrictum votorum congregationis habitae super aestimatione domorum*; and see BAV, *Codice Chigi*, M VIII, LXI, ff. 239–240 e 283–286.

walls (*muri e cementi)* the owner must be compensated only "for the income produced by renting the business [...] to the sum of 8 scudi and 10 scudi and even 12 scudi, more or less, in different cases". The sum in this instance was not halved.

However, De Rossi writes that if one had to assess a magnificent building, a palace adorned with noble *fab(b)rica e cimenti*, erected on a costly site, the sum of the annual rent, added to the already considerable value of the building and land, could only be re-evaluated at 2,5–3 percent. The resulting sum was to be halved in this case.

These examples clearly express the intent of giving the expropriated owner compensation for the violation of his rights. Bernini explained the meaning of this passage by commenting during the Congregation meeting: "the prices (compensation, ed.), which seem exorbitant, are a result of the will to buy property using force, so if the Owner of these houses receives a much higher price than he would normally be able to sell for, it is owed to him, because his (property, ed.) has been taken". He continued: "the Popes have provided for the disconsolate by giving him the 6th of the fair price"[22].

However, De Rossi's calculating method created a strong bias that favoured buildings in the suburbs. Only Bernini (and it would be interesting to investigate this aspect of his work) proposed steps to remedy this flaw, which would favour the expropriating authority. He suggested the option of applying the benefits originally established to safeguard the dispossessed owners (half of the sum of the land, buildings and rent) to the expropriator as well. When the expropriator wished to buy property in the suburbs, according to the calculation based on income that was not halved, he ended up paying a considerably higher price than market value. Bernini's suggestion that even in these cases, fair compensation should be calculated in the same way (halving only the annuity) in this instance to benefit the expropriating authority. The Congregazione della Fabbrica di San Pietro did not express an opinion on this proposal, for fear that lowering the price of buildings in the suburbs would foment discontent among the population[23].

Therefore, during the seventeenth century in Rome, no universal and proven method for assessing fair compensation existed. What does surprise

22 Güthlein, "Quellen aus dem Familienarchiv Spada", *art. cit.*, p. 240.
23 *Idem*, p. 241.

us is discovering that the popes, in spite of their undoubted sovereignty *Urbi et Orbi*, in order to expropriate property, were forced to give compensation, whereby the property was estimated to be worth more than its actual value would have been on the free market, in a sale between private parties. In order to persuade owners to give up their properties, the pope had to resort to financial gratification that went beyond the market price. The whole concept of private property (*dominium*), which had been inherited from Roman law, was disrupted by this practice. These laws had never tolerated limitations, even when they came from the government and were of public interest.

In this sense, Bernini's reflection on the practice of overestimating properties for compensation is enlightening. He considered it an indemnity to compensate moral damages, the violation of an individual right. It was still considered a violation in 1865, when Giuseppe Pisanelli, the spokesman for the law on expropriation law (No. 2359) defined it as literally "an injury to personal property".

It is obvious that such expensive compensation, full of delays and legal disputes, must have made Alexander VII's vast demolition campaign a complicated, costly and impractical undertaking, even though it was a requisite for carrying out the grandiose projects of this pope, who hoped to become the new Alexander the Great, founder of a new city.

"For Service of the most August and of the Public". Expropriations and the Building of the Mercantile Spaces in Trieste in the XVIIIth Century

DANIELE ANDREOZZI

1. In the early 1700's Emperor Charles VI of Habsburg made up his mind about the need to have at his disposal a war naval fleet in order to be able to play the role of a superpower on the European theatre. Although deprived of the necessary financial resources, he devised various projects designed to create an imperial commercial fleet, which in turn would lead to the development of a military fleet to which it would provide means, resources, men and skills. The port of Trieste, imperial outpost in the Mediterranean and Adriatic seas, was chosen as the preferred spot for the implementation of such projects. At that time Trieste was a small city of about 5,000 people and the presence of other territorial powers had always blocked its expansion towards the inner areas while the Serenissima Republic of Venice opposed Trieste's expansion towards the Adriatic sea. Trieste also had a very limited infrastructure both for its urban center and for its commerce and navigation. In fact, the city was the site of marginal flows of traffic done by boats that had limited capacity and size and that shipped in the interstices left open by the Venetian rules which tended to reserve to the Serenissima the bulk of the Adriatic trade. These flows, because of their typology, had never demanded meaningful projects for the port. That was also due to the fact that the most part of these trades were done by merchants who were not residing in Trieste and were utilising the port, during favourable moments, as a connective point in their circuits. The local patriciate, with very limited power and resources, was limited to offering space, guaranteeing rudimental management and counting on profits coming from tariffs imposed on merchandise in transit and from city's offices. Therefore the city lacked the financial resources, the know-how, and the traditions needed to sustain development of commercial activities. From this starting point a deep process of transformation changed Trieste rapidly. Its population increased to

30,000 inhabitants and it became the site of a group of merchants and entrepreneurs coming from various parts of the Italian Peninsula, Levant, Continental Europe, and the Balkans and capable to dominate in land and maritime traffic. Such transformation dealt obviously with the city infrastructure as well as the urban aspect[1].

In 1719 Charles VI instituted a "privileged company", the "Oriental Company", of which he and some members of the aristocracy in his court were shareholders. He had given this Company a central position in the city government, in a semi-public role, and tasked it with developing the mercantile traffic, especially with the Levant, and the manufacturing sector. Moreover, the Emperor decided to start the construction of the infrastructures in order to achieve such results: port, dockyard, lazaretto, spaces dedicated to commerce, customs, communication routes, and areas dedicated to the living quarters of merchants and artisans who were choosing to relocate their activities to Trieste. Over time those factors helped in creating next to the sea a new district, later named "Theresian", opposed to the old town that slightly climbed to the inner area on the hills the near the Karst and was surrounded until the middle of the 1750's by the walls that reinforced the physical separation of the local patriciate and the magistrates of the town community[2].

From the second decade of the 1700s the spaces chosen by the imperial bureaucracy for the construction of infrastructures, dockyard, homes, and warehouses were those until then occupied by saltpans. During a process that lasted many years, the saltpans were expropriated and the new district and

1 On the history of Trieste in the XVIII century, see Finzi Roberto, Panjek Giovanni (a cura di), *Storia economica e sociale di Trieste*, vol. I, *La città dei gruppi 1719–1918*, Lint, Trieste, 2001; Finzi Roberto, Panariti Loredana, Panjek Giovanni (a cura di) *Storia economica e sociale di Trieste*, vol. II, *La città dei traffici 1719–1918*, Lint, Trieste, 2003 and Andreozzi Daniele, Gatti Carlo (a cura di) *Trieste e l'Adriatico. Uomini, merci e conflitti*, Edizioni Università di Trieste, Trieste 2005.

2 On this, see Andreozzi Daniele, "'Quale generatione di fiera si pensi introdurre'. Spazi dei commerci e pratiche dei mercanti a Trieste e nel Litorale austriaco nei primo decenni del Settecento", in Andreozzi Daniele, Panariti Loredana, Zaccaria Claudio (a cura di), *Acque, terre e spazi dei mercanti. Istituzioni, gerarchie, conflitti e pratiche dello scambio dall'età antica alla modernità*, Trieste, Editreg, 2009, pp. 113–139 and Panjek Alexander, "Chi costruì Trieste. Edilizia infrastrutture, mercato immobiliare e sevizi tra pubblico e privato (1719–1918)", in Finzi, Panariti, Panjek (a cura di), *Storia economica e sociale di Trieste, op. cit.*, pp. 643–690.

the accompanying infrastructure were built. It is a well known fact. It has sometimes been interpreted as the result of the enlightened and modernizing imperial will and in such case the emphasis is placed on the expropriation; and it has at other times been interpreted as the sign of the imperial respect to the local society and in such case the emphasis is placed on the compensations paid to the expropriated owners[3]. Above all, this episode has been placed in the traditional view of the city's history. Such view paints Trieste as an artificial creature of centralising and modern imperial politics, unhinging the preceding order of the Ancien Regime. The expropriation and the building of the district are viewed as a fundamental part of these politics. However, new hypothesis can now be formulated. In the Trieste of the Eighteenth century the role of the state appears a lot more marginal and, if anything, it is during the following century, the Nineteenth, that the state emerges as a leader in the city's history[4].

In fact, between the XVII and the XVIII centuries, with the further weakening of Venice's ability to control the Adriatic sea, a deep redefinition of the quantitative and qualitative hierarchies of the commercial routes had taken place. Coastal trade had become a central element in the definition of economic spaces and the ships of small and midsize centres of both coasts of that sea and of the Mediterranean had given rise to a very dense network of trade based around a multitude of small and midsize ports and even natural landings. In those circumstances, the politics of the Habsburg's were affected by scarcity of resources, strong discontinuity, and lack of alignment between goals and means employed. Those politics were sometimes aimed at unreachable goals; they appear out of step with the times, and modelled on myths and examples, like Venice and the privileged companies, belonging to a fading past. The last to arrive on the sea, the Emperor showed its characteristics belonging to the Ancien Regime even in its relations with the periphery which was managed only through chains of mediation. This does not imply that the flows of

3 On this, see Panjek, *Chi costruì Trieste, op. cit.*, pp. 644–647; for the debate focusing on the saltpans, see Marina Pozzetto, "Il dibattito per l'espropriazione delle saline di fuori Porta Riborgo e di Valdirivo, avvenuto nel 1731", in *Archeografo triestino*, XIX (1934), pp. 231–256 and Irene Iacchia, "I primordi di Trieste moderna all'epoca di Carlo VI", in *Archeografo triestino*, XXXVI (1919), pp. 81–160.

4 Andreozzi Daniele, "Il peso delle parole. Linguaggi di esclusione e linguaggi di inclusione nella storia di Trieste", in Scarciglia Roberto (a cura di), *Trieste multiculturale. Comunità a linguaggi di integrazione*, Bologna, Il Mulino, 2011, pp. 13–38.

material and immaterial resources from the centre were not essential for the development. It means instead that such resources turned out to be crucial in the interaction with the powers of the sea that, having placed Trieste in their circuits, through manipulation, shape them to suit their goals. Now, the ability to see the city's growth not as an artificial creation of the politics of Charles VI but as a complex result of the interaction between the strategies of Vienna, of the local community, and of mercantile and sea forces, opens up the possibilities for alternative interpretation of those expropriations as well[5].

The history and the myth of such growth appear multifaceted and complex and seem to relate closely to another story and another myth, that of modern ownership. That ownership, openly confronting the divided, fragmented, affected and limited ownership of the Ancien Regime, presented itself strong with its rights, unique, certain, free from outside influences, and totally available to the will of its owner. As the history of the Trieste's growth, such presentation displays quite a few mythical elements. Modern ownership, in fact, from the offset – in parallel with the evolution of the state and the economy – was immediately affected again, limited and then fragmented and divided[6]. During the nineteenth century, such trajectory in Trieste also faced the birth of the corporation and the debate on its consequences on the ownership itself. In this context, the factual reconstruction of the process of expropriation of the salt-pans can help us in understanding the actual mechanisms of the development of Trieste in the eighteenth century and can, perhaps, even help us in drawing a more complex, less linear and less teleological history of modern ownership.

In fact, a dispute opened around the concept of ownership and its use among different interests and views: the state interests, which were going back to the notions of absolutism in its eighteenth century manifestations; those belonging to the local community that, inspired by the contractual models of the Ancien Regime, defined itself as "Public"; and those of the merchants who, being at the heart of the economic dynamics of the Eighteenth century

5 On this, see Andreozzi, "'Quale generatione di fiera si pensi introdurre'", *art. cit.*, pp. 113–139; Id., "Tra Trieste, Ancona, Venezia e Bologna. La canapa e il commercio nell'Adriatico del '700, in Andreozzi, Gatti (a cura di), *Trieste e l'Adriatico*, *op. cit.*, pp. 153–201; Id, "Gli 'urti necessari'. Dalla manifattura all'industria (1718–1914)", in Finzi, Panariti, Panjek (a cura di), *Storia economica e sociale di Trieste*, *op. cit.*, pp. 541–600.

6 Grossi Paolo, *Proprietà e contratto*, in Fioravanti Maurizio (a cura di), *Lo stato moderno in Europa*, Laterza, Roma–Bari, 2002, pp. 118–128.

Adriatic, were later described, sometimes with teleological exaggerations, as individualist and members of a modern bourgeoisie. The payments made to the old owners, the new fate of the grounds, and the costs and obligations imposed on the new users and/or new owners of those areas solidified the outcome of the dynamics in play among the powers (political, economic and social) determining which were the collective and Public interests, the individual ones, and those of the Prince. So, even during the process that resulted in the mythical entrepreneurial and bourgeois Trieste, the ownership still shows signs of being multifaceted, prone to division and faded.

2. In 1717 Charles VI proclaimed the freedom of navigation on the Adriatic sea against the Venice's mercantilist rules on the commercial trade and on the military shipping. In 1719 he elevated Trieste and Rijeka to the rank of free ports and started the "Oriental Company" with the headquarters in Vienna and Trieste. In 1720 the Company was dealing with the city, the "Public", its settling in Trieste. It had, in fact, to establish the conditions of its stay and to obtain a space in order to locate a dockyard to start the construction of its fleet. The city was very much in favour of settling because, "being short of means [...], limited in its territory and lacking in subjects who were quite poor", it was hoping to gain significant advantages. In particular, the local patriciate was counting on fattening up its income with the tariffs and the management of the city offices that would have seen its profit rise thanks to the thickening of the flows of merchandise. So the city allowed the Company to use the land outside "the door of Riborgo" along the city walls and all the way to the port. This was the site where awhile back the saltpans of "Snel", which had been abandoned twenty years previously, were located. The concession did not include any form of payment and, to confirm the interest of the local community in the success of the project, the city contributed one thousands florins, guaranteed from the profit derived from the oil tariff, to the improvements that the Company would have done in that area. The local patriciate had different priorities; the agreement, in fact, established that the site remained the "reason" and "property" of the "Public" and under its civil and criminal jurisdiction as all of those who worked there, regardless whether they were from Trieste or elsewhere. Furthermore, the Company was not allowed to import or sell wine. Safeguarding in this way the sources of income of the patriciate, the pact was completed with the definition of a few minor points: the Company was permitted to impede

access to the location but had to guarantee, in case of necessity, access to the citizens and it was held responsible for the upkeep of the roads and the canals crossing the area. Such canals transported the garbage and sewage of the urban centre. The Company was also allowed to utilise the city walls in order to lean construction sites on them while assuming responsibility for safety, especially in case of fire[7].

Harmony was just superficial, however, and the newly stipulated pacts were immediately contested. A new formulation gave the Company more authority regarding the closing of access to the area and the right to sell wine at retail level as Trieste noblemen and religious individuals could do. In this context, the confirmation of the Company's intention to not want to leave the jurisdiction of Trieste but simply to want to be "considered" equally just like all the other citizens and noblemen, if it was trying to sweeten the bitter pill the patriciate had been forced to swallow, still it must not have been enough to reassure it. In fact, the Company shortly came back refusing the agreement and offering another one, in twelve points.

The imperial bureaucracy, fearing that the quarrel could become an obstacle to the "increase of commerce", found itself mediating between the fighters paying attention to the "happiness" of the Company and of the City. The twelve points would hardly have pleased the patriciate. If the ownership of the area remained with the city, the jurisdiction of the city community was being sharply revised. It maintained competence in criminal matters, but the "control of the people of the ships" and of the those who worked for the Company was being transferred into the hands of this latter and, furthermore, all "disputes concerning commerce" of "merchants" and "traders" had to be moved to the new "tribunal of exchange", which was in the orbit of the Company itself. The Company, in addition, demanded the right of being able to sell wine without having to pay any tariff and to open a tavern; it also asked for a reduction of the tariff placed on olive oil, more freedom to build and on the control of the point of access and, considering it had to care for the upkeep of the roads in

7 On the agreements and the disputes relating to the saltpans of Snel see Archives of the Republic of Slovenia, Ljubljana, As 730, Gospostvo Dol, book 158, pp. 728–740 (1720–1723). On the Oriental Company see Bussolin Giovanni, *Della imperiale privilegiata compagnia orientale nel secolo scorso e del Lloyd austro-ungarico nel secolo presente. Studio storico*, Trieste, Herrmanstorfer, 1882, pp. 29–164 and Andreozzi, "'Quale generatione di fiera si pensi introdurre'", *art. cit.*, pp. 118–129.

the area, it asked that the citizenry did the same for the streets used to move goods. The agreement, based on an unstable balance between a sort of eminent collective "public" ownership and a sort of collective semi-private / semi-state ownership, was impossible to reach because of those demands. So the decision made in Graz in 1723 by the Habsburg bureaucracy to impose the company point of view on the city did not put an end to the dispute. It was the failure of the Company and the consequent vanishing of it that brought an end to the dispute towards the end of the 1720s[8].

3. With the field cleared of the presence of the Oriental Company, the patriciate's hopes of being able to utilize the free port in order to increase the flow of commerce to be exploited by using traditional methods come to the fore again. This was also due to the fact that the imperial magistrates put the fixer Fortunato Cervelli from Ferrara in charge of drawing up plans for the revival of the port; if, on the surface, such plans were in line with the imperial objectives, they also hid other interests rooted in Adriatic commercial networks. So the patriciate could acquire sufficient room for itself within the new plans. The hypothesis devised by Cervelli was based on the creation of a system of fairs able to connect Europe, the Padana Plain, Trieste and the Levant. In reality, the only fair that actually opened was in Trieste each August for four years (from 1730 until 1733). It was located on the same site where for a few years the dockyards had been operating and that later on was assigned to its new use without any apparent contrast. So when, in concomitance with the opening of the first fair, the idea of expanding the space dedicated to trade by using other areas still occupied by saltpans was considered, the patriciate seemed always favourable to the imperial projects. Only in 1740s the defeat of the local patriciate became evident, and his attitude changed sharply[9].

In the wake of Fortunato's projects, the idea of buying up the saltpans next to the city and turning them to a different use was gaining acceptance in Vienna since at least 1729. The idea was to drain them for sanitary reasons (they

8 On the failure of the company see Andreozzi, "'Quale generatione di fiera si pensi introdurre'", *art. cit.*, pp. 125–129.

9 Caracciolo Alberto, *Fortunato Cervelli ferrarese "neofita" e la politica commerciale dell'Impero*, Giuffre, Milano, 1962; Andreozzi, "'Quale generatione di fiera si pensi introdurre'", *art. cit.*, pp. 130–139.

caused fever and miasma and merchants who had come for the first fair had even complained about the risk of malaria) and economic reasons (they were not highly productive). The thought of using them to build warehouses "and make profit through merchants" was entertained, especially in order to allow "merchants and foreigners" that would have come to the city adequate spaces to locate activities and living quarters. The past experience of the Oriental Company was probably revisited with the intention of building a separate district from the jurisdiction of the city in order to build the necessary infrastructures for trade, manufacturing plants and craft shops, and the house of the people employed in those sectors. This time, however, the saltpans were active and owned by private citizens and the strategy chosen by the imperial bureaucracy was to buy them. In fact, "deeming necessary for the public benefit the acquisition of the saltpans next to Riborgo of this city", in January of 1730 Charles VI gave the order to purchase the saltpans via a "regulated contract". The whole affair was put in the hands of the Commission sent to Trieste to attend the start of the fair, delegated by the Inspectorate of Commerce. This was the magistracy to which was assigned the task of overseeing the development of commerce in the city. The Commission arrived in Trieste early in 1730 and started looking for an agreement, "being unable to force the owners of saltpans to agree to a contract"[10].

The negotiation turned out to be neither brief nor easy. However, when evaluated according to the Ancien Regime's criteria, it was not particularly complex or time consuming. Examining the course of the negotiation allows us to see the strategies of the actors involved and to assess their motivations, goals, and achievements or losses. So we are also able to evaluate the process of acquisition performed by the imperial bureaucracy in its relations with the local society and with the policies devised by the centre. Among the actors involved in the situation, the city community was the one that kept the lowest profile along with the patriciate that controlled it. As a matter of fact, unlike

10 On the events concerning the saltpans of Riborgo see Archives of State, Trieste, Intendenza commerciale, 183, Saline, cc. 1r–47r (1730–1733) and 43, "Contrati seguiti con li fondali e consorti delle saline appresso Riborgo e in Valle de Rivo comprate in esecutioni delle clementissime cesaree resolutioni di sua sacra cesarea cattolica real Maestà", cc. 1r–49r (1731). Unless otherwise stated, all data, events, facts and quotations concerning the saltpans of Riborgo come from these two sources.

what had happened in the early 1720s, it did not intervene in the deal and the sources do not give us an idea of what its opinion of the deal was. Moreover, the negotiation involved a very limited group of owners, some of them not even of the city arena, rather than the patriciate as a whole. In those circumstances the community was favourable to the imperial projects particularly regarding the start of the free fair from which it hoped to make important profits. Therefore the sale of the saltpans did not hurt the general interests of the patriciate or the role that commerce and salt production had in the city economy. All of this allows us to suppose that the community did not oppose to the sale and, instead, helped in convincing the owners not to defend the personal interest at the detriment of those of their class. That is probably that some of the owners referred to when, while accepting the start of the negotiation with the state, motivate such choice and their "good will" with the desire to satisfy the imperial wishes and to contribute to the interest of the "Public"[11].

Obviously, much more present on the scene were the owners. However, the identities of the owners were not immediately revealed but become known with different time and modalities. In order to understand this we must begin by the description of the objects of the negotiation: the saltpans. They were divided into "fondamenti", productive units themselves also fractioned in evaporation pools called "capitini" or "cavedini". "The *fondamento* was surrounded by channels where salt water flowed and connecting mouths placed among the various *capitini* allowed the worker to let the desired amount of water flow to each *capitino*"[12]. Therefore, every "fondamento" was an autonomous production unit and the capitini that were part of it had to be managed organically. In charge of this and of the management of the saltpans and production of salt was the "fondale". The saltpans eyed by the Emperor were situated between the walls of the city and the sea, outside of the door of Riborgo and next to the area of the dockyard built by the Oriental Company in Val di Rivo. They were subdivided by seven foundations for a total of 228 "capitini". They were headed up by five "fondali": Camilla Bonomo, who was represented during the

11 In the sources of Trieste the term "public" is usually used to identify the city and the city community.

12 Fanfani Tommaso, "Il sale nel Litorale austriaco dal XV al XVIII secolo. Un problema nei rapporti tra Venezia e Trieste", in Di Vittorio Antonio (a cura di), *Sale e saline nell'Adriatico (secc. XV–XX)*, Napoli, Giannini, 1981, pp. 201–202.

negotiation by her own son Giovanni Vito Bonomo, Antonio Civrani, Guglielmo Bonomo, Giacomo Dolcetti and Alessandro Dolcetti (see Table 1)[13].

Table 1. The Saltpans Eyed by the Emperor

"Fondamento"	"Fondale"	Numbers of "capitini"
1	Camilla Bonomo born Civrani	40 (37)*
2	Camilla Bonomo born Civrani	33
3	Camilla Bonomo born Civrani	17
4	Guglielmo Bonomo	32
5	Antonio Civrani	46
6	Giacomo Dolcetti	36
7	Alessando Dolcetti	24

* Three "capitini" were eliminated to build canals and to improve the water circulation.

The "fondali" had been spotted by consulting the registers of the salt warehouse. In fact, in 1696 Vienna had introduced the monopoly on salt and, beginning from that year, the various salt producers had to hand the salt being produced over to the imperial warehouse based "on a five year contract that could be silently renewed"[14]. The register, though, did not record all of those who possessed that right but only those in charge of the single productions units, the "fondali" who also managed the plant for other "consorti" (consorts). The "consorti" were individuals, families or religious institutions that held different rights on the saltpans. This way during the negotiations those who had that right were suddenly multiplied unveiling the complete geography of the rights over the property only during the final stages of the talks (see Table Appendix 1).

13 The Civrani and Bonomo did not own any other saltpan, while the Dolcetti were "fondali" of another "fondamento" with 45 "capitini" (Fanfani, *Il sale nel Litorale austriaco dal XV al XVIII secolo*, *op. cit.*, p. 204).

14 Fanfani, "Il sale nel Litorale austriaco", *art. cit.*, p. 195.

The affected saltpans were all connected to the wealth of two families belonging to the local patriciate: the Civranis and the Dolcettis. It is evident that the fragmentation of the saltpans was mostly the result of the practice of utilizing such type of possessions to give women dowry when, marrying or entering a religious institutions, they were exiting their families.

However, it is difficult to evaluate the full scope and sense of such strategies. We do not know exactly how and when those possession had been formed, neither the reasons for which some of the saltpans were charged with a tithe in favour of the Habsburg Chamber. Antonio Crivani had acquired his early "capitini" in 1709 from another member of his family, Andrea; the first transfer made by the Dolcettis, the one to the St. Cyprian monastery, dates from 1685 and Camilla's wedding must have taken place around that time, that the same wedding that originated the possession. After that, and within the course of two generations, the number of consorts and consequently the fractioning of the rights over the foundations, appear to increase considerably. However, this could also be an optical illusion. In reality, in some cases the saltpans, acting as a form of warranty for the satisfaction of the debt contracted with the dowry and the payment of interests, were part of a complex mechanism of fictitious sales – actual credits – that had to be closed with the redemption of the good that had been handed over at a pre decided price[15].

Such practices could have been assisted even further by the introduction of the monopoly: the value of the salt given to the warehouse formed a capital on which the "fondali" gained a yearly interest of around 5–6 %; such interest was well suited to be used in such a mechanism. This way the negotiation with the state would have photographed a segment of a process extending through time without showing its full development. It could also have revealed a moment of difficulty for a family, as in the case of the Dolcettis who, besides suffering the less than prosperous conditions of some of its own members, still had to redeem the saltpans that had been pawned during the previous century and had let go

15 Camilla died in 1737; on this see Fanfani, "Il sale nel Litorale austriaco", *art. cit.*, p. 205. On the fictitious sales and repurchase agreements see Corazzol Gigi, *Fitti e livelli a grano. Un aspetto del credito rurale nel Veneto del '500*, Milano, Franco Angeli, 1979. For example, the deals between Antonio and Giovanni Vito Bonomo and the Jesuits and between the Monastery of St. Cyprian and the Dolcettis were openly fictitious sales and repurchase agreements.

of part of the "capitini" to forces external to the city, like the Venetian noble Zen family and the Monastery of Bistra. The vicissitudes of three families can only allow us to suppose that, due to the scarcity of available real estate, the saltpans had an important role within the mechanisms connected to the wedding market of the patriciate. However, there is no doubt that the production of salt within the economic system of Trieste was changing and this could led to different types of attitudes regarding the use and management of that type of good.

In fact, from at least the second half of the previous century imported salt had acquired an ever increasing importance in Trieste. So, at the beginning of the eighteenth century, it was superior in quantity, quality, and value to the local variety. The traffic, involved in the import and consequent re-export of the mineral and in a complex interweaving between smuggling and legal trade, had become the determining economic element and the product of Trieste, besides the local consumption, it served to elude Venetian laws by blending with the imports and, particularly after 1696, to elude the Habsburg laws as well. Regardless of the fact that the saltpans had lost importance related to what they were producing, they were useful for trade. In fact, they allowed the merchants to move across borders and state regulations avoiding tariffs and prohibitions and exploiting price differentials. While reinforcing such role, the saltpans were also setting off the decadence as productive plants[16].

So the projects, aiming at importing salt from the Kingdom of Naples, from Sicily and from Tripoli and then re-exporting towards Lombardy or to inner regions of the Empire, gained strategic value as part of the economic policies devised to promote the growth of Trieste, and the local production lost relevance[17]. In this context, the imperial bureaucracy started the acquisition of seven "fondali" (13,4 % of those present in the city) with their 228 "capitini" (14,6 % of the 1561 that were active) that in 1725 had produced 2674 *stara* of salt (13 % of Trieste's total production).

16 Rossetti Domenico, "Delle saline di Trieste. Considerazioni sulla loro storia e legislazione", in *Archeografo triestino*, XVIII (1892) pp. 119. Rossetti wrote that between 1690 and 1725 there was a sharp fall in salt production; this fall increased further between 1725 and 1780. See also Fanfani, "Il sale nel Litorale austriaco", *art. cit.*, pp. 186–210.

17 On these projects see, for example, Archives of State, Trieste, Intendenza commerciale, 553, 4 (1732).

Table 2. The Productivity of the Saltpans[18]

	"Fondale"	1725		1728		1730	
		stara	lire	stara	lire	stara	lire
1	Camilla Bonomo	395	1,481	644	2,415	161	504
2	Camilla Bonomo	415	1,556	733	2,748	195.5	734
3	Camilla Bonomo	271	1,016	508.5	1,906	156	585
4	Guglielmo Bonomo	402.5	1,510	509.5	1,910	177	664
5	Antonio Civrani	647.5	2,429	1,160.5	4,289	309	1,159
6	Giacomo Dolcetti	309	1159	475	1,781	209	784
7	Alessandro Dolcetti	234.5	881	250.5	940	78	291
	Total sum	2,674.5	10,032	4,281	15,989	1,285.5	4,721

	"Fondale"	1732		1735	
		stara	lire	stara	lire
1	Camilla Bonomo	–	–	–	–
2	Camilla Bonomo	–	–	–	–
3	Camilla Bonomo	–	–	–	–
4	Guglielmo Bonomo	282	1,059	187	701
5	Antonio Civrani	–	–	–	–
6	Giacomo Dolcetti	367	1,376	274.5	1,030
7	Alessandro Dolcetti	104.5	392	44	185
	Total sum	753.5	2,827	505.5	1,916

Source: Fanfani, "Il sale nel Litorale austriaco", *art. cit.*, pp. 204–205.

After the negotiation that had been started had fallen apart, in March the Commission made the "fondali" an offer in order to jumpstart the deal. The Commission had calculated an average of the revenue paid for the salt that

18 The staio (plural stara or staia) is a capacity measure equivalent to 83,31 litres in Venice and Trieste; see Martini Angelo, *Manuale di metrologia, ossia misure, pesi e monete in uso attualmente e anticamente presso tutti i popoli*, Torino, Loescher, 1883, p. 796 and Hocquet Jean-Claude, *Il sale e la fortuna di Venezia*, Roma, Jouvence, pp. 557–563. In the deals concerning the saltpans one florin was equivalent to 5 *lira*.

every one had given the warehouse during the past ten years and utilising such average it had decided the value of the single saltpans. The offer was immediately turned down. The reasons for the rejection were based on some disagreement over the methods followed to calculate the average. Above all there was the fact that, in addition to the revenue from the salt given to the authorities, the saltpans were bringing in additional earnings: fishing, the use of buildings standing there and, especially, the salt used directly by the families of the owners or given by them as "gifts" to friends and relatives[19].

In reality the calculation of given salt must have been quite inaccurate as a form of yardstick in order to figure out the exact profitability of the saltpans because the state monopoly inserted itself in complex strategies in which import, export, smuggling and consumption were all important elements. Even the productive peak recorded in 1728 and the following decline recorded in 1730, besides the climatic conditions, could perhaps have been explained with the imperial attentions towards the saltpans, attention that could well have caused rumours [20].

Whatever the case may be, in August, while continuing the negotiations on the account of the Habsburg by the "counterscribe" of the Office of the salts, Pietro Tognana, the "fondali" announced, as previously mentioned, that they were ready to sell for "service of the most August [Charles VI] and of the Public good [the Community of Trieste]". Moreover, instead of making a counter offer as had been asked of them, they declared themselves to be ready, albeit with some reservation, to accept a fair estimation[21]. So in order to satisfy imperial aspirations and for the "care of the owners as well", on the 18 of that month the Commission put "the judges and rectors of the city of Trieste", expression of the citizenry, in charge of choosing "two able and accomplished adjustors". Two more were chosen by the Office of salt. Two days later the four of them – Domenico Sofia and Giuseppe Braun, who were chosen by the first group, and Tommaso Senzik and Michele Daneu, who were chosen by the second – officially swore to "give the right estimation [...] or lose their souls" and

19 The Commission had previously asked "fondali" to propose a price but they had not responded.

20 On the peak and the decline of production see Fanfani, "Il sale nel Litorale austriaco", *art. cit.*, p. 204.

21 Above all, such reservations concerned the defence of the dower rights.

"putting aside any regard for fear, friendship, hate, persecution or envy nor to get distracted from the truth by friendship, complacency, promises, hopes, damages or anything else". Their compensation, as customary, was established to be 1 % of the total estimate. Between the 21 and the 23 of August the calculation was completed. Due to internal forces within the city, the estimates turned out to be extremely favourable to "fondali" whose interests, also because of the ways in which the adjustors were paid, happened to coincide with those of the adjustors. The Commission found the discrepancy between the new estimates and the previous proposals to be too much. So, in order to obey the precise orders coming from its superiors that demanded to obtain a more advantageous price, it gave Tognana the task of obtaining a "discount" from the owners of about a quarter of the value of the estimate. In case of a refusal, Tognana would have had to "inform them of the fact that the Commission had decided in favour of the discount". Furthermore, if the amount due was not released by the authorities, the creditors would have been entitled to 5 % interest and the directive of not allowing a higher interest had also come from the centre.

Within two days the "counterscribe" had made a round of consultations obtaining, despite the "firm" will expressed by the Commission, a general refusal. Every one turned down the discount. Crivani, who did not want to "profit" but neither "be damaged" offered a discount of about 8 % (500 florins); Guglielmo Bonomo said he could not satisfy the request due to dowry obligations and only agreed to deduct from the total amount the tithe due to the imperial Chamber; Giacomo Dolcetti declared his inability to decide due to many having claims on his "fondale" and, in any case, he requested a new estimate because he felt he had been damaged by the previous one; Alessandro, speaking also for his sister, proposed a reduction of 10 % over the "capitini" they were entitled to; Giovanni Vito Bonomo turned down the possibility of any discount.

The negotiation stalled for a few months until when, in April 1731, the Commission resurfaced again by sending a report containing further proposals to Vienna. Despite the "zeal" with which the matter had been handled, the acquisition of the saltpans had not taken place because of "the difficulties of some of the *fondali* who stood firmly in their position without allowing for any discount". So the Commission, "acknowledging the stated opposed reasons", and "balancing all difficulties for the advantage of the Treasury as for that of the protection of the owners", had elaborated new offers that considered the plurality of those who were holding rights; they were twenty among individuals, religious associations and noble Venetians and all of them were now revealed. We summarize them here, "capitino" by "capitino", based on the enumeration that we have adopted in the tables:

1. Didio Giuliani, who owned six "capitini", declared himself willing to accept a discount of about 16 % of the value of the stimate. The Commission proposed to accept the offer and to convince the other consorts, still opposed to it, to do the same;
2. Camilla Bonomo had agreed to a 9 % discount. The Commission proposed to accept it and to convince the other consorts to do the same;
3. The Commission was proposing to pay the entire amount of the estimate, minus the total sum of the capital on which the tithe was paid to the Habsburg Chamber, and assigning an interest rate of 6 % to Giovanni Vito Bonomo until the state had repaid its debt;
4. Guglielmo Bonomo had proposed to deduct the amount of the tithe to the Habsburg Chamber from the estimate (4600 liras from 16000) and had offered a further 900 liras discount (about 5 %); the Commission proposed to accept;
5. Civrani had offered a reduction of 500 florins from 6144 (about 8 %) and had asked for 6 % interest and the promise to receive the entire amount paid in cash within three months from the moment of his request; the Commission also proposed to accept this deal;
6. In this case the Commission proposed to reduce the estimate by subtracting the tithe paid to the Habsburg Chamber (1440 *lire*), thereby lowering the total amount down to 2266 florins from the 2270 of the original estimate. It was a very complicated situation due to the presence of the noble Venetians Zen who had never manifested their intentions, along with the Benedectine nuns of St. Cyprian, who were bound to the Dolcettis by a "repurchase agreement".
7. Alessandro Dolcetti, also acting for his sister Maria, had proposed a discount of about 9 % and had asked for an interest rate of 6 %; this offer too had found the Commission in agreement. The Abbott of the Monastery of Bistra instead had only asked for 42 *stara* of salt yearly, something that the Commission found extremely advantageous.

These proposals, that the Commission, as it established from the beginning of the report, had elaborated almost from a position of equidistance between the Emperor's interests and the rights of the private citizens, were the only way possible in order to overcome "the difficulties met in this sale agreement as this subdelegated Commission was not able to force the *fondali* to agree to the contract". As a matter of fact the Commission did not have the power to force them and its efforts, made in order to meet their needs while at the same time pleasing Vienna, looking to show that some concession had been made, were still fruitless.

It was necessary to wait until September in order to remove the various obstacles that prevented a solution to the situation. At that point, following further pressure coming from the centre, the Commission, that could not place hope in any other course of action, decided to close the matter. A last round of talks with the "fondali" and others holding rights did not result in anything new and every one reaffirmed their position. In a final report, in order to justify the poor result in the eyes of their superiors, the Commission basically recognized the reasons of the "fondali" and of those who claimed rights over the "capitini", be they due to dowry rights or contracts of purchase that covered loans. So, between September 14 and 15, the contracts of purchase were drawn up. The estimates made by the able and accomplished adjustors were basically respected and along with them the rights contained in the contracts stipulated between the "fondali" and the others who held rights (tables 3 and 4)[22].

The comparison among the estimates, the offers, the counter offers, and the final price shows how the local society was able to defend its own interests. In fact, the demands it had made during the course of negotiations were granted, while the requests made by the Habsburg magistracies were denied. In the cases in which the bigger discounts were approved (Civrani and Guglielmo Bonomo), the concession of a higher interest rate guaranteed the revenues of the "fondali" and the whole network of obligations joining "fondali" and consorts (debts, credits, dowry, repurchase agreement) was recognized and confirmed.

22 On the complex relationships between the Habsburg bureaucracy, stationed in Trieste, and the local powers see Andreozzi Daniele, "Tra centro e periferia. Pasquale Ricci e la Commissione sulle manifatture e fabbriche del Litorale (1763–1766)", in Andreozzi, Gatti (a cura di), *Trieste, op. cit.*, pp. 123–151. These relationships were reinforced by shared interests.

Table 3. The Sales

"Fonda-mento"	"Consorti"	Number of "capitini"	Sale results	Price (in florins)
1	Camilla Bonomo	14	Sold at the price established by the estimate	1,666 5% interest
	Didio Giuliani	6	Sold at the price established by the estimate	714 5% interest
	Daniele Francol	3	Sold at the value given at the moment of the concession of the dowry	365 5% interest
	Antonia Zucchelli	9	Sold at the price established by the estimate (Angela is considered usufructuary and Giovanni Vito Bonomo the owner)	1,071 5% interest
	Jesuits	5	Sold at the price established by the estimate (Giovanni Vito Bonomo is considered the owner of goods pawned to the Jesuits)	595 5% interest
2	Camilla Bonomo	18	Reduction by 8% of the price established by the estimate	2,044 5% interest
	Antonio Burlo	5	Sold at the value given at the moment of the concession of the dowry	623 5% interest
	Monastery of St. Cyprian	7	Sold at the value given at the time the "capitini" were originally purchased	862 5% interest
	Daniele Francol	3	Sold at the value given at the moment of the concession of the dowry	366 5% interest
3	Giovanni Vito Bonomo	17	Sold at the price established by the estimate (from it the value of the tithe will have to be deducted according to a latter negotiation)	2,247 5% interest
4	Guglielmo Bonomo	32	Sold at the price established by the estimate minus the value of the tithe (liras 1,600) and a 6% reduction	2,560 5% interest (first year); 6% interest (beginning the second year)

"Fonda-mento"	"Consorti"	Number of "capitini"	Sale results	Price (in florins)
5	Antonio Civrani	46	8% reduction	5,544 5% interest (first year); 6% interest (beginning the second year)
6	Monastery of St. Cyprian	6	Sold at the value given at the moment of the concession of the dowry	377 5% interest
	Venetian nobles Zen	18	No reported sale	–
	Dolcetti brothers	12	No reported sale	–
7	Alessandro Dolcetti	8	Reduction by 10% of the price established by the estimate	408 5% interest
	Maria Dolcetti	8	Reduction by 10% of the price established by the estimate	408 5% interest
	Monastery of Bistra	8	Sold for 42 stara of salt yearly	–

Table 4. Comparison among the Diverse Proposals and the Final Price

"Fondali"	Estimates (in florins)	Discounted price (in florins)	Final proposal (in florins)	Final price (in florins)
1	4,403	3,300	3,700	4,411
2	4,114	3,086	3,740	3,895
3	2,247	1,686	2,247 minus the value of the tithe	2,247 minus the value of the tithe
4	3,050	2,288	2,550	2,560
5	6,044	4,533	5,500	5,544
6	2,720	2,040	2,226	No reported sale
7	1,360	1,020	816 and 42 stara of salt yearly	816 and 42 stara of salt yearly

As a matter of fact, if the use of the saltpans within these complex relationships does not allow us, due the many factors that could have influenced it, to compare the price expressed in the contracts stipulated among the representatives of the social reality of Trieste to the ones reached with the Emperor in mere "economic" terms, the safe guarding of the social (and economic) ties built around the saltpans shows the resistance of the city.

Maybe the owners of the saltpans would not have wanted to let them go, but what pushed them towards acceptance of the agreement were the good terms negotiated more than imperial pressure; these terms safeguarded their personal interests and the expectations of the all patriciate in the economic development of the city, supporting the interests of their class.

At any rate, Charles VI became the owner of at least 195 "capitini". From that moment the "fondamenti" di Antonio Civrani and of Camilla and Giovanni Vito Bonomo halted production. Those belonging to Guglielmo Bonomo and Alessandro Dolcetti stayed active but came under the control of the state. The "fondamento" belonging to Giacomo, instead, maybe less appealing due to the presence of the Venetian nobles, remained partially unsold and continued to produce salt on the account of the Dolcettis[23]. In total, the Emperor had paid 19,473 florins and 42 *stara* of salt. However, the saltpans were not immediately utilised; the land reclamation proceeded very slowly and it was necessary to wait for many years, at least until the second half of the century, before the new district became relevant in size. Still, for a long time, the rights of ownership remained fluid within the district and the Habsburg bureaucracy, in allowing the use of that area that had been acquired only with difficulty, made use of various models: division of the property into *dominium utile* and eminent domain, rentals, perpetual rent, sales, and free concessions.

23 Fanfani, "Il sale nel Litorale austriaco", *art. cit.*, p. 204.

Appendix 1. The Rights Burdening the Saltplan

"Fonda-mento"	"Fondale"	"Consorti"	Number of "capitini"	Reason of ownership
1	Camilla Bonomo born Civrani	Camilla Bonomo	17	–
		Didio Giuliani	6	–
		Daniele Francol	3	In the name of his wife Marianna Bonomo; for dower rights
		Baroness Antonia Zucchelli born Bonomo (Gradisca resident)	9	For dower rights
		Jesuits	5	–
2	Camilla Bonomo born Civrani	Camilla Bonomo	18	–
		Antonio Burlo	5	In the name of his wife Maria Caterina Bonomo; for dower rights
		Monastery of S. Cyprian (Trieste)	7	For dower rights
		Daniele Francol	3	In the name of his wife Marianna Bonomo; for dower rights
3	Camilla Bonomo born Civrani*	Giovanni Vito Bonomo	17	–
4	Guglielmo Bonomo*	Guglielmo Bonomo	32	In the name of his wife Giulia Civrani; for dower rights
5	Antonio Civrani	Antonio Civrani	46	–
6	Giacomo Dolcetti*	St. Cyprian monastery (benedectine nuns)	6	For dower rights
		Venetian nobles Zen	18	–
		Dolcetti brothers	12	–
7	Alessandro Dolcetti	Alessandro Dolcetti	8	–
		Maria Dolcetti, widow Iurco, in the name of her minor children	8	For dower rights
		Monastery of Bistra (nowadays in the Republic of Slovenia)	8	–

* The "capitini" were burdened by a tithe in favour of the Habsburg Chamber.

Confiscations puis indemnisation des nobles émigrés (1792-1826) dans le district de Rochefort (Charente-Inférieure, France)

Denis Gandouet

Une législation hésitante voire contradictoire et en perpétuel renouvellement

Le débat sur la vente des biens des émigrés s'ouvre au mois de janvier 1792. Les députés de la Législative mesurent, d'emblée, « l'explosivité » de cette question. En effet, l'Etat, en décidant d'aliéner le patrimoine des nobles qui émigrent, s'arroge des biens privés, ce qui va à l'encontre du principe énoncé dans la Déclaration des droits de l'Homme et du Citoyen de 1789 qui fait de la propriété un droit inviolable et sacré. Par ailleurs, cette expropriation heurte la conscience de nombreux députés, bourgeois et grands propriétaires pour la plupart.

Cependant, un décret du 9 février 1792 décide le séquestre des biens fonciers des émigrés. Cette décision est confirmée, après beaucoup d'hésitations, par la Législative le 30 mars 1792: à la veille de la déclaration de guerre contre l'Autriche est décrétée la confiscation du patrimoine de tous les émigrés qui ont quitté le territoire français depuis le 1er juillet 1789[1].

Dès le début du conflit, la France connaît d'importantes difficultés militaires – les Autrichiens pénètrent dans le Nord du royaume au début du mois de juillet 1792 – et, dans ce contexte, l'Assemblée Législative déclare la « patrie en danger » le 11 juillet[2]. La guerre a alors des répercussions sur les débats concernant le sort des émigrés – incorporés aux troupes qui envahissent le

1 Bodinier Bernard, Teyssier Éric, Antoine François, *L'événement le plus important de la Révolution. La vente des biens nationaux en France et dans les territoires occupés, 1789-1867*, Paris, Société des études Robespierristes et Éditions du CTHS, 2000 (Mémoires et documents d'histoire de la Révolution française), p. 28 et pp. 390-391.

2 Biard Michel, Dupuy Pascal, *La Révolution française, Dynamiques, influences, débats, 1787-1804*, Paris, Armand Colin, 2004, p. 206.

territoire national – à l'Assemblée. Le principe de la vente des biens des émigrés est décrété le 27 juillet 1792[3], deux jours seulement après le manifeste de Brunswick, rédigé par un émigré, qui menace les parisiens d'extermination si ces derniers s'en prenaient à la personne du roi[4].

Les motivations qui ont poussé les députés à franchir le Rubicon sont multiples. Il s'agit, tout d'abord, de faire payer la guerre à ceux qui se sont engagés aux côtés des « Ennemis de la Révolution » et qui sont donc tenus comme responsables du conflit. La vente du patrimoine des émigrés doit alors couvrir les dépenses militaires de la France. La patrie punit ainsi ses traîtres et, d'une pierre deux coups, coupe les vivres à ces ennemis de la France en vendant leurs châteaux et autres propriétés. Mais, il s'agit aussi pour les députés de rassembler les Français dans ce combat contre les forces réactionnaires. Et, parmi les citoyens français, ceux qui veulent éviter un retour à l'Ancien régime synonyme de lourdes ponctions fiscales pesant sur les terres qui grevaient leur capacité à investir dans le foncier, ce sont les paysans. Or, la vente des biens des émigrés est une opportunité formidable pour la République qui naît: elle peut assouvir le désir profond des paysans défavorisés de devenir propriétaire et, en même temps de calmer l'état d'agitation qui règne dans les campagnes[5], mais elle peut aussi permettre « d'élargir la base sociale des partisans de la Révolution ». En ce sens, par le décret du 2 septembre 1792, la Législative adopte le principe du morcellement du patrimoine des émigrés, c'est-à-dire que les biens sont vendus en de multiples petits lots (lotissement). Mais selon ce décret, les ventes ont lieu selon le système des enchères, donc au plus offrant. Cette disposition avantage, bien évidemment, les paysans aisés et les bourgeois d'autant plus que, dans les faits, le décret laisse une grande liberté d'action aux administrations des districts chargées de la vente effective des biens nationaux, pour fixer les limites du morcellement « le plus utilement possible »[6]. Nombreux sont ceux qui décident de ne pas fractionner les fermes des émigrés…

3 Bodinier, Teyssier, Antoine, *L'événement le plus important de la Révolution, op. cit.*, pp. 390-391.

4 Martin Jean-Clément, *La Révolution française, 1789-1799, une histoire socio-politique*, Paris, Belin, 2004, p. 154.

5 En effet, les campagnes connaissent, en cet été 1792, des révoltes anti-seigneuriales. Les paysans demandent la suppression définitive de tous les droits féodaux, décision qui n'interviendra qu'en 1793.

6 Bodinier, Teyssier, Antoine, *L'événement le plus important de la Révolution, op. cit.*, pp. 28 et 390-391.

La République proclamée, la vente des biens nationaux reste un enjeu politique entre les deux tendances politiques qui s'affrontent à la nouvelle Assemblée, la Convention, à savoir: les Girondins et les Montagnards. Aux commandes de la République dès septembre 1792, les Girondins tentent de s'appuyer sur les campagnes. Ainsi, le 4 mars 1793, il y a un débat intense entre les groupes à la Convention sur la division effective des biens des émigrés. Puis, le 4 avril suivant, un décret impose le retour au morcellement des biens avant leur mise en vente et suspend les ventes de fermes. Les grandes demeures doivent être morcelées le plus possible. Les Montagnards, qui ont renversé les Girondins le 3 juin 1793, prennent aussi des décisions sur la question des biens des émigrés pour s'assurer le soutien de la paysannerie[7].

Les modalités définitives de la vente des biens des émigrés sont alors adoptées par les décrets des 25 juillet et 22 novembre 1793 (législation n. 1). La vente aux enchères au chef-lieu de district est confirmée. Le morcellement des domaines est décidé. Le bien est payé en dix termes égaux, le premier dans le mois qui suit la vente, les neuf autres chaque année, avec un intérêt de 5 %. Enfin, la Convention attribue des bons de 500 livres aux « patriotes indigents » et aux défenseurs de la patrie qui ne possèdent pas de terre et qui ne paient aucun impôt. Cette somme est remboursable sans intérêts sur vingt ans. Elle permet aux pauvres de participer aux ventes aux enchères et de devenir propriétaire[8]. Ainsi, après plus d'un an de débats acharnés, parfois contradictoires, et dans un contexte intérieur (révolte fédéraliste, contre-révolution en Vendée et dans l'Ouest de la France) et extérieur (guerre contre l'Autriche et la Prusse) très difficile, la vente des biens des émigrés commence.

7 *Ibid.*, pp. 28-29 et 392-393.

8 *Ibid.*, pp. 29 et 393-394 et Caron Pierre, Desprez François, *Recueil de textes législatifs et administratifs concernant les biens nationaux,* Paris, volume II (01/01/1792-30/06/1793), 1930; volume III (01/07/1793-06/03/1796), 1944.

La vente des biens des émigrés dans le district de Rochefort (1793-1804)

Les biens sont évalués d'après le prix du bail ou, à défaut, par deux experts, un de l'administration, l'autre représentant l'acheteur potentiel. Lorsque la vente est décidée, le bien fait l'objet d'une publicité par affiche pour que personne ne puisse en ignorer l'existence. Les affiches sont placardées au chef-lieu de district et dans la commune concernée par la vente d'un bien. Les deux séances d'adjudication (la première étant celle de « présentation » des biens; la seconde étant l'adjudication définitive) se déroulent en présence de deux officiers municipaux de la commune de situation des biens. Les séances démarrent sur la mise à prix correspondant à l'estimation. Et les enchères peuvent alors être criées.

Dans le district de Rochefort (qui comprend 54 communes soit une superficie totale de 78.500 ha), les ventes s'étalent du 30 octobre 1793 au 20 mars 1804. Dans cet intervalle, 637 adjudications sont nécessaires à la vente de 5.144 ha (6,6 % de la superficie du district). Les autorités du district s'avèrent très efficaces puisque les biens sont vendus rapidement. En effet, lorsqu'en août 1794 l'administration marque une pause, 355 lots (soit 55,7 % du nombre total de lots vendus) et 2.284,5 ha (44,4 % de la superficie totale vendue) ont déjà été adjugés. Et en septembre 1795, quand le district suspend les ventes et clôt la liste des lots qui tombent sous le coup de la législation n. 1, 597 lots et 4.506 ha sont déjà vendus, c'est-à-dire que 93,7 % du nombre total d'adjudications et 87,6 % de la superficie globale sont vendus moins de deux ans après le début des opérations d'aliénation. Un autre élément démontre la rapidité des ventes: les biens des émigrés furent adjugés au cours de 93 séances: 66 eurent lieu entre octobre 1793 et septembre 1795, ce qui fait un rythme d'une séance d'adjudication tous les 10 jours – intervalle très rapproché convenons-en –, séances au cours desquelles on vend, en moyenne 9 lots. Les lots tombant sous le coup des autres législations sont peu nombreux (40 lots soit 6,3 % du nombre total d'adjudication et 637,6 ha soit 12,4 % de la superficie totale)[9]. Ils concernent

9 Archives Départementales de la Charente-Maritime, série Q 107, Procès verbaux (PV) d'enchères et d'adjudications de biens de seconde origine (30 juillet 1793 – 29 floréal an III) et série Q 108, Procès verbaux d'adjudications de biens de toute origine (lois du 12 et 27 prairial an III), Thermidor an III/fructidor an III; séries Q 175-176, actes de ventes (loi du 28 ventôse an IV) entre le 15 prairial an IV et le 28 frimaire an VII; séries

principalement les biens des parents d'émigrés dont la succession fut ouverte le 28 avril 1795 et la vente issue du partage des biens indivis avec des émigrés, décidée le 17 août 1796[10].

Au total, ce sont 154 immeubles qui furent vendus, dont 78 fermes (50,6 % du nombre d'immeubles), 14 moulins (9,1 %), 16 maisons dans le centre ville de Rochefort (10,4 %), 21 châteaux ou maisons de maître (13,6 %). Le reste (16,2 %) est constitué de maisons et de granges situées en milieu rural ou dans les bourgs ainsi que deux halles, 4 fours (dont deux banaux), un magasin et une fabrique de tuiles. 129 immeubles furent adjugés entre 1793 et 1795 soit 83,8 % du parc immobilier des émigrés[11].

On observe, entre la législation n. 1 et les autres législations de vente, une différence notable entre le nombre de lots et la taille des biens vendus. Entre 1793 et 1795, un lot fait, en moyenne, 7,5 ha alors qu'entre 1796 et 1799, un lot contient 15,9 ha. Cet écart, du simple au double, relève de l'originalité principale de la première période des ventes: le lotissement des propriétés lors des adjudications. Cela explique le paradoxe apparent de cette première période de vente: on vendit 9 fermes sur 10 (69 sur 78) entre 1793 et 1795 mais la taille moyenne des lots est moindre que pour les législations suivantes car à partir de 1796, on ne morcela plus les exploitations. Cette mesure de lotissement explique également qu'en 1793-1795, 1 lot sur 3 compte moins de 1 ha; 1 lot sur 2 moins de 2 ha et 3 lots sur 4 moins de 5 ha. La situation change radicalement dès septembre 1795 (dernier mois des adjudications de la première période): le lotissement est supprimé.

Des biens très divers furent soumis au lotissement: les fermes bien sûr, mais aussi des parcelles de prés, de labours ou de bois, et cela, quelle que soit leur taille de départ, qu'elles soient petites ou grandes. Cependant, pour les plus grandes exploitations agricoles, les autorités du district conservèrent une superficie

Q 181-182, affiches et PV de premières enchères et d'adjudications entre le 13 germinal an V et le 28 thermidor an VI; série Q 183, PV de premières enchères et d'adjudications entre le 26 pluviôse an VII et le 6 thermidor an VII et série Q 187, PV de premières enchères et d'adjudications an XII-1807.

10 Bodinier, Teyssier, Antoine, *L'événement le plus important de la Révolution*, *op. cit.*, pp. 29 et 30.

11 Archives départementales de la Charente-Maritime, séries Q 107-108, Q 175-176, Q 181-182, Q 183 et Q 187.

Figure 1. Nombre de lots vendus, mois par mois, dans le district de Rochefort, entre octobre 1793 et mars 1804

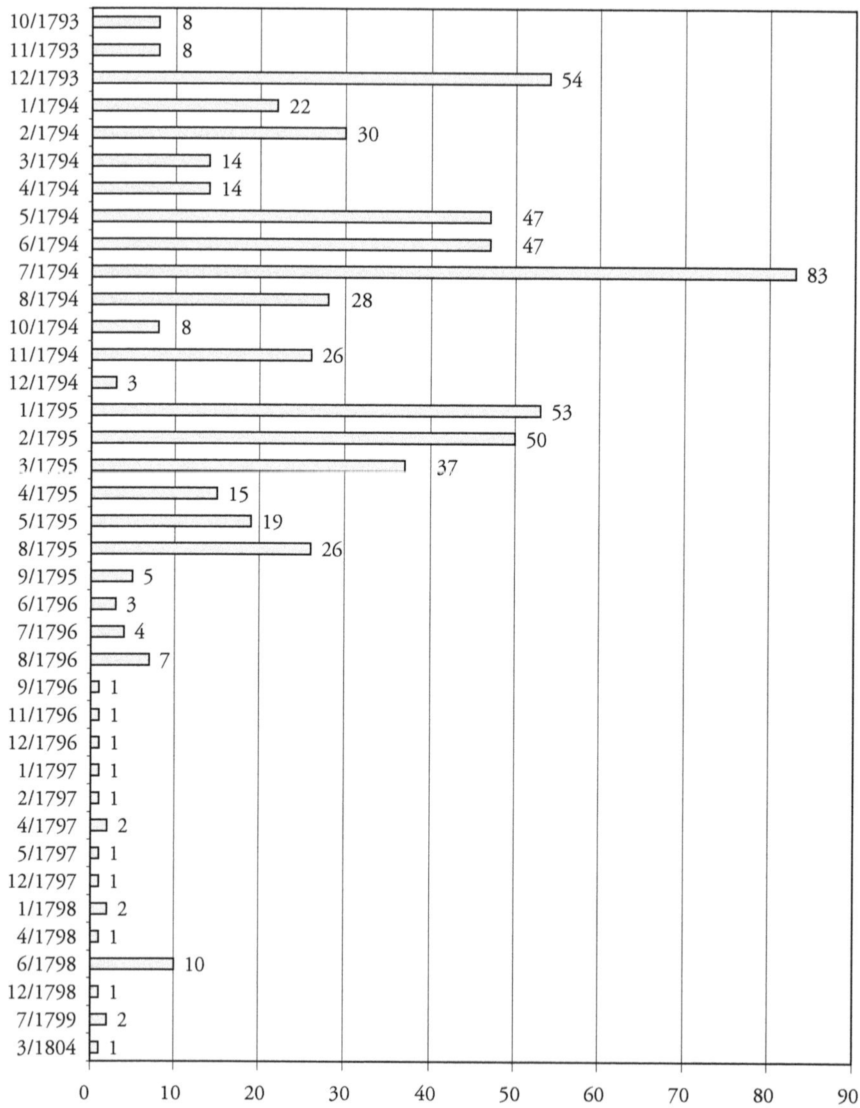

Source: Voir note n. 9.

Figure 2. La vente des biens des émigrés, mois par mois, en hectares, dans le district de Rochefort

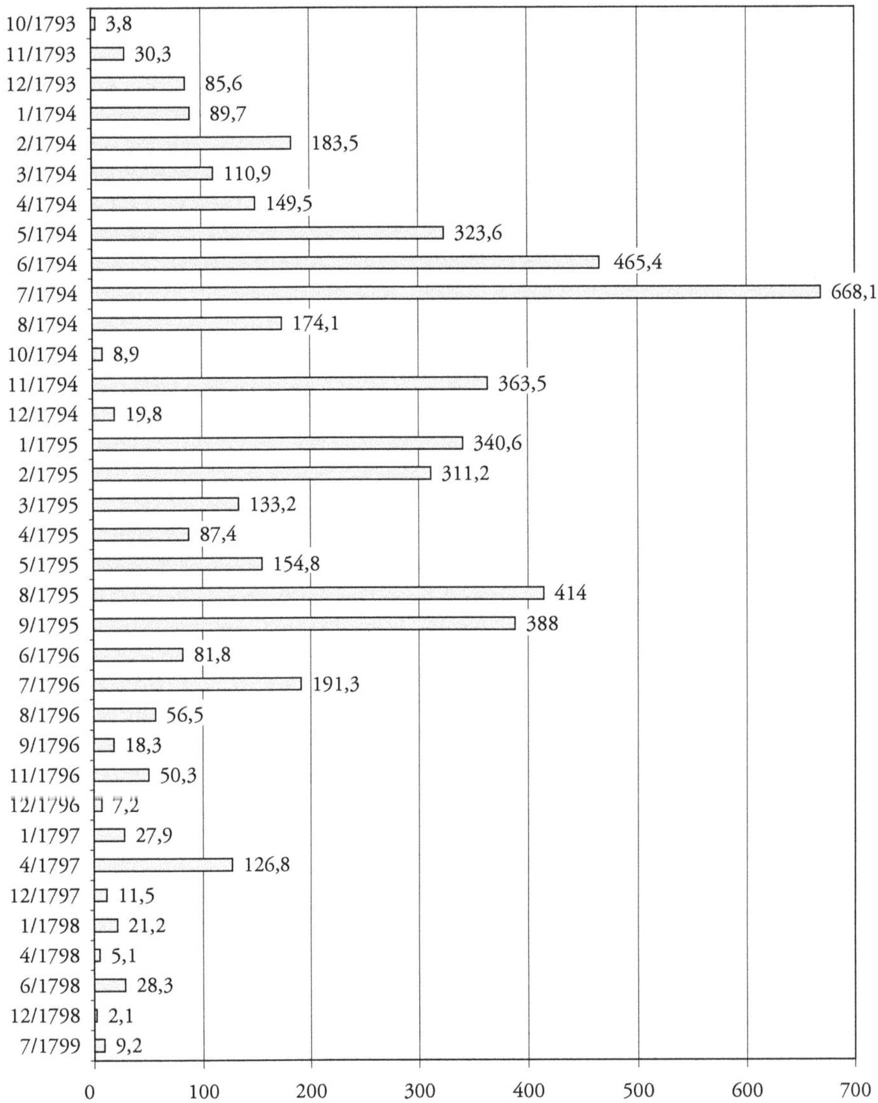

Source: Voir note n. 9.

assez significative autour des bâtiments de la ferme et ne fractionnèrent que les champs en périphérie de propriété. Pour les petites exploitations, le lot qui contient le corps de ferme est vendu en premier. La superficie de ce lot est très souvent plus importante que les lots qui suivent. Mais, le premier lot ne comprend parfois que les bâtiments de la ferme ou bien ces derniers ne sont entourés que par moins d'un hectare. Hormis les lots concernant les bâtiments fermiers ou des châteaux/maisons nobles, les lots d'un même bien sont adjugés ordinairement par tranche de 5 ha maximum (en 10 lots environ). Mais, très souvent ces lots ont une superficie inférieure à 2 ha. Ainsi, ce réel souci de lotissement s'exerça sur une longue période: il témoigne sans doute, parmi les dirigeants du district, de sympathies « montagnardes ».

Les ventes des biens des émigrés débutèrent le 30 octobre 1793 alors que pour 100 livres-papier on obtient plus que 45 livres numéraires. En effet, ces ventes se déroulent dans un contexte inflationniste – la monnaie papier, l'assignat, s'effondrant[12] – ce qui va grever le bilan financier des ventes pour l'Etat.

Les administrateurs s'alignèrent sur le phénomène inflationniste en 1795. En effet, les estimations furent assez « basses » la première année de vente (octobre 1793-août 1794; année où l'on adjugea 44,4 % des biens des émigrés): 1.382.448 livres pour 2.284,5 ha soit une estimation moyenne de 605 livres l'hectare alors que les 2.221,5 ha aliénés entre octobre 1794 et septembre 1795 furent estimés à 2.525.627 livres, soit une moyenne de 1.137 livres l'hectare. Ainsi, d'une année sur l'autre, les prix d'estimation furent multipliés par 1,9 et ce n'est pas dû à une plus grande valeur des biens adjugés en 1795. Si les prix d'estimation suivirent la courbe de l'inflation, cela suggère que les prix d'adjudication grimpèrent très vite eux aussi. Les prix d'estimation sont multipliés par 2,2 par rapport aux prix courants d'adjudication dans la première année de vente et par 2,9 au cours de la seconde année alors que, cette année là, on a anticipé la dévaluation de l'assignat. Après des enchères relativement raisonnables jusqu'en août 1794, les prix s'emballent à partir de fin 1794 pour atteindre des sommets en 1795.

L'Etat tente de lutter contre l'inflation galopante en adoptant une nouvelle législation en 1796. Après une suspension des adjudications décidée le 21 novembre 1795, l'Etat met en place, par le décret du 18 mars 1796, de nouvelles

12 Voir l'annexe 1 en fin d'article.

Figure 3. Prix d'estimation, prix d'adjudication courant et réel, mois par mois, pour la première période de vente, dans le district de Rochefort

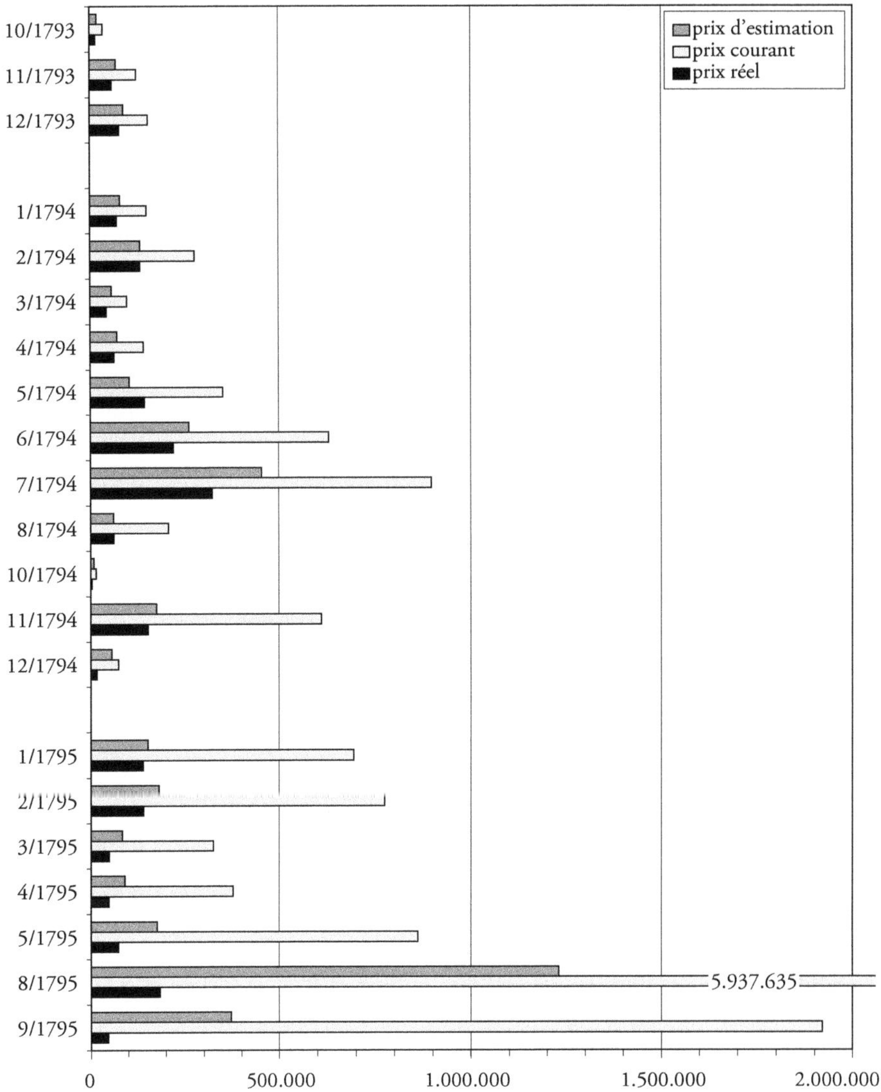

Source: Archives départementales de la Charente-Naritime, séries Q 107-108 et séries Q 175-176.

modalités de ventes. L'assignat ayant perdu toute valeur, les biens des émigrés sont acquis par le biais d'une nouvelle monnaie-papier: le mandat territorial, créé le même jour. Le système des enchères est supprimé, il est remplacé par des ventes sur simple soumission au chef-lieu de département. Le prix de vente est estimé à 22 fois le revenu de 1789 pour les terres et 18 fois pour les bâtiments. Un quart du bien est payé à la soumission. Deux autres quarts dans les deux décades qui suivent (soit dans les 20 jours suivant), le dernier quart dans les seize mois[13].

Mais ces nouvelles modalités sont à l'origine des pires gaspillages car les enchères ne sont plus là pour limiter les effets de l'inflation, le mandat territorial se dépréciant encore plus rapidement que l'assignat. Pour cette seconde législation, les prix d'adjudication furent 22,4 fois supérieur aux prix d'estimation (1.162.000 livres contre 56.875)!

Finalement, le 4 février 1797, le mandat territorial est officiellement démonétisé. C'est le retour officiel à la monnaie métallique. La dévaluation de l'assignat et l'inflation galopante font que les prix courants d'adjudication ne correspondent pas à grand-chose. Ainsi, il faut prendre en compte les prix réels pour juger du véritable bilan financier des ventes des biens des émigrés. Les prix réels sont, presque toujours, inférieurs aux prix d'estimation même dès la première année de vente. Entre octobre 1793 et août 1794, le prix réel des ventes (soit 1.200.678 livres) ne correspond qu'à 86,9 % du prix d'estimation. Ce rapport est négatif mais il n'est pas trop mauvais, les autorités du district vendant les biens des émigrés à un assez bon prix (526 livres l'hectare, prix sans inflation). En revanche, la situation se détériore grandement à l'été 1795. En effet, la seconde année, le rapport entre le prix réel (851.023 livres) et le prix d'estimation (2.525.627) n'est plus que de 33,7 %! A partir de 1795, on peut affirmer que le district de Rochefort perd de l'argent (prix moyen d'un hectare entre octobre 1794 et septembre 1795: 383 livres seulement alors que de grandes exploitations sont vendues). Globalement, l'écart final entre le prix d'estimation et le prix réel d'adjudication est de 0,53 pour la première période de vente (où l'on vendit presque 9 ha sur 10 de biens d'émigrés), c'est-à-dire que le produit final des opérations de vente entre 1793 et 1795 ne représente que la moitié de la valeur des estimations[14].

13 Bodinier, Teyssier, Antoine, *L'événement le plus important de la Révolution*, *op. cit.*, p. 30.

14 Archives Départementales de la Charente-Maritime, séries Q 107-108 et Q 175-176.

Entre 1793 et 1795, le district de Rochefort vendit les biens des émigrés pour la somme globale de 14.610.524 livres et, entre 1796 et 1804, pour la somme de 1.735.848 livres (le tout exprimé en prix courant). Le prix réel de ces opérations financières, entre 1793 et 1795 est de 2.051.692 livres mais pour la période 1796-1804, nous ne connaissons l'ampleur exacte de l'inflation que jusqu'au 28 juillet 1796, date à laquelle l'émission de l'assignat cessa. Entre le 10 juin et le 20 juillet 1796, on vendit 6 lots qui rapportèrent en prix réels 22.163 livres. Ainsi, le bilan global est le suivant: entre 1793 et 1804, le montant des adjudications, en prix courant, s'élève à 16.346.372 livres. Le bilan, en prix réel, est délicat à juger. Pour comparer ce qui peut l'être, disons simplement qu'entre le 30 octobre 1793 et le 20 juillet 1796, le district de Rochefort vendit les biens d'émigrés pour 2.073.945 livres (prix réel) alors qu'à la même période, le montant de la somme en prix courant atteint 14.632.687 livres. L'instabilité monétaire ne cessant que sous le Consulat, on peut affirmer que les lots furent véritablement « bradés » à partir d'août 1795, la situation ne cessant de se détériorer. Le prix réel d'un hectare, en moyenne, entre 1793 et juillet 1796 est de 434 livres seulement. Ce chiffre est assez fiable puisqu'il concerne 92,9 % de la superficie vendue (soit 4.779,1 ha)[15].

Ce prix révèle véritablement ce que fut la vente des biens des émigrés dans le district de Rochefort: une catastrophe financière, d'autant plus que cette vente a mobilisé une partie des administrations communales, du district et du département pendant plusieurs années pour faire face au bon fonctionnement des opérations d'inventaire, de séquestre, de gestion des propriétés nationales et de ventes. Ceci eut également un coût important, à déduire des « bénéfices » des ventes[16].

Relativisons ce bilan en disant que politiquement, cette vente permit à la Convention de réaliser son objectif principal: financer la guerre à l'intérieur et à l'extérieur de la France grâce, en plus, au patrimoine de ses ennemis. Si l'on tient compte de cela, peu importe si les biens des émigrés ont été vendus

15 Archives Départementales de la Charente-Maritime, série Q 107, Procès verbaux (PV) d'enchères et d'adjudications de biens de seconde origine (30 juillet 1793 – 29 floréal an III) et série Q 108, Procès verbaux d'adjudications de biens de toute origine (lois du 12 et 27 prairial an III), Thermidor an III/fructidor an III; séries Q 175-176, actes de ventes (loi du 28 ventôse an IV) entre le 15 prairial an IV et le 28 frimaire an VII.

16 Auzou Etienne, *La vente des biens nationaux de première et deuxième origines dans le district de Caudebec-en-Caux, 1791-1856*, Maîtrise, Rouen, 1991, p. 138.

rapidement et à des prix « bradés » car, non seulement, ils n'ont rien coûté à l'Etat mais, ils ont aussi permis de consolider la République et de vaincre les forces contre-révolutionnaires[17].

Les 637 lots et les 5.144 ha furent appropriés par 348 acquéreurs. En moyenne, chaque acquéreur a donc enlevé 14,8 ha, chiffre assez élevé qui permet de relativiser la portée de la mesure du lotissement. Dans les faits, les écarts entre les acheteurs sont exacerbés. L'élite des acheteurs (ceux qui ont acquis plus de 100 ha) forme un groupe de 11 individus qui s'est arrogé 60 lots (9,4 % des lots; 5,5 lots par acquéreurs en moyenne), 1.688 ha (soit 32,8 % de la surface totale aliénée) et 28 immeubles (soit 18,2 % du nombre total d'immeubles vendus), surtout des fermes (24, soit 30 % du nombre d'exploitations agricoles)! Plus largement, les 20 plus gros acquéreurs emportèrent 2.387 ha soit près de la moitié de la superficie mise en vente (46,4 % exactement) et 38 immeubles (soit un immeuble sur 4). Outre les 20 plus gros acquéreurs de biens d'émigrés, 27 autres individus, ceux qui ont acquis plus de 50 ha et qui font figure, encore, de gros acquéreurs, remportèrent 1.147 ha.

1.147 ha soit 22,3 % de la superficie aliénée. 44 personnages ont acquis entre 20 et 50 ha. De fait, ces individus peuvent être considérés comme des acheteurs importants, de second rang tout de même. Ils enlevèrent 912 ha soit 17,7 % de la superficie aliénée. Les 243 acquéreurs restants (70 % des acheteurs), ceux de moins de 20 ha et que l'on peut qualifier de « petits acquéreurs », enlevèrent 697 ha (13,5 % de la superficie totale des ventes)[18]. Le lotissement n'a donc pas produit tous les effets escomptés. Certes, beaucoup de gens modestes ont pu participer aux ventes, par le biais des dispositifs expliqués dans la première partie, mais ils se sont partagés les « miettes du gâteau », prenant les lots que la bourgeoisie et les paysans aisés ne s'arrachaient pas.

On ne connaît pas la profession de 16 individus soit 4,6 % du nombre d'acquéreurs. Ils achetèrent 19 lots (3 % du nombre total de lots) et 61,2 ha soit 1,2 % de la superficie aliénée[19].

Deux-cent-quinze paysans (dans le tableau « cultivateur » + « propriétaire rural » soit 61,8 % du nombre d'acquéreurs) s'approprièrent 2.188,5 ha (soit

17 Bodinier, Teyssier, Antoine, *L'événement le plus important de la Révolution*, *op. cit.*, p. 329.

18 Archives départementales de la Charente-Maritime, séries Q 107-108, Q 175-176, Q 181-182, Q 183 et Q 187.

19 Archives départementales de la Charente-Maritime, séries Q 107-108, Q 175-176, Q 181-182, Q 183 et Q 187.

Tableau 1. Acquisitions de biens fonciers (en ha) de seconde origine selon la profession dans le district de Rochefort

Profession	Nbre acheteurs	Nbre de lots	Superficie totale	Pct. superf.	Nbre fermes	Exploitation superficie
Cultivateur	157	264	1.098,5014	21,4	16	509,1096
Propriétaire:						
rural	58	105	1.089,9986	21,2	14	508,7968
urbain	14	30	374,3127	7,3	5	251,7143
Négociant	16	46	809,3220	15,7	12	602,0630
Marchand	33	80	671,6731	13,0	14	475,0336
Artisan	13	15	51,2432	1,0	1	38,8042
Homme de loi	7	16	172,3031	3,3	2	78,2637
Profession de santé	1	1				
Fonctionnaire	6	10	183,0044	3,6	2	156,7817
Militaire	8	31	280,7176	5,5	4	158,2083
Veuve-seule	9	2	6,1540	0,1		
Monde de la mer	4	8	12,65	0,2		
Noble	6	10	332,7599	6,5	8	294,7065
Inconnue	16	19	61,1978	1,2		
Total	348	637	5.143,8378	100,0	79	3.073,4817

Source: Voir note n. 9.

42,5 % de la superficie aliénée) en 369 lots (57,9 % du nombre total de lots vendus et 1,7 lot par acquéreur en moyenne). En moyenne, chaque paysan acquiert 10,2 ha (ce qui est inférieur à la moyenne générale). Ils remportèrent 30 fermes (38 % des exploitations) et, plus largement, ils enlevèrent 62 immeubles (40,3 % du parc immobilier adjugé) soit, dans le détail: 9 châteaux ou maisons de maître, 30 corps de ferme, 8 maisons, 10 moulins, 3 granges et 2 fours banaux. Mais certains propriétaires ou cultivateurs tirèrent leur épingle du jeu, ce qui suggère des acquisitions fort inégales au sein du monde paysan (on recense 8 paysans parmi les 20 plus gros acquéreurs de biens de seconde origine). Dans le détail, chaque propriétaire rural, qu'on peut qualifier de paysan aisé a acquis, en moyenne, 18,8 ha alors qu'un cultivateur (« petit paysan ») n'a enlevé que 7 ha en moyenne, encore ces modestes travailleurs de la terre ont-ils profité du lotissement. Leurs acquisitions auraient été réduites à la portion congrue si cette mesure n'avait pas été appliquée[20].

La bourgeoisie devance la paysannerie. 102 bourgeois (29,3 % du nombre d'acquéreurs) enlevèrent 237 lots (37,2 % du nombre de lots et une moyenne de 2,3 lots par acquéreur) et 2.607,5 ha soit 50,7 % de la superficie acquise. La bourgeoisie remporta 41 fermes (51,9 % du nombre d'exploitations). En moyenne, un bourgeois acquiert 25,3 ha (ce qui est supérieur à la moyenne générale). Mais, quelques acquéreurs se distinguent: on retrouve 11 bourgeois parmi les 20 principaux acquéreurs de biens d'émigrés. Au total, la bourgeoisie acheta 73 immeubles (47,4 % du parc immobilier vendu): 13 châteaux ou maisons de maître, 41 fermes, 9 maisons, 3 moulins, 2 halles, 2 fours, un magasin, une prison et une fabrique de tuiles. Dans le détail, la haute bourgeoisie (propriétaires urbains et négociants, soit 30 personnes) s'est concentrée sur les biens à forte valeur ajoutée (fermes et châteaux), ce qui explique qu'elle s'est rendue maître de près d'un quart de la superficie totale vendue (23 % exactement). Un grand bourgeois a acquis 39,5 ha en moyenne alors qu'un membre de la moyenne et de la petite bourgeoisie (marchand, homme de loi, profession de santé, militaire, fonctionnaire, artisan) n'a enlevé que 19 ha[21].

Il convient d'aborder une catégorie d'individus particulière: la noblesse. Six nobles (1,7 % du nombre d'acquéreurs) enlevèrent 10 lots (1,6 % du nombre de lots) mais 332,8 ha soit 6,5 % de la superficie vendue. Ce qui confère une telle emprise foncière à la ci-devant noblesse, c'est l'acquisition de 8 exploitations agricoles (10 % du nombre des fermes). On recense un noble parmi les 20 plus gros acquéreurs de biens de seconde origine. Au total, les nobles achetèrent 16 immeubles (10,3 % du parc immobilier aliéné): 3 châteaux ou maisons de maître, 8 corps de ferme, 4 maisons et un moulin. Les ci-devant nobles – ils résident en ville ou à l'extérieur du district de Rochefort – ont cherché, dans la mesure du possible, à racheter une partie du patrimoine familial. C'est, par exemple, le cas de Bénigne Augustine Françoise Le Tellier Montmirail, qui racheta deux domaines appartenant à son fils Polycarpe de la Rochefoucaud, d'une superficie totale de 201 ha[22].

20 Archives départementales de la Charente-Maritime, séries Q 107-108, Q 175-176, Q 181-182, Q 183 et Q 187.

21 Archives départementales de la Charente-Maritime, séries Q 107-108, Q 175-176, Q 181-182, Q 183 et Q 187.

Tableau 2. Nombre d'immeubles acquis selon la profession

Profession	Châteaux/ maisons de maître	Fermes	Maisons	Moulins	Autres	Total
Marchand	7	14	1	1	3	26
Négociant	1	13	1		2	17
Propriétaire:						
urbain	1	5	1	2	1	10
rural	8	14	3	2		27
Cultivateur	1	16	5	8	5	35
Homme de loi	1	2				3
Militaire	3	4	2			9
Artisan		1	3		1	5
Noble	3	8	4	1		16
Fonctionnaire		2				2
Profession de santé			1			1
Inconnue			3			3
Total	25	79	24	14	12	154

Source: voir Tableau 1.

L'analyse géographique montre la courte « victoire » des citadins dans ces ventes. On ignore le domicile de 14 acquéreurs seulement (4 % du nombre d'acquéreurs) qui enlevèrent 7 lots. Ces derniers ne remportèrent que 31,8 ha soit 0,6 % de la superficie adjugée[23].

86,5 % des acquéreurs (soit 301 personnes) sont domiciliés dans le district de Rochefort. Seulement 9,5 % des acquéreurs (33 personnes) habitent dans d'autres districts. Leur présence peut s'expliquer par la volonté de spéculer, la taille des fermes des émigrés qui est importante ou l'absence de biens dans la commune de ces « étrangers proches ». Mais, ces 33 personnes « étrangères »

22 Archives départementales de la Charente-Maritime, séries Q 107-108, Q 175-176, Q 181-182, Q 183 et Q 187.

23 Archives départementales de la Charente-Maritime, séries Q 107-108, Q 175-176, Q 181-182, Q 183 et Q 187.

enlevèrent tout de même 30 immeubles (19,5 % du nombre total d'immeubles aliénés), 66 lots (10,4 % du nombre de lots) et 1.055,5 ha soit 20,5 % de la surface totale aliénée[24].

88 acquéreurs sont domiciliés en ville: de fait, 25,5 % des acquéreurs sont des citadins. Les acquéreurs des villes enlevèrent 209 lots soit 32,8 % du nombre global des adjudications. Répartis en huit villes (Rochefort, Tonnay-Charente et Surgères dans notre district et Saint Jean d'Angély, La Rochelle, Saintes, Orléans et Paris), ils emportèrent 2.583,9 ha soit 50,2 % de la superficie aliénée dont 34,2 % proviennent d'individus étrangers au district de Rochefort (soit 882,7 ha)[25].

Enfin, 246 acquéreurs sont domiciliés en milieu rural: de fait, 70,7 % des acquéreurs sont des ruraux. Les acquéreurs des « champs » enlevèrent 421 lots soit 66,1 % du nombre de lots vendus. Mais, au total, ils ne remportèrent « que » 2.527,9 ha soit 49,1 % de la surface aliénée dont 6,8 % proviennent d'individus étrangers au district (soit 172,8 ha)[26]. Partout en France, sauf dans le district de Rouen, les ruraux sont nettement majoritaires en nombre mais il n'en va pas de même quant à la valeur ou à la taille de leurs acquisitions[27]. Neuf ruraux font tout de même partie des 20 plus gros acquéreurs de biens de seconde origine.

Le 3 mars 1800, la liste des émigrés est clôturée et c'est le début des radiations. Le 26 avril 1802, l'amnistie des émigrés qui rentreront avant le 23 septembre de la même année est décidée[28].

24 Archives départementales de la Charente-Maritime, séries Q 107-108, Q 175-176, Q 181-182, Q 183 et Q 187.

25 Notons que les Rochefortais dominèrent les ventes dans la moitié sud du district. Ils enlevèrent, globalement, 1.124,6 ha (21,9 % de la superficie totale), 117 lots (18,4 % du nombre total de lots), 17 maisons et 17 fermes (22,1 % du nombre d'immeubles). Les habitants de Surgères dominent quant à eux la moitié nord du district: 742,4 ha (14,4 %), 36 lots (5,7 %), 3 maisons et 13 fermes (10,4 %). A titre d'information le plus gros acquéreur de biens d'émigrés est un négociant de Surgères, Samuel Lebouc, qui emporta 306,3 ha et quatre fermes. Archives départementales de la Charente-Maritime, séries Q 107-108, Q 175-176, Q 181-182, Q 183 et Q 187.

26 Archives départementales de la Charente-Maritime, séries Q 107-108, Q 175-176, Q 181-182, Q 183 et Q 187.

27 Bodinier, Teyssier, Antoine, *L'événement le plus important de la Révolution*, *op. cit.*, p. 245.

28 *Ibid.*, pp. 29-31.

L'indemnité du « Milliard » (1825) : une compensation pécuniaire pour les anciens émigrés

La noblesse, à l'issu de ce processus de vente, n'est pas ruinée mais est tout de même appauvrie. Après « l'intermède » révolutionnaire et napoléonien, les Bourbons, par la personne de Louis XVIII, rétablissent la monarchie. Le nouveau régime s'appuie sur la noblesse pour gouverner le pays et entend donc contenter les anciens émigrés et leurs familles, en tentant de leur trouver une compensation à la perte de leur patrimoine. Néanmoins, devant l'ampleur du transfert foncier qu'a représenté la vente des biens des émigrés, Louis XVIII ne peut remettre en cause les adjudications effectuées par la République. Toutes les couches de la société, y compris des nobles, s'étaient enrichies. Revenir sur ces aliénations constituait un danger politique, une étincelle susceptible d'allumer une nouvelle révolution. Ainsi, Louis XVIII, par la Charte de 1814, reconnaît l'irrévocabilité des ventes, ce qui apaise tous les propriétaires de biens d'émigrés. En revanche, par la loi du 5 décembre 1814, les biens qui n'avaient pas été aliénés sont restitués à leur propriétaire.

Néanmoins, ces restitutions ne satisfaisaient pas pleinement les émigrés, d'autant qu'un nombre important d'entre eux avait tout perdu. Ils réclamaient alors une indemnisation. Louis XVIII en accepta le principe et son successeur, Charles X prit la décision de donner une compensation financière aux anciens émigrés, ses plus fidèles alliés politiques, par la « loi du Milliard », le 27 avril 1825[29].

La loi a pour objectif d'indemniser le plus justement possible les « expropriés » mais cela dans la limite des moyens financiers dont dispose l'Etat à cette époque. La loi ne prend en compte que les biens fonciers et immobiliers (exit le mobilier et les rentes) et les évalue en tenant compte de l'inflation en vigueur au moment des adjudications. Les biens vendus avant mai/juin 1795, sont remboursés sur la base du prix d'adjudication, réduit en numéraire (au cours de l'assignat). Pour les adjudications postérieures à cette date, les autorités prennent le revenu de 1790 et le multiplie par 18[30].

29 *Ibid.*, pp. 271-272.
30 *Ibid.*, p. 272.

La loi définit également les conditions pratiques pour être indemnisé. Les expropriés, leurs descendants ou héritiers disposent d'un délai d'un an pour constituer un dossier (pièces justificatives à fournir: preuves de leur état civil, procès-verbaux d'adjudications, actes de rachats éventuels) qu'ils doivent transmettre au préfet[31].

Au sommet de l'échelle administrative, le Conseil d'Etat se prononce sur la recevabilité des dossiers, après avis d'une commission spécialement instituée pour cette indemnisation. Les oppositions furent nombreuses. L'élaboration des bordereaux d'indemnités (dossiers qui récapitulent les dates de vente, la description du bien – superficie, situation –, les prix, les paiements) est difficile à réaliser pour les fonctionnaires qui doivent «jongler» avec les différentes procédures utilisées au moment des ventes mais aussi avec l'inflation de l'époque pour calculer le prix de la compensation finale. Les premiers dossiers sont déposés dès le mois de mai 1825 et les derniers en avril 1826 comme la loi l'autorise[32].

Les bordereaux d'indemnité donnent tout à la fois la valeur des biens vendus et recouvrés pour tous les biens de l'émigré situés non seulement dans le département de la Charente-Inférieure mais aussi dans les autres départements quand il y a des biens. Au chercheur d'isoler les biens qui concernent le district de Rochefort. Les dossiers qui aboutirent et qui concernent des individus dont les biens sont situés, partiellement ou totalement, dans le district de Rochefort sont au nombre de 37. Le montant brut de l'indemnité concernant ces 36 émigrés, leurs descendants ou héritiers (un des émigrés compte deux dossiers) atteint 1.612.780 francs (valeur des biens sis uniquement dans le district de Rochefort). 10 émigrés cumulent 682.667 francs de dettes.

L'indemnité n'est pas délivrée sous forme de capital mais prend l'aspect d'une rente perpétuelle de 3%. A l'échelle nationale, la plupart des indemnités sont faibles ou moyennes. C'est aussi le cas dans le district de Rochefort. Cela ne doit pas surprendre car ces indemnités correspondent à la valeur – peu élevée au final – des biens aliénés. La modicité de certaines indemnités paraît suspecte mais certains n'ont pas touché grand-chose parce que leurs biens avaient été bradés[33]. A titre d'exemple, Polycarpe de la Rochefoucaud semble être victime de cette braderie: de Rochechouart possédaient 2 fois moins de superficie

31 Le délai est de deux ans pour les individus qui ne résident pas en Europe.

32 *Ibid.*, p.273.

33 Bodinier, Teyssier, Antoine, *L'événement le plus important de la Révolution*, *op. cit.*, p.277.

Tableau 3. Valeur de l'indemnité brute (en francs) versée aux émigrés pour les biens situés dans le district de Rochefort

Nom de l'émigré	Valeur indemnité brute	superficie concernée	Nom de l'émigré	Valeur indemnité brute	superficie concernée
Mallat de la Bertinière	15.000	21,4	Grelier dit Concize	7.632	hôtel particulier
Soeurs d'Orvilliers	6.300	hôtel particulier	Dupaty, veuve Turpin	7.200	hôtel particulier
Carré dit Candé	63.343	221,6 ha	Prou de Monroy	21.850	64 ha
Bernard de Marigny	25.632	52 ha	Roullin	12.609	13 ha
Bidé Maurville de l'Angle	17.467	28,4 ha	de Saint Orens	19.269	61,9
Froger jeune l'Eguille	225.580	375,3 ha	Mesnard	37.790	75 ha
La Perrière Roiffé	111.652	275 ha	Guillouet D'orvilliers	16.200	hôtel particulier
Polycarpe la Rochefoucaud	121.865	676,5 ha	Froger aîné l'Eguille	132.075	160,4ha
Jean Fçois la Rochefoucaud	4.100	9,2	Cullant	38.411	225,4 ha
La Guarrigue La Tournerie	25.200	hôtel particulier	Astier, veuve Voutron	7.515	27,9 ha
La Roche Saint André	28.114	53 ha	Voutron Nicolas	13.392	302,2 ha
Polignac	2.682	6,6 ha	Gabarret, veuve Raymond	5.153	27,9ha
Fleuriant	11.206	7,2 ha, 3 maisons	Laguarrigue frères	1.462	
St Michel Dunezat	27.503	35,1 ha	Bidé Maurville de la Funelière	168.979	264,9ha
De Brémont Lecomte	10.000		La Laurencie Leffort	7.651	105,6ha
Rigaud Vaudreuil	6.390	hotel particulier	Bouet Duportail	157	0,5 ha
Rochechouart	287.056	331,1 ha	De Pont des Granges	12.771	60,6 ha
Prévôt Traversais	93.713	264,3 ha	Rémond	19.125	56,9ha

Source: Archives Départementales de la Charente-Maritime, séries Q307-Q312, Bordereaux d'indemnité du Milliard et pièces annexes. Ordre d'inscription au registre de la préfecture. Données calculées par l'auteur. Pour information, voici les autres principaux patrimoines (en ha), vendus au cours de la Révolution: la famille Green de Saint Marsault (229), Beaucorps (199), La Rochejacquelein, le chef vendéen (156), Jean Saint Georges (144), les frères Delpy de la Roche (126), Daitz de Mesmy (116), la Roche du Maine (105), Delaage (90), La Laurencie (86,5), Saint Habre (76), Caqueray de Valmenier (57), Huon de Rosne (57) Chadeau de Laclochetterie (50).

foncière mais la valeur de son patrimoine est estimée le double de celui de la Rochefoucaud. En effet, la moitié des domaines de ce dernier fut vendue après août 1795 alors que le patrimoine de de Rochechouart fut dispersé au début des opérations … Mais pire, une vingtaine d'émigrés du district de Rochefort dont les biens avaient été aliénés ne reçurent aucune indemnité: plus d'héritiers, non dépôt de demande d'indemnisation, refus de l'administration?

Les expropriés sont, globalement, indemnisés. Mais, on l'a dit, le mobilier[34], les rentes, ainsi que les fermages (qui n'ont pas été touchés par les émigrés de la date de confiscation jusqu'au moment où ils ont pu en reprendre possession) ne sont pas concernés par l'indemnisation. Ainsi, privés pendant trente ans des revenus de leurs rentes et fermages, beaucoup d'émigrés se sont endettés pour mener, tant bien que mal, existence. Autre limite de cette loi: le montant de la rente (3 %) est peu élevée si on le compare à la situation en usage avant la Révolution, période où le revenu des terres était estimé à environ 5 % de leur valeur en capital. Par ailleurs, cette rente n'étant associée à aucune terre fit des émigrés des « rentiers sans terre » et beaucoup ont essayé de s'en séparer[35].

Pour l'Etat, la loi est lourde financièrement: il s'engage à verser, à perpétuité aux expropriés, une rente de 3 % (même si, le temps passant, le poids diminuera). Selon André Gain, cette rente, au total, aurait coûté 630 millions à l'Etat[36], un chiffre inférieur à la compensation financière octroyée par Charles X. Cependant, l'Etat s'est engagé à rembourser une partie des dettes des émigrés et a donc été perdant quand le passif était supérieur à la valeur de l'indemnité brute qu'il avait versée[37].

34 Le mobilier de chaque émigré a été vendu en moyenne pour 3.960 livres dans le district de Rochefort, mais pour certains émigrés, la vente s'élève à plusieurs dizaines de milliers de livres. Voir Archives Départementales de la Charente-Maritime, séries Q 195-200, inventaires, procès-verbaux de ventes, mainlevées et états divers de meubles de deuxième origine.

35 Bodinier, Teyssier, Antoine, *L'événement le plus important de la Révolution*, *op. cit.*, p. 277.

36 Gain André, *Autour du milliard des émigrés: rachats des émigrés et indemnité accordée*, Paris, Société d'impressions typographiques, 1930.

37 Bodinier, Teyssier, Antoine, *L'événement le plus important de la Révolution*, *op. cit.*, p. 278.

Annexe 1. Dévaluation de l'assignat et du mandat territorial dans le département de la Charente-Inférieure. Pour 100 livres-papier, on obtient en numéraire à la date de …

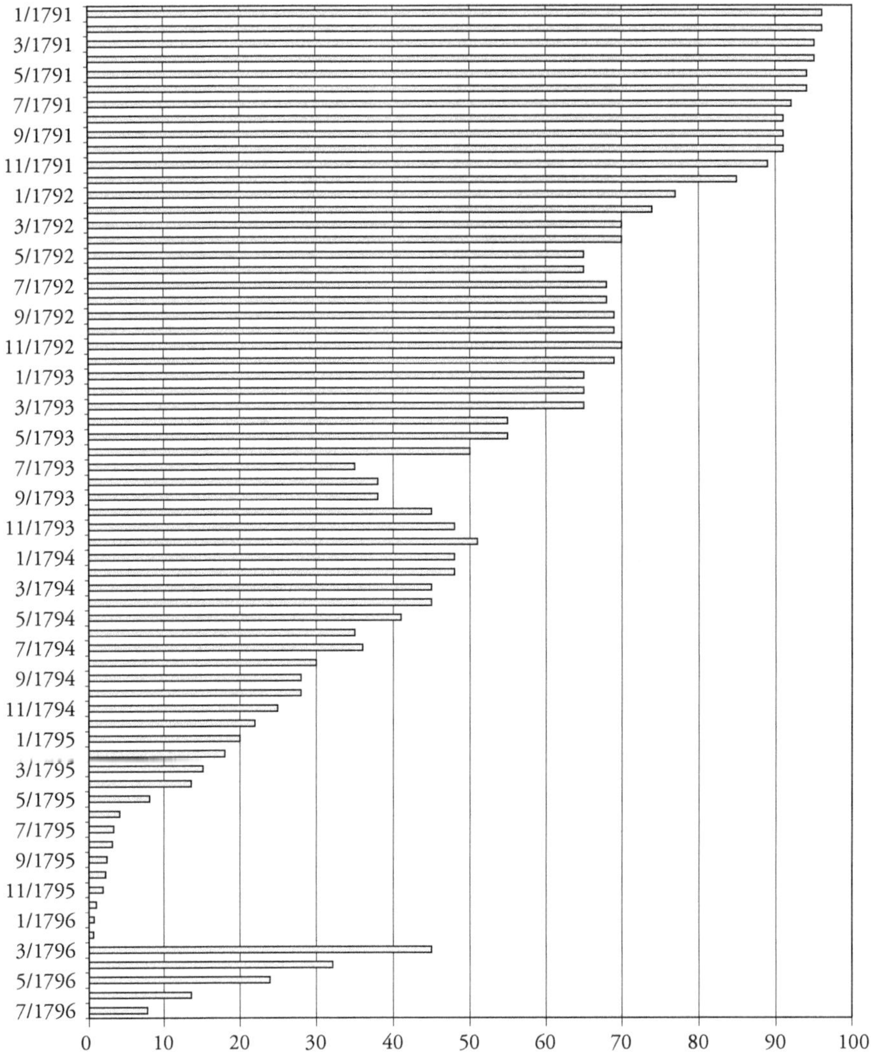

Source: Graphique réalisé par l'auteur d'après Pierre Caron, *Tableaux de dépréciation du papier-monnaie*, Paris, Imprimerie Nationale, 1909, pp. 87-88.

Annexe 2. Les principaux acquéreurs de biens d'émigrés dans le district de Rochefort

NOM, Prénom	Profession / Domicile	Superficie (en ha)	Immeubles
LEBOUC, Samuel	Négociant / Surgères	306,3308	métairie de la Boissonnerie et halles (Surgères); Cabane des Côteaux (St Louis de la Petite Flandre); Cabane de Bois Tableau (Muron); métairie de Courbuisson (St Saturnin du Bois)
LE TELLIER-MONTMIRAIL, Bénigne Augustine Françoise	Noble /Paris	201,0295	Domaine d'Aguré: métairies du Bois Hardy et de la Clavière; domaine de la Bougraine: métairies des Trois rois et de Bourlot (Saint Saturnin du Bois)
VILLEDON, Gabriel	Lieutenant de gendarmerie / Saint Jean d'Angély	163,4220	Le château de Moragne, métairies Dupoteau, de la Liardière et de Tout-Vent (Moragne)
FENIS, Jean François	Propriétaire / Saint Germain de Marencennes	160,0544	Cabane du Rocher (Saint Louis de la Petite Flandre), maison et métairie des Bugaudières (Saint Germain de Marencennes)
RAULT, Jean François	Propriétaire / Rochefort (les Broussailles)	147,0115	Cabane du Petit Couvent (Ardillières); une maison, n° 1146 rue de la République (Rochefort)
GOUGAUD, Pierre	Cultivateur / Breuil-Saint-Jean	129,3188	Métairies de l'Angle et de Châlons (Ardillières)
ALLET Pierre	Propriétaire / La Rochelle	126,2738	Domaine du Magnou (Fouras et Saint Laurent de la Prée)
JUIN, Christophe	Notaire puis négociant / Marsais (Boisse)	123,5922	Métairie de Roiffé (Saint Germain de Marencennes), métairie de l'Houmeau du Coux (Ardillières)
AUDRY, François	Propriétaire / Chambon (Marlonges)	116,3104	Métairie de la Pagatrie (Chambon et Virson)

NOM, Prénom	Profession / Domicile	Superficie (en ha)	Immeubles
PELLETREAU, François	Négociant / Rochefort	111,7970	Cabane du Bois d'Arlet (Tonnay-Charente)
ROBERT, Jean	Cultivateur / Rochefort (les Chartres)	103,0789	métairie de Bois Carteau et cabane de la Tisselle (Ciré)
DUPONT, François Benoît	Commissaire des fontes de l'artillerie de la marine / Rochefort	92,8222	Maison et métairie du Frêne (Puy-du-Lac)
MECHINET, Samuel Pierre	Propriétaire / Thairé	88,8906	un domaine (Voutron)
RICHARD, Alexis	Inspecteur de la régie nationale / La Rochelle	81,7802	Cabane de Roquet (Ciré)
PELLETREAU, Jean François	Négociant / Rochefort	75,9813	Cabane des Tourettes (Moragne)
MOLLIERE, Pierre	Greffier de la justice de paix /Rochefort	75,0015	Cabane ou métairie de Mariou (Ciré)
PARONNEAU, Louis Charles	Négociant / La Rochelle	73,1638	Cabane des Arènes (Voutron)
BRIZARD Pierre	Boucher / Rochefort	72,1382	Cabane de la Platière (Voutron)
POULET, Pierre Jacques	Cultivateur / Benon	70,6696	Domaine de Chambon

Source: Archives départementales de la Charente-Maritime (voir note n. 9). RAULT Jean François et FENIS Jean François ont acheté ensemble 72 ha 82 a 19 ca (2 prés); Jean ROBERT a acquis la cabane de la Tisselle de 46 ha 15 a 47 ca avec CHAIGNEAU Paul, cultivateur au Thou; Christophe JUIN a acquis la métairie de Roiffé (80 ha 85 a 63 ca) avec Pierre MARCHESSEAU, marchand à Marsais; Louis Charles PARONNEAU a acquis la cabane des Arènes de 62 ha 90 a 72 ca avec François SEIGNEUREIN, cultivateur à St Vivien; Jean GIRAUD a acquis la métairie de la Morinière avec Louis SOLLEAU, cultivateur à St Louis de la Petite Flandre. Pour une liste exhaustive des acquéreurs de biens nationaux dans le district de Rochefort, se reporter à Gandouet Denis, *La vente des biens nationaux de première et de seconde origines dans le district de Rochefort (1791-1804)*, mémoire de maîtrise d'histoire, Université de La Rochelle, 2003.

III

Models and Practices of Expropriation in the Contemporary Age

Modèles et pratiques de l'expropriation durant l'époque contemporaine

From Barons to Peasant Farmers: The Privatisation of Feudal Lands in Southern Italy in the Nineteenth Century

Paola Nardone

During the course of the eighteenth century, as part of the process of the Enlightenment, the political and economic power of the baronial class and the Church were downsized as Western European States became increasingly securlarized.

This development was particularly slow and difficult in southern Italy, where the authority of the feudal lords and the Church had grown considerably over the years. Thanks to the concessions made by the various sovereigns, these social classes had accumulated extensive privileges which, in point of fact, prevented the State from exercising its sovereignty over the country, thereby hindering any economic growth or civil progress.

At the turn of the century, Neapolitan society was still organised along essentially feudal lines, based on a centuries-old stratification of customs, traditions and rights (but also usurpations and arrogance) which had brought about a paradoxical situation: the people were subject to the "government of two masters"[1].

The authority of the sovereign was in fact significantly restricted by that of the feudal lords and the Church, both of which enjoyed immunity with respect to royal power, and legal and financial rights over the king's subjects, but above all, both possessed huge landed interests. In particular, it was estimated that the Church occupied between half and three quarters of the entire Kingdom[2],

1 Villani Pasquale, *Mezzogiorno tra riforme e rivoluzione*, Roma-Bari, Laterza, 1974, p. 156. For more on this subject see Galasso Giuseppe, "L'ultimo feudalesimo meridionale nell'analisi di Giuseppe Maria Galanti", in *Rivista Storica Italiana*, 2 (1983), pp. 262–281.

2 Perrella Alfonso, *L'eversione della feudalità nel napoletano: dottrine che vi prelusero storia, legislazione e giurisprudenza*, Bologna, Forni, 1909, p. 400. According to calculations made by Genovesi Antonio, "Discorso sull'agricoltura (1764)", in De Rosa Gabriele (a cura di),

while the feudal lords – who at the turn of the century represented a truly exiguous number of the population of southern Italy[3] – exercised their "control" over 1940 of the 1994 State *universitas* or hamlets[4], imposing their authority over a larger number of subjects than those subject to the sole judgement of the crown. It was presumed in fact that, excepting the capital, 70% of Neapolitans were subject to feudal jurisdiction and only 30% to royal jurisdiction[5].

Restricting our analysis to the case of feudal lands and to the events that led to their privatisation, we must remember that the excessive power of the barons stemmed essentially from the high concentration of feudal possessions[6]. Such property brought with it extensive power and big profits (which, if added to those of the Church were even greater than those of the monarchy[7]), and consequently, over time the feudal question became the "major issue" of the Kingdom and in a vain attempt to restrict their political power, the crown "was several times forced to fight against the barons" to try and prevent them from accumulating estates. One of the first endeavours in this direction was made in 1536 when Charles V, forced to intervene to restrict the abuses and usurpation all too often committed against the communal lands[8], proceeded to issue

Feudalità, clero e popolo nel Sud attraverso le visite pastorali del '700, Napoli, L.S.E., 1969, p. 37, the Church owned two thirds of all the farmlands in the Kingdom.

3 Trifone Gabriele, *Feudi e demani. Eversione della feudalità nelle provincie napoletane*, Milano, S.E.L., 1909, pp. 142–144, indicates that in 1791 the kingdom's population numbered 4,950,533; 31,000 were feudal lords, 26,000 judges, 12,400 doctors, 90,000 men of the Church and the rest "lowly-bred populace".

4 Perrella, *L'eversione della feudalità nel napoletano, op. cit.*, p. 400.

5 Villani, *Mezzogiorno tra riforme e rivoluzione, op. cit.*, p. 199.

6 *Ibid*, pp. 195–196. Rao Anna Maria, *Il Regno di Napoli nel Settecento*, Napoli, Guida, 1983, p. 120. "The richest and most powerful barons numbered just 600 with only a few dozen families at the top [...] about ninety barons exercised their jurisdiction over nearly 2,000,000 people".

7 As the calculations of Ludovico Bianchini go to show in Bianchini Ludovico, *Della storia delle finanze nel Regno di Napoli*, Napoli, Tip. Flautina, 1835, vol. III, p. 51, Villani, *Mezzogiorno tra riforme e rivoluzione, op. cit.*, p. 195 and Galasso, "L'ultimo feudalesimo meridionale", *art. cit.*, p. 277.

8 Among the many definitions of domain is that of the Terra di Lavoro dividing Commissioner, Del Greco Camillo, *Dei demanii nelle provincie meridionali d'Italia*, Vasto, 1885, p. 16, where the domain is defined as "any extension of land, over which the citizens of one or more *universitas* exercise civic usage; it is split into feudal, communal and ecclesiastical according to whether the property belongs to the State, the *universitas* or hamlet or the Church".

an edict intimating the Notables to relinquish unlawfully occupied lands, and for this purpose created a special Feudal Commission to settle any disputes[9].

The various provisions adopted over time to free the usurped lands and increase the number of landowners[10] did not bring about any tangible results until the end of the eighteenth century. The Kingdom was still a country in which private property was almost non-existent[11]. The land was split up to include crown lands, feudal lands and free estates, most of which was personal (rather than feudal)[12] property of the feudal lords themselves. Only a few small allotments were freehold – *quod ad aliquem pleno jure pertinent* –, and most of these were located around the towns and villages. All the rest was communal, feudal, Church and royal land[13].

This situation had critical effects on agricultural and social progress: there were many forms of exploitation and appropriation practised by the seigneurs. There were very few middle-class landowners (the so-called civil class) and this meant that food production was low.[14] Finally, the peasants were reduced to being serfs[15], thanks to the proliferation of unfair agrarian contracts[16].

9 Valente Angela, *Gioacchino Murat e l'Italia Meridionale*, Torino, Einaudi, 1965, p. 279.

10 A summary of the laws on the domain issue can be found in Liberati Gianfranco, "I demani nel Mezzogiorno continentale tra giurisprudenza e prassi", in Massafra Angelo (a cura di), *Il Mezzogiorno preunitario. Economia, società, istituzioni*, Bari, Dedalo, 1988, pp. 565–602.

11 That "The free landowner did not exist or was very rare at the time of Charles Bourbon" is the opinion of Michelangelo Schipa, recalled by Ricchioni Vincenzo, *Studi storici di economia dell'agricoltura meridionale*, Firenze, Macrì, 1952, pp. 5 and 7; Ricchioni, in disagreement with Schipa, maintains that private property in the Kingdom was much more common that imagined.

12 *Ibid*, p. 9, "personal property which should be considered as private property but which often the feudal lords purposely confused with feudal property", above all to avoid paying taxes to the municipalities.

13 Fortunato Giustino, *Badie Feudi e Baroni della Valle di Vitalba*, Manduria, P. Laicata, 1968, vol. I, p. 197.

14 Schipa Michelangelo, *Il Regno di Napoli al tempo di Carlo di Borbone*, Napoli, Pierro, 1904, p. 202.

15 Galanti Giuseppe Maria, Assante Franca and Demarco Domenico (a cura di), *Della descrizione geografica e politica delle Sicilie*, Napoli, ESI, 1969, p. 420.

16 These were perpetual, levelling and long-lease contracts, Nitti Francesco Saverio, "La distruzione dei pubblici demani in Basilicata e in Calabria", in De Rosa Gabriele, Cestaro Antonio (a cura di), *Territorio e società nella storia del Mezzogiorno*, Napoli, Guida, 1973, p. 611.

Centuries of opposition to progress in the land sector had prevented the formation of that agricultural middle class required for the economic development of the Kingdom, preventing the process of conversion of the wealth accumulated in previous "profit activities" in immovable property. This was a process that had started in some countries of western Europe by the late seventeenth century[17]. The fact is that at least until the French decade of the Kingdom of Naples, "the land was not merchandise"[18]. On the contrary, it was often precisely such conditions that triggered mechanisms of violation and usurpation of areas which, not belonging to individual citizens but to the entire community, appeared somewhat more vulnerbale: the common lands.

These were land areas which, being of public domain, were naturally and freely open to the civic uses required for the needs of material existence; frequently however, the very ease of access to the land gave rise to damaging acts and usurpations on the part of outsiders and of the joint-owners themselves[19]. Moreover, even when such situations did not occur, the carrying out of servitude was often equally difficult. This occurred when the right to civic use of a communal land was granted to inhabitants of several municipalities or also neighbouring fiefs. A situation of promiscuity was thus triggered which led to a precarious and disorderly ownership, which actually prevented the production of wealth and only served to worsen the living conditions of the poorer classes.

Civic uses were practised on all categories of land; for centuries an unbreakable relationship had existed in the Kingdom between commons and such servitudes. The *ius receptum* was the principle whereby a commons, by its very

17 Romano Ruggero, *Opposte congiunture. La crisi del Seicento in Europa e in America*, Venezia, Marsilio, 1992, p. 9; on the dynamics of the "refeudalization" process see Wallerstein Immanuel, *Il sistema mondiale dell'economia moderna*, Bologna, il Mulino, 1982, vol. II, p. 34, ff; Bloch Marc, *I caratteri originali della storia rurale francese*, Torino, Einaudi, 1973, p. 163. On the concept of accumulation of the middle class and relative investments in land in the 19th century, see Bonelli Franco, "Il capitalismo italiano. Linee generali d'interpretazione", in *Storia d'Italia. Dal feudalesimo al capitalismo*, Torino, Einaudi, 1978, pp. 1196–1202.

18 Kula Witold, *Teoria economica del sistema feudale. Proposta di un modello*, Torino, Einaudi, 1977, p. 21. In the eighteenth century, Adam Smith, in his most famous work on nature and the wealth of nations, talking about the free market, also condemned the private property bonds enforced by closed systems like that of the Church and barony, which represented obstacles to economic growth.

19 Fortunato, *Badie Feudi e Baroni della Valle di Vitalba*, *op. cit.*, p. 197.

nature, was necessarily encumbered by civic uses[20]. Consequently, the populations that inhabited the fiefs also benefitted from such rights to the land inasmuch as a fief could not exist without civic use[21]. Part of the fief, besides the "defences", i.e., those areas – usually woodland and pasture, fenced in or closed – on which the feudal lord did in fact prevent civic use, were also the commons which, being originally public property granted by the king to the barons, could be used by the rural population.

The violation of the property by the barons could, therefore, occur in several ways. The first case, and perhaps the most frequent, consisted in the usurpation of civic use, meaning the tendency to transform the feudal land into a defensive unit. This occurred because, over time, the feudal lord tried to fence in, or otherwise make inaccessible to the local population, increasingly larger plots of his feudal possessions, and by so doing prevented the exercising of servitudes on such lands[22]. A second violation consisted in the actual occupation of other people's land (Church, municipality and private land). This often involved the communal lands and the unlawful occupation took place by force or with the complicity of dishonest local administrators, both by means of false sales and by means of the exercising of civic use where this was not allowed[23]. Such illegal actions were made possible by the state of weakness and dependency of the population, by the disorderliness and ambiguity of the laws, by the omnipresence of mixed lands and by the fact that the usurped lands were often located in geographic areas far away from the "arm of the law"[24].

20 Tranasi Michele, *La nascita della proprietà privata*, Foggia, Leone, 2002.

21 Nitti, "La distruzione dei pubblici demani in Basilicata e in Calabria", *art. cit.*, p. 610.

22 Numerous documents certifying the usurpations of civic uses are kept in the State Archives of Chieti (hereinafter: ASCh), Land Acts, Municipality of Vacri, b. 1, f. 6. It must be pointed out that the usurpations committed by the feudal lords did not only involve lands but also the rights and taxes that went with them; on this subject see Galanti, *Della descrizione geografica e politica delle Sicilie*, *op. cit.*, p. 420.

23 Despite everything Valente, *Gioacchino Murat e l'Italia Meridionale*, *op. cit.*, p. 280, points out that in 1806, when French troops occupied the Kingdom, about 3,000 trials were under way for abuse of feudal lands.

24 Petrusewicz Marta, *Latifondo. Economia morale e vita materiale in una periferia dell'Ottocento*, Venezia, Marsilio, 1990, pp. 47–49 describes the situation of the Sila, the home of usurpation *par excellence*, and, in speaking about the Baracco estate, reveals that the family was involved in legal disputes with over 53 Calabria municipalities, accused of usurpation of public land.

Neapolitan reformers had struggled against such violations of the land and in favour of the formation of private property free of feudal ties and encumbrances, as well as guaranteed by the laws of the State. During the course of the eighteenth century, they had asked the monarchy, first implicitly and then directly, for the abolition of the feudal system[25]. A first significant step towards the privatization of feudal lands was taken by the successor of Filangeri, Melchiorre Delfico[26] from Abruzzo.

Delfico lived and worked in a very particular context in the province of Teramo where, at the end of the century, the large feudal estates had broken up for "biological" reasons and most of them had returned into the hands of the king[27]. Taking advantage of the fall of the oldest and most powerful feudal lord, the duke of Acquaviva, and of the favour in which the monarchy appeared to hold the reformers, Delfico became the spokesperson for the reformist ideas circulating in Neapolitan cultural circles, which saw the economic rebirth of the Kingdom tied to a new concept of property and labour. Interpreting the hopes of the lesser aristocracy and local patricians, and anxious to take possession of the assets of the former barons, but without the means to acquire them all at once, in 1790 he suggested to the monarchy that jurisdiction should be taken away from those fiefs of the Kingdom which had returned to the charge of the Inland Revenue due to the lack of legitimate heirs and that these lands

25 Villani Pasquale, "Il dibattito sulla feudalità nel Regno di Napoli da Genovesi al Canosa", in *Studi sul Settecento Italiano*, Napoli, Istituto Italiano Studi Storici, 1968, pp. 252–331.

26 Delfico Melchiorre, *Riflessioni su la vendita de' feudi*, Napoli, Porcelli, 1790. On Delfico's role in the revolutionary events at the end of the eighteenth century, see Carletti Gabriele, "Melchiorre Delfico e il decennio rivoluzionario 1789–1799", in Russo Umberto, Colapietra Raffaele, Muzzi Paolo (a cura di), *Il 1799 in Abruzzo*, L'Aquila, Colacchi, 2001, vol. II, p. 1155–1181.

27 The duke of Atri, Rodolfo d'Acquaviva had died without leaving any male heirs and despite having tried to avoid devolution to the Inland Revenue in 1775, the Royal Chamber had proceeded to seize all the feudal and other property of the Atri family. In Abruzzo, at the end of the century, the king was not only the owner of the estates of the Acquaviva family, but also of those of the Farnese family and of the feudal complex of the former Medici fiefs, as well as of other minor fiefs. Incarnato Gennaro, "Crisi signorile, ripresa regia e speranze borghesi nel tardo '700 teramano", in *Aprutium*, 1982/0, pp. 16–20. Del Bono Giovanni, "La feudalità nel 1799 in Abruzzo", in *Il 1799 in Abruzzo*, *op. cit.*, pp. 784–787, makes a detailed estimate of the minor fiefs devolved starting in 1760 up to the law dated 25 April 1799.

should be placed on the market as private properties. The proposal was accepted in 1791, when the Council of Finances decided to sell these lands as free lands and in several lots, so as to promote the spread of private property[28].

Hence a process of land privatization began which, while limited[29], was in some ways consistent with the anti-feudal line of Tanucci[30]. It revealed the intentions of the reformers to reduce the power of a competitor with the State, and also to create a new landed middle class made up of medium-sized landowners (but not, at this point, many small farmers). Small holdings did not find favour with the reformers because they were tied to forms of land exploitation that often ended in degradation[31].

In point of fact, nothing changed and land ownership in the Kingdom (together with feudal power) remained the same until the arrival of the French.

It was only thanks to French government policies that a change in land distribution came to southern Italy: for the first time, the creation of a small farm holding became part of government policy[32]. In this respect, the lands were taken away from the barons in two distinct stages: a first and more incisive stage with the law passed in 1799 (the concrete effects of which are not assessable in view of the very short life of the Neapolitan Republic); and a second less vigorous stage following the occupation of 1806, which showed its effects for a good part of the nineteenth century.

In the first case, the public authorities tried to implement a real expropriation of the feudal lands subject to civic uses. By law, such lands belonged entirely to the Municipality within which they were located. Any disputes about such lands between the former barons and the communal authorities were automatically settled in favour of the *universitas*, which acquired full

28 Rao, *Il Regno di Napoli nel Settecento, op. cit.*, p. 122.

29 We should not over-estimate the action of the crown because its magistrature often turned out to be a harder opponent than the old feudal lords, cf. Incarnato, "Crisi signorile", *art. cit.*, p. 14.

30 Tanucci tried to restrict the sale of fiefs and keep those devolved to the Inland Revenue within the royal domain. A summary account of the topic can be found in Rao, *Il Regno di Napoli nel Settecento, op. cit.*, pp. 116–123.

31 Incarnato, "Crisi signorile", *art. cit.*, p. 23 and pp. 30–31.

32 Even though in actual fact, Woolf Stuart, "La storia politica e sociale", in *Storia d'Italia. Dal primo Settecento all'Unità*, Torino, Einaudi, 1973, p. 227 states that "no intention existed to re-distribute the lands at the expense of the nobles". The idea was to free the municipalities and the peasants from the legal subjection of the barons.

ownership of such assets[33]. It was, therefore, the State *in primis* which, for reasons of general interest, acquired the feudal land, confiscating it *ipso iure* from the former feudal lords and assigning it to the municipalities.

The law of 1806, whereby a first concrete step was taken towards the privatisation of feudal lands, was less general and less drastic, even as regards its guidelines. In fact, only the legal rights to feudal lands were abolished initially, while the ownership of the land remained in the hands of the former feudal lords, just as (luckily) civic uses remained unchanged for the local population. It was only with other subsequent regulatory measures that the procedures were established by means of which part of the former feudal lands were reintegrated into the communal lands and then privatised through the establishment of real rights of usufruct in favour of the peasant class.

From the very beginning, there was a greater benevolence on the part of the new French government towards the former barons, In fact, the abolition law of 1806 sanctioned the principle whereby the right to claim the lands belonged to the individual *universitas*; as had been the case in 1799. It was no longer envisaged that the State would assign such lands to the municipalities *ope legis:* now the local institutions had to start proceedings against the former feudal lords.

These would have been presided over by a special court, the feudal Commission, with the participation of the representatives of all the parties involved (municipalities, feudal lords, inland revenue and government). In the event of the case being won by the municipalities, these would have received a share of the former feudal lands, calculated with an eye to the type of civic use existing at the time of the coming into effect of the abolition law.

Having outlined the general procedure whereby, during that first phase, small farm holdings were to have been created from the lands that once belonged to the barons, we can go on and make a number of observations.

First of all, it is a good idea to recall the admirable work done by the government which, thanks to the speeding up of proceedings, managed to hear about 29,000 cases[34] in just a few years. In fact, the Ministry of the Interior

33 Cuoco Vincenzo, *Saggio storico sulla rivoluzione napoletana del 1799*, Roma-Bari, Laterza, 1980, p. XLII.

34 Valente, *Gioacchino Murat e l'Italia Meridionale*, *op. cit.*, p. 280. According to Perrella, *L'eversione della feudalità nel napoletano*, *op. cit.*, p. 442, there were 2,180 cases to be heard.

ordered the Intendants to map all the lands of the provinces[35]. This document was promptly sent to the feudal Commission and resulted in the latter pressing the Intendants to solicit the representative of the municipalities, whose areas were within the former fiefs, to report all the litigations already pending under the old government (and lying in the law court of the abolished Royal Chamber) for all matters relating to the usurpations but, also, so they might start proceedings in order to uphold their rights and those of single individuals to the former feudal lands[36].

Many obstacles presented themselves immediately. In particular, a fierce struggle had to be made against the strong opposition of the former barons who occasionally took advantage of the ignorance of the people to continue to behave as if nothing had changed, pretending not to be aware of their new situation and of the feudal system abolition law[37]. Another common form of resistance consisted in inducing the communal representatives to hide the royal decrees, or even go so far as to deny the existence of previous cases, or even those in progress at the time of the French occupation[38], and the existence of property or rights violated by the former barons. This was possible because these individuals took part in the political life of the local communities as magistrates, i.e., those acting as "communal controllers"[39], and managed, thanks to their economic clout, to subjugate the other local officials who, in many cases, could not even read or write.

Frequently however, this abuse of power was discovered and reported, thanks above all to the watchful eye of the government which ordered the Intendants to closely monitor the situation so that all the towns could claim

35 ASCh, Land Acts, General Affairs, b. 187/III, 1808–1812, f. 69, sub-sect. 9.

36 *Ibid.*, sub-sect. 36. In this respect, Valente, *Gioacchino Murat e l'Italia Meridionale*, *op. cit.*, p. 284 quotes the case of the Intendant of L'Aquila: on 4 December 1809, thanks to his pressing request, 21 municipalities had started proceedings to protect their rights against the barons.

37 *Ibid.*, p. 285. In Abruzzo in 1808, in the case of the citizens of Pratola Peligna, the former baron was demanding the abolished *jus habitationis* and the personal day right from the citizens.

38 As the voluminous files relating to the proceedings and trials in progress in the law court of the abolished Royal Chamber and the numerous arrests of citizens who had dared denounce them go to show; cf. ASCh, Land Acts, General Affairs, b. 187/III, 1808–1812, b. 69, sub-sect. 36.

39 *Ibid.*

their rights. The mayors and the officials of the municipalities that favoured the barons against the interests of the community were severely punished.

Despite these obstacles and other seemingly endless problems associated with the splitting up of the former feudal lands, a broad anti-baron front grew up consisting of nearly all the *universitas* of the Kingdom. These claimed lands and rights because, as one of the most famous maxims of the feudal Commission read: *ubi feuda ibi demania, ubi demania ibi usus*, and wherever there was civic use, part of the land was to legally become the property of the municipality before being shared out among its citizens.

To speed up and facilitate the sharing out process of the former feudal lands (and all state lands) in 1809, Murat appointed and sent to the provinces of the Kingdom special Commissioners charged with solving all the problems relating to "mass division"[40]. It was also ruled that the will of the Commission was to be sovereign and that sentences were to be executed whatever the opposition. The possibility also existed of turning to the State Council. Such a procedure had no suspensive effects, however, and even in the event of the Council upholding a "misdemeanour", the party involved would only have had to pay a fine, which in any case had to be refunded within a period of 10 years[41].

Secondly, it must be considered that during the trial phase, the former feudal lords did everything possible to defend the fiefs in an attempt to prevent their lands being taken over by the municipalities. They even tried to trick the French officials and a lot of pressure was put on the communal attorneys, to the extent that, even though the latter knew that they were liable to prosecution, they sometimes refused to uphold the rights of the municipalities. They used the excuse of having numerous other engagements and failed to present themselves before the feudal Commission[42].

Attempts to deceive the Commissioners were made during the course of the trials by producing false witnesses and intentionally erroneous estimates of the lands involved in the disputes, drawn up by obliging surveyors.

The bearing of false witness was aimed at extending the defences or tenancies on the feudal land as much as possible, or else at degrading the types of

40 ASCh, Land Acts, General Affairs, b. 188/I, 1809–1883, f. 1.

41 *Ibid.*, art. 5.

42 Various cases of this kind are to be found in ASCh, Land Acts, Municipality of Vacri, b. 2, f. 16.

bondage existing on the land or, finally, at increasing the portion of communal land belonging to the baron.

Such false statements or evidence were made and produced in the so-called "verbal trials" when, for example in the first case, the former baron had the magistrates or the citizens themselves, who could often not read or write, state that on a more or less extensive part of the feudal land, they had not in fact practised any form of civic use for some time. Such circumstance resulted in the land no longer being considered communal land and implied its taking on the quality of "defence": as such, according to the abolition law, it could not be divided up and was, therefore, assigned in free ownership to the former feudal lord (with a trifling fee to be paid to the municipalities).

In the second case, the bearing of false witness was intended to show that for some years, the communal land had been subject to farm contracts of the perpetual tenancy type. In such a situation, the law protected the tenant farmers, hence the lands affected by such land tenure systems were not including in the sharing out procedure with the municipalities and remained in the hands of the barons.

In the third case, we find falsifications aimed at discrediting the type of civic use existing over the fief at the time the abolition law was passed, i.e., in August 1806. In fact, the presence of civic use not only represented the indispensable condition for the sharing out of the lands, but also the "measure" used by the feudal Commission to calculate the portion of the land which was to pass out of the hands of the former feudal lords into those of the municipalities[43]. In the sharing out process, the importance taken on by these rights was such that the use of a univocal principle had to be established. For this purpose, the Napoleonic government finally went about re-ordering and classifying the many civic uses applicable in the Kingdom, reducing them essentially to three categories: essential, useful and communal[44]. In the first case, the law ruled

43 Demarco Domenico, *Il crollo del Regno delle due Sicilie. La struttura sociale*, Napoli, ESI, 2000, p. 6, immediately indicates a first injustice. The rules whereby sharing out was conducted were not based on the rights which the barons and citizens originally had to the lands but on those existing at the time the law was passed, rights that increased in the hands of the barons and were drastically reduced for the citizens.

44 A detailed classification of the single categories of civic uses can be found in: ASCh, Land Acts, General Affair=s, b. 188/I, 1809–1883, f. 1, more specifically Title III, *Separazione in massa delle terre demaniali tra' padroni di esse, ed i Comuni per gli usi, che questi vi*

that the *minimum* fee to the municipalities corresponded to one quarter of the entire land. This amount could be increased to include one third or even half the lands; in the other two cases, the *minimum* was equivalent to half the land, but if the Commission thought fit, it could include up to three quarters of the lands being split up[45].

By changing the type of civic use, the share belonging to the parties was considerably effected. It was precisely this frequently used option that triggered a series of endless disputes between the *universitas* and the former feudal lords, disputes that continued well past the Restoration in the ordinary law courts.

In the last case under examination, the bearing of false witness tended to aim to prove the existence of rights (usually grazing rights) which the former feudal lord exercised over the communal land. This way, when these lands were split up between the citizens, a share would go to the baron; to be precise, the law ruled that the baron was to receive "a portion equal to that of the holder of joint rights, who was to receive the largest quantity"[46].

Examples of the bearing of false witness and corruption during the splitting up of the feudal lands continue to be found in numerous documents kept in the State Archives and go to show just how strong and deep-rooted the economic-political power of the barons was, despite the abolition process taking its course throughout the French Decade.

In this respect, we should mention as an example the former fief of Guardiabruna in the district of Lanciano in Abruzzo Citeriore, because in this particular case reality was completely distorted. The local authorities, but also many citizens, to please the former barons, swore before the government officials that the communal land had originally been a feudal estate and that, over the following years, the baron, in an act of benevolence towards the local population, had granted it for use by farmers who, in bad faith, had taken it over and left the baron with grazing rights only. Despite these testimonies, the feudal

rappresentano, art. 11–16. Here, for the sake of brevity, we shall just say that the essential civic uses concerned everything strictly necessary for the personal use of citizens, the useful ones regulated a series of customs relating to production and economic activities. Finally, land uses contemplated participation in the harvesting of the fruits in the domain of the estate.

45 *Ibid.*, art. 16.

46 Lepre Aurelio, *Storia del Mezzogiorno d'Italia. Dall'Antico Regime alla società borghese (1657–1868)*, Napoli, Liguori, 1986, vol. II, p. 191.

Commission still managed to assign a part of this area to the municipality, but after the sentence another trick was played. The public officials and the local land surveyors produced a series of documents whereby, by means of the falsification of the account of the natural conditions of fertility of the soil, they managed to ensure the baron was given the best of the lands. The citizens complained because the land given to the municipality was so unyielding that it could not even be used to graze goats. In fact, after the division of the land, the condition of the citizens worsened to the point that they had no alternative but to pack their bags and leave the area forever[47].

In other words, the difficulties raised by the noble classes were such that even when communal land was identified with certainty before the feudal Commission, this would often seem to disappear without trace[48].

Quite apart from the example just mentioned and despite the numerous obstacles encountered during the first "mass division" phase relating to the former feudal lands, with the subsequent division into lots, a memorable land redistribution process was underway. It was to have significant economic and social consequences (in relation to which historians have often expressed contrasting opinions[49]). Only a few years earlier, such an event would have been totally unimaginable: this was the creation of an agrarian society made up of myriad small landowners[50].

47 ASCh, Land Acts, General Affairs, b. 187/III, 1808–1812, f. 69, sub-sect. 36.

48 Dell'Olio Michele, "Tracce demaniali", in *Mappe e Territorio. Insediamenti umani e demaniali a Scerni*, Villamagna (Ch), Tinari, 1994, p. 46.

49 Authors who express a negative opinion of the division into lots are, for example, Giustino Fortunato, "La questione demaniale nell'Italia meridionale", in Id., *Il Mezzogiorno e lo Stato Italiano*, Bari, Laterza, 1911; Demarco, *Il crollo del Regno delle due Sicilie*, *op. cit.*; Trifone, *Feudi e demani.*, *op. cit.*; Saladino Antonio, *Saggi di storia civile e storia delle istituzioni pubbliche nel Regno di Napoli*, Roma, The research centre, 1981; Villani Pasquale, "Il catasto di Carlo di Borbone negli studi dell'ultimo ventennio", in *Annali della Facoltà di Lettere e Filosofia di Napoli*, vol. 2 (1952), p. 23. A less severe opinion is expressed by authors like Franchetti Leopoldo, *Condizioni economiche e amministrative delle province napoletane*, Bari, Laterza, 1985; Tocci Giovanni, *Terra e riforme nel mezzogiorno moderno*, Bologna, Patron, 1971; Bevilacqua Piero, *Breve storia dell'Italia Meridionale dall'Ottocento ad oggi*, Roma, Donzelli, 1993. The topic is summed up by Woolf, "La storia politica e sociale", *art. cit.*, p. 228, who underscores that the abolition of feudalism created a number of small holdings but that the biggest benefits went to the rural middle class.

50 Lepre, *Storia del Mezzogiorno d'Italia*, *op. cit.*, p. 196.

By dividing the land up into lots – also known as the "French system of division by heads"[51], the legislator effectively shared out the former feudal lands, reintegrated in the communal lands, to the peasant farmers. Thus it was that the process of privatization of fiefs and the creation of small holdings – either free or easily redeemable – was completed[52].

In actual fact, though the government expected to divide up all the lands by 1809[53], the operation instead proved very difficult and went on, in alternate phases, well beyond the point of Italian unification[54]. Strong resistance came from the most disparate social classes, starting with the peasant farmers themselves right up to the former feudal lords (who considered their rights had been downtrodden); the struggle was also and above all against the rising agrarian and State middle class[55], often unwittingly helped by the French government.

And when the struggle against the dividing up of the land into lots was perpetrated by the recipients themselves, i.e., the so-called "communist" peasant

51 Nitti, "La distruzione dei pubblici demani in Basilicata e in Calabria", *art. cit.*, p. 613. The splitting up into lots was to have been between all citizens of any age, gender and social status. If the lands to be split up were not extensive enough to allow such division, this was to have been done by families; finally, if the land was not enough to go round, the less well-off citizens were to be preferred.

52 The division into lots did not establish specific property rights for the peasant farmers but rather a right of usufruct, such as emphyteusis: for the use of the assigned land, a rent was to be paid to the municipality, as well as the land tax charged by the State.

53 As provided by the decree dated 3 December 1808 containing the instructions to comply with the law dated 1 September 1806 and the decree dated 8 June 1807, on the division of lands.

54 Palmieri Walter, "Introduzione", in Id. (a cura di), *Il Mezzogiorno agli inizi della Restaurazione*, Roma-Bari, Laterza, 1993, p. IX. It is hard to estimate how many former feudal lands were split up among the new owners because exact data for all the provinces is not available. Bevilacqua, *Breve storia dell'Italia Meridionale, op. cit.*, p. 4, estimates that mass division between 1806 and 1860 involved about 600,000 hectares of land; the sharing out into lots between private individuals amounted to over 205,000 hectares for a total of about 116,000 lots (we do not know, however, how much land came from the feudal, communal and Church lands). Finally Nitti, "La distruzione dei pubblici demani", *art. cit.*, p. 623, estimates that between 1860 and 1890 about 260,000 hectares of land were split up.

55 The landed middle class, the large landowners, the animal farmers and the municipal administrators were totally against splitting up by lots, and aspired instead to the direct ownership of the lands and could not stand the fact that these might be assigned to the peasant farmers, Villani, *Mezzogiorno tra riforme e rivoluzione, op. cit.*, p. 207.

farmers, the reasons were to be found mainly in principles of social justice and community interests. Consider, for example, the fact that the dividing up of the commons was a system already tried out in the Borbonic period and that in some places it had turned out to be a complete failure[56], or, and this was the most frequent case, in some municipalities the conviction existed that the assignment of small lots would not solve the problems of the peasant farmers, nor compensate them for the loss of their entitlement to exercise civic uses[57] on which the economy of the entire community was founded. In point of fact, the risk existed of considerably worsening the living conditions of the people[58].

If on the other hand, the sharing out into lots was opposed by the other social classes, this represented a struggle within the communities, in which the competing factions were, on the one hand, the landowners anxious to enlarge their property and, on the other, the landless peasant farmers who aspired to become landowners. This discord eventually took on both political and social connotations, making popular conflicts in the Kingdom even more bitter. These tensions developed to the point of violence and led to the so-called "land issue" which after the unity of Italy became a part of the greater and more complex "southern issue"[59].

56 In this respect, see the case, for Abruzzo, of Torre de' Passeri in 1792, described by de Pompeis jr. Ermanno, *Torre de' Passeri tra Sette e Ottocento. Storia di una famiglia borghese*, Villamagna (Ch), Tinari, 1995, p. 95.

57 Sometimes, by splitting the land into small lots, there was no land suitable for grazing and crop growing. Where on the other hand, the land exceeded the needs of the population, it was often more convenient to use the lands for grazing rather than split them up, also because such land was often hilly and far away from the town.

58 Besides the land, the peasant farmers also had to be given the capital needed to grow the crops, pay the rent and the land tax; the lack and bad government of the Monti Frumentari (there were just 500 at the time of the French occupation) placed those who had been given the lots in the hands of the money lenders and often forced them to cultivate the land intensely before abandoning it due to loss of natural soil fertility (and after destroying all the existing woodland). The conditions of poverty of the peasant farmers were such that some municipalities refused to split the land up into lots, as occurred for example in the province of Teramo, cf. Teramo State Archive, Original acts of the Provincial Council, b. 1, f. I. It was at this point that the government began to be asked to grant the shares to wealthier persons able to exploit them better; this proposal was not met with favour by Minister Zurlo who expressed his opinion formally in the ministerial decree dated 29 January 1812, cf. Nitti, "La distruzione dei pubblici demani", *art. cit.*, p. 618.

59 Saladino, *Saggi di storia civile e storia delle istituzioni pubbliche*, *op. cit.*, p. 44.

In the specific case of Abruzzo, the idea of creating small peasant farm holdings, which had stemmed from the so-called "ancient land divisions" (dating back to the Decade), was to a large extent made futile by the sale of the single properties, once the "prohibitive clause"[60] expired.

In particular, the work of the distributing Commissioner for Abruzzo, Giuseppe de Thomasis, charged with dividing up the land, had led to the creation of around 30,000 small lots, as well as to the foundation, with 600 former feudal share tenants, of the municipality of Ateleta[61]. By 1811, the situation still favoured the small owners. The Murat "statistics" show the widespread presence of medium and small landowners, especially in the province of Chieti where, after the land division, there were no more estates for community and promiscuous use[62].

This situation failed to spur the agricultural sector. The excessive splitting up of the land together with a lack of capital and failure to introduce new farming methods did not allow a satisfactory organisation of the farming enterprise; no innovations were implemented; rather the conflict between crop farming and sheep farming grew worse[63] (with a sharp drop in the number of sheep),

60 To prevent the peasant farmers' share being transferred to the wealthy landowners, Minister Zurlo issued a prohibitive clause forbidding the sale and the mortgaging of the shares during the ten year period after assignment. In some areas of the Kingdom, the limit was even higher and during the first four years, even leasing the land was forbidden in some cases. The clause immobilized "lands that had died" in the opinion of Giacomo Racioppi, quoted by Villari Rosario, *Il Sud nella storia d'Italia*, Bari, Laterza, 1961, p. 164. The aim was to prevent the rural classes from falling to proletariat level but the legal prohibition had controversial and damaging effects, Demarco, *Il crollo del Regno delle due Sicilie*, *op. cit.*, p. 144.

61 Grilli Egidio, *Giuseppe de Thomasis: la vita e le opere*, Roma, tip. della Tribuna, 1900, p. 592.

62 Demarco Domenico, *La 'statistica' del Regno di Napoli nel 1811*, Roma, Accademia Nazionale dei Lincei, 1988, vol. I, p. 28, 136, 244. See also Del Re Giuseppe, *Descrizione topografica, fisica, economica, politica de' reali domini di qua del Faro*, Napoli, Pietà de Turchini, 1830–1836, vol. I, pp. 133–134, shows that in Abruzzo Citeriore there was a considerable increase in the number of small and medium landowners which exceeded that of the larger landowners.

63 For the agricultural reforms seen from an economic viewpoint, cf. D'Elia Costanza, "La ragione delle riforme. Agricoltura e nuovo diritto nel Mezzogiorno francese", in D'Elia Costanza, Salvemini Raffaella (a cura di), *Riforma e Struttura. L'impatto della dominazione napoleonica nel Mezzogiorno fra breve e lungo periodo*, Napoli, CNR, 2008, pp. 13–26.

deforestation increased and, above all in the Teramo area, so did emigration in the agro Romano[64]. It is not surprising then that, starting in 1821, the year of the expiry of the prohibition to transfer land shares imposed by the French, the free land market took on new life, with a series of exchanges whereby the nobles and the middle-class did good business[65].

The mass sale of the shares and the state of poverty of the peasant farmers (often indebted with the buyers themselves) weighed heavily on the price of the lands, which had initially been fairly low and well below market value. Starting in 1824 on the other hand, prices began to rise and in 1827 they were close to real prices[66]. At the end of the century, a number of government investigations into the state of land operations reported a significant fall in the number of small landowners as a result of the transfer of peasant farmlands, especially in the province of Chieti and, to a lesser extent, in that of Teramo; in the L'Aquila area on the contrary, the land shares remained stable and were not transferred[67].

A more articulate ownership situation in the region took shape instead following the subsequent land divisions made by the Borbonic government and those of the post-unity period[68]. In these cases, the data on land shares "held" by peasant farmers is more encouraging: in 1884, about 5,087 small farms were still owned by the share-holders of L'Aquila, 4,728 by those of Teramo, while

64 On the topic, besides Demarco, *La 'statistica' del Regno di Napoli nel 1811*, *op. cit.*, p. 28, 136 and 244, see also Jovacchini Maria Teresa, "Aspetti economico-sociali dei contratti agrari in Abruzzo alla fine del sec. XVIII", in *Rivoluzione francese e Governo Napoleonico in Abruzzo (1789–1815). Dalla Rinascenza Teramana al Riformismo Murattiano*, Teramo, Centro Abruzzese di Ricerche Storiche, 1992, pp. 67–71.

65 In this respect, Fortunato, "La questione demaniale nell'Italia meridionale", *art. cit.*, p. 88, wrote: "The only beneficial effects of splitting up the land into shares in southern Italy has been for the monopoly of the lands in the hands of the owners".

66 Nardone Paola, *Denaro e terra. La 'modernità' di un latifondo ottocentesco (secc. XVII–XIX)*, Milano, Franco Angeli, 2004, pp. 104–105.

67 The result of the investigations is indicated by Ricchioni, *Studi storici di economia dell'agricoltura meridionale*, *op. cit.*, pp. 166–169.

68 Starting in 1811, the functions of the Land Distribution Commissioners were transferred to the Intendants and, in January 1861, to "Special Commissioners" appointed to terminate the land division operations within the same year. In 1862, the Prefects were appointed to share out the land and the entire operation passed under the control of the Ministry of the Interior and the Ministry for Agriculture, Industry and Trade.

there is no precise data for the province of Chieti, even though it appears that most of the shares continued to be owned by locals[69].

Generally speaking, including for the Abruzzo region as well, the supposition that regulated the formation of farm ownership in southern Italy remains true, i.e., that "land shares were a *permanent* foundation of small holdings only when [they were able] to be transformed into vineyards or orchards, or else used for growing other types of trees or shrubs".[70] The consolidation of small ownership was closely tied to the changes made to the agricultural landscape. Such changes were, to some extent, easier to make only in the late nineteenth century when, following a growing awareness of the promotion of the agrarian culture, sustained thanks to the long-term and extensive efforts of the Economic Societies, together with a greater impulse given to the agricultural world by the credit system (comforted by the rise in prices of food products brought about by the population increase), the peasant farmers were placed in the position, but also given the means, to produce better crops and implement better land management[71]. In some areas of southern Italy, this translated into the consolidation of small peasant holdings which all too often, due to lack of means, had been

69 Ricchioni, *Studi storici di economia dell'agricoltura meridionale, op. cit.*, p. 170. During the Seventies, Professor Antonio Saladino promoted a series of dissertations on land division in Abruzzo Citeriore, especially that, in two volumes, of Bozzelli Franca, *Per un contributo allo studio della questione demaniale in Provincia di Abruzzo Citra (1806–1860),* academic year 1973/1974 deposited at the ASCh. This pinpoints the situation of land division in Abruzzo Citeriore between 1806 and 1863 and shows that of the 121 provincial municipalities, only 54 obtained mass division during the Decade, while out of a surface area of 102,242 hectares, the lands taken away from the former feudal estates only amounted to 28,103 hectares. The extension of the shared out lands (including former Church and communal land) was little less than 12,000 hectares split into 8,987 lots.

70 The Salandra report is highlighted by Ricchioni, *Studi storici di economia dell'agricoltura meridionale, op. cit.*, pp. 166–177. In particular in the province of L'Aquila, the shares had been used for vineyards with "satisfactory results", while in the province of Chieti, besides vineyards, olive groves and cereal crops had also been planted with "good results". Finally, in the province of Teramo the new crops were: vineyards, olive groves, orchards, artificial meadows and, in restricted areas, also cereals, and results were "excellent".

71 In the years after the Restoration, strong agrarian activism took place in the Kingdom in answer to the agricultural crisis caused by the opening up of European markets; Petrusewicz Marta, "Agromania: innovatori agrari nelle periferie europee dell'Ottocento", in Bevilacqua Pietro (a cura di), *Storia dell'agricoltura italiana. Mercati e Istituzioni,* Venezia, Marsilio, 1991, vol. III, p. 295.

abandoned or transferred to the advantage of the extension of pre-existing landed estates and those of the agrarian middle-class[72].

In conclusion, the transfer of the land from the feudal lords to the peasant farmers, once completed, did not by itself create the conditions for the transformation of the land ownership structure in southern Italy. In order for ownership to become certain and rooted and for it to fortify and offer opportunities of economic growth, adequate supporting policies were required which, unfortunately, were conspicuously lacking in the first half of the nineteenth century, thereby frustrating a greater part of the revolutionary endeavours made by the French government. Only after the unity of Italy did the State give greater attention to the agricultural sector which, in some areas of southern Italy, resulted in the more stable presence of small peasant farm holdings.

72 Such event did not give rise to automatic agricultural progress in the Kingdom; De Rosa Luigi, *Conflitti e squilibri nel Mezzogiorno tra Cinque e Ottocento*, Roma-Bari, Laterza, 1999, p. 194.

L'expropriation d'utilité publique pour cause de risque naturel dans les départements alpins et algériens, seconde moitié du XIXe siècle

Nicolas Krautberger

L'expropriation a été relativement peu abordée par les historiens qui l'ont plus souvent traitée de manière annexe dans des travaux s'intéressant à l'histoire de la notion d'utilité publique. Mais l'expropriation a fait l'objet de nombreuses études techniques produites par les juristes, depuis le XIXe siècle jusqu'à nos jours[1]. Cette généalogie discursive est particulièrement cohérente. Elle peut aisément tenir lieu d'histoire de la notion. Néanmoins, en proposant une législation continue de l'expropriation d'utilité publique au XIXe siècle, cette généalogie tend principalement à naturaliser une catégorie juridique en masquant le faisceau de pratiques effectives auxquelles se rattachait l'expropriation.

Depuis 1789 et la Déclaration Universelle des Droits de l'Homme et du Citoyen, en France toute atteinte à la propriété privée est susceptible d'une attaque en justice. Entre la violation et l'expropriation de la propriété, la déclaration de l'utilité publique permet de faire passer l'intérêt général avant l'intérêt particulier. Juridiquement, l'utilité publique ne peut être invoquée qu'à propos de circonstances exceptionnelles qui permettent de ramener l'expropriation dans le droit commun afin de l'appliquer légalement. Il s'agit d'une mesure

1 Parmi d'autres: Vomarne Georges, *De l'expropriation pour cause d'utilité publique en Algérie*, Alger/Paris, Dubos et Challamel, 1865; Doumenjou Hippolyte, *Question forestière. Critique du projet de loi de l'application de l'expropriation pour cause d'utilité publique aux reboisement et gazonnement des montagnes*, Foix, Pomiès, 1877; Crépon Théophile, *Code annoté de l'expropriation pour cause d'utilité publique: France, Algérie et colonies: loi du 3 mai 1841, lois diverses, ordonnances et décrets*, Paris, Marescq, 1885; Jacques Adrien, *Du régime de l'expropriation pour cause d'utilité publique en Algérie*, Thèse, Paris, Université de Paris 1901; Étienne Auguste, *La Notion d'expropriation. Son évolution*, Thèse, Nîmes, Université de Montpellier, 1926; Chevallier Paul, *L'Expropriation d'urgence*, Thèse, Montdidier, Université de Paris, 1927.

mobilisée par des politiques d'exception. Ces politiques recoupent bien entendu les situations de guerre, qui ne seront pas abordées directement dans cet article.

L'expropriation d'utilité publique dont il sera ici question concernera au premier chef la propriété non-nationale d'immeubles en grande partie ruraux. Sur ces propriétés, l'expropriation impliquait la mise en œuvre d'une série de travaux publics de la part de l'État. Outre l'ensemble des situations se rattachant aux politiques d'aménagement urbain et routier dont elle fut l'outil privilégié, l'expropriation d'utilité publique fut appliquée à grande échelle dans deux contextes particuliers: la colonisation de l'Algérie et la restauration des terrains de montagne en métropole. Dans ces deux cas particuliers, il s'agira de montrer comment et pourquoi l'expropriation de la propriété foncière non-nationale a reposé sur l'institutionnalisation social-historique d'un contexte d'urgence environnementale.

Le droit de l'expropriation d'utilité publique en France

Sous l'Ancien Régime, l'expropriation des particuliers par le souverain tombait sous la notion générale de « retrait d'utilité publique ». Ce *retrait* de la propriété s'exerçait principalement pour l'ouverture des chemins et canaux et pour le dessèchement des marais. Il était admis qu'en dédommagement, on attribuait une indemnité au propriétaire pour rembourser la valeur réelle de l'immeuble ainsi qu'une fraction en *sus* comme compensation du sacrifice imposé[2].

Au cours du XIXe siècle, l'économie générale de la législation sur l'expropriation s'articula sur trois points principaux: le principe de *déclaration* de l'utilité publique, le principe de *responsabilité* de l'État et le principe du paiement préalable des *indemnités* d'expropriation[3]. La première formulation juridique date de 1791 et de l'article 17 de la Déclaration Universelle des Droits de l'Homme et du Citoyen: « La propriété étant un droit inviolable et sacré, nul ne peut en être privé si ce n'est lorsque la nécessité publique l'exige évidemment, et sans la condition d'une juste et préalable indemnité »[4]. L'article 545

2 Crépon Théophile, *Code annoté de l'expropriation pour cause d'utilité publique: France, Algérie et colonies: loi du 3 mai 1841, lois diverses, ordonnances et décrets*, Paris, Marescq, 1885.

3 Delbez Louis, *La compétence contentieuse en matière d'emprises administratives sur les propriétés privées*, Thèse, Paris, Université de Montpellier, 1926.

4 Cité dans Crépon, *Code annoté de l'expropriation pour cause d'utilité publique*, *op. cit.*, p. XI.

du Code civil reprit ce principe sans régler précisément la procédure: qui était en charge de prononcer l'utilité publique, qui fixait le montant des indemnités d'expropriation, et surtout qui réglait ces indemnités?

Par son titre 2, la loi du 16 septembre 1807 attribua l'ensemble de ces tâches à l'administration, ce qui causa un certain nombre de contentieux. La loi du 8 mars 1810 chargea l'administration de déclarer l'utilité publique tandis que les tribunaux vérifiaient la légalité de la déclaration et prononçaient l'expropriation tout en fixant le montant des indemnités[5]. Avec la loi du 7 juillet 1833, suivant l'importance et la nature des travaux, la déclaration de l'utilité publique revenait soit au pouvoir législatif (loi), soit au pouvoir exécutif (décret). L'administration devait quant à elle déterminer après enquête préalable les propriétés sur lesquelles devait porter l'expropriation. Le pouvoir judiciaire seul avait la capacité de prononcer l'expropriation et le devoir de régler les indemnités. La nouveauté de 1833 résidait dans le transfert de l'évaluation du montant de l'indemnité, du tribunal à un jury spécial de propriétaires.

La loi du 3 mai 1841 confirma ce principe tout en organisant la possibilité d'une déclaration d'utilité publique en cas d'urgence. Le titre *Dispositions exceptionnelles* permettait «de prendre possession des terrains non-bâtis soumis à l'expropriation, lorsqu'il y aura urgence spécialement déclarée par une ordonnance royale, et sous la condition de la consignation d'une somme dont le montant aura été fixé par un jugement»[6]. A partir de loi de 1841, plusieurs textes sont venus étendre les situations susceptibles de déclaration de l'utilité publique qui restaient jusque là cantonnées à l'aménagement urbain et aux dessèchements des marais[7]. Toutes les dépossessions prononcées sous cet empire devaient reposer sur l'intérêt général et ne pouvaient s'appliquer qu'aux

5 Vomarne, *De l'expropriation pour cause d'utilité publique en Algérie*, *op. cit.*, p. 6.

6 Crépon, *Code annoté de l'expropriation pour cause d'utilité publique*, *op. cit.*, p. XIII.

7 Les routes nationales (loi du 21 mai 1842), les chemins de fer (loi du 15 juillet 1845), l'assainissement des logements insalubres (loi du 13 avril 1850), la voirie urbaine (décret du 26 mars 1852), les places de guerre (décret du 23 septembre 1853), le libre écoulement des eaux de drainage (loi du 10 juin 1854), les travaux militaires (loi du 22 juin 1854), les servitudes relatives aux magasins à poudre de la guerre et de la marine (loi du 22 juin 1854), la conservation des eaux minérales (loi du 14 juillet 1856), le reboisement des montagnes (loi du 28 juillet 1860), le gazonnement des montagnes et les chemins vicinaux (loi du 8 juin 1864, articles 7 et 1-2) cf. Crépon, *Code annoté de l'expropriation pour cause d'utilité publique*, *op. cit.*, pp. 389-430.

immeubles. Elles entraînaient obligatoirement la mise en œuvre de travaux publics aux frais de l'État et l'attribution d'une indemnisation aux propriétaires dépossédés.

Dans les colonies françaises, l'expropriation d'utilité publique suivait une législation parente. En Algérie, l'expropriation fut d'abord réglée par les arrêtés des gouverneurs généraux successifs[8]. Le titre IV de l'ordonnance royale du 1er octobre 1844, ainsi que le titre IV de la loi du 16 juin 1851 sur la propriété foncière en Algérie fixèrent par la suite toute la législation en la matière pour le reste du XIXe siècle[9]. Plusieurs éléments différaient néanmoins entre la métropole et sa principale colonie. En Algérie, l'établissement de l'utilité publique comme la déclaration de l'expropriation ne se faisaient pas par décret mais par décision du ministre de la Guerre. Le règlement de l'indemnité ne dépendait pas d'un jury de propriétaires, mais d'un tribunal civil de première instance selon un jugement souverain et sans appel en ce qui concerne la fixation du montant de l'indemnité. L'expropriation pouvait être prononcée pour tout un faisceau de causes sans équivalent en métropole[10]. De la même manière qu'en métropole et à peu près à la même période, l'ordonnance algérienne de 1844 prévoyait (chapitre V) une possibilité de « prise de possession en cas d'urgence » (articles 61 à 71).

Les traces archivistiques laissées par l'expropriation d'utilité publique en France au XIXe siècle doivent donc être cherchées dans les sources judiciaires. En règle générale, les documents concernent une multitude de cas particuliers, majoritairement urbains[11]. Néanmoins, l'État français recourût aux procédures d'expropriation d'utilité publique de manière systématique et à grande échelle dans deux contextes particuliers: d'abord pour les nécessités de la colonisation de l'Algérie dès la conquête d'Alger en 1830, puis, dans les régions de montagne, pour la lutte contre la torrentialité.

8 Il s'agit des arrêtés du 17 octobre 1833, du 4 novembre 1841 et du 15 janvier 1842. Voir, Crépon, *Code annoté de l'expropriation pour cause d'utilité publique*, *op. cit.*, p. 431.

9 Vomarne, p. 9 et ss.

10 Pour la fondation des villes, villages ou hameaux, ou pour l'agrandissement de leur enceinte ou territoire; pour l'établissement des ouvrages de défense; pour l'établissement de fontaines; pour l'ouverture de route, cf. Crépon, *Code annoté de l'expropriation*, *op. cit.*, p. 432.

11 Le Syndicat des expropriés s'efforçait par exemple de rassembler périodiquement tous les cas d'expropriation engendrés par l'aménagement haussmannien de Paris dans le *Bulletin de l'expropriation pour cause d'utilité publique*, durant les dernières années du XIXe siècle.

L'expropriation d'utilité publique en Algérie

Au XIXe siècle, le statut de la terre en Algérie est indissociable d'un long processus par lequel l'État français mit aux mains des européens une partie importante du territoire algérien et la quasi majorité des terres arables et des forêts. Cet accaparement foncier connut son apogée entre 1871 et 1900, avec la colonisation officielle, mais s'appuyait sur près de quarante années de conquête militaire et de répression des insurrections par le biais d'une législation d'exception[12]. Quarante années au terme desquelles le domaine national français en Algérie compta plus de 6,5 millions d'hectares d'immeubles ruraux dont près de 3 millions d'hectares de forêts[13]. Ce processus s'appuya en partie seulement sur les procédures d'expropriation d'utilité publique. Ce vaste transfert foncier s'est en effet opéré suivant deux procédures parentes de l'expropriation: soit par négociation (vente à l'amiable), soit par confiscation (expropriations et séquestres).

Aux principes d'une colonisation d'utilité publique

De la prise d'Alger jusqu'en 1871, l'État français, largement épaulé sur le terrain par ses troupes armées, procéda à l'élaboration juridique et à l'application de ce que l'historiographie qualifie de processus de *domanialisation*[14]. Grâce à un certain nombre de mesures juridiques et d'actes de gouvernement ponctuels, l'État s'appropria d'abord toutes les terres du *beylik*, c'est à dire les terres appartenant autrefois à l'administration ottomane, ainsi que toutes les forêts. La lente cristallisation de la propriété collective et privée du droit romain par dessus les classifications indigènes (*arch*, *melk*, *habous*) s'opéra par différentes

12 Peyerimhoff de Fontenelle Henri, *Enquête sur les résultats de la colonisation officielle de 1871 à 1895: rapport à Monsieur Jonnart, gouverneur général de l'Algérie*, Alger, Imprimerie Torrent, 1906, p. 10. Ce que Sari appelle pour sa part le processus de « dépossession des fellahs ». voir, Sari Djilali, *La dépossession des fellahs (1830-1962)*, Alger, Société nationale d'édition et de diffusion, 1978.

13 Djebari, *La France en Algérie: bilans et controverses. La genèse d'un capitalisme d'État colonial*, Alger, Office des Publications Universitaires, p. 111.

14 Cf. Sari, *La dépossession des fellahs (1830-1962), op. cit.*; Djebari, *La France en Algérie: bilans et controverses, op. cit.*; Rahmani Ahmed, *Les biens publics en droit algérien*, Alger, Les Éditions Internationales, 1996; Khalfoune Tahar, *Le domaine public en droit algérien: réalité et fiction*, Paris, l'Harmattan, 2004.

procédures[15] au cours desquelles la cadastration des terres, la recension et la distribution des titres de propriété firent émerger un certain nombre de terres vacantes ou mal possédées aux alentours des périmètres de colonisation, que les commissaires avaient pour directive de rattacher directement au domaine national.

À partir de 1871, la propriété privée, indigène comme européenne, ayant été suffisamment constituée, le processus de domanialisation changea de régime avec le recours exceptionnel aux emprises administratives telles que l'expropriation. Entre 1871 et 1895, la colonisation officielle reposa sur la mise à disposition des colons de 428 périmètres répartis sur près de 650.000 hectares de terre dont la quasi totalité passa par le domaine privé de l'État avant d'être redistribuée[16]. L'origine de ces terres se répartissait comme suit: 13% (de ces 643.546 hectares) revenaient aux procédures d'expropriation d'utilité publique, tandis que 36% étaient le fruit des séquestres.

Les différentes voies coloniales de dépossession foncière

Dans le cas des 85.291 hectares concernés, l'expropriation fut appliquée suivant l'article 19 de la loi du 16 juin 1851. Ne pouvant porter que sur les propriétés particulières, son application n'était pas aussi simple qu'en métropole: elle nécessitait de constituer les diverses formes de propriétés foncières indigènes en propriété privée afin que chaque procédure d'expropriation concernât une parcelle dûment située et un propriétaire parfaitement identifié. Ce qui était réalisé en grande partie après le passage des dernières commissions du senatus-consulte en 1870. Mais comme le fit remarquer Peyerimhoff, ni la coercition ni le règlement obligatoire en argent ne furent de rigueur[17]. Le prix des terres

15 Il s'agit des commissions des transactions et partage (1844-1848), de cantonnement (1858-1860) et du senatus-consulte (1863-1870), cf. Ageron Charles-Robert, *Les Algériens musulmans et la France (1871-1919)*, Paris, PUF, 1968.

16 Il faut noter que ce chiffre représente la superficie de terres employée à la constitution des lots individuels de la colonisation officielle (allotissement). Il est de loin inférieur à la superficie totale des terres sur laquelle l'État imposa son emprise pour former le domaine public, au titre duquel il faut compter les terrains communaux, les pépinières, les réseaux de communication (chemins de fer notamment), les forêts domaniales et les plans d'eau.

17 Il convient ici de garder à l'esprit que Peyerimhoff, dont les chiffres de ce travail sont extraits, était un fervent promoteur de l'œuvre coloniale française en Algérie, cf. Sari, *La dépossession des fellah, op. cit.*, p. 77.

Figure 1. Origine des 643.546 hectares de terres mis à disposition de la colonisation officielle par l'État en Algérie entre 1871 et 1895

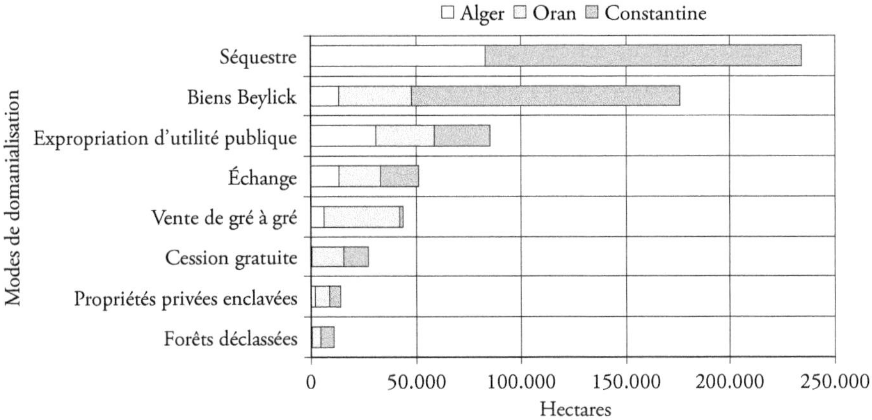

	Alger	Oran	Constantine	Total
Séquestre	83.096	135	151.144	234.375
Biens Beylick	14.000	34.156	128.010	176.166
Expropriation d'utilité publique	31.076	27.473	26.742	85.291
Échange	13.618	19.907	17.558	51.083
Vente de gré à gré	6.157	35.953	1.833	43.943
Cession gratuite	581	15.043	11.765	27.389
Propriétés privées enclavées	2.082	7.035	5.001	14.118
Forêts déclassées	774	4.053	6.354	11.181
Total	151.384	143.755	348.407	643.546

Source: Henri de Peyerimhoff de Fontenelle, *Enquête sur les résultats de la colonisation officielle de 1871 à 1895: rapport à Monsieur Jonnart, gouverneur général de l'Algérie*, Alger, Imprimerie Torrent, 1906, p. 77.

fixé par le tribunal, un grand nombre d'indigènes acceptait une compensation en nature, en échange de terres de moins bonne qualité puisées dans les ressources du domaine privé de l'État[18]. Sur les 85.291 hectares expropriés, 38.000

18 Cela concerna en l'occurrence les 50.000 hectares de terres de la catégorie « Échange » dans le figure 1.

auraient été obtenus à l'amiable: la possibilité juridique d'expropriation servit largement à amener les nouveaux propriétaires à négocier avec l'administration des Domaines. Ce procédé ne doit pas être confondu avec les achats de terres que l'État avait la possibilité de faire en dehors de l'emprise juridique de l'utilité publique (cela concerne les 14.000 hectares de propriétés isolées dans de vastes ensembles domaniaux et les 44.000 hectares de terrains négociés de gré à gré).

Chacune des parcelles à exproprier faisait l'objet d'un simple arrêté préfectoral qui suivait la constitution d'un dossier comprenant un plan d'ensemble et les justificatifs de propriété. « L'expropriation après entente à l'amiable est certainement de toutes les procédures d'achat la mieux adaptée aux conditions spéciales de la propriété indigène, et, notamment, au nombre des détenteurs et à la confusion de leurs droits »[19]. Dépendant pour une large part des rapports de force entre indigènes et autorités coloniales et de la nature des terres en question (agricoles, prés, friches, forêts), le montant moyen des indemnités à l'hectare sur la période variait fortement entre les différents départements: 50 francs dans l'Oranais, 86 dans l'Algérois et 96 dans le Constantinois[20].

Néanmoins, comme le montre la Figure 1, une large partie des terres domanialisées (près de 230.000 hectares) en Algérie le fut par différentes procédures de séquestres qui, à la différence de l'expropriation d'utilité publique et de l'achat à l'amiable, était une mesure répressive d'exception menée par l'État à l'encontre de la propriété foncière privée comme collective.

Le séquestre des terres incendiées

Le recours au séquestre, bien que juridiquement possible depuis 1842, se systématisa réellement à la suite de l'insurrection de Mokrani en 1871. Cette mesure exceptionnelle comportait trois volets: elle consistait en une amende collective attribuée aux tribus insurgées (10 millions de francs au total pour l'insurrection de 1871). S'ensuivait le séquestre des propriétés des acteurs principaux de la révolte, en exécution de l'ordonnance du 31 octobre 1845 (environ 55.000 hectares). Enfin, les autorités appliquaient le séquestre collectif édicté par arrêté du Gouverneur Général à l'encontre des collectivités reconnues coupables

19 Peyerimoff, *Enquête sur les résultats de la colonisation*, *op. cit.*, p. 83.

20 Pour une étendue statistique de 3.532 fr., cf. Peyerimhoff, *Enquête sur les résultats de la colonisation officielle de 1871 à 1895*, *op. cit.*, p. 84.

d'insurrection (environ 600.000 hectares). Avec la loi du 17 juillet 1874 sur les incendies, l'État colonial opéra un renversement crucial pour sa politique d'acquisition de terres, notamment dans les régions montagneuses. Alors que les incendies étaient jusque là considérés comme les conséquences des insurrections, cette loi assimilait tout incendie à un acte insurrectionnel, appliquant ce que les journaux radicaux et les grands concessionnaires de chênes-liège réclamaient en vain depuis les années 1860 contre le « complot de la torche ». Avec l'institutionnalisation de la responsabilité collective, le séquestre devint « un acte de force, à caractère pénal très apparent »[21]. Les sanctions prévues consistaient à appliquer des amendes aux tribus riveraines, à séquestrer les forêts incendiées et à en interdire le pâturage pendant six ans au moins[22]. Avec la loi forestière du 9 décembre 1885, qui fait suite aux violents incendies de 1881, les broussailles furent assimilées aux forêts ce qui permit de criminaliser toute pratique de pâturage et de défrichement, et en cas d'incendie, de domanialiser des terres ignorées jusque là par la loi de 1874[23]. La loi de 1885 permit notamment d'exproprier les derniers indigènes titulaires d'un titre de propriété *melk* (privé) sur des enclaves[24]. Finalement, on doit noter que « les terres du séquestre n'ont été appréhendées et conservées en nature qu'en vue de la constitution des centres de colonisation officielle »[25].

La Figure 2 tente de rendre compte du mécanisme très complexe par lequel l'État français a pu violer la propriété, au prétexte de l'utilité publique de la colonisation dans un contexte d'urgence environnementale créé par les incendies.

En dehors des achats de terres à l'amiable faits sur les crédits ordinaires de la colonisation qui ne sont pas concernés par la notion d'utilité publique, il convient de noter que les ressources nécessaires à l'expropriation pouvaient provenir soit d'une ligne budgétaire spéciale de la colonie[26], soit du rachat par les tribus dépossédées de certaines de leurs terres séquestrées. Ceci explique en partie le décalage entre une période (1871-1875) d'explosion des séquestres

21 *Ibid.*, p. 177.

22 Nouschi André, *Enquête sur le niveau de vie des populations rurales Constantinoises de la conquête jusqu'en 1919: Essai d'histoire économique et sociale*, Paris, PUF 1961, p. 482.

23 Guyot Charles, *Rapport sur l'établissement de forêts de protection*, Impr. L. Pochy, 1913, p. 6.

24 Sari, *La dépossession des fellahs (1830-1962)*, *op. cit.*, p. 82.

25 Peyerimhoff, *Enquête sur les résultats de la colonisation officielle de 1871 à 1895*, *op. cit.*, p. 117.

26 « Dépenses sans lien direct avec la colonisation », d'après les sources de Peyerimhoff, *Enquête sur les résultats de la colonisation*, *op. cit.*, p. 506.

Figure 2. Dépense publique occasionnée par le processus de domanialisation pour la colonisation officielle en Algérie entre 1871 et 1895 (répartition par origine des budgets)

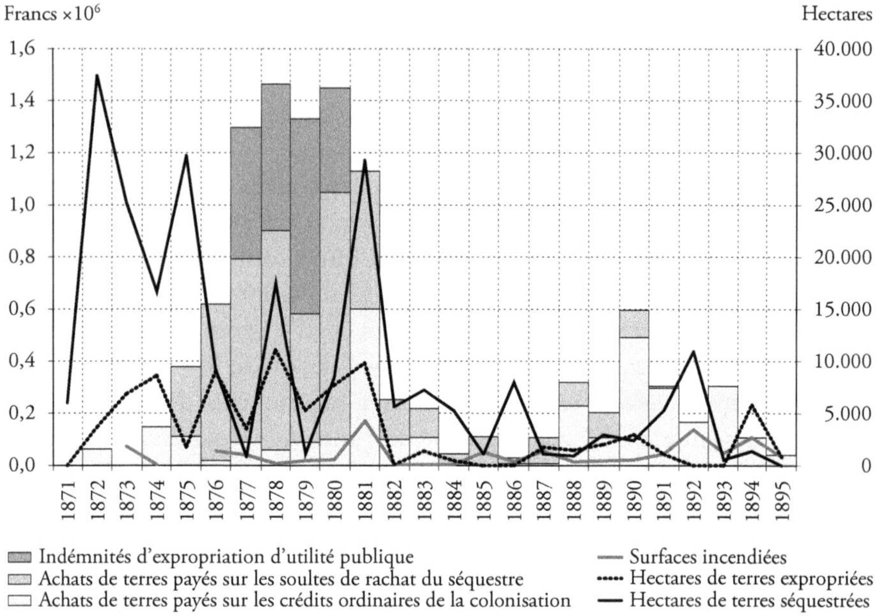

extraordinaires de terres, et une période (1875-1882) d'accumulation et de mise à disposition des moyens financiers que nécessitait l'expropriation « légale » des propriétaires indigènes qui augmente régulièrement entre 1871 et 1881. Ce système aboutit à la situation paradoxale déjà mise en lumière par certains historiens[27], dans laquelle les tribus séquestrées finançaient elles-mêmes l'expropriation des propriétés *melk* possédées par des propriétaires indigènes.

27 Cf. Nouschi, *Enquête sur le niveau de vie des populations rurales*, *op. cit.*; Ageron, *Les Algériens musulmans et la France (1871-1919)*, *op. cit.*; Sari, *La dépossession des fellahs (1830-1962)*, *op. cit.*

L'expropriation d'utilité publique dans les Alpes

En métropole, l'idéologie du reboisement d'utilité publique fonctionnait sur la mise en cause de l'incurie pastorale dans la production des inondations catastrophiques. Au XIXe siècle, la sylviculture européenne accordait une place cruciale aux forêts dans la régulation du régime des eaux: qu'il s'agisse de l'absorption des pluies torrentielles, de la préservation des sources ou encore de la répartition annuelle et géographique des précipitations sur la Terre. Selon les experts, ces phénomènes auraient été accentués en fréquence et en intensité par ce que le code forestier qualifiait depuis 1827 d'abus de jouissance et de déboisements intempestifs. Les pratiques agricoles des communautés de montagne étaient responsables du ravinement des sols du fait qu'elles consommaient le bois (surpopulation) tout en l'empêchant de repousser (surpâturage). La restauration de ces territoires à l'état où les auteurs anciens les avaient décrits – toujours avant 1789 – nécessitait la mise en œuvre d'un vaste programme de modernisation économique passant par un changement profond des modes de vie alpins et d'une redéfinition des produits de l'industrie pastorale (la fruitière et le gruyère).

Utilité publique et « dangers nés et actuels »

La loi du 28 juillet 1860 (complétée par celle du 8 juin 1864) sur le reboisement des montagnes avait pour objet la protection des sols contre les ravages des eaux. C'était une loi particulièrement autoritaire, votée par un régime libéral fermement attaché à la propriété privée mais bien décidé à conserver l'intérêt général en cas de situations exceptionnelles. Elle prévoyait deux types d'interventions sur les parcelles à risque dont l'État n'était pas le propriétaire direct. Soit un encouragement en subventions et en nature (graines et plants) pour les travaux facultatifs de boisement effectués par les propriétaires eux-mêmes (commune comme particulier); soit une obligation d'effectuer les travaux déclarés d'utilité publique par décret du Conseil d'État, au sein de « périmètres de restauration »[28].

28 Estimés à plus d'un million d'ha. de terrains à reboiser en 1861, les ressources financières mises à disposition de l'Administration des Forêts devaient lui permettre de réaliser environ 80.000 ha. de reboisement en dix ans cf. Vicaire Henri, *Reboisement des montagnes – Compte rendu des travaux de 1861*, Paris, Imprimerie Nationale, 1862, p. 6.

Pour ce dernier type de travaux, les propriétaires étaient mis en demeure de les exécuter[29]. En cas de refus ou d'incapacité d'engager les dépenses, souvent importantes (barrages, digues, clayonnages, terrasses, seuils ...), l'État pouvait se substituer à eux. Les propriétaires particuliers, pouvaient donc être expropriés, conformément aux dispositions de la loi du 3 mai 1841, et pouvaient retrouver leurs propriétés soit en remboursant les frais de restauration augmentés par les indemnités d'expropriation et les intérêts, soit en abandonnant la moitié des terrains reboisés à l'État dans les cinq années suivant la date d'achèvement des travaux. Pour les communes, elles n'étaient pas expropriées mais l'État conservait la jouissance des terrains reboisés jusqu'au remboursement complet des avances. Elles pouvaient d'ailleurs recouvrer leurs droits gratuitement, en échange de la moitié des terrains reboisés.

Sous l'empire de la loi de 1860, 219 périmètres furent décrétés d'utilité publique, s'étendant sur 139.000 hectares[30], pour une dépense publique totale de 11,5 millions de francs[31]. En raison du montant souvent élevé de ces travaux, l'État se retrouvait ainsi capable, par simple prescription, d'exproprier de grandes superficies de territoire. Les intérêts des populations rurales s'en trouvaient lésés attendu que, dans bien des régions, la forêt constituait une pièce maîtresse du système rural. En étendant les périmètres protégés et les couverts forestiers, l'État devenait responsable du recul des terrains de parcours sur lesquels reposait l'économie pastorale montagnarde.

Par la loi du 4 avril 1882 sur la restauration et la conservation des terrains de montagne, les agents forestiers perdirent la possibilité d'intervenir où bon leur semblait, et durent limiter leurs actions aux terrains présentant des « dégradations du sol et des dangers nés et actuels » – notion qui venait encadrer celle d'utilité publique. Ces nouveaux périmètres n'étaient plus constitués par décret,

29 Demontzey Prosper, « Rapport sur l'exécution de la loi du 4 avril 1882 », in *Bulletin – Ministère de l'Agriculture: documents officiels, statistique, rapports, comptes rendus de missions en France et à l'étranger*, vol. 6, 1887, p. 412.

30 139.000 hectares dont seulement 26 % avait été reboisés ou regazonnés en 1882, et dont par ailleurs, la moitié avait été rendue à leurs propriétaires dès la promulgation de la loi de 1882 via la procédure de révision des périmètres, cf. Demontzey, « Rapport sur l'exécution de la loi du 4 avril 1882 », *art. cit.*, p. 419.

31 Guichet Maurice, *Des droits de l'usufruitier dans les bois et forêts (Dr. Rom.); Droit français. Législation de la restauration et de la conservation des terrains en montagne*, Thèse, Nancy, Université de Nancy, 1887 p. 29.

mais représentaient le fruit d'une longue procédure d'enquête couronnée ou non d'une loi. « C'est le retour au droit commun »[32]. L'utilité publique des travaux de restauration devait être établie à l'échelle des bassins versants des rivières torrentielles. L'administration forestière devait désigner les terrains à restaurer au moyen d'une enquête dans chaque commune concernée. Elle établissait un procès-verbal de reconnaissance, dressait un plan de la parcelle, réalisait des tableaux de parcelles par nature de sol et par type de propriétaire et, enfin, proposait un avant-projet des travaux à réaliser. Le dossier constitué était envoyé au préfet. Les avis des conseils municipaux et généraux étaient joints à ceux d'une commission spéciale où siégeaient, à côté d'élus, deux représentants des grands corps d'État. À partir de ce dossier, le Ministre faisait préparer un projet de loi statuant sur l'utilité publique des travaux. Quand celle-ci était adoptée par le Parlement, les travaux obligatoires pouvaient être engagés aux mêmes conditions que sous la loi de 1864, par les soins de l'administration et aux frais de l'État. Ce dernier devait par conséquent acquérir les terrains concernés, soit à l'amiable, soit par expropriation. Particuliers et communes pouvaient alors être expropriés définitivement: les restitutions n'étant plus envisagées à aucun moment du texte de la loi[33].

Entre 1860 et 1887, 37.500 hectares de terrains avaient été domanialisés, dont 41 % par expropriation d'utilité publique, et il était projeté de domanialiser encore 32.000 hectares sur la période 1887-1897[34]. Ce qui fut largement réalisé puisque l'État se serait approprié près de 300.000 hectares de terrains de montagne pour cause d'utilité publique entre 1860 et 1914 selon les sources officielles[35].

32 Demontzey, « Rapport sur l'exécution de la loi du 4 avril 1882 », *art. cit.*, p. 414; Daubrée Lucien, 1909, *Reboisement et gazonnement des montagnes – Compte rendu des travaux de 1869 à 187 – Procès-verbaux de la commission forestière des Alpes*, Paris, Imprimerie Nationale, IV.

33 Mesure toujours régie par la loi de 1841, l'État pouvait cependant étaler le paiement des indemnités d'expropriation sur dix exercices (article 21 de la loi de 1882). Pour les communes, cela ne posait pas de problème; pour les gros propriétaires, cela représentait un placement juteux grâce aux 5 % d'intérêt; mais la répartition sur dix ans du paiement des faibles montants dus aux petits propriétaires représentait quasiment une perte sèche et occasionnait de nombreuses plaintes, cf. Demontzey, « Rapport sur l'exécution de la loi du 4 avril 1882 », *art. cit.*, p. 418.

34 « État n. 4 » in Demontzey, « Rapport sur l'exécution de la loi du 4 avril 1882 », *art. cit.*, p. 423.

35 CNRS, *Les Eaux et forêts du 12e au 20e siècle*, Paris, Éd. du CNRS, 1987, p. 582.

Figure 3. Terrains acquis par l'État au 31 décembre 1886 dans le cadre de la politique de reboisement et de restauration des terrains de montagne

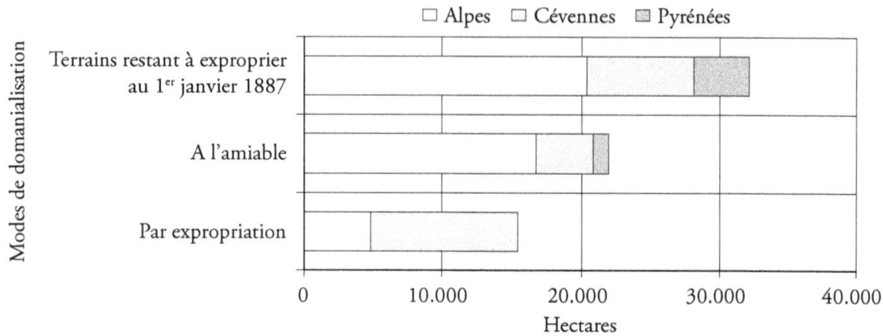

	Alpes	Cévennes	Pyrénées	Total
Terrains restant à exproprier au 1er janvier 1887	20.379	7.739	4.011	32.129
A l'amiable	16.752	4.107	1.130	21.989
Par expropriation	4.894	10.560	0	15.454
Total	42.025	22.406	5.141	69.572

Source: Etat n. 2, in Prosper Demontzey, « Rapport sur l'exécution de la loi du 4 avril 1882 », *Bulletin – Ministère de l'Agriculture: documents officiels, statistique, rapports, comptes rendus de missions en France et à l'étranger*, vol. 6, 1887, p. 422.

Les deux voies principales de dépossession foncière en métropole

Finalement, à l'instar de l'Algérie, l'État a relativement peu exproprié par rapport à ce que lui permettaient les lois (celle de 1860 notamment), préférant largement acheter à l'amiable les parcelles périmétrées au grès des circonstances[36] ou encore encourageant les travaux facultatifs par des subventions[37]. Les quelques

36 Cela se voit dans l'extrême morcellement des terrains de l'État, cf. Daubrée, *Reboisement et gazonnement des montagnes, op. cit.*, p. 188.

37 Dans le cas des communes, les travaux en question coûtèrent 7 millions de francs (subventionnés à 23 % par les départements et à 55 % par l'État) et portèrent sur 54.000 ha. de reboisement. Dans le cas des particuliers, il fut question de 5 millions de francs pour 53.000 ha. de reboisement subventionnés à 5 % par les départements et à 37 % par l'État, cf. Daubrée, *Reboisement et gazonnement des montagnes, op. cit.*, pp. 208 et 211.

22.000 hectares de terrains achetés à l'amiable dans les périmètres décrétés d'utilité publique ont été acquis par l'État depuis 1860, selon la loi du 3 mai 1841 qui régissait les cessions à l'amiable avant ou après jugement d'expropriation. Là encore, l'expropriation fut largement utilisée comme une menace par l'Administration pour encourager les particuliers à vendre leurs terrains. Six hectares acquis à l'amiable sur dix seulement tombaient sous le coup d'un périmètre d'utilité publique: les quatre restant étaient négociés de gré à gré avec les particuliers par les forestiers, au sein d'un contexte – généralisé et connu de tous – d'acquisition systématique de l'État. Si l'utilité publique ne constituait pas un facteur discriminant, elle rendait néanmoins possible cette offensive foncière généralisée de l'État à l'égard des terrains de montagne.

Expropriations et acquisitions à l'amiable, tout en portant sur des superficies et des territoires différents, coutèrent autant au gouvernement. Les indemnités allouées par les jurys des commissions d'enquête d'utilité publique aux propriétaires expropriés s'élevaient, en 1887, à 5 millions de francs, à peu près également distribués entre communes et particuliers: pour 1,3 million dans les Alpes et 3,7 millions dans les Cévennes – soit un prix moyen à l'hectare respectivement de 268 francs contre 357. Ces chiffres soulignent nettement la différence de traitement entre communes et particuliers:

Dans les Alpes, les terrains expropriés étaient communaux à plus de 80 % et l'hectare communal était indemnisé à hauteur de 156 francs contre 758 pour le particulier. Dans les Cévennes, les particuliers étaient concernés à 33 % mais l'indemnisation d'expropriation de l'hectare communal restait dans un rapport de 6/10 avec celle des particuliers (290 contre 492 francs).

De l'autre côté, pour les 22.000 hectares de terrains acquis à l'amiable que la crise des systèmes de production agricole libérait littéralement dans certaines hautes terres comme les Cévennes entre 1880 et 1914[38], cela représentait aussi un investissement public de 5 millions de francs, à peu près également répartis entre les Alpes et les Cévennes (2 millions pour chacune des régions). Ceci donnait une moyenne nationale de 132 francs à l'hectare[39] masquant des disparités régionales et locales importantes: du simple au double entre Alpes et

38 Poupardin Denis, Nougarède Olivier et Larrère Raphaël, *La constitution du domaine privé de l'État sur les hautes terres du Lingas et de l'Aigoual*, Rungis, INRA,1988, p. 31.

39 « État n. 3 » in Demontzey, « Rapport sur l'exécution de la loi du 4 avril 1882 », *art. cit.*, p. 422.

Figure 4. Étendue et types de propriétaires concernés par les expropriations pour cause de reboisement et de gazonnement d'utilité publique en France entre 1860 et 1887

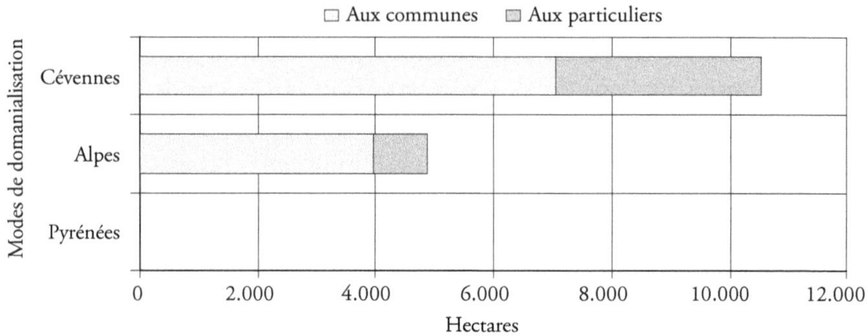

	Aux communes	Aux particuliers	Total
Cévennes	7.067	3.492	10.559
Alpes	3.983	910	4.893
Pyrénées	0	0	0
Total	11.050	4.402	15.452

Source: Etat n. 4, in Prosper Demontzey, « Rapport sur l'exécution de la loi du 4 avril 1882 », *Bulletin – Ministère de l'Agriculture: documents officiels, statistique, rapports, comptes rendus de missions en France et à l'étranger*, vol. 6, 1887, p. 423.

Cévennes, et de 150 à 1.000 francs entre communes cévenoles selon la nature des terrains par exemple[40].

Ainsi, en règle générale, l'expropriation était toujours plus dispendieuse que l'achat à l'amiable, d'autant plus lorsqu'elle concernait des terrains particuliers et que ces terrains étaient plus petits. Dans ce cadre, le principal problème de l'administration forestière fut de trouver les ressources financières propres et suffisantes pour prendre en charge la politique foncière engagée par la loi de 1882. Ainsi, le mot d'ordre administratif est rapidement devenu pragmatique: « déclarer d'utilité publique, le plus rapidement possible à l'ensemble des

40 Poupardin, *La constitution du domaine privé de l'État*, *op. cit.*

périmètres et attendre les offres des propriétaires ou entamer avec eux, sans se presser, des négociations en vue d'aboutir autant que possible à des cessions amiables »[41].

La mise en défens des terrains à risque

Limitant les prérogatives véritablement forestières des agents administratifs, la loi de 1882 les invitait par ailleurs à une plus grande intervention dans la gestion des étendues pastorales. En dehors des périmètres de restauration réservés aux parcelles menaçant les routes ou les villages, la loi de 1882 prévoyait dans son Titre II la *mise en défens* de certains terrains de parcours pour une période ne pouvant excéder dix années, à charge de dédommager les propriétaires de cette privation temporaire. La mise en défens concernait « les terrains dont l'état de dégradation n'est pas encore assez avancé pour nécessiter des travaux de restauration »[42]. Cela signifiait l'interdiction absolue de jouissance d'une parcelle sans distinction aucune de propriété[43]. À la différence de la mise en périmètre de reboisement sous la loi de 1882, elle était prononcée par décret du Conseil d'État, renouant ainsi avec l'arbitraire et l'exception de la loi de 1860. De même, sur les terrains moins dégradés encore, l'administration forestière pouvait les soumettre à la *règlementation du pâturage* par simple décision administrative, du moment que ces parcelles étaient situées dans l'une des communes dont les noms étaient inscrits dans le tableau annexé au règlement d'administration publique. La différence entre expropriation et mise en défens, réside dans le principe: alors que la première implique un chantier de travaux publics matérialisant la nécessité, la seconde peut tout autant violer la propriété privée, mais en prescrivant au contraire de ne rien faire à l'égard de ces parcelles. Cette pratique de mise en défens peut donc être rapprochée de la mise sous séquestre des terres incendiées en Algérie.

L'estimation des surfaces passées sous le régime pastoral et celles sanctuarisées par la mise en défens est plus complexe. Aucun document d'ensemble n'en fait le récapitulatif. Seule une compilation des archives communales pourrait

41 Demontzey, « Rapport sur l'exécution de la loi du 4 avril 1882 », *art. cit.*, p. 430.
42 *Ibid.*, p. 415.
43 Guichet, *Des droits de l'usufruitier dans les bois et forêts (Dr. rom.)*, *op. cit.*, p. 124.

en donner un chiffre global, sachant qu'on dispose d'une liste nominative de toutes les communes où ces mesures avaient été appliquées[44].

Conclusion

La courte étude qui précède montre que dans les Alpes comme en Algérie, entre 1840 et 1900, l'État français a mené à l'égard de la propriété foncière non-nationale, une offensive juridique et pratique, que l'on pourrait qualifier de véritable «processus de domanialisation». Ce processus s'est appuyé en partie sur l'expropriation pour utilité publique, mais pas seulement. Étant donné que l'expropriation restait une procédure exorbitante du droit commun, elle ne pouvait être mise en œuvre par l'État qu'au sein de contextes d'urgence bien spécifiques servant rétrospectivement à légitimer l'emploi de tels expédients juridiques – colonisation/guerre, puis incendies en Algérie, inondations catastrophiques dans les régions de montagne. Les risques naturels ont alors servi d'une manière ou d'une autre à incarner ces circonstances exceptionnelles.

On a pu observer aussi que l'expropriation d'utilité publique s'accompagna de part et d'autre de la Méditerranée des deux mêmes voies de dépossession annexes: l'une, consensuelle, souvent justifiée par des exigences comptables et par la recherche d'un apaisement des tensions locales – l'achat à l'amiable en situation d'utilité publique; l'autre, dissensuelle, toujours reliée à l'existence d'un état d'exception propre à légaliser l'exercice de mesures répressives à l'égard des biens des particuliers – le séquestre et la mise en défens. L'étude de l'expropriation doit donc à tout prix prendre en compte cette part non négligeable de vente forcée de terres et de confiscation qui n'apparaît pas directement dans les sources officielles de l'expropriation.

Enfin, ce rapprochement conduit évidemment à chercher une procédure parente des séquestres en métropole. Les mesures de mise en défens dans les communes alpines consistaient comme le séquestre à interdire toute jouissance d'une parcelle. Il s'agissait bien d'une confiscation de tout droit de propriété et de droits d'usage. Cependant, la métropole ne connaissait pas le contexte

44 Elles sont au nombre de trois cents, cf. Guyot, *Rapport sur l'établissement de forêts de protection*, *op. cit.*, p. 4 et Guichet, *Des droits de l'usufruitier dans les bois et forêts (Dr. rom.)*, *op. cit*, p. 412.

d'exception propre à la colonie; la mise en défens n'impliquait pas la même conception du temps que le séquestre; mais surtout, les mises en défens n'étaient pas rachetables, elles ne permettaient pas à l'administration de dégager le volant financier nécessaire aux indemnités d'expropriation. Le séquestre reste une mesure juridique non-légale propre à l'état d'exception colonial.

Enfin, si le processus de domanialisation a été abordé par certains historiens dans le cadre de la colonisation de l'Algérie, aucun rapprochement n'a encore jamais été opéré avec les pratiques similaires de l'administration sur les territoires de montagne en métropole. Aussi pourrait-on proposer un schéma synoptique de ce processus auquel les mesures d'expropriation ont contribué durant la seconde moitié du XIXe siècle. L'intérêt serait alors que de futures recherches sur le sujet puissent le préciser, lui indexer de nouveaux cas pour finalement le modifier substantiellement.

Figure 5. Schéma synoptique du processus de domanialisation mis en œuvre par l'État français dans les Alpes et en Algérie au cours de la seconde moitié du XIXe siècle

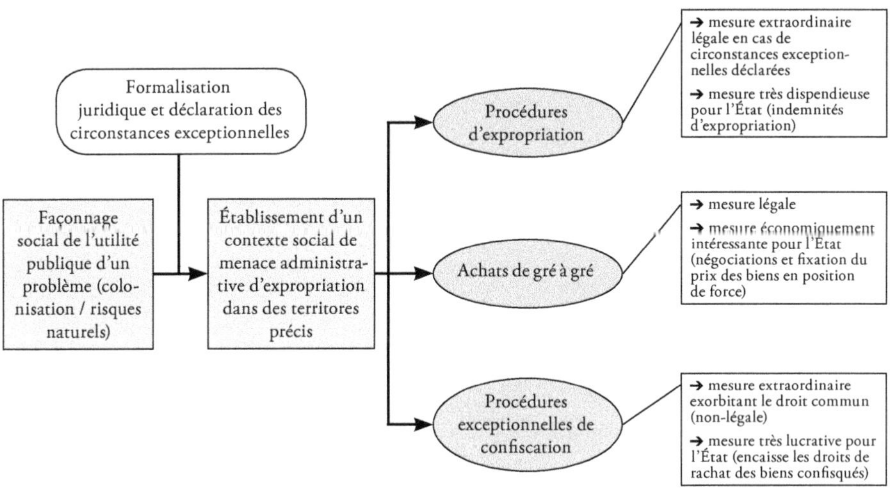

Expropriation for Public Use: Construction of the Railway Line in Abruzzo

Natascia Ridolfi

The construction of the railway line in Abruzzo was made possible by the activity of expropriation The legal institution of expropriation has its principles in the Italian Constitution which on the one hand protects private propriety and on the other preserves the right of expropriation for the benefits of general interests[1]. This is considered as an unavoidable necessity of political, economic and social solidarity to which the citizen-owner is subject. This is recognised by compensation determined by the value of the land and by the profits it produces on the basis of the market[2].

The first act, which governs the expropriation proceedings related to the railway, was the Royal Decree no. 281 of 2 October 1861 issued with an adjoining regulation, in occasion of the construction of the railway in the Napoletane[3] province, which proposed, among other things, the guidelines of the Preunitarian decree focusing on the realization of the railway in Apulia[4].

A general regulation on expropriation for public use was issued only in 1865: Law no. 2359 of 25 June. It consists of over one hundred articles and regulated

1 Finocchiaro Giuseppe, "Costituzione della Repubblica Italiana. Articoli 42–43", in *Codice civile e leggi complementari: giurisprudenza, schemi e tabelle*, Milano, Il Sole 24 ore, 2004, pp. 10–11.

2 Through expropriation "the administration authority can transfer the property of a good from a private, subject, who is the owner, to a public body or other private subject who is entitled by law, that is, who has obtained the declaration of public use for a general project presented". Ardizzone Ugo, "Dichiarazione di pubblica utilità", in *Enciclopedia di Diritto*, XII, Milano, Giuffrè, 1964, p. 391.

3 The Regulation was made up of 27 articles which regulated the expropriation in each part, from the compilation of the register to the estimation of the compensation. "Regio decreto n. 281 del 2 ottobre 1861", in *Raccolta ufficiale delle leggi e dei decreti del Regno d'Italia*, vol. I, Torino, Stamperia Reale, 1861, pp. 1131–1139.

4 "Decreto del 28 febbraio 1856", in *Collezione ufficiale delle leggi napoletane*, 1856, I term, pp. 106–109.

in detail the entire process of expropriation from the occupation of the land to the payment of compensation underlining the public use of the railways besides the social value of the service offered[5]. As to the indemnification, it was subject to further changes, indeed Law no. 2892 of 1885, issued in occasion of the redevelopment of the city of Naples[6], brought regulations for the variations of evaluation of the compensations for expropriation: the estimate was based "on the average value of the property expropriated and the aggregation rents of the last decade"[7].

The expropriation of the assets related to the railway works, besides the fact that they gave life to substantial production, resulted in the "Law on the provisions laid down by law and regulation regarding expropriation for public use", issued by the President of the Republic (Decree no. 327[8] of 8 June 2001), and had an important role also in the economic and financial field. Indeed, the commitment of funds on the part of the State was particularly significant for the railway companies and private individuals, but more relevant were the repercussions on the land. The passage of the railway interested both the agricultural and industrial sectors, as it subjected farmland and industrial sites to expropriation procedures.

The introduction of railways in Abruzzo was supported by several factors related to the development of the national policy framework and to local development. This infrastructure allowed the central authorities to travel to and relate faster with Southern Italy and therefore facilitated immediate application of the directives and instructions of the central bodies. The military also benefited from the railway lines: they allowed the national army to get hold of

5 "Legge n. 235925 del giugno 1865", in *Raccolta ufficiale delle leggi e dei decreti del Regno d'Italia*, vol. XII, Torino, Stamperia Reale, 1865, pp. 1477–1513.

6 This law was issued following the diffusion of the cholera outbreak in the summer of 1884 and it aimed to redevelop the insalubrious area of the city. It regulated the expropriation as well as the compensation for the houses confiscated. Feola Marcello, *L'espropriazione per pubblica utilità. Profili generali*, Roma, Formez, 2002, s.p. (http://db.formez.it/storicofontinor.nsf/8804ae899ac04f.7c12569f.0030aaca/404F4E3084436E88C1256C5A002E36D9/$file/saggio%20f.ola.pdf).

7 "Legge n. 289215 del gennaio 1885", in *Raccolta ufficiale delle leggi e dei decreti del Regno d'Italia*, Roma, 1885, vol. 74, pp. 43–51.

8 "Testo unico delle disposizioni legislative e regolamentari in materia di espropriazione per pubblica utilità", in *Gazzetta Ufficiale*, 189 (2001) Ordinary Supplement n. 211.

the men living in South Italy. More important was the social impact that the railway had, helping to stamp out the phenomenon of banditry[9]. The railway lines had a positive impact also on the economical and commercial development of the territory and for this reason the local political party had strongly supported the project. In fact, while the Adriatic railway line was part of the national project to connect the northern part of Italy to the South, superceding the logic of merely local interests, continuous pressure was exercised for the construction of the regional railway lines[10].

The Adriatic railway underwent constant changes from the initial plans. It was to be built along the coast and in some parts drew dangerously near the shore. The original[11] route, which was to cross the hills, was put aside for another less expensive project which had broadly the same characteristics and the same objectives[12]. The coast line, which was contracted out to the *Società*

9 For a further and more attentive study on the railway in Abruzzo refer to: Gorgoni Lanzetta Lucia, Millevolte Giovanna, "Da un nodo ferroviario nascita di una grande città", in Lorenzetti Roberto (a cura di), *La questione ferroviaria nella storia d'Italia*, Roma, Editori Riuniti, 1989, pp. 63–65.

10 Giuseppe Devincenzi had a particular interest in the development of the regional railway lines although he recognized the importance of the two great national railway lines, the Adriatic and the Celano, and he waited for the "Popoli-L'Aquila-Rieti railway line and Teramo and Lanciano short distance lines". For further study on the Senator Devincenzi concept concerning the viability of these projects, refer to Nicola Romualdi, "G. Devincenzi e la viabilità ordinaria comunale nella regione", in *Atti del 2° Convegno Giuseppe Devincenzi nel Risorgimento e nella politica post-unitaria,* Teramo, 29–30 June, 1972, Teramo, Edigrafital, 1974, p. 152. While for the study of the domestic railway lines refer to: Sabatini Gaetano, "La creazione del sistema ferroviario in un'area marginale: l'Abruzzo tra Ottocento e Novecento", in Sabatini Gaetano (a cura di), *La rivoluzione dei trasporti in Italia nel XIX secolo. Temi e materiali sullo sviluppo delle ferrovie tra questione nazionale e storia regionale*, L'Aquila, Amministrazione Provinciale, 1996, pp. 206–209.

11 Panfilo De Riseisn was one of the major supporters of the pre-Unification railway project: he commissioned Vincenzo Antonio Rossi, engineer and great expert of the Reign, to create the Abruzzo rail track, that had to "assume the function of collector of the railway flow from the Valli del Tordino, Aterno-Pescara and Sangro, in order to enhance the trade towards north until Tronto, and toward south until San Severo and towards Naples". For further in-depth studies refer to Mercurio Franco, "Reti di comunicazione e formazione delle gerarchie territoriali", in Costantini Massimo, Felice Costantino (a cura di), *L'Abruzzo*, Torino, Einaudi, 2000, pp. 829–830.

12 The railway track "drawing near the shore did not have any negative aspects and did not require the demolition of part of the mountains for tunnels nor did it give any problems

Strada Ferrate Meridionale by the government, was built in a short time: in 1863, after just two years, the Abruzzo railway track celebrated its opening and in 1866 it was the turn of Apulia[13].

The procedure for the expropriation was divided into two phases: a preliminary one which consisted of the occupation of the land, and a definitive one which involved the effective act of transfer of the property. Before proceeding to the discharge of the expropriation act in favour of the *Società Strade Ferrate Meridionali*, the State, having possession of the land concerned, examined the relevant conditions and opportunities. In this phase an initial estimation of the goods was based on the extension, nature and economic destination of the property. That resulted in the assignment of a value which usually changed over the course of the full procedure. In fact, the expropriation gave rise to the recognition of compensation that consisted of, besides the estimation of the land value, a measure of compensation designed to reimburse the landowners for their economic discomfort in the period between the possession of the land and its expropriation.

There were about twenty municipalities interested in the construction of the Abruzzo railway line, some of which were not located directly on the coast. Initially, the provinces of Teramo and Chieti were involved but in 1927 the province of Pescara joined. The locations through which the Adriatic line runs, as well as the dates of the expropriations, are indicated in Table 1.

Although the construction of the infrastructure was brought about very quickly, it needed different typologies of intervention: the first, which consisted of track designing and positioning of the track materials was finished in the 1860s and the expropriations of land were quite consistent, as shown in Table 2.

Our data processing indicates that the area expropriated was about 2 million square meters, equivalent to Lit 350,000 of that period[14].

---

for inclinations of the ground: the obstacles of the watercourses were overcome without adopting particular measures". See Gorgoni Lanzetta, Millevolte, "Da un nodo ferroviario nascita di una grande città", *art. cit.*, pp. 67–68.

13 *Ibid.*

14 It is important to state that many proceedings did not bear the exact extension of the land expropriated but only their assessments. Therefore, we have proceeded to a general estimate of the missing areas which have been expropriated.

Table 1. Municipalities of the Abruzzo Region Interested in the Expropriation for the Construction of the Adriatic Rail Line

Municipality	Date
Colonnella	1864, 1863, 1862
Tortoreto	1864, 1866, 1922
Giulianova	1864, 1863, 1900
Montepagano	1861
Mutignano	1865
Atri	1861, 1863
Silvi	1865, 1908, 1915
Città Sant'Angelo	1865, 1886
Montesilvano	1865, 1900, 1900
Castellamare Adriatico	1865, 1870, 1872, 1873
Pescara	1861, 1912, 1908
Francavilla al mare	1864, 1955
Torrevecchia Teatina	1956
Ortona a mare	1864, 1903, 1916, 1919
San Vito Chietino	1954, 1865, 1863
Rocca San Giovanni	1865, 1864, 1917, 1923, 1924, 1926, 1927
Fossacesia	1889, 1907, 1956
Torino di Sangro	190..., 1865, 1864, 1865, 1924
Paglieta	1954
Vasto	1865, 1921, 1920
San Salvo	1907, 1922

Source: Data processing from: State Archive of Teramo (henceforth: ASTe), Prefettura, Serie I, Categoria XXI, Inventario II, *Elenchi e Verbali*, buste 2-3-4-5-6, and the State archive of Chieti (henceforth: ASCh), Prefettura, Categoria XXI, I Versamento, *Elenchi e verbali*, buste 133-134, IV Versamento, buste 154-156-157-158-159-160-161-162-163, V Versamento, buste 251-253-255 and 256.

The interventions performed after the opening of the line were varied but the only objective was to stabilize the railway; indeed, immediately after the inauguration of the Ortona-Foggia track on 9 November 1863 in the presence of Vittorio Emanuele II, the Società Strade Ferrate Meridionali had to intervene with settlements and consolidations, in particular on those tracks close to the

Table 2. Expropriations during the First Phase of the Construction of the Adriatic Railway (1861–1865)

Municipalities	Dates	Interventions	Lands expropriated (m^2)	Indemnity (lire)
Colonnella	1864	Railway construction		41,100.79
	1862	Ramp construction	1,392.02	2,798.77
	1863	Railway shift	1,331.98	391.71
Tortoreto	1864	Railway construction	132,248.74	21,746.75
Giulianova	1864	Railway construction	45,394.62	23,486.98
	1863	Ramp construction	1,863.26	566.89
Montepagano	1861	Railway construction	172,753.27	24,916.79
Mutignano	1865	Railway construction	345,838.09	15,671.18
Atri	1861	Railway construction	66,073.47	2,008.86
Silvi	1862	Railway construction	45,107.44	17,065.98
Città Sant'Angelo	1865	Railway construction		8,388.90
Montesilvano	1861	Railway construction	76,284.68	9,086.37
Castellamare Adriatico	1863	Railway construction	61,392.80	17,112.93
Pescara	1861	Railway construction		13,749.18
Francavilla al mare	1864	Railway construction	202,944.00	32,301.38
Ortona a mare	1864	Railway construction	65,642.90	24,882.30
San Vito Chietino	1865	Railway construction	34,691.00	55,294.07
Rocca San Giovanni	1864	Railway construction	225,502.78	11,952.77
Torino di Sangro	1864	Railway construction	58,516.00	9,138.31
	1865	Railway construction		5,350.71
Vasto	1865	Railway construction	39,577.00	10,550.07
Total			1,576,554.05	337,011.62

Source: Data processing from: ASTe, Prefettura, Serie I, Categoria XXI, Inventario II, *Elenchi e Verbali*, b. 2-3-4-5-6, and ASCh, Prefettura, Categoria XXI, I Versamento, *Elenchi e verbali*, b. 133-134, IV Versamento, b. 154-156-157-158-159-160-161-162-163, V Versamento, b. 251-253-255 and 256.

coast and exposed to sea storms[15]. In Table 3 there is a synthesis of expropriations for these interventions.

Table 3. Expropriations for the Consolidation of the Adriatic Railway (1863–1865)

Municipalities	Dates	Interventions	Expropriated area (m^2)	Indemnity (lire)
Montesilvano	1863	Ramp and guard box construction	3,295.44	265.57
	1865	Railway premises construction and stagnant water reclamation	12,683.51	6,493.64
Castellamare Adriatico	1863	Ramp and guard box construction	2,005.85	812.43
Ortona a mare	1864	Consolidation works	59,073.38	9,953.55
	1864	Consolidation works	45,471.92	6,678.00
San Vito Chietino	1863	Layout hill overhanging tunnel	1,484.03	278.79
	1865	entrance Realization cliff		2,100.00
Torino di Sangro	1865	Station structure	2,951.00	639.26
Total			126,965.13	27,221.24

Source: Data processing from: ASTe, Prefettura, Serie I, Categoria XXI, Inventario II, *Elenchi e Verbali*, b. 2-6, and ASCh, Prefettura, Categoria XXI, I C Versamento, *Elenchi e verbali*, b. 133-134, IV Versamento, b. 154-156-157-158-159-160-161-162-163, V Versamento, b. 251-253-255 and 256.

Railway stabilization required the expropriation of over 125,000 square meters of land, in terms of money this amounted to 28,000 Italian Lire. Nevertheless, the stabilization of the Adriatic line did not guarantee the success of the

15 The Società Strade Ferrate Meridionali actually finished the work on schedule in order to collect the cash prize equivalent to one million Lire allotted by the government; although a few sections were only provisional. For further depth-ins refer to: Cioci Adriano, *Storia delle ferrovie in Abruzzo dalle origini ai giorni nostri*, L'Aquila, Adelmo Polla Editore, 1997, p. 21.

Table 4. Expropriations for Improvement and Upgrading of the Railway Sections (1866–1924)

Municipalities	Dates	Interventions	Land expropriation (m^2)	Indemnity (lire)
Tortoreto	1866	Railway stand construction in Vibrata	2,204.49	529.14
	1922	Rural rail station construction	1,619.00	4,857.00
Giulianova	1900	Rail extension at station	979.30	714.65
Atri	1866	Extension railway bridge	827.50	75.42
Silvi	1908	Change of destination railway station in Silvi	1,078.00	1,508.71
	1915	Construction goods station and third railway track	2,021.50	4,981.40
Città S. Angelo	1886	Construction road parallel to railway line	369.00	110.70
Montesilvano	1866	Construction service buildings and yards	7,978.43	508.13
	1900	Extension second line	2,590.82	681.63
Castellamare	1866	Construction of service buildings and forecourts	18,503.24	8,451.13
Pescara	1872	Extension station forecourt in Pescara	1,374.35	297.81
	1873	Work for transport towards north of the level crossing	46,791.86	17,466.55
	1908	Different kinds of work	1,430.00	740.00
	1915	Different kinds of work	2,509.00	5,696.00
Fossacesia	1907	Station refurbishment	624.16	332.74
	1907	Water station refurbishment	1,003.00	2,989.33
Torino di Sangro	1924	Pit and tunnel construction	3,919.00	647.45
Vasto	1921	Expropriation aquifers to supply station	46.11	2,923.00
San Salvo	1907	Extension third line for freight service expansion	3,318.00	445.96
Total			97,567.76	49,099.75

Source: Data processing from: ASTe, Prefettura, Serie I, Categoria XXI, Inventario II, *Elenchi e Verbali*, b. 2-3-4-5-6, and ASCh, Prefettura, Categoria XXI, I Versamento, *Elenchi e verbali*, b. 133-134, IV Versamento, b. 154-156-157-158-159-160-161-162-163, V Versamento, b. 251-253-255 and 256.

system, and there were to be more interventions and the infrastructure had to undergo improvement work and upgrading between the end of the nineteenth and the beginning of the twentieth century. These measures had to be taken to accompany and support the trade networks that were growing both along the coast and in the hinterlands. Table 4 outlines the expropriation for this reason.

Throughout this first phase, which took over fifty years, 98,000 square meters of land was expropriated at a cost of 50 thousand lire, giving the railway line its present "look". From the second half of the twentieth century the Adriatic railway network has been upgraded through electrification interventions; the following table indicates the relative expropriations.

Table 5. Expropriations for the Modernisation of the Adriatic Railway (1954–1955)

Municipalities	Dates	Interventions	Area expropriated (m^2)	Indemnity (Lire)
Francavilla al mare	1955	Railway electrification	13,310.00	90,195.00
Ortona	1954	Railway electrification	166,791.00	
Fossacesia	1955	Railway electrification	50,585.00	189,158.00
Total			230,686.00	279,353.00

Source: Data processing from: ASTe, Prefettura, Serie I, Categoria XXI, Inventario II, *Elenchi e Verbali*, b. 2-3-4-5-6, and ASCh, Prefettura, Categoria XXI, I Versamento, *Elenchi e verbali*, b. 133-134, IV Versamento, b. 154-156-157-158-159-160-161-162-163, V Versamento, b. 251-253-255 and 256.

The cost for the electrification works on the 230 thousand m^2 of land occupied was approximately 280,000 lire. During this stage, however, the Cassa per il Mezzogiorno (Fund for South Italy) had a decisive role financing the electrification works in the Bari-Pescara section, and this was completed in 1957[16]. It is also important to remember that during this period the institution

16 The expenditure supported by Cassa per il Mezzogiorno for the electrification works of the Bari-Foggia-Pescara railway line, including equipment, facilities, and other services, as well as the locomotives, amounted to 20 billion lire. For further details refer to: Serra

of expropriation was not the only one to be used; more than once, the State granted itself the right of easement which provided a "perpetual" compensation as payment to the landowners.

Table 6. Extension of Lands Subjected to Perpetual Servitude (1956)

Municipalities	Dates	Lands subjected to easement	Indemnity (lire)
Torrevecchia Teatina	1956	53,554.00	207,866.00
Fossacesia	1956	99,792.00	316,809.00
Paglieta	1956	18,753.00	50,667.00
Total		172,099.00	575,342.00

Source: Data processing from: ASCh, Prefettura, Categoria XXI, V Versamento, *Elenco Torrevecchia Teatina del 1956,* b. 255; *Elenco Fossacesia del 1956,* b. 251; *Elenco Paglieta del 1956,* b. 256.

As shown in Table 6, the landowners who were given an easement compensation lived in hill towns adjacent the coast; it was not convenient for the State to buy the land given the ancillary works so they simply obtained the use of the land instead. Over 170,000 square meters of land (at a cost of 600,000 lire) was subjected to easement for electrification works. The location of the Adriatic railway line along the coast and the particular morphology of the land required continuous intervention and maintenance. The necessary stabilization and containment of landslides required further expropriations (see Table 7):

The most frequent interventions were related to consolidation and reforestation, settling landslides and making excavations designed to protect the railway line[17]. For this reason, in the early twentieth century, the expropriated land amounted to 150,000 m^2, at a cost of almost 100,000 lire. In point of fact, the

Paolo, "Opere ferroviarie e marittime", in AA.VV., *Cassa per il Mezzogiorno. Dodici anni 1950–1962, La viabilità,* vol. IV, Bari, Laterza, 1962, pp. 131–140.

17 The consolidation works concerned the groundwater landslides which occurred in close proximity to Ortona, at km 373,400 and km 382 in Rocca San Giovanni. ASCh, Prefettura, Categoria XXI, IV Versamento, *Verbale di esproprio per lavori di consolidamento della falda franosa ai km 373,400 e 374'285 della Bologna-Otranto,* b. 157, fascicolo 2894, and Prefettura, Categoria XXI, IV Versamento, *Verbale di esproprio per lavori di consolidamento*

Table 7. Expropriations for Consolidation Works during the Twentieth Century

Municipalities	Dates	Interventions	Expropriated area (m2)	Indemnity (lire)
Ortona	1919	Groundwater and landslides	602.00	1,099.35
Rocca San	1917	Groundwater and landslides	3,373.20	918.79
Giovanni	1923	Consolidation and reforestation	44,029.00	21,001.90
	1924	Consolidation and reforestation	105.39	6,148.07
	1926	Consolidation and reforestation	47,727.00	32,711.00
	1927	Consolidation and reforestation	44,687.00	30,842.10
Vasto		Construction guard ditches	3,823.00	216.45
San Salvo	1922	Construction guard ditches	3,858.00	2,600.00
Total			148,204.59	95,537.66

Sources: Data processing from: ASTe, Prefettura, Serie I, Categoria XXI, Inventario II, *Elenchi e Verbali*, b. 2-3-4-5-6, and ASCh, Prefettura, Categoria XXI, I Versamento, *Elenchi e verbali*, b. 133-134, IV Versamento, b. 154-156-157-158-159-160-161-162-163, V Versamento, b. 251-253-255 and 256.

Adriatic railway line along with its installation and subsequent interventions, needed a great quantity of expropriated land and in the following table there is a summary of all the phases of expropriation.

The area expropriated for public use consisted of nearly 2,200 000 square meters of land[18], with capital of over 800,000 lire allocated over time as compensation[19] (see Table 8). Although all the expropriations were carried out to allow different interventions and to meet the needs of general interest, there were 2,200 square kilometres of land expropriated for only 123 km of actual railway line. In fact the land expropriated allowed not only for the line but for accompanying facets of infrastructure and facilities such as stations, parking areas, warehouses, etc.

della frana al km 382 della linea Castellamare Adriatico-Foggia fra le stazioni di S. Vito, Lanciano e Fossacesia, documento n. 158153, b. 162, fascicolo 2985.

18 ASTe, Prefettura, Serie I, Categoria XXI, Inv. II, *Elenchi e Verbali*, b. 2-3-4-5-6, and ASCh, Prefettura, Categoria XXI, I Versamento, *Elenchi e verbali*, b. 133-134, IV Versamento, b. 154-156-157-158-159-160-161-162-163, V Versamento, b. 251-253-255 and 256.

19 *Ibid.*

Table 8. Summary of Expropriations for the Adriatic Railway Line (1861–1956)

Municipalities	Dates	Interventions	Land expropriations (m^2)	Indemnity (lire)
Colonnella	1864	Railway construction		41,100.79
	1862	Ramp construction	1,392.02	2,798.77
	1863	Railway shift	1,331.98	391.71
Tortoreto	1864	Railway construction	132,248.74	21,746.75
	1866	Railway stand construction in Vibrata	2,204.49	529.14
	1922	Rural rail station construction	1,619.00	4,857.00
Giulianova	1864	Railway construction	45,394.62	23,486.98
	1863	Ramp construction	1,863.26	566.89
	1900	Rail extension at station	979.30	714.65
Montepagano	1861	Railway construction	172,753.27	24,916.79
Mutignano	1865	Railway construction	345,838.09	15,671.18
Atri	1861	Railway construction	66,073.47	2,008.86
	1866	Extension railway bridge	827.50	75.42
Silvi	1862	Railway construction	45,107.44	17,065.98
	1908	Change of destination railway station in Silvi	1,078.00	1,508.71
	1915	Construction goods station and third railway track	2,021.50	4,981.40
Città Sant'Angelo	1865	Railway construction		8,388.90
	1886	Construction road parallel to railway	246.00	110.70
Montesilvano	1861	Railway construction	76,284.68	9,086.37
	1863	Ramp and guard box construction	3,295.44	265.57
	1865	Railway premises construction and stagnant water reclamation	12,683.51	6,493.64
	1866	Buildings and forecourts construction	7,978.43	508.13
	1900	Extension second line	2,590.82	681.63

Table 8 continued

Municipalities	Dates	Interventions	Land expropriations (m²)	Indemnity (lire)
Castellamare Adriatico	1863	Railway construction	61,392.80	17,112.93
	1863	Ramp and guard box construction	2,005.85	812.43
	1866	Buildings and forecourts construction	18,503.24	8,451.13
Pescara	1861	Railway construction		13,749.18
	1872	Extension forecourt in Pescara	1,374.35	297.81
	1873	Work for transport towards north of the level crossing	46,791.86	17,466.55
	1908	Different works	1,430.00	740.00
	1915	Different works	2,509.00	5,696.00
Francavilla al mare	1864	Railway construction	202,944.00	32,301.38
	1955	Railway electrification	13,310.00	90,195.00
Ortona a mare	1864	Railway construction	65,642.90	24,882.30
	1864	Consolidation works	59,073.38	9,953.55
	1864	Consolidation works	45,471.92	6,678.00
	1916	Extension station	14,950.00	9,375.68
	1919	Groundwater and landslides	602.00	1,099.35
	1954	Railway electrification	166,791.00	
Fossacesia	1907	Station structure	624.16	332.74
	1907	Water station refurbishment	1,003.00	2,989.33
	1955	Railway electrification	50,585.00	189,158.00
San Vito Chietino	1865	Railway construction	34,691.00	55,294.07
	1863	Layout hill overhanging tunnel entrance	1,484.03	278.79
	1865	Cliff structure		2,100.00
Rocca San Giovanni	1864	Railway construction	225,502.78	11,952.77
	1917	Groundwater and landslides	3,373.20	918.79
	1923	Consolidation and reforestation	44,029.00	21,001.90

Table 8 continued

Municipalities	Dates	Interventions	Land expropriations (m²)	Indemnity (lire)
Rocca San Giovanni (continued)	1924	Consolidation and reforestation	105.39	6,148.07
	1926	Consolidation and reforestation	47,727.00	32,711.00
	1927	Consolidation and reforestation	44,687.00	30,842.10
San Salvo	1907	Extension third line for freight service expansion	3,318.00	445.96
	1922	Construction guard ditches	3,858.00	2,600.00
Torino di Sangro	1864	Railway construction	58,516.00	9,138.31
	1865	Railway construction		5,350.71
	1865	Station structure	2,951.00	639.26
	1924	Pit and tunnel construction	3,919.00	647.45
Vasto	1865	Railway construction	39,577.00	10,550.07
	1921	Expropriations aquifers to supply station	46.11	2,923.00
		Construction guard ditches	3,823.00	216.45
Total			2,196,423.53	813,006.02

Source: Data processing from: ASTe, Prefettura, Serie I, Categoria XXI, Inventario II, *Elenchi e Verbali*, b. 2-3-4-5-6, and ASCh, Prefettura, Categoria XXI, I Versamento, *Elenchi e verbali*, b. 133-134, IV Versamento, b. 154-156-157-158-159-160-161-162-163, V Versamento, b. 251-253-255 and 256.

The activities of expropriations were not simple to carry out and complex procedure requests as well as long legal fights were supported by the valuations of experts. In most cases landowners were completely against expropriations: almost all the dispossessed contested the meagre compensations in view of the loss of a part of ownership which represented an integral part of their assets and that resulted in a reduction in income value. This kind of opposition from the landowners assumed the form of a contrasting actions by small and medium landowners towards the railway companies, supported by the government through the important institutional role of the prefect who was called in, not only for the discharge of the definite expropriation but also during the procedural phase which concluded with the acceptation of the compensation[20]. This amount was subjected to many controversies between the dispossessed landowners and the prefect, and there were many disputes relating to the iniquity of the money compensations as an adequate estimation of the values[21].

Furthermore, we must not forget that the lands expropriated were cultivated and they represented for many farming families their only means of survival, as well being part of the family assets. Most of the lands situated on the hills had different productive capacities compared to those near the sea, which were basically sandy. In the municipality of Chieti the lands expropriated were cultivated with olive groves and vineyards, products of a certain significance in local farming. Table 9 shows the typology of the lands expropriated.

20 Tramontano Luigi (a cura di), *Codice delle leggi amministrative*, Milano, Hoepli, 1998, p. 1339, 1347.

21 The estimations of the compensations were calculated through parameters which differed according to the expert. For example, the land expropriated near Rocca San Giovanni for consolidation works due to landslides was designated as "industrial", but because it involved the extraction of clay it was considered primarily rural and was therefore estimated at less than its real economic value, resulting in low compensation. ASCh, Prefettura, Categoria XXI, IV V Versamento, *Verbale del Prefetto*, b. 154, fascicolo 2832–2848.

Table 9. Typology of the Lands Expropriated

Municipalities	Typology lands expropriated
Colonnella	Cultivated
Tortoreto	Cultivated – uncultivated
Giulianova	Cultivated
Monterpagano	Cultivated – sandy
Mutignano	Uncultivated – pasturage
Atri	Cultivated – sandy
Silvi	Sandy
Città Sant'Angelo	Cultivated
Montesilvano	Cultivated – sandy
Castellamare	Cultivated – sandy
Pescara	Cultivated – vineyards
Francavilla al mare	Cultivated – vineyards
Torrevecchia Teatina	Cultivated
Ortona	Cultivated – vineyards – olive groves
San Vito Chietino	Cultivated – uncultivated
Rocca San Giovanni	Cultivated – olive groves – uncultivated
Fossacesia	Cultivated – vineyards – olive groves
Torino di Sangro	Cultivated
Paglieta	Cultivated – vineyards
Vasto	Cultivated – olive groves
San Salvo	Uncultivated

Source: Data processing from: ASTe, Prefettura, Serie I, Categoria XXI, Inventario II, *Elenchi e Verbali*, b. 2-3-4-5-6, and ASCh, Prefettura, Categoria XXI, I Versamento, *Elenchi e verbali*, b. 133-134, IV Versamento, b. 154-156-157-158-159-160-161-162-163, V Versamento, b. 251-253-255 and 256.

It is obvious that most of the lands that underwent the disposition were intended for typical coastal cultivation, in particular for wine and oil production[22]; only a limited area of land was sandy and therefore it was uncultivated. Figure 1 shows this distinction.

Figure 1. Typology of the Lands Expropriated

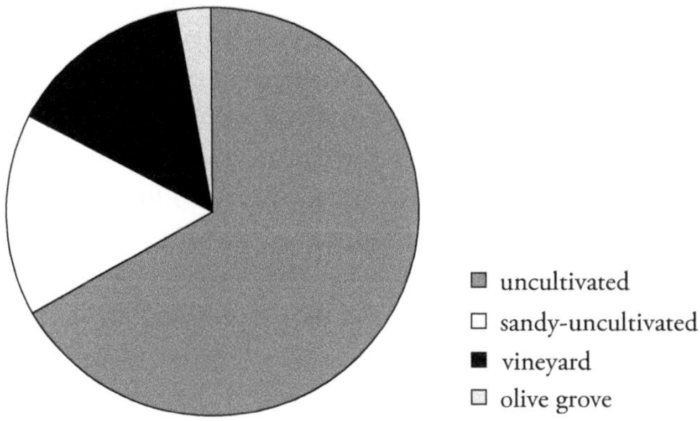

Source: Data processing from: ASTe, Prefettura, Serie I, Categoria XXI, Inventario II, *Elenchi e Verbali*, b. 2-3-4-5-6, and ASCh, Prefettura, Categoria XXI, I Versamento, *Elenchi e verbali*, b. 133-134, IV Versamento, b. 154-156-157-158-159-160-161-162-163, V Versamento, b. 251-253-255 and 256.

Furthermore, as mentioned, the primary objective of the expropriations, which conformed to the principal of public use, was not the economical and industrial development of the region. Indeed, this attitude was confirmed by two of the most important industries of the territory: Krios, a well-established company from Turin which produced refrigeration for wine and must and Nazareno Verrocchio furnace, a factory manufacturing building materials. The two factories were located between the municipalities of Castellamare Adriatico and Pescara[23].

22 Istituto Nazionale di Economia Agraria, *La distribuzione della proprietà fondiaria in Italia: Abruzzi e Molise*, Roma, Edizioni Italiane, 1947, pp. X–XI.

23 Krios industry stretched over an area of around 8600 square meters and it produced on average 100 thousand hectolitres of wine and must, while the Verrocchio furnace industry

The expropriations of the two industrial sectors in the first decade of the twentieth century were designed to facilitate the expansion and general layout of the Castellamare Adriatico station. The loss of the industries was considerable in terms of prestige as well as economically, and more given that Italy was going through the process of industrialization to which the Abruzzo region could not fully contribute. The two leading industries on the market at that time were: Società Applicazioni Frigorifiche Krios, the first industry in Italy using low temperature methods for the wine ageing process; and Hoffmann furnace, belonging to Nazareno Verrocchio, which boasted a production of 5 million pieces per year and was very much esteemed abroad[24].

As to the sum of money-compensation proposed to the two industries new changes of rules, enacted after the period of Unification, were taken into account: estimation criteria were set out as in Law 25 June 1865 which allowed the expert the discretion of estimation according to "the prices in free negotiation", following the substitution of other criteria as to Law 7 July 1907 which instead provided the estimation of the property based on the "average of the commercial value and the aggregation rents in the last decade, as long as they were dated to the corresponding annual rent"[25]. Essentially, the damage was to be considered on the basis of the commercial value and the loss of profit in a ten-year rental period[26].

covered an area of 9,000 square meters and produced around 5 million bricks on average. For further detail refer to: Benegiamo Marcello, "Le economie parallele. Pescara e la Valle dal decollo al primato (1890–1940)", in AA.VV., *Era Pescara,* Pescara, Pierrecongress, 1993, pp. 140–142.

24 ASCh, Prefettura, Serie I, Categoria XXI, IV Versamento, 1908–1936, *Relazione di perizia circa la stima dei beni siti nei comuni di Pescara e Castellamare Adriatico da espropriarsi per pubblica utilità dalle Ferrovie dello Stato*, b. 160, fascicolo 2941.

25 ASCh, Prefettura, Serie I, Categoria XXI, IV Versamento, 1908–1936, *Relazione di perizia circa la stima dei beni siti nei comuni di Pescara e Castellamare Adriatico da espropriarsi per pubblica utilità dalle Ferrovie dello Stato*, b. 160, fasc. 2941.

26 From the survey Krios was entitled to a market price equal to 31,279 40 lire and a cadastral revenue equal to 960 30 lire while the industry belonging to Verrocchio had a market price equal to 32,648 30 lire and a cadastral revenue equal to 9,104 87 lire. The true value of the goods expropriated were calculated on the average of the two evaluations and according to other supplementary elements. *Ibid.*

Figure 2. Cadastral Plan of the Sites of the Two Industries: Krios and Verrocchio.

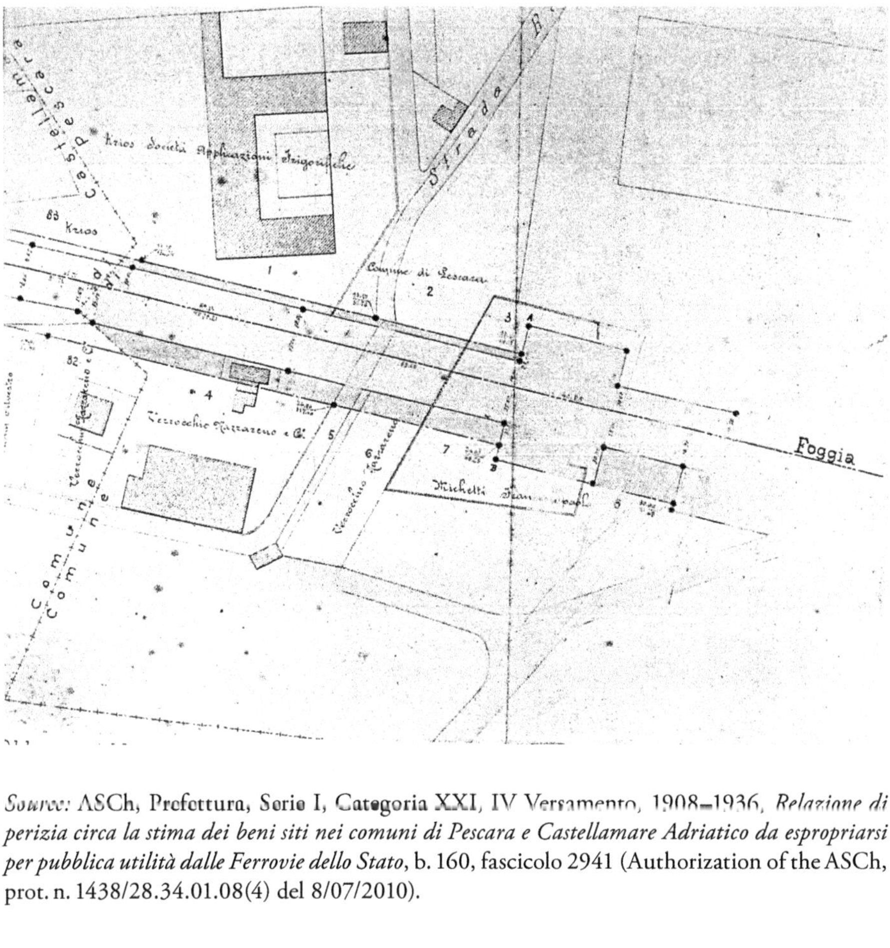

Source: ASCh, Prefettura, Serie I, Categoria XXI, IV Versamento, 1908–1936, *Relazione di perizia circa la stima dei beni siti nei comuni di Pescara e Castellamare Adriatico da espropriarsi per pubblica utilità dalle Ferrovie dello Stato*, b. 160, fascicolo 2941 (Authorization of the ASCh, prot. n. 1438/28.34.01.08(4) del 8/07/2010).

During the expropriations both industries pointed out more than once that the economic damage they underwent was caused not only by the loss of the property of the building but by the interruption of the highly profitable production process. The indemnities relative to the expropriation of the industrial sites were inferior to the real estimation, although the property estimation criteria were considered somewhat antiquated and were set as shown in Table 10.

Table 10. Property Expropriated Related to the Industries: Krios and Verrocchio

Company	Property	Indemnity
Krios	Parcel no. 1	632.85
	Parcel no. 83	940.00
Total		1,572.85
Verrocchio	Parcel no. 6	595.13
	Parcel no. 4	3,430.52
	Parcel no. 82	466.67
Total		4,492.32

Source: ASCh Prefettura, Serie I, Categoria XXI, IV Versamento, 1908–1936, *Relazione di perizia circa la stima dei beni siti nei comuni di Pescara e Castellamare Ad. da espropriarsi per pubblica utilità dalle Ferrovie dello Stato*, b. 160, fascicolo 2941.

Fortunately the expropriations of the two industries, Krios and Verrocchio, were isolated cases. Consequently, we can confirm that the Adriatic railway supported the economic development of the region through providing a direct connection with the rest of the country and it intensified trade along the coast as well as in the hinterlands.

There were drawbacks due to the expropriations, however. For example, the environmental damage to the municipality of Pescara was significant; in fact, following the expropriations some areas were used to provide rubble for the construction of the track and at the end of the completion of the railway track those areas were abandoned and turned into pools of water and marshes by the rain, further damaging the already marginal coasts exposed to severe conditions[27].

However, the expropriations also had positive effects on the financial framework of the region, thanks to the unexpected and immediate sum of cash available to be given to landowners, who could benefit from the money in a timely fashion.

27 ASCh, *Atti del consiglio Provinciale di Abruzzo Citeriore*, 1862–1863, Chieti, Tip. Del Vecchio, 1863, p. 11 ff.

The overall benefits of the introduction of the new infrastructure were not immediately evident, however. The full practical value of the developments went unrealised for a number of years as they were under-utilised. The railway was not fully used for the transportation of people or for trade. The initial difficulties related to the instability of the railway network, the failure of the railway station to receive goods as well as the limited number of regional connections.

From 1879, however, the change from mail to passenger transport opened a new era, characterized by important trade traffic and a major tourist resort development which modified the aspect of many local coastline towns[28]: new hotels, better connections with the hinterlands and a major awareness of the wider economic climate marked the passage of the Abruzzo region into the twentieth century[29].

Even the employment situation benefited from the significant commitment of the government: new categories of workmen such as porters, warehouse keepers and carters were employed in the new railway stations, which also attracted the attention of middle-class merchants and a number of adventurers in search of easy profits[30]. Another less positive effect of the costal development was its contribution to the migration of workers from the mountainous areas of the region, intensifying the phenomenon of the depopulation of the hinterlands already compromised by a difficult economic situation.

The expropriations, therefore, in the light of the sacrifice of individuals, brought changes to the Adriatic railway: from a simple network, as it was conceived at the beginning, to an important instrument of economic and social growth for the territory. The railway line has, over 150 years, changed from a simple rail infrastructure to a more complex and appropriate system, characterized by logistic and commercial supports projected towards the future.

28 Cioci, *Storia delle ferrovie in Abruzzo*, *op. cit.*, p. 25.

29 For further-in-depths refer to: Pierucci Paola, "Strutture balneari ed attività economiche lungo la costa", in Di Vittorio Antonio, Barciela Lopez Carlos, Massa Paola (a cura di), *Il patrimonio industriale marittimo in Italia e Spagna. Strutture e territorio*, Genova, De Ferrari, 2009, pp. 364–365.

30 For further in-depths regarding effects of the railway in the city of Pescara refer to: Gorgoni Lanzetta, Millevolte, "Da un nodo ferroviario nascita di una grande città", *art. cit.*, pp. 76–77.

Expropriation as a Planning Tool. Limitations and Contradictions: The Town Plan for the Central Neighbourhoods of Padua (1921–1927)

Stefano Zaggia

Throughout the nineteenth century Padua maintained an urban structure that was almost identical to the one that emerged at the time of the fall of the Venetian State. The urban agglomeration did not undergo major expansion and continued to remain stable within the walls mapped out in the first half of the 16th century. In fact, the choices made in the modern era were to have a strong impact on the city's subsequent development: the defensive system was not only extensive (encompassing around eleven kilometres of fortifications), but almost hald of the enclosed area was undeveloped (cultivated land, fields, gardens). On the threshold of the 20th century, the city was still entirely within the walls, maintained as a customs frontier and characterised by large empty spaces which could be used for a building expansion project, but this solution was never considered. Until 1901 the city continued to have one of the lowest population densities in Italy, second only to Reggio Calabria. The lack of necessity meant that the possibility of completely demolishing the walls to make room for urban expansion was never taken into consideration[1].

The overall urban structure of the city, therefore, only witnessed a few evolutionary events during the 19th century. An initial important change was, however, the creation of the Padua-Mestre railway line (1842), the first section of the line connecting the territories of Lombardy-Veneto from Milan to Venice. The works led to the construction of a station inside the city walls, an initiative which involved projecting an image of the city beyond the magisterial line of the fortifications. This facilitated the creation of an industrial area close to the railway junction, but at the same time created problems in terms of how

1 Zaggia Stefano, "Dis-armare e attrezzare la città: mura, strade, edilizia a Padova tra Otto e Novecento", in *Città e storia*, IV, n. 2 (2009), pp. 387–401.

to properly and functionally connect the city centre with the new important infrastructural area[2].

After the unification of Italy and following the national law of June 1865, the city immediately equipped itself with a *Piano regolatore edilizio* (Town Plan) that was finally approved in 1872. This plan outlined some of the main developments needed to organise the road system and internal urban spaces. The report accompanying the graphs only put forward considerations on the internal structure of the city's urban fabric. Nonetheless, this seemed to set the tone for the ideas that would form the basis of the subsequent town plan for the period following the First World War[3]. The designated commission, in fact, did not see any need to expand outside the usual limits of the urban aggregate. The commission concentrated its attention on modernising the narrow streets of the city. They were "extremely irregular and unruly beyond all description". To be made even "adequate and passable … [they] would first need to be almost completely demolished".[4]. However, it was decided to make only limited improvements to the roads and to set guidelines which would outline how the transformation of city buildings was to proceed. The commission's highly negative assessment of the physical characteristics of the city's buildings continued to be a key factor in the subsequent development of urban planning.

Only some of the building works set out in the Building Plan of 1872 were implemented in the years to follow, whereas other unplanned major urban operations were executed, such as the re-routing of a section of the river near the church of S. Sofia[5]. In the meantime, the city entered into a phase of rapid expansion in demographic terms (the population almost doubled) and socio-economic terms. At the threshold of the new century, an issue which had been neglected by the previous planning operations resurfaced: the establishment of a straight connection between the train station and the city centre, gathered

2 Puppi Lionello, Universo Mario, *Padova,* Roma Bari, Laterza, 1982, pp. 213–217; Zaggia, "Dis- armare", *art. cit.*

3 Puppi, Universo, *Padova, op. cit.,* pp. 229–235; Calabi Donatella, "L'urbanistica di fine Ottocento in un ventennio di attività della Giunta Municipale", in Zucconi Guido, Castellani Francesca (a cura di) *Camillo Boito. Un'architettura per l'Italia Unita,* catalogo della mostra, Marsilio, Venezia, 2000, pp. 35–39.

4 *Commissione del Piano Regolatore della città di Padova. Relazione,* Padova, 1873.

5 Donvito Vincenza Cinzia, "Progetti a scala urbana", in Zucconi, Castellani (a cura di) *Camillo Boito, op. cit.,* pp. 47–49.

around the historical piazzas, with the City Council, the Café Pedrocchi and the University. This is how the idea to create a wide and straight road axis for connecting the train station and the piazzas was born. The works to create the *rettifilo* (straight stretch of road), later called the Corso del Popolo, began in 1905[6]. They involved cutting away a large part of the wall curtain, the building of a bridge and the demolition of building sectors through small operations of expropriation and direct purchase. Deeply affecting the urban structure, this new directive modified the traditional entry route into the city and ultimately obscured the visage of the urban limits that was maintained for centuries by the northern curtain.

This led to the creation of an affluent strip along the new large road axis which was characterised by the construction of houses for middle to upper class people, the introduction of new public buildings (Savings Bank and Post Office) and new services (garages)[7]. The results were mixed: on the one hand, the new axis effectively met the need to connect vital parts of the city, but on the other hand it did not solve the problems of relations between urban elements which were in competition because of incompatible structural scales and functions. This conflict was highlighted in 1927 by Antonio Nezi who defined the Corso del Popolo as "An arrow pointing directly at the heart of the city"[8].

The above-mentioned operations provide a background against which it is possible to classify and define the town planning proposals formulated in the period following the First World War. As already observed, the Plan for Padua is interesting because of the confrontation inherent in the aim of catering for the needs which were presumed to characterise modern life in the old city[9]. In some way this case study is paradigmatic due to the way the debate on the city evolved in Italy, suspended between integral conservation and radical

6 Universo Mario, "Padova Liberty", *Storia della città,* n. 3 (1978), pp. 49–66; Puppi, Universo, *Padova, op. cit.*, p. 246.

7 Universo Mario, "L'architettura della 'Padova nova'", Puppi Lionello, Zuliani Fulvio (a cura di), *Padova. case e Palazzi*, Vicenza, Neri Pozza, 1977, pp. 271–295, pp. 287–291.

8 Nezi Antonio, "Sistemazioni urbane e questioni edilizie: Padova, il piano regolatore e la zona monumentale", *Emporium*, vol. LXV, 14 (1927), pp. 185–194.

9 Bottini Fabrizio, "Padova e la formazione della cultura urbanistica italiana nel periodo tra le due guerre", in *Storia Urbana*, a. XIV, n. 52 (1990), pp. 165–193.

transformation. It also marks a turning point by virtue of the fact that it became a topic of national debate.

Urban planning in the early decades of the century was based on a series of regulations proposed by Italian law of the late 19th century, and drew inspiration from a series of concrete operations that had already been executed in some of the most important Italian cities such as Florence, Milan, Naples and Venice[10]. The first technical tools for intervening on building fabrics date back to 1865 and were mainly a result of the law for the *Piano per il Risanamento della città di Napoli (Plan for the Redevelopment of the City of Naples)* of 1885[11]. This legislation triggered a debate that for decades featured a mind-set which encouraged the preservation of the historical urban environment at the expense of social health considerations. These problems could only be addressed through the complete demolition and restoration of historic buildings. In this context, expropriation was the crucial implementation tool[12].

The conception of the new plan for Padua can be traced back to 1902 when the City Council decided to set-up a commission to draft a plan for redeveloping an area on the outskirts of the city centre, near the old Jewish ghetto, situated to the south of the municipal piazzas[13]. At that time, this theme of restoration and redevelopment of the former closed Jewish neighbourhood also interested cities such as Rome, Florence and Verona[14]. In any case, attention was drawn away from this project by the start of another urban operation: the creation of a straight connection with the station, the *rettifilo* (straight section of road).

10 Zucconi Guido, *La città contesa. Dagli igienisti sanitari agli urbanisti (1855–1942)*, Milano, Jaka Book, 1989 (1999[2]); Calabi Donatella, *Storia dell'urbanistica europea*, Milano, Bruno Mondadori editore, 2008, pp. 56–58.

11 Giuntini Andrea, "Gli ingegneri sanitari e l'utopia igienista", Giuntini Andrea, Minesso Michela (a cura di), *Gli ingegneri in Italia tra '800 e '900,* Milano, Franco Angeli, 1999, pp. 117–128; Calabi, *Storia dell'urbanistica, op. cit.*, pp. 75–77; Zucconi, *La città contesa, op. cit.*, pp. 49–54.

12 Calabi, *Storia dell'urbanistica, op. cit.*, pp. 94–96; also: Calabi Donatella, *Storia della città. L'età contemporanea,* Venezia, Marsilio, 2005, pp. 125–129.

13 *Atti relativi all'approvazione del Piano regolatore edilizio,* Società Cooperativa Tipografica, Padova, 1925, pp. 9–10; Castelli Roberto, "Gli sviluppi urbanistici", in Munari Carlo (a cura di), *Padova tra le due Guerre,* cat. della mostra, Padova, Cassa di Risparmio di Padova e Rovigo, 1988, pp. 34–45.

14 Calabi, *Storia della città, op.cit.*

The theme of the Town Plan was taken up again at the end of the First World War: in the last months of 1918 the Council authorised the City Administration to include in the 1902 Redevelopment plan of the city centre a vast area situated to the north of the historical piazzas (the so-called neighbourhood of Santa Lucia), which had been partially damaged during the war. This led to the approval of a project in the following year aimed at redeveloping some blocks around the Church of Santa Lucia through demolitions, mapping of new roads and building reconstructions[15]. On this occasion, the City Council also alluded to possible agreements with private companies for executing the expropriation works required to implement the project. However, the proposal formulated was rejected by the Provincial Council who wanted a more organic scheme that could "inserito nel contesto generale della città [fit more smoothly into the overall plan for the city]"[16].

This subsequently led to the drafting of another plan – *Piano Regolatore Edilizio per il risanamento e la sistemazione di due Quartieri Centrali e per la costruzione di un quartiere giardino in località Vanzo (Town Plan for the Redevelopment and Organisation of two Central Neighbourhoods and for the construction of a garden district in the locality of Vanzo)* – by the municipal technical office, managed by Tullio Paoletti. Presented at the Council Meeting of 2 August 1921, it was immediately approved. The technical report identified the aim of the town plan: "hygienic and moral" restoration by means of "una radicale modificazione nella struttura dei Quartieri Centrali [A radical change in the structure of the Central Neighbourhoods]" involving around 110 thousand square meters[17]. It aimed at organising both zones to the north and south of the piazzas (the neighbourhood of St Lucia and the Ghetto) by demolishing (i.e. *sventrare* or "gutting out" according to health terminology) most of the existing buildings and creating two large piazzas in the middle of each neighbourhood where large road axes could converge. It also called for extending some existing piazzas (such as Piazza Garibaldi).

15 Torresini Donatella, *Padova 1509–1969 gli effetti della prassi urbanistica borghese,* Venezia-Padova, Marsilio editori, 1974, p. 64; Universo Mario, "Padova negli anni Venti", in *Storia della citta,* n. 11 (1979), pp. 63–76.

16 Quoted in Universo, "Padova negli anni Venti", *art. cit.*, p. 64.

17 *Ibidem.*

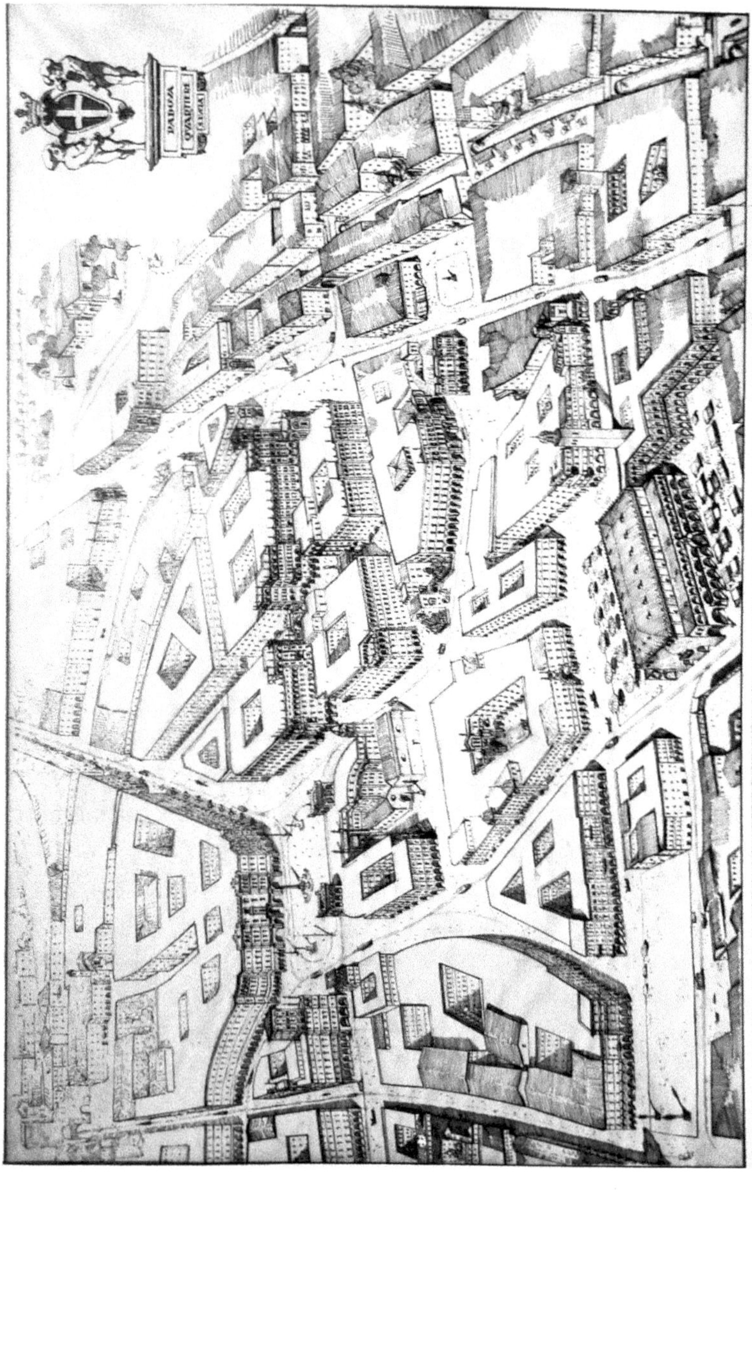

Figure 1. Town Plan of Padua (1924): Perspective View of the New Squares and Buildings

Source: Biblioteca Civica di Padova.

At the same time, plans were made to urbanise a large undeveloped area within the city walls located to the south of Prato della Valle – the area of Vanzo – in order to create a garden district in compliance with the "modern regulations" on system infrastructures: sewers, gas pipes, water, public lighting, etc. It was necessary to 'arrange a sufficient number of houses for the population evicted' from the redeveloped neighbourhoods of the city centre. It was estimated that the on-site works would take 25 years to complete: a first phase of 13 years to prepare the northern area around St Lucia and to start the works in Vanzo; a second phase of 5 years to work on the zone near Piazza delle Erbe; and a final third phase of 7 years to completely demolish and rebuild the Ghetto area[18].

The mechanism proposed to execute the works was mainly based on the tool of expropriation by zone, with explicit reference to the 1865 law and above all the 1885 law for the redevelopment of Naples[19]. In order to substantiate the reference to this legislation, the planners focused strongly on the hygiene issues that characterised the layout of the city centre. The analysis of the zones involved in the intervention, as well as the debate by the City Council, tediously highlighted the aspects of physical degradation: "luride topaie [...]abitazioni insalubri [...] strade strette [...] trivii mefitici [...] promiscuità [...] prostituzione [...] malnutrizione" *[lurid dumps [...] unhealthy homes [...] narrow streets [...] filthy crossroads [...]. Promiscuity [...] prostitution [...] malnutrition]* and the subsistence economy of these urban areas[20]. The debate that preceded the approval of the Council Meeting justified the adoption of the law for Naples as a 'preventive' measure for the possible spreading of infective diseases.

In view of the foreseeable impact of these demolition works on the consolidated urban structure, the technical report guaranteed to preserve and protect the architectural aspects of the areas to be redeveloped with a clause that in actual fact impeded its precise implementation: the protection did not include

18 [Comune di Padova], *Piano regolatore edilizio per il risanamento e la sistemazione di due quartieri centrali e per la costruzione di un 'quartiere giardino' in località 'Vanzo'*, Società Cooperativa Tipografica, Padova, 1921; Universo, "Padova negli anni Venti", *art. cit.*, pp. 65–66; Franzin Elio, *Luigi Piccinato e l'antiurbanistica a Padova 1927–1974*, Saonara (Padova), Il prato, 2004, pp. 18–19.

19 Giuntini, "Gli ingegneri sanitari", *art. cit.*, pp. 122–126.

20 *Atti relativi all'approvazione del Piano Regolatore edilizio*, Padova, Società Cooperativa Tipografica, 1925, pp. 21–23.

"those aspects that obstructed the layout of the roads"[21]. This point, relating to the protection of monuments, was ambiguous and faced some opposition from other administrations involved in the approval procedure: the provincial council meeting, in fact, asked to take into consideration the preservation of some buildings placed under the protection of the law; while the Second Section of the Upper Council for Antiques and Fine Arts also criticised the demolition of a "large part of the old city" based on a report by Gustavo Giovannoni and Ludovico Pogliaghi. Despite these objections, the plan was approved by Law No. 1043 of 23 July 1922. Some changes were introduced by the commission, mainly relating to protecting existing monuments, and requesting that the detailed intervention plans were first approved by the Undersecretary of Fine Arts[22].

To realise the Plan, therefore, the City Council entered into an agreement with a Building Corporation: APE (Società Anonima per l'Edilizia) was specifically set up and managed by the engineer Gino Peressutti, a professional operating in Padua and an advocate of the first project created in 1919[23]. Following an initial security from the Corporation in accordance with articles 12 and 13 of the Naples Law, the agreements called for the City Council to declare the central neighbourhoods and the Vanzo area as "public interest zones" in order to take advantage of the special legal conditions. The city council then committed itself to expropriate around 105,000 square meters of land in order to create the necessary infrastructure (roads, piazzas, sewers, lighting). The areas involved would remain the property of the city council. Of the areas expropriated, 43 thousand square meters were designated for public works, while around 65,500 were earmarked for "rebuilding works". According to the data provided by the technicians, the operations involved evacuating 1,961 people from a total of 769 families. Plans were also made to expropriate just over 188 thousand square metres of land in the zone of Vanzo, at a cost of 15 Italian lire/square meter, half of which would have been allocated to the construction of roads[24].

21 *Ibid.*

22 Universo, "Padova negli anni Venti", *art. cit.*, p. 68; Franzin, *Luigi Piccinato, op. cit.*, p. 20.

23 *Ibid.*; Faggioni Giuseppe, "Note sull'architettura di Gino Peressutti. Gli anni degli esordi", in Pietrogrande Enrico (a cura di), *La costruzione della città. Architettura a Padova nei primi quarant'anni del Novecento*, Saonara (Padova), Il prato, 2007, pp. 19–48.

24 Universo, "Padova negli anni Venti", *art. cit.*, pp. 65–66.

Figure 2. *Piano particolareggiato per il Quartiere di Santa Lucia* (1924). Map of St. Lucia's Neighbourhood with the Buildings to be Expropriated and Demolished and the New Blocks to be Built

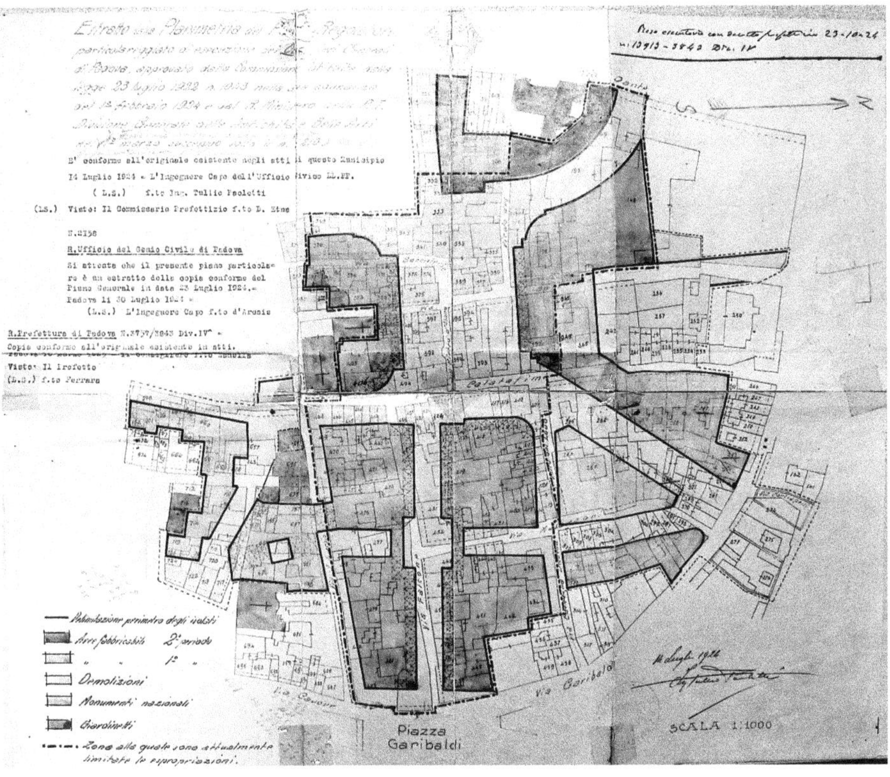

Source: Archivio Generale del Comune di Padova, *Lavori pubblici,* Piano regolatore, b. 50. Published with the kind permission of the Comune di Padova, no. 1 (17/02/2012).

With the agreements signed with the APE Building Corporation, the city council committed itself to sell the development areas for a cost equal to the average expropriation price, which was estimated at around 200 lire/square meter, and later increased to 260 lire. According to the calculations made, the operations would have seen the city council having to pay out 9.5 million lire[25].

25 *Atti relativi all'approvazione, op. cit.*, p. 29.

As in other urban planning activities, and starting from the Naples law, the role of the agreements is crucial as a decisive element for implementing the urban transformations. As highlighted by Guido Zucconi: "attraverso le convenzioni, i privati sono chiamati a dare una fisionomia a piani concepiti in termini schematici [...]. Attraverso la convenzione i municipi possono delegare ad altri gli oneri e i fastidi rappresentati dalle pratiche di esproprio e di sfratto, pur garantendosi un livello sufficiente di ordine e di qualità nella fabbricazione" [The agreements call upon private entities to give a physiognomy to plans conceived in schematic terms [...]. The city councils use the agreement to delegate to others the charges and problems represented by the practice of expropriation and eviction, even guaranteeing itself a sufficient level of order and quality in the production][26].

Therefore, the mechanism of expropriation and rebuilding, via the agreement with one single company, was not irreconcilable with Padua's political desire for reallocating economic resources to the building sector and related activities. As witnessed, the intention to stimulate the city's economic recovery was certainly present, made possible by the start-up of a building cycle[27]. The monopolistic choice, nevertheless, combined with the farfetched ambition of renewal manifested by the plan immediately brought to light its economic and urban-planning limitations. In fact, the actual value of the properties emerged right at the start of the first expropriation works as being equal to 500 lire per square meter[28].

The approval of the Town Plan with the Royal Decree made it possible to commence the implementation operations. The next move was to draft the execution plan for the first round of works to be executed in the zone of Santa Lucia. This was approved in October 1924. The Building Corporation which, according to the agreement stipulated with the City Council, was to manage all the demolition and rebuilding works, was also officially set-up (Società Anonima Padovana Edilizia). The expropriation procedures were based on estimates made according to the laws for Naples: the purchase value was set by averaging the venial value (often determined by the likely cost for the

26 Zucconi, *La città contesa*, *op. cit.*, p. 54.

27 Roverato Giorgio, "L'età contemporanea", in Gullino Giuseppe (a cura di), *Storia di Padova*, Sommacampagna (Verona), Cierre, 2009, pp. 241–324, pp. 281–285.

28 Franzin, *Luigi Piccinato*, *op. cit.*, p. 21.

entire job and in the absence of a precise calculation of the annual income) with the legal value (based on the value of the rent or on the net taxable income of the asset). Very accurate archival documents remain of the estimates and evaluations made in 1925 by the engineer of the project, Mr. Sarocco[29]. These documents contain descriptive reports, calculations and often photographs of the properties (most of which now no longer exist)[30].

Figure 3. Photographic Survey of Buildings to be Expropriated (1925)

Source: Archivio Generale del Comune di Padova, *Lavori pubblici,* Piano regolatore, b. 50. Published with the kind permission of the Comune di Padova, no. 1 (17/02/2012).

29 Archivio Generale del Comune di Padova (AGCPd), *Lavori pubblici,* Piano regolatore, b. 50, fasc. n.n.

30 Fabris Giuseppe, "La sorte di alcune case storiche nelle demolizioni del centro di Padova", in *Emporium,* vol. LXVIII, nov. (1928), pp. 321–324; Gaudenzio Luigi, "Aspetti di un quartiere scomparso", in *Padova e la sua Provincia,* a. XII, n. 2, feb. (1966), pp. 8–11.

Nevertheless, the start-up of the plan immediately triggered a reaction from some of the citizens and an extensive national debate ensued. Firstly, the owners of the houses involved in the expropriation attempted to take legal action, but this was rejected by the Prefect[31]. The basic conception of the plan was then criticised by many sides, based mainly on the choice to demolish the historical sites that were previously expropriated and to reconstruct them according to new standards. The local voice for this strong opposition was an association called *Antenorei Lares.* This group progressively broadened the critical front by also involving political and cultural exponents such as Corrado Ricci, Gustavo Giovannoni, and Roberto Papini[32]. In the meantime, to respond to some of the criticism, the City Council quickly prepared a plan to expand the city beyond the walls. This was translated into law in 1925. The land was essentially based on an expansion grid without any kind of regulating principle, and showed all the instrumentality of the operation.

This subsequently led to the formulation of alternative proposals in 1927 consisting of a report by Daniele Donghi (supported by *Antenorei Lares*) and by a group of young graduates of the Architectural School of Rome ("Gruppo Urbanisti Romani"), headed by Luigi Piccinato and supported by Gustavo Giovannoni, which was later illustrated in the pages of 'Architettura e Arti Decorative' (Architecture and Decorative Arts)[33]. This project aimed at resolving a specific case which at that time was the object of national debate, and also sought to propose a "model for the building start-up of Italian cities". This method would no longer involve demolition of historic areas, but rather an expansion regulated by new neighbourhoods and the subsequent scaling back of the old city centre[34].

In the meantime, expropriation and demolition works continued in the neighbourhood of Santa Lucia. However, the practical implementation caused the emergence of significant economic and organisational difficulties, deriving

31 AGCPd, *Lavori pubblici*, Piano regolatore, b. 50; Universo, "Padova negli anni Venti", *art. cit.*, p. 71.

32 Franzin, *Luigi Piccinato, op. cit.*, pp. 22–28.

33 [Gruppo Urbanisti Romani] "Relazione al piano regolatore e di ampliamento della Città di Padova", in *Architettura e Arti Decorative*, a. VII, fasc. 1–2 (1927), pp. 17–30.

34 Giovannoni Gustavo, *Vecchie città ed edilizia nuova,* Torino, UTET, 1931; Zucconi Guido, "Gustavo Giovannoni, Vecchie città ed edilizia nuova, 1931. Un manuale mancato", in Paola di Biagi (ed.), *I classici dell'urbanistica moderna,* Roma, Donzelli, 2002, pp. 57–69.

from the valuation errors made during the formulation of the expropriation plan. It appeared clear that the figures proposed did not correspond to reality. For example, the cost of 200 lire per square meter proposed for the expropriation works was estimated at more than double this actual cost[35]. The land costs, however, were revealed to be too high and the Building Corporation declared bankruptcy and closed. All the charges fell back onto the City Council.

The public expropriation device was the only operating tool adopted and the only way envisaged to implement the urban renewal but it was disconnected from any realistic assessment of the economic and social conditions of the city, as well as from the requirements of development. It proved to be completely ineffective. The only speculative elements, namely the private interests and special economic requirements, that the local administration hoped to use as an engine for the change, proved to be counterproductive and were based mainly on an out-dated concept of the project. For example, Cesare Albertini had already warned the congress of municipal engineers in 1924 that "oggi non è più possibile pensare ai cosiddetti sventramenti centrali, che assorbono enormi capitali e molte volte sacrificano i quartieri più caratteristici ed artistici tramandatici del passato" [*The so-called demolition of the city centre could no longer be taken into consideration because it would absorb enormous capitals and place great sacrifices on the most characteristic and artistic neighbourhoods handed down to us from the past*][36]. He supported the alternative need to consider new locations for the public buildings and for the formation of secondary centres.

In fact, the re-building of the demolished zones and the creation of a new piazza (the current Piazza Insurrezione) extended for over ten years and was only made possible by the inflow of capital coming from Public Bodies[37].

Piccinato clearly interpreted the result of the operations in this way: "così Padova presentava gli studi per la piazza che occuperà parte dell'area delle demolizioni centrali. È questo proprio il caso tipo di un piano di trasformazione che, male concepito, ha finito per ridursi, là dove la speculazione edilizia ha avuto ragione di tutto, alla realizzazione di un solo dettaglio: quello di una piazza avulsa dall'organismo della città" [*Padua presented the plans for the piazza that will occupy part of the area of the central demolitions. This is a typical case of*

35 Universo, "Padova negli anni Venti", *art. cit.*, p. 72.

36 Quoted in: Bottini, "Padova e la formazione della cultura urbanistica", *art. cit.*, p. 169.

37 Universo, "Padova negli anni Venti", *art. cit.*, p. 72.

Figure 4. The Area of St Lucia after the Demolition

Source: Biblioteca Civica di Padova.

a transformation plan that, badly conceived, ended up reducing itself, where the building speculation became the reason for everything, to the completion of only one detail: that of a piazza separated from the organism of the city][38].

The unresolved, ambiguous relationship between the fragment of the "new city" established in this context and actual city functions forced a rethinking of the town plan and a national competition was launched in 1932 to restore the city[39]. However, this did not succeed in restitching the tears produced in the city's organic fabric, and did not lead to the creation of an efficient and adequate infrastructure system to meet developing needs.

38 Piccinato Luigi, "Il 'Momento Urbanistico' alla Prima Mostra Nazionale dei Piani Regolatori", in *Architettura e Arti Decorative*, a. IX fasc. 5–6 (1930), pp. 195–235, pp. 205–206.

39 Marconi Plino, "Concorso per il Piano Regolatore di Padova", in *Architettura,* XII, fasc. II, febr. (1935), pp. 109–125; Franzin, *Luigi Piccinato, op. cit.*, pp. 36–38.

Wheat-Storage in Fascist Italy: Evolution and Policies

Manuel Vaquero Piñeiro

Introduction

A central feature in the general framework of economic policy pursued by the fascist regime in Italy was the strengthening of agriculture and the full exploitation of national agricultural resources. The Battle for Wheat ("*la battaglia del grano*") and The Battle for Land ("*la bonifica integrale*"), which were the subject of massive propaganda campaigns, were the fundamental interventionist actions undertaken by the regime. The unfolded from top to bottom and deeply influenced the entire rural productive system[1]. During the 1920s and 1930s, in an effort to achieve self-sufficiency in food and to reduce imports, the state assumed absolute power over agricultural policy. The rules of the free market were practically eliminated, transforming many economic agents into passive performers without any degree of autonomy[2]. It is our intention

1 Orlando Giuseppe, "Progressi e difficoltà dell'agricoltura", in Fuà Giorgio (a cura di), *Lo sviluppo economico in Italia. Storia dell'economia italiana negli ultimi cento anni*, vol. III. *Studi di settore e documentazione di base*, Milano, Franco Angeli, 1978, pp. 19–103 (especially pp. 43–46).

2 For some recent discussions of fascist agricultural polices: Preti Domenico, "La politica agraria del fascismo. Note introduttive", in *Studi storici*, XIV, 4 (1973), pp. 803–869; Tattara Giuseppe, *Cerealicoltura e politica agraria durante il fascismo*, in Toniolo Gianni (a cura di), *Lo sviluppo economico italiano 1861–1940*, Roma-Bari, Laterza, 1973, pp. 373–406; Fano Ester, "Problemi e vicende dell'agricoltura italiana tra le due guerre", in *Quaderni storici*, 29/30 (1975), pp. 468–496; Cadeddu Alberto, Lepre Stefano, Socrate Stefano, "Ristagno e sviluppo nel settore agricolo italiano (1918–1939)", in *Ibidem*, pp. 497–518; Cohen John S., "Fascism and Agriculture in Italy: Policies and Consequences", in *The Economic History Review*, 21, 1 (1979), pp. 70–87; Corni Gustavo, "La politica agraria del fascismo. Italia e Germania", in *Studi storici*, 28, 2 (1987), pp. 385–421; Nützenadel Alexander, *Landwirschaft, Staat und Autarkie. Agrarpolitik im faschistischen Italien*, Tübingen, M. Niemeyer, 1997; Stampacchia Mauro, *Ruralizzare l'Italia: agricoltura e bonifiche tra Mussolini e Serpieri 1928–1943*, Milano, Franco Angeli, 2000; Zaganella Marco, *Dal*

here to demonstrate how governmental organizations, professional categories, cooperatives and other associations, in order to reach the goals pre-established by state authorities, had to become the leading actors in a wider process of rationalization and simplification of the Italian agricultural sector. In this context, emphasis must be placed on the institutions of storage and warehousing, "typical fascist institutions of the new economy" as defined by Mussolini, who saw in them a revolutionary tool to control and regulate production[3].

Wheat-Storage: From Voluntary to Obligatory

During the Second Congress of Agricultural Associations, which was held in 1925, the issue of building cooperative silos of grain as a means of regulating the domestic market for wheat was confronted[4]. Although there were already some of these silos in Italy in the mid-twenties, they were not very common, especially in comparison with some countries (such as the USA or Canada) where there was a much stronger tradition of grain silos managed by cooperatives. While farmers argued that collectivisation would slow agricultural production, there were also technical considerations relating to skill levels, questions over the availability of financial resources, and a lack of suitable storage buildings[5]. The issue came back to the forefront with the outbreak of the agricultural crisis in the 30s.

In 1930 a sales office for wheat opened in Naples. It aimed to work directly with the manufacturers of cereals, agricultural cooperative associations, the Italian federation of agricultural associations and the National Fascist Confederation of farmers[6]. Although only 66,264 quintals were deposited in the first year, wheat-storage itself experienced rapid growth due to falling prices and the contraction of international trade. Wheat-storage was invoked as the only medium for effectively disciplining the domestic market[7]: in 1932 five

Fascismo alla DC. Tassinari, Medici e la bonifica in Italia tra gli anni Trenta e Cinquanta, Siena, Cantagalli, 2010.

3 *Giornale di agricoltura della domenica*, 9 maggio 1937.

4 *Giornale di agricoltura della domenica*, 22 marzo 1925.

5 *Ibid.*

6 Archivio di Stato, Perugia, Archivio Società economico-agraria, b. 32.

7 *Ibid.*

million quintals of wheat with a value of 387 million Italian lire were stored; three years later nearly eight million quintals were stored out of a total domestic produce of 42 million Italian lire[8]. If at first the storage was voluntary, leaving manufacturers the freedom to deliver the goods, there was soon a clear change of direction[9]: in fact, in the wake of an increasingly hostile state policy towards the free initiative of producers and buyers, public authorities assumed a much more pronounced role in the performance of brokerage functions. This increasing state intervention was taking place in a climate characterized by intensifying charges of speculation and the presumed presence of "saboteurs of the economic policy of the regime"[10]. There was a growing conviction among the ranks of agricultural organizations that the only possible course of action to reduce waste and stop the continuous decline in agricultural profits was to enact legislation giving the state the power to regulate the "national framework and rationale of the wheat", thereby removing the presence of uncontrolled, free market initiatives[11].

The practice of wheat-storage, as constituted around 1930, illustrated the central tenets of corporatism and the intention of overcoming class divisions within the world of work[12], and the policies taken in this regard met the stringent requirements of an increasingly uncompetitive economy that was

8 *Federazione italiana dei Consorzi Agrari. 1892–1952*, Roma, Ramo Editoriale degli Agricoltori, 1953, pp. 91–102; Galli Renato, "I consorzi nell'economia agraria. Linee di dinamica corporativa", in *Atti del primo congresso nazionale di diritto agrario*, Firenze, tip. editrice Mariano Ricci, 1935, pp. 503–523.

9 Pagani Luigi, *Dagli ammassi volontari agli ammassi obbligatori. Per la disciplina del mercato del grano*, Venezia, Istituto Federale delle Casse di Risparmio delle Venezie, 1936, pp. 15–23.

10 "Il regime a protezione degli agricoltori. Le speculazioni degli accaparratori stroncate con gli ammassi di grano", in *Il Messaggero*, 2 agosto 1936, p. 2.

11 *Sul disciplinamento del mercato nazionale dei frumenti*, Milano, Federazione nazionale fascista di panificatori, piccoli pastai ed affini, 1935, p. 3; Volpi Alessandro, "La circolazione dei prodotti", in Cianferoni Reginaldo, Ciuffoletti Zeffiro, Rombai Leonardo (a cura di), *Storia dell'agricoltura italiana*. Vol. III. *L'età contemporanea*, Firenze, Polistampa, 2002, pp. 285–332 (especially. pp. 319–329).

12 Franck Louis, *Il corporativismo e l'economia dell'Italia fascista*, a cura di Nicola Tranfaglia, Torino, Bollati Boringhieri, 1990 (French edition in 1934); Cassese Sabino, *Lo Stato fascista*, Bologna, il Mulino, 2010, pp. 121–124; Gagliardi Alessio, *Il corporativismo fascista*, Roma-Bari, Laterza, 2010.

vulnerable to international forces[13]. Before the tightening of trade relations in the wake of the introduction of this autarkical ideology[14], the legal framework concerning wheat storage underwent a further significant change. The law of May 21, 1934, n. 821, ordered the mills to use a percentage of the national wheat in the milling process[15]. Following the entry into force of law of June 24, 1935, n. 1049, special committees (*centri ammassi provinciali*) that had to administer the activity of the wheat storage operators began to operate in each Italian province under the supervision of the Ministry of Agriculture,. The next step was the law of 16 March 1936, n. 392, which was designed to regulate the collective sale of wheat. Soon after, obliterating any glimmer of free enterprise in the wheat trade. the law of June 15, n. 1273 made wheat storage obligatory; from now on "the national wheat production, and of the colonies and introduced into the kingdom, and that might be introduced from abroad in temporary import" was to be delivered to the institutional storage operators for the collective sale. An exclusion could be made from the obligation to deliver the wheat based on the needs of owners and employees, to a maximum of 3 quintals each, and the quantities useful for planting a maximum of 2 quintals per hectare of cultivation. The transport of wheat occurred thirty days after the threshing[16]. The person who delivered the grain (called *conferente*) received a certificate stating the quantity, quality, density, impurities and other characteristics of the wheat delivered. Attached to this document was the authorization to be paid by the bank for the wheat[17].

After the entry into force of the law on "totalitarian discipline of prices", which was the true cornerstone of fascist economic policy[18], neither the producers nor any other pivate interest could market wheat. Since they could no

13 Ciocca Pierluigi, *Ricchi per sempre? Una storia economica d'Italia (1796–2005)*, Torino, Bollati Boringhieri, 2007, pp. 204–218.

14 Gagliardi Alessio, *L'impossibile autarchia: la politica economica del fascismo e il Ministero scambi e valute*, Soveria Mannelli, Rubbettino, 2007.

15 Frassoldati Carlo, *Gli ammassi obbligatori*, Roma, Osservatorio Italiano di Diritto Agrario, 1941, p. 36.

16 Fragola Umberto, *Gli ammassi collettivi di prodotti agrari*, Roma, Confederazione fascista degli agricoltori, 1938; Rizzuti Antonio, *Gli ammassi collettivi di prodotti agrari*, Roma, Confederazione fascista degli agricoltori, 1938.

17 Frassoldati, *Gli ammassi obbligatori*, *op. cit.*, p. 39.

18 Brizzi Alessandro, *Economia e politica agraria*, Bari-Città di Castello, casa editrice dott. Luigi Macrì, 1942, pp. 58–60.

longer operate on a free market[19], there was no choice but to bring the crops to the nearest wheat-storage centre. The result was a mixed public-private regime, which shared many of the traits and contradictions that characterized the relationship between fascist ideology and economic practice[20]. On one hand, there was private ownership of land and crops, but, on the other, marketing and distribution of profits was under the control of the state.

The wheat-storage network assumed a key role in state agriculture policy with Italy's entry into the war in 1940. The national storage institute, which was created in a period of depressed prices, became a tool used to enforce price moderation and to manage the rationing of food[21]. There was a parallel surge in intervention by the central and local authorities, who were concerned at the increasing tendency of manufacturers to evade the law[22]. Faced with this worsening situation, the answer proposed by the fascist regime was to tighten the mesh of the controls, creating a multitude of new advisory boards which imposed a further bureaucratization of economic life[23]. In 1941 the "Ministerial Commissioner for the acceleration of the obligatory storage of cereals" came into operation at the national level, while at the local level, control was entrusted to the municipal committees that oversaw the delivery of grain to storage facilities[24]. Simultaneously, the amount of wheat to be retained for personal use was reduced to 65 kg; it was also established that the police, trade unions, cooperatives, and agricultural associations should be involved in denouncing, if even anonymously, "traitors to the homeland".

If we leave aside the Italian experience and look at the situation around Europe during the 1930s, it is clear that other countries were implementing

19 Federico Giovanni, "Mercato", in de Grazia Vittoria, Luzzatto Sergio (a cura di), *Dizionario del fascismo*, Torino, Einaudi, 2002–2003, vol. II, pp. 119–123.

20 Maier Charles S., *Alla ricerca della stabilità*, Bologna, il Mulino, 2003, pp. 107–127.

21 Toscano Mario, "Agricoltura", in *Annali dell'economia italiana,* IPSOA, 9, 2 (1983) pp. 61–63.

22 Archivio di Stato, Perugia, Prefettura. Atti, b. 392.

23 Segreto Luciano, "Industrial Capitalism and Politica Constraints: the Bureaucratization of Economic Life during the Fascist Regime", in Kobrak Christopher, Hansen Per H. (eds.), *European Business, Dictatorship and Political Risk 1920–1945*, New York, Berghahn, 2004, pp. 223–234.

24 *Riordinamento degli enti economici dell'agricoltura e dei Consorzi agrari*, Edizioni di attualità, Roma, 1942, pp. 24–25.

policies aimed at strictly controlling the supply chain of wheat. In Spain, beginning in 1937 (before the end of the Civil War), the "Servicio Nacional del Trigo" began operation[25]. For its part, the Soviet Union[26], in the name of the fight against speculation and the easy money that the affluent peasants and "kulaks" had made between the 20s and 30s, began to work on persuading farmers of the benefits of bringing wheat to the state collection centres (the *zagotovki*) and in creating a much more rigid bureaucratic and administrative framework, with the full involvement of the Party and the whole apparatus of political and administrative operations aimed at "taking the grain". In 1932 the "Committee for storage" began to operate, while local delivery of wheat to *zagotovki* remained in the hands of commissioners and managers who imposed a reign of terror and fierce repression in a desperate attempt to overcome the resistance of the peasant population, independent or collectivized, who opposed the removal of all available grain.

Even in European countries ruled by democratic regimes and with solid market economies, the 30s saw the establishment of public institutions responsible for implementation of control policies, primarily in regard to the price and distribution of staple foods[27]. In France, at the time of the Popular Front government, the law of 15 August 1936 established the "Office National interprofessionnel du blé". In Great Britain the 1932 Wheat Act aimed to give farmers a minimum price for each crop[28].

25 Barciela López Carlos, *La agricultura cerealística en la España contemporánea: el mercado triguero y el Servicio Nacional del Trigo*, Madrid, Universidad Complutense, 1981; Id., *"Ni un español sin pan". La red nacional de silos y graneros*, Zaragoza, Prensa Universitaria de Zaragoza, 2007. For the Germany, Corni Gustavo, *La politica agraria del nazionalsocialismo (1930–1939)*, Milano, Franco Angeli, 1989.

26 Lewin Moshe, *Contadini e potere sovietico dal 1928 al 1930*, Milano, Franco Angeli, 1972, pp. 180–185; Id., *Storia sociale dello stalinismo*, Torino, Einaudi, 1988, pp. 135–148; Carr Edward H., Davies Robert William, *Le origini della pianificazione sovietica 1926–1929*. I. *Agricoltura e industria*, Torino, Einaudi, 1972.

27 For a general overview on protectionist measures in the Thirties, Frassoldati, *Gli ammassi obbligatori, op. cit.*, pp. 21–33; see Keynes John Maynard, "The Policy of Government Storage of Food-Stuffs and Raw", in *The Economic Journal*, XLVIII (1938), pp. 449–460.

28 Roberts S. G., "The Wheat Act 1932", in *The Manchester School*, 4, 1 (1933), pp. 41–54. On English agriculture before the crisis of 1929, Collins E. J. T., "Agriculture in a free trade economy Great Britain 1870–1930", in Villani Pasquale (a cura di), *Trasformazioni delle società rurali nei paesi dell'Europa occidentale e mediterranea*, Napoli, Guida editori, 1986, pp. 59–80.

This panorama of European nations also reveals profound differences. Compared to the rest of Europe (excluding the Soviet Union), the Italian situation emerges as one in which free enterprise found itself embroiled in an increasingly dense web of controls and prohibitions. The combination of events in Italy, including the serious international crisis, the authoritarian tendency of the Fascist regime and the flaws of an economic structure that depended on the state, ended up producing a degree of "public intervention in size [...] exceptional"[29]. At this point, to better understand the problems of obligatory grain storage in Italy, the relationship between the wheat and the stored product should be examined. This relationship differed from region to region according to the magnitude of production, average yield, the type of land ownership, its systems of management, the diet of the population, and supervision by competent authorities.

Table 1. Stored Wheat in Italy (Thousands Quintals)

Years	Wheat products	Stored wheat	%	Years	Wheat products	Stored wheat	%
1935	42,000	7,700	18,3	1941/42	70,702	33,725	48,0
1936/37		27,428	44,9	1942/43	65,753	31,169	47,0
1937/38	80,635	39,338	49,0	1943/44	65,103	29,498	45,0
1938/39	81,838	41,139	50,6	1944/45	64,508	26,930	42,0
1939/40	79,709	41,243	52,0	1945/46	41,765	10,471	25,0
1940/41	71,042	33,265	47,0	1946/17	61,256	22,704	37,0

Source: L'ammasso del grano nelle campagne 1936–1939, Roma, Istituto Centrale di Statistica del Regno d'Italia, 1939; *Annuario statistico dell'agricoltura italiana, 1936–1938*, vol. 1. *1939*, Roma, Istituto Centrale di Statistica del Regno d'Italia, Roma, 1940, pp. 342–343; *Annuario statistico ... 1939–1942*, Roma, Istituto Centrale di Statistica del Regno d'Italia, 1948, pp. 318–319; *Annuario statistico ... 1943–1946*, Roma, Istituto Centrale di Statistica del Regno d'Italia, 1950, pp. 436–437.

29 Castronovo Valerio, *Storia economica d'Italia. Dall'Ottocento ai giorni nostri*, Torino, Einaudi, 1995, pp. 301–307.

Some initial quantitative findings help to highlight the nature of grain storage as an instrument of political power and economic interventionism[30]. Omitting the data for 1935, the year before the entry into force of the law on mandatory collective masses, between 1936 and 1943,210,000 thousand quintals of wheat were moved to storage facilities. Considering Italy as a whole, in percentage terms, the total share of all the wheat produced that was in storage went from 45% in 1936/37 to 52% in 1939/40. During the war period, from 1940/41 to 1943/44, the share remained essentially stable at around 45–47%, but the national figure hides differences between the various regions of the country. While the north-central regions continued to ensure an abundant flow of wheat harvest, in 1942/43 the South experienced a serious decline (26% in Puglia and 53% in Sicily).

At the end of World War II the country's wheat production collapsed: the wheat harvest was just over 40 million quintals (a 36% decline) and in these circumstances, the storage facilities, many of which were seriously damaged during the fighting, received just 10 million of quintals of cereals (60 % less than the previous year). These numbers illustrate the dramatic conditions in Italy at the start of post war reconstruction, and how urgent it was to revive the production and distribution of grain. A significant increase was reported in 1946/47, when the gross marketable production increased by 45% and the wheat stocks in storage exceeded one hundred percent.

Before 1941 the highest percentage of stored wheat was found in northern Italy (58–63%) and the largest support came from Lombardy, Veneto and Emilia, which provided more than half of the wheat stored in Italy.I In some provinces, such as in Milan, the wheat in storage exceeded 95%. In the central regions the percentage fell to 42–45%, while in the South it did not even reach 40%. Sicily, at close to 43%, was an exception in the South[31]. It seems evident that what influenced these figures was that on small peasant farms, the percentage of stored wheat was lower due to family consumption. Family consumption in southern Italy could absorb almost the entire grain harvest. In contrast, areas located north of the Po, which were characterized by big

30 On "ruralization" as the ideology of fascism, see Preti, "La politica agraria del fascismo. Note introduttive", *art. cit.*, pp. 834–840.

31 *L'ammasso del grano nelle campagne 1936–1939*, Roma, Istituto Centrale di Statistica del Regno d'Italia, 1939, p. 23.

farms and reduced consumption of wheat per capita, were able to create the conditions for the delivery of nearly the entire harvest. In order to increase gross production, mechanization and the widespread use of chemical fertilizers allowed large cereal producers, and not only in the north, to cultivate all available land, since they were sure they could sell the entire harvest on the national market.

Legal Aspects of Wheat-Storage

The storage grain attracted the interest of specialists in agricultural law, who in the late 30s devoted much research to the theme[32]. In political circles, it was widely believed that the practice of the storage would create a large number of legal questions[33]. The law of 1936 that had made storage mandatory had not established clearly the rights and obligations of the parties (private, State, credit institutions) involved[34]. Neither could it be denied that there was a direct relationship between the obligation of delivery and the increase in the black market and smuggling[35]. It was, therefore, clear that the expulsion of private transactions and the concentration of the whole distribution chain in the hands of the state created conflicts involving huge vested interests. The result was a public service which was legally controversial and ambiguous.

At the beginning of the wheat storage plan, there was talk of an "expropriation or confiscation in the interest of public economy"[36]. A similar assessment

32 Frassoldati, *Gli ammassi obbligatori*, *op. cit.*, pp. 78–103.

33 Fiorentino A., "Gli ammassi granari obbligatori", in *Rivista di diritto agrario*, 2–3 (1938), pp. 284–306.

34 Senin Angelo, "Struttura e disciplina degli ammassi granari obbligatori", in *Rivista di diritto agrario*, 1 (1937), pp. 39–84; Tassinari Giuseppe, "Compiti autarchici dell'agricoltura", in *Nuovi Annali dell'Agricoltura*, XX (1940), pp. 5–7; Fragola Umberto, "L'ammasso nei suoi aspetti dogmatici", in *Atti del secondo congresso nazionale diritto agrario*, Roma, Edizioni Universitarie, 1939, pp. 562–570; Carlo Frassoldati, "Trasferimenti coattivi ed ammassi obbligatori di prodotti agricoli", in *Ibid.*, pp. 570–595.

35 Barciela López Carlos (ed.), *Autarquía y mercado negro: el fracaso económico del primer franquismo 1939–1959*, Barcelona, Crítica, 2003.

36 Ferrara F., "Gli ammassi obbligatori di prodotti agricoli", in *Studi in memoria di Bernardino Scorza*, Roma, soc. ed. del Foro Italiano, 1940, pp. 319–344; "Ammasso", in *Enciclopedia*

stemmed from the fact that after 1936 the right to free enjoyment of property was eliminated. The producers lost the ability to regain full possession of the goods and the law recognized only the right to collect money that was the economic equivalent of the goods sold. In exchange for the sale of the property, there was a corresponding right to obtain payment of a compensation price. This price, however, depended on neither the seller nor the buyer, but was set by the State. So to many juridical experts the storage obligation was a clear case of "property violated", leading to the forced sale of property and to the fact that political power replaced private economic practices.

Organisation and Operation

The management of storage facilities was entrusted to the "Ufficio centrale ammasso" under the Ministry of Agriculture and Forestry: it had as its primary object the National supply, the rational distribution of the product and the stabilization of a fair price. As part of this system in the years preceding the war, centres emerged for the storage and marketing of agricultural commodities and raw materials other than those of plant origin developed and animal feed (oil, rice, corn, cheese, chestnuts, potatoes, oil, saffron, silk cocoons[37], wool, hemp, leather, cotton, tobacco, sunflower seeds, essence of bergamot). In addition to legal doubts, the whole system of storage depended on a regular cash flow. The centres, at the time of receiving the goods for storage, were required to advance a portion of the proceeds that were thought likely to derive from the sale. So, the need to have a large degree of liquidity created a strong bond between the storage centres and banks[38]. There was another important aspect: the system of obligatory storage reflected the base price to be paid per quintal at the time

---

agraria italiana, I, Roma, Federazione italiana dei consorzi agrari – Ramo editoriale degli agricoltori, 1952, pp. 418–421.

37 Bof Frediano, "Antefatti, origine e sviluppo iniziale degli essiccatoi cooperativi bozzoli in Friuli", in *Storia economica*, X, 1–2 (2007), pp. 5–51.

38 Pagani Luigi, *Funzione presente e futuro degli ammassi granari e dei relativi anticipi creditizi*, Venezia, Istituto federale delle Casse di Risparmio delle Venezie, 1934. In the case of Spain, the financing of *Ammassi* increased the public debt and the circulation of money. Barciela López Carlos, *La financiación del Servicio Nacional del Trigo: 1937–1971*, Madrid, Banco de España, 1981.

of delivery. However, since there were differences among the various production areas of the country, the experts and the Ministry found themselves in agreement on the need to set a price on a provincial basis so as to reflect this diversity, and taking into account the expectations of producers. The Bank of Italy, wishing to curb the expectations of the Ministry of Agriculture, sought to impose a policy of caution and to avoid an excessive increase in the volume of money in circulation, which would put at risk the stability of prices. According to official estimates, which were calculated to include advances, the ministry was demanding about 2 billion lire[39].

The creation of storage facilities required the rental or the construction of warehouses, many of them located in the vicinity of railway lines. From the standpoint of building structures to be used, the increase in production following the "Battle of Wheat" imposed the need for spacious and adequate buildings[40], so as to keep wheat in good condition. This contributed to the development of a specific field of literature devoted to the manufacture of industrial equipment for the storage of wheat[41]. The first national law aimed at encouraging the construction of silos and warehouses for wheat dates back to July 1, 1932. To recoup costs quickly, the law promoted systems for preserving agricultural products other than wheat.

The distribution in Italy and its colonies of warehouses and silos is a matter of undoubted importance because the availability of substantial financial resources allowed the formation of a large integrated real estate from hundreds of buildings scattered across the country. Some data will help us to understand the scale of the phenomenon in 1932 when more than 200 million Italian lire was used in the construction of 760 warehouses, while the budget of the

39 Cova Alberto, "Il credito all'agricoltura dalla unificazione alla seconda guerra mondiale: alcune considerazioni", in D'Attorre Pier Paolo, De Bernardi Alberto (a cura di), *Studi sull'agricoltura italiana. Società rurale e modernizzazione*, Milano, Fondazione G. Feltrinelli, 1994, pp. 37–61; Cova Alberto, Galli Anna Maria (a cura di), *La Cassa di Risparmio delle Provincie Lombarde dalla fondazione al 1940*, Roma-Bari, Laterza, 1991, (especially vol. II: *Il Novecento* a cura di Alberto Cova, pp. 148–149).

40 Mango Achille, *La conservazione dei cereali*, Piacenza, Federazione italiana consorzi agrari, 1931; *La conservazione dei cereali (frumenti) nei granai e nei silos. Necessità di una regolamentazione statale*, Roma, Federazione nazionale fascista dei panificatori, piccoli pastai ed affini, 1937.

41 Chapperon Renzo, *Silos e magazzini per ammassi granari. Progettazione, costruzione, gestione*, Udine, Istituto delle Edizioni Accademiche, 1936.

Ministry of Agriculture and Forestry in 1940 shows an expenditure of 400 million Italian lire to be paid over ten years for the building and equipping of warehouses and storage facilities[42]. At the time of the war in Italy there were 793 buildings in operation by grain-dependent agricultural consortia, with a capacity of over 13 million quintal, and there was a plan to build 321 other structures with the capacity for another 5 million quintal[43].

The mass storage of grain soon created the conditions for the development of specialized companies dedicated to the design and construction of large silos[44]. The "Società Magnaghi & Bassanini" was able to design large and modern silos, demonstrating this capacity by building structures in Rome, Naples, Cagliari and Piacenza, and also the facilities located in smaller towns such as Portogruaro, Prato, Tarquinia, Orvieto and Umbertide. Another company that was active in the Milan area was the "Società Italiana Costruzioni Agricole Industriali", which, in addition to basic construction, also undertook to provide the mechanical equipment for storage. Other companies were Noli or S.I.M.A., both based in Milan and involved in the construction of rational and well-equipped storage facilities. Buildings constructed for the storage of wheat in the 30s fully reflected the theories on the subject of workplace environments and the creation of healthy, bright and comfortable spaces, able to convey a "clear sense of logic and order". The orderly architectural design gave to the observer "a favourable impression, difficult to forget, of order, fairness and care with which the company carried out its tasks and the solidity of the company itself"[45]. The use in the construction of wheat storage buildings of arches, towers, and other elements typical of fascist architecture,– in concrete structures which required the use of massive mechanical equipment – had the added effect of demonstrating through the silos the achievements of fascism.

These storage facilities benefitted from a favourable tax regime but were also subject to many expenses arising from the purchase of trucks and transport

42 *Giornale dell'agricoltura della Domenica*, 11 agosto 1940.

43 *Giornale dell'agricoltura della Domenica*, 21 giugno 1940 and 1 dicembre 1940.

44 Murè A., "Il granaio dell'urbe", in Torelli Landini Enrica (a cura di), *Roma. Memorie della città industriale. Storia e riuso di fabbriche e servizi nei primi quartieri produttivi*, Roma, Fratelli Palombi, 2007, pp. 238–243; Vaquero Piñeiro Manuel, "I silos granari in Italia negli anni Trenta: fra autarchia economica e soluzioni architettoniche", in *Patrimonio industriale*, V, 7 (2011), pp. 56–68.

45 Masi Fausto, "Fabbricati industriali", in *Casabella*, X, 110 (1937), pp. 40–45.

vehicles, in addition to disinfection, insurance, lighting, heating and staff salaries. There was also another more intractable problem: in the absence of a rigorous selection and division, the goods received were often mixed indiscriminately and at the expense of its most valuable components[46].

Table 1 shows the apparent resilience demonstrated by the whole Italian system of storage during the war[47]. Obviously, there is no intention to underestimate, much less ignore, the strategies followed by the rural population to evade the required contribution: a set of solutions were devised to allow continuous repression-avoidance[48]. But beyond individual or collective behaviour, the difference in the volume of wheat delivered before and after the war shows that a new and diverse reality was forming. If before 10 June 1940 the discipline of the storage system had virtually erased the freedom of trade, market practices being harnessed in a complex network of laws and prohibitions, with the opening of hostilities and the gradual imposition of a war economy, the storage operators now had access to cash, and this was of great importance in the eyes of the rural population. Not surprisingly, until the harvest of 1942/43 there were no significant changes[49]. In fact, large sections of the rural population could even accumulate savings due to the rising prices, as well as from the subsidies for men under arms, and, specifically, by operation of the storage itself, which each year paid the operators without bearing the risks of transactions made in a context dominated by the war.

If we now look at the price of wheat (Table 2) before and after the 1936 Law on obligatory storage, there was a clear upward trend in the price of wheat up to 1927, and a rise in terms of the lire at the time, which was particularly

46 Toniolo Gianni, *L'economia dell'Italia fascista*, Roma-Bari, Laterza, 1980, pp. 307; Cohen Jon S., "Rapporti agricoltura-industria e sviluppo agricolo", in Ciocca Pierluigi, Toniolo Gianni (a cura di), *L'economia italiana nel periodo fascista*, Bologna, il Mulino, 1976, pp. 379–407.

47 Nützenadel Alexander, "Economic Crisis and Agriculture in Fascist Italy, 1927–1935. Some New Considerations", *Rivista di storia economica*, XVII, 3 (2001), pp. 289–312.

48 Canali Gianfranco, "Una società rurale in guerra: note sulle campagne umbre durante la seconda guerra mondiale", *Proposte e ricerche*, XIV, 33 (1994), pp. 69–95; Ciuffetti, Augusto, Di Sano Luigi, *Criminalità e giustizia tra economia di guerra e società (1940–1946)*, in Brunelli Luciana, Canali Gianfranco (a cura di), *L'Umbria dalla guerra alla Resistenza*, Foligno-Perugia, Istituto per la Storia dell'Umbria Contemporanea, 1998, pp. 30–48.

49 Cova Alberto, *Cremona e la sua provincia nell'Italia Unita*. vol. I. *La storia economica*, Milano, Giuffré, 1984, pp. 242–244.

significant in the years 1920–1921 and 1925–1926. As noted, the revaluation of the lira that was adopted by the regime with the speech at Pesaro[50], sanctioned the start of a very different phase: food prices fell until 1934, when they began a slow climb. Now the consequences of the operation of obligatory storage and the application of a price imposed by the Ministry of Agriculture become clearer. So, in 1936 the price tied to free markets ended and a system completely subject to political power began. In the first two years the price of wheat was modified, but what is clear is that between 1936 and 1938, following the entry into operation of the storage policy, the nominal price of wheat underwent a wholesale increase of 17%. After the first two years the price of a quintal of wheat underwent further changes and settled down at 135 lire until the early forties. 1941 saw a 15% rise in the price of wheat due to state aid. In subsequent years, the incentive mechanism based on awards and grants in support of producers' incomes remained in force and the quintal of stored wheat reached the nominal price of 750 lire in 1945–1946. Immediately after the war, under the weight of inflation, the wholesale price of wheat reached 2,250 lire per quintal in 1947.

Wheat Storage after the Second World War

The history of grain storage was not interrupted by the end of World War II and in the decades after the war a new chapter unfolded, even if philosophy behind it remained constant[51]. Immediately after the war, under the definition of a new agricultural policy, it was thought that the main problem to be solved was the revision of prices of wheat to meet the expectations of the producers. For a short period of time, under the Law of October 5, 1945, n.721, storage became voluntary instead of obligatory, but just a year later, at the congress of the Christian Democracts, Alcide De Gasperi wrote about the need to restore a

50 Cova Alberto, *Cremona e la sua provincia nell'Italia Unita*. vol. I. *La storia economica*, Milano, Giuffré, 1984, pp. 242–244.

51 Sinatti D'Amico Franca, "Lo Stato e le politiche agricole", in Bevilacqua Piero (a cura di), *Storia dell'agricoltura italiana in età contemporanea*, III. *Mercati e istituzioni*, Milano, Franco Angeli, 1991, pp. 427–470.

Table 2. Average Wholesale price of the Quintal Of Wheat in Italy

Year	Lire (nominal value)	Year	Lire (nominal value)	Year	Lire (nominal value)
1913	28	1925	181	1937	117
1914	29	1926	200	1938	128
1915	40	1927	140	1939	135
1916	38	1928	135	1940	145
1917	43	1929	130	1941	165
1918	56	1930	127	1942	195
1919	69	1931	101	1943	235
1920	90	1932	111	1944	350
1921	115	1933	93	1946	750
1922	118	1934	86	1947	2,250
1923	102	1935	105		
1924	121	1936	111		

Source: Giacomo Acerbo, *La economia dei cereali nell'Italia e nel mondo*, Milano, Hoepli, 1934, p. 881; *Giornale di agricoltura*, n. 21, 26 maggio 1947.

strict discipline to the supply of wheat, adding that the return to the obligatory storage system was strongly supported by the Allies. The words of the Christian Democrat politician found practical implementation with a Ministerial Decree of 27 May 1946, which restored obligatory storage and renamed the system as the "granary of the people" (*i granai del popolo*). From that point, the municipalities began to receive the Italian edition of "Economic Notes", a publication of the United Nations Relief and Rehabilitation Administration, which provided information on the progress of provincial storage. However, despite the strict controls imposed by law enforcement and the bureaucracy, the rural population tried to escape the obligation of delivering grain to the state operated system. Aside from the obvious economic damage involved, the fact remained that the principles and methods used by the state echoed the very recent fascist authoritarianism[52].

52 Forti Carla, *Dopoguerra in provincia. Microstorie pisane e lucchesi (1944–1948)*, Milano, Franco Angeli, 2007, pp. 238–240.

According to the detractors of the current system, it was necessary to clarify who benefited by keeping this system of obligatory storage. The conflict of interest was between the small landowners who, even after the fall of fascism, found themselves in a system that forced them to sell to the state, and the industrial sectors, which under the storage system and the control of prices for the raw material, were able to control labour costs and increase their profits[53]. In a system marked by a profound mingling of public and private interests, storage continued to be the instrument used to make a massive transfer of financial resources to agricultural interests. In 1947, the subsidized prices were much higher than in 1938. At the same time, the existence of storage facilities in the hands of agricultural associations (*Consorzi agrari*) encouraged the sale of large quantities of chemical fertilizers and agricultural machinery.

The delivery mechanism did not vary in any way from that organized in 1936 until the harvest of 1949–50, the year in which the mandatory regime of storage was changed to give to farmers the freedom to voluntary deliver the wheat to agricultural associations. These new arrangements were introduced by the final law n. 1235, dated 7 May, 1948, which established that the storage operations were voluntary; the utilization, transformation and sale of agricultural products were entrusted to cooperatives, *Consorzi agrari*, which are now clearly recognized as subjects of private law. The *Consorzi agrari* had been the subject of much criticism; they were accused of having accumulated vast real estate assets under fascism. Rather than reform, the new legislation confirmed the pre-eminent position of the *Consorzi agrari* in the wheat sector. In this way, the opportunity for reforming the sector and for opening the grain market to free competition[54] became more difficult.

The history of grain storage calls into question issues such as the positions taken up by the various political parties and unions, and the line followed by the popular farmers' organizations when they were called on either to reject relationships with agricultural institutions which had colluded with fascism, or to use them to ensure the movement of essential commodities. It also brings into focus the relationship that is created between the free market and the

53 Cetti Carlo, *Il sistema degli ammassi e dei raduni di bestiame (Una delle follie del fascismo)*, Partito dei Rurali d'Italia, Como, Il ginepro, 1946.

54 Rossi-Doria Manlio, *Rapporto sulla Federconsorzi*, Bari, Laterza, 1963, p. 144.

controlled market[55]. Under the tight control of the "Federconsorzi" and "Coltivatori diretti"[56], the reasons cited for not dismantling the system of storage, in front of a country exhausted by poverty and unemployment[57] were the usual ones – namely the difficult adjustment of agriculture markets, the inferiority of the farmers to the large intermediaries, the fight against speculation, and the preservation of national interests pursued by perpetuating a strict protectionist discipline[58].

The storage facilities run by Catholic trade unions created a particular political situation, because the system proved to be a powerful electoral machine in the creation of a consensus, especially in a period marked by sharp ideological contrasts. Some numbers help us understand the size of the phenomenon: between 1947 and 1951, about 14 to 15 million tons of wheat on average was delivered for storage, and the proprietors (*conferente)* numbered more than seven hundred thousand individuals[59].

As we learned from the raging controversy that accompanied the development of Federconsorzi in the 60s and 70s, the storage situation contributed

55 De Cecco Marcello, "La politica economica durante la ricostruzione 1945–1951", in Woolf Stuart J. (a cura di), *Italia 1943/50. La ricostruzione*, Roma-Bari, Laterza, 1975, pp. 283–318.

56 Barbadoro Idomeneo, *La Federconsorzi nella politica agraria italiana*, Roma, Editoriale sindacale italiana, 1961; Rossi Ernesto, *La Federconsorzi e lo Stato*, Firenze, La Nuova Italia, 1963; Ventura Angelo, "La Federconsorzi dall'età liberale al fascismo: ascesa e capitolazione della borghesia agraria 1892–1932", in *Quaderni storici*, XII, 36 (1977), pp. 683–733; Fontana Severina (a cura di), *La Federconsorzi tra stato liberale e fascismo*, Roma-Bari, Laterza, 1995; De Marzi Renato, *Grano e potere: la Federconsorzi, cento anni di lotte per il dominio sulle campagne*, Bologna, Edagricole, 1987; Mottura Giovanni, *Il conflitto senza avventure. Contadini e strategia ruralista nella storia della Coldiretti*, Milano, Fondazione G. Feltrinelli, 1994; Rossi Ernesto, *Viaggio nel feudo di Bonomi*, Roma, Editori Riuniti, 1965.

57 Ciocca, *Ricchi per sempre?, op. cit.*, pp. 228–239.

58 Serpieri Arrigo, *Istituzioni di economia agraria*, Bologna, Edizioni Agricole Bologna, 1956, pp. 152–154; Fabiani Guido, *L'agricoltura italiana tra sviluppo e crisi (1945–1985)*, Bologna, il Mulino, 1986, p. 99; Petri Rolf, *Storia economica d'Italia. Dalla Grande guerra al miracolo economico (1918–1963)*, Bologna, il Mulino, 2002, pp. 266–272.

59 Istituto Centrale di Statistica, *Annuario statistico dell'agricoltura italiana 1947–1950*, Roma, Tipografia Fausto Failli, 1953, pp. 645–648. Between 1949 and 1961 there was over 240 million quintals of wheat stored, Rossi-Doria, *Rapporto sulla Federconsorzi*, *op. cit.*, p. 75.

to immobility[60] and was one of the pillars of the agricultural policy of the Italian Republic. This system, in fact, proved to be a key mechanism in creating conditions for the positioning of the peasant masses in political parties and unions.

60 Fabiani, *L'agricoltura italiana tra sviluppo e crisi*, *op. cit.*, pp. 103–105; Cova Alberto, *Economia, lavoro e istituzioni nell'Italia del Novecento. Scritti di storia economica*, Milano, Vita e pensiero, 2002, p. 635. About Spain see, Fernández Prieto Lourenzo, *El apagón tecnológico del franquismo: estado e innovación en la agricoltura del siglo XX*, Valencia, Tirant lo Blanc, 2007; Pujol Josep (ed.), *El Pozo de todos los males: sobre el atraso en la agricoltura española contemporánea*, Barcelona, Crítica, 2001.

IV

Expropriations and Seizures in the Colonies and after the Colonies

Expropriations et confiscations dans le monde colonial et post-colonial

De la liberté comme violation de la propriété privée: indemnités et abolitions de l'esclavage dans le Nouveau Monde (1777-1888)

Frederique Beauvois

De 1777 à 1888, les abolitions de l'esclavage dans le Nouveau Monde affranchissent plus de sept millions d'esclaves sur une population américaine composée en 1850 de 59 millions d'individus. Cette rupture inédite avec un mode de production universel et pluriséculaire touche la main d'œuvre servile la plus importante numériquement au monde et engage définitivement les Amériques dans la voie du travail libre.

Une majorité d'Etats juge nécessaire d'accompagner ce phénomène révolutionnaire de dédommagements. En effet, des indemnités sont prévues dans les lois d'abolition en faveur de ceux qui en subissent les dommages. Dans les Amériques, ce sont les propriétaires d'esclaves qui sont considérés comme la partie lésée, qu'il s'agit donc de dédommager. Loin d'être un cas isolé, il s'agit ici de la généralité. La valeur capitalisée en 2007 de ces indemnités n'atteint pas moins de trois milliards de dollars. Si les propriétaires d'esclaves sont généralement dédommagés de la libération de leurs biens humains, les esclaves quant à eux doivent se contenter pour solde de tout compte de leur liberté nouvellement acquise et toute relative.

La conciliation entre le respect de la propriété des planteurs et le droit à la liberté des esclaves par l'octroi d'une indemnité n'allait cependant pas forcément de soi. Cela explique l'absence d'indemnisation relevée dans certains cas. L'étude de l'argumentaire tant anti abolitionniste que abolitionniste concernant l'indemnité permettra de mettre en lumière les spécificités de la propriété de l'homme, son origine, ses limites, ainsi que les difficultés rencontrées par les Etats décidés à abolir l'esclavage face au caractère sacré de la propriété privée.

Si une hiérarchie des valeurs les plus centrales de notre société moderne devait être établie, la notion de liberté en occuperait sans doute la première place. Considéré aujourd'hui comme une des composantes les plus essentielles de l'humanité, le droit à la liberté a cependant été longtemps nié au plus grand nombre. En effet, il y a moins de deux siècles, humanité et liberté ne sont qu'un oxymore[1]. Arthur Young estime au 18e siècle que la plus grande partie de la population mondiale est réduite en esclavage[2], la privation de liberté étant susceptible de revêtir plusieurs formes: esclavage, servage, péonage, hilotisme, etc. Longtemps, des individus ont ainsi été considérés comme constituant la propriété d'autres hommes. Cette chosification de l'être humain n'apparait alors comme scandaleuse qu'à une minorité d'esprits éclairés.

Cette étude se propose d'examiner les caractéristiques de cette perception matérialiste de l'homme, ainsi que ses limites, par le biais des abolitions de l'esclavage dans le Nouveau Monde. Les Amériques constituent donc le champ géographique d'investigation, le cadre chronologique s'étendant de 1777 – année de la première abolition dans le Vermont, Etat du nord des Etats-Unis – à 1888, date de l'émancipation finale au Brésil.

De l'esclave comme propriété

Jusqu'aux abolitions du 18e et du 19e siècles, l'esclave est considéré légalement comme une chose, au même titre que la terre, les bêtes de sommes, ou les instruments d'exploitation d'une plantation. Les « codes noirs » caractérisent la nature de la propriété servile et règlementent son usage dans les colonies du Nouveau Monde. L'esclave y est défini comme un bien mobilier ou immobilier[3]. Il est ainsi généralement perçu comme une propriété et traité comme tel partout dans les Amériques.

1 Drescher Seymour, "Abolitionist expectations: Britain", in Temperley Howard (ed.), *After slavery: emancipation and its discontents*, London, Routledge, 2000, p. 41.

2 Seuls 33 millions d'individus sur un total de 775 sont libres. Cf. Young Arthur, *Political essays concerning the present state of the British empire; particularly respecting I. Natural advantages and disadvantages. II. Constitution. III. Agriculture. IV. Manufactures. V. The colonies and VI. Commerce*, London, W. Strahan and T. Cadell, 1772, p. 20.

3 L'esclave est par exemple défini comme un bien par l'article 44 du code noir français. Sur la nature immobilière de la propriété servile, voir Peytraud Lucien, *L'esclavage aux Antilles françaises avant 1789, d'après des documents inédits des archives coloniales*, Paris, Librairie Hachette et Cie, 1897, pp. 247-265.

Le vol ou l'exportation d'un esclave hors de la colonie sans le consentement de son maître est puni de mort. L'esclave marron est châtié comme un voleur puisqu'en fuyant son maître, il le vole de sa propre personne. Son être même appartient à son propriétaire et non à lui-même. La propriété servile est régie par les mêmes normes que n'importe quel autre bien. Elle se transmet de génération en génération, par héritage, mariage ou par le biais des créances. L'esclave peut représenter une garantie pour un prêt, être acheté à crédit, saisi ou faire l'objet d'une assurance[4]. L'esclave est donc considéré comme une propriété à part entière et tout à fait commune.

Le devoir de l'Etat étant de protéger les biens personnels de ses citoyens de tout dommage susceptible d'y être causé, il relève de sa responsabilité de préserver la relation exclusive du maître avec ses esclaves. La perception matérialiste de l'esclave a ainsi comme conséquence de conférer à l'esclavage un caractère d'intouchabilité qui complique fortement toute procédure d'affranchissement des esclaves.

D'une abolition comme expropriation

Une abolition libérant les esclaves signifie une atteinte aux biens serviles dans lesquels les maîtres ont investi des capitaux sous le couvert de la loi. Par le biais de l'émancipation, l'Etat porte donc préjudice à une propriété légale qu'il était pourtant censé protéger, ce qui n'est pas sans poser problème. Cette conjoncture d'intérêts conflictuels a cependant fait l'objet d'un texte de loi qui prévoit un protocole en vue de la réquisition des biens de particuliers.

En effet, bien que l'inviolabilité de la propriété soit stipulée dans la constitution, l'Etat est parfois contraint de transgresser les lois qu'il est chargé de

4 L'épisode du Zong en est une célèbre illustration, voir Oldham James, "Insurance litigation involving the Zong and other British slave ships, 1780-1807", in *Journal of legal history*, 28 (2007), pp. 299-318, Webster Jane, "The Zong in the context of the eighteenth-century slave trade", in *Journal of legal history*, 28 (2007), pp. 285-298 et Rupprecht Anita, "A limited sort of property: history, memory and the slave ship Zong", in *Slavery & abolition*, 29 (2008), pp. 265-277. Sur les assurances contractées sur les esclaves pendant le passage de l'Atlantique, voir Rupprecht Anita, "Excessive memories: slavery, insurance and resistance", in *History workshop journal*, 64 (2007) pp. 6-28.

faire respecter. L'aliénation étatique des biens d'un particulier est connue législativement sous le terme français d'expropriation, qui signifie littéralement « hors de la propriété », de *compulsory purchase* en Grande-Bretagne, d'*eminent domain* ou d'*appropriation* aux Etats-Unis et d'*expropiación* en espagnol.

Dans le cadre d'un aménagement du territoire ou de réformes des structures existantes, le principe de l'expropriation a comme objectif la transformation de la société en vue de son adaptation aux exigences dictées par le progrès, tout en sauvegardant ses fondations. Elle doit ainsi permettre de protéger le droit de propriété tout en le limitant.

Cette mission n'est pas des plus simples. Le principe d'expropriation touche à l'une des bases les plus fondamentales de la société, investissant un des « lieux » les plus sensibles du *pactum societatis* qu'est le respect de la propriété. Ecartelée entre le respect des droits donnés et la nécessité d'être efficace, l'expropriation représente ainsi un sujet épineux pour les législateurs de l'époque, que Tocqueville qualifie au 19e siècle de « grand champ de bataille »[5]. Si l'expropriation est susceptible d'apparaître comme une solution aux difficultés que pose une abolition, elle ne constitue pas un remède universel à tous les maux et pose plus d'un problème.

Afin de pallier à ses dérives potentielles, sa procédure est strictement réglementée. Identiques dans la majeure partie des constitutions occidentales, ses conditions sont ainsi résumées: « Nécessité, pour légitimer l'atteinte à la propriété privée, d'une raison dûment justifiée d'intérêt public, et l'obligation d'indemniser le propriétaire préalablement à la prise de possession »[6]. Utilité publique et indemnité sont donc les deux pré requis nécessaires à une expropriation légitime.

L'esclave étant considéré comme une propriété, son aliénation est ainsi présentée comme constituant une expropriation des droits de son propriétaire légitime sur le plan légal, puisqu'elle a comme conséquence de le priver de la jouissance de son bien. C'est la raison pour laquelle des lois stipulent depuis

5 Lacche Luigi, « L'expropriation pour cause d'utilité publique en France au 19e siècle. Origines et développement d'un modèle juridique », in: Société Jean Bodin pour l'histoire comparative des institutions, *L'expropriation: 2e partie Moyen-Age et temps modernes,* Bruxelles, De Boeck Université, 2000, p. 80.

6 Le Loup de Sancy L., « Etude sur l'expropriation pour cause d'utilité publique en Angleterre, en Belgique, en Prusse, en Italie, en Espagne et dans la Confédération suisse », in *Bulletin de la société de législation comparée,* 1 (1877), p. 25.

l'Antiquité une indemnité en faveur du propriétaire dépossédé partiellement ou totalement de son bien servile suite à une série de figures: décès causé par autrui, emprisonnement à vie, peine capitale ou affranchissement.

Ces dispositions sont reprises dans les codes noirs appliqués dans la majeure partie des colonies françaises, britanniques, espagnoles, néerlandaises et danoises[7]. Tout dommage, partiel ou total, affectant la capacité de travail de l'esclave ou portant atteinte à sa vie doit être indemnisé. L'emprisonnement, la mutilation ou la mort d'un esclave suite à une décision législative ou d'une traque de marrons donnent ainsi lieu à des dédommagements[8]. Le but initial de cette disposition est d'éviter qu'un maître ne tente de soustraire un esclave criminel à la justice afin de préserver ses biens. Sa conséquence est de consacrer l'inviolabilité de la propriété servile.

Entre propriété et liberté

Cette conception matérialiste de l'esclave n'emporte cependant pas l'adhésion de tous et connaît dès son instauration des salves d'attaques qui se fortifient dès le dernier quart du 18e siècle. La légitimité du système esclavagiste est en effet remise en question par les idéaux de liberté hérités du siècle des Lumières. La volonté affichée des abolitionnistes de mettre un terme au commerce des esclaves, ainsi que les émancipations des Etats du nord des Etats-Unis, ébranlent les fondations du système servile.

7 Goveia Elsa V., *The West Indian slave laws of the 18th century*, Barbados, Caribbean University Press, 1979, p. 50.

8 Un règlement de Saint-Domingue datant de 1710 prévoit le dédommagement des esclaves tués en marronnage, voir *Dissertations sur le droit public, des colonies, françaises, espagnoles, et anglaises, d'après les Lois des trois nations, comparées entre elles*, Genève, Knapen, 1778, p. 329. La 47e clause d'une loi édictée en 1767 dans la colonie britannique de Saint-Vincent prévoit le remboursement des esclaves blessés, mutilés ou tués lors de la traque de marrons, voir les propos du parlementaire Francis à la Chambre des Communes lors de la présentation de sa motion pour la réglementation des conditions de vie et de travail des esclaves dans les colonies britanniques. Aux Etats-Unis, il est rapporté que les tribunaux ont l'habitude des plaintes des propriétaires de marrons tués par les chasseurs chargés de les capturer, voir Goodell William, *The American slave code, in theorie and practice; its distinct features shown by its statutes, judicial decisions, and illustrative facts*, London, Clarke, Beeton and Co, 1853, p. 217.

Si jusqu'alors les affranchissements ne relèvent que de cas particuliers et individuels, il est désormais question d'abolir l'institution même de l'esclavage. Plus ou moins résistantes aux coups portés par les abolitionnistes selon les lieux concernés, les structures serviles dans leur globalité sont menacées, et, à terme, condamnées. Le monde bascule dans la voie des émancipations de masse et la suppression définitive du système esclavagiste en place dès la fondation occidentale du Nouveau Monde.

Si le Législateur a édicté un certain nombre de règles concernant le respect de la propriété dans l'esclave et l'affranchissement, il n'a pas envisagé l'éventualité d'une émancipation de masse, par laquelle tout un pan de la propriété coloniale serait annihilé. Nul protocole n'a été prévu pour une dépossession à une si large échelle des planteurs. S'il n'existe pas de réglementation particulière à une abolition générale, les dispositions légales générales stipulent que toute expropriation d'un bien privé par l'Etat doit s'accompagner d'une indemnité.

Cependant, cette perspective d'une abolition comme expropriation est remise en question par les nouvelles données humanistes héritées du siècle des Lumières. Jusqu'alors, le principe de propriété dans l'homme n'était pas réellement discuté. C'est à l'aube des processus abolitionnistes que la représentation de l'esclave comme chose bascule réellement dans la controverse. L'esclavage entre alors en confrontation directe avec le concept de liberté. Cette rencontre constitue un point de rupture dans l'équilibre longtemps en place de l'esclavage.

Ce champ d'expérimentation peut être qualifié d'« extrême » puisqu'il confronte la notion de propriété à ses propres contradictions internes, par la mise en concurrence de deux des principes les plus fondamentaux de notre société que sont la propriété et la liberté. L'observation de l'interaction entre ces deux notions doit permettre d'éclairer les limites de l'une et de l'autre dans les mentalités du 19e siècle.

Aujourd'hui comme hier, liberté et propriété sont considérées comme sacrées et intouchables. Profondément ancrées dans les mentalités occidentales, ces deux notions remontent aux sources de notre société. C'est la raison pour laquelle l'une et l'autre se côtoient dans la quasi totalité des textes de loi fondateurs de nos Etats modernes[9]. Quelles que soient leur culture politique, leur communauté

9 Voir la clause 29 de la *Magna carta libertatum*, charte britannique des libertés du 13e siècle, le 5e amendement de la Déclaration des droits – *Bill of Rights* – édictée en septembre 1789 par le 1er Congrès des Etats-Unis, et l'article 2 de la « Déclaration des droits de l'homme et du citoyen » de 1791.

linguistique, leur conception du rôle de l'Etat et des relations entre les individus et la société, l'ensemble des constitutions occidentales s'accordent en effet sur le caractère sacré tant de la liberté que de la propriété. Ces éléments centraux sont perçus comme préludant à tout pacte social. En adhérant à une communauté d'hommes, tout individu acquiert le droit à la protection de sa liberté et de ses biens par cette même collectivité.

Ces deux éléments semblent au prime abord plutôt complémentaires que concurrents. Le droit de propriété implique de disposer de sa liberté, et le droit de liberté de la possession de son propre corps et ainsi des fruits de son travail. Chaque concept représente donc une condition élémentaire de l'autre. John Locke n'affirme rien d'autre lorsqu'il énonce que "every man has a property in his own person [...]. The labour of his body, and the work of his hands [...] are properly his"[10]. Ces deux notions semblent ainsi généralement plus ou moins intimement liées.

Il existe cependant une occurrence – sans doute unique – dans laquelle liberté et propriété sont soudainement et parfois violemment mises en concurrence. Il s'agit du cadre de l'esclavage et de ses abolitions. L'esclavage constitue en effet une situation paroxysmique de l'opposition entre liberté et propriété. La perception matérialiste de l'esclave constitue la négation de son humanité, et par conséquent de son droit à la liberté. Dans le contexte des émancipations, le droit de possession des uns sert à légitimer la privation de liberté des autres, justifiant leur maintien dans l'esclavage. Suite aux abolitions, les maîtres sont dépossédés de leur propriété servile par le simple fait du recouvrement de leur liberté par les esclaves. Liberté et propriété s'opposent ainsi, l'un prenant le pas sur l'autre. Le phénomène d'une abolition constitue ainsi un champ d'expérimentation unique dans lequel se confrontent deux principes constitutifs des sociétés modernes.

Si l'esclave est une chose, son propriétaire a droit à une indemnité d'expropriation. Si par contre il est un homme, son maître n'a aucun droit à un dédommagement pour avoir dépouillé autrui de son droit fondamental à la liberté, perçue par certains tout au long de l'histoire comme une des composantes les plus essentielles des droits de l'homme[11]. La privation de liberté – privilège

10 Locke John, *Two treatises of government*, London, C. and J. Rivington, 1824 [1690], p. 145.

11 Voir entre autres exemples le Digeste de Justinien de 530, *Pandectae Justinianeae, in novum ordinem digestae*, Paris, Dondey-Dupré, 1823, p. 69; Llorente J.-A., *Œuvres de Don*

primaire et fondamental de tout être humain – entre ainsi en concurrence direct avec le droit naturel. Les lois de la nature précédant le droit des hommes, elles l'invalident quand elles s'y opposent.

Cette contradiction existant entre l'état de privation de liberté que confirme la loi des hommes avec l'ordre naturel des choses a comme conséquence de remettre en question la légitimité de la propriété servile en dépit de sa légalité. Les abolitionnistes soutiennent qu'une distinction doit être faite entre la notion de légalité qui découle des lois en vigueur dans une société et celle de légitimité qui trouve son origine dans le droit naturel, dans la raison et dans la morale. La première ne peut prétendre à prendre le pas sur la seconde, le droit naturel primant nécessairement sur celui des hommes et ne pouvant donc souffrir aucune dérogation. Même légal, le système servile ne peut être considéré comme légitime. La contestation du statut de chose de l'esclave par l'affirmation de son humanité a ainsi comme conséquence de récuser l'assimilation d'une abolition à une expropriation.

Entre propriété et homme

L'antagonisme diamétral existant entre ces deux définitions de l'esclave comme chose ou comme homme s'alimente du flottement perceptible entre la caractérisation officielle de la propriété servile comme biens communs et l'usage pratique qui en est fait. La théorie et la pratique sont parfois en contradiction l'une de l'autre, ce qui entretient le doute quant à la nature de l'esclave. L'inébranlabilité de la conception matérialiste de l'esclave comme chose n'est en effet pas sans fissures. Si les codes noirs définissent l'esclave comme une propriété tout à fait commune, une recherche poussée plus en détails indique que ce constat ne va pas forcément de soi. Certains aspects observables dans la pratique démontrent que les choses sont en réalité bien plus compliquées qu'elles ne paraissent au prime abord.

Barthélemi de Las Casas, Evêque de Chiapa, défenseur de la liberté des naturels de l'Amérique, 2, Paris, Eymery, 1822, pp. 56-57, Bodin Jean, *Les six livres de la République*, Paris, Gabriel Cartier, 1608 [1576], p. 279, Locke *Two treatises of government, op. cit.*, p. 143 ou encore Hutcheson F., *A system of moral philosophy, in three books (vol. 2)*, London, Longman, 1755, pp. 294-295.

En premier lieu, les codes noirs contiennent des clauses stipulant des sanctions à l'égard des maîtres ayant maltraité ou tué leurs esclaves. Ces règlements protègent théoriquement l'esclave de la toute puissance de son maître et constitue une limite à la possession absolue du maître sur son bien humain. Les biens inanimés ne bénéficient naturellement pas de telles faveurs, qui paraîtraient bien inutiles si elles devaient s'appliquer à l'usage d'objets exclusivement matériels.

Ce n'est cependant pas l'humanité de l'esclave qui lui vaut de bénéficier de cette protection, mais sa nature d'être vivant, commune à tout animal. Les règlements serviles ne sont en effet pas les seuls à énoncer des peines contre des propriétaires maltraitants. Les lois concernant les bestiaux par exemple sont également riches de stipulations concernant la responsabilité de ceux qui y portent dommage.

La possibilité d'assujettir des choses vivantes à une volonté externe a toujours soulevé les questions les plus fondamentales quant à la propriété. Les êtres non seulement humains mais vivants ont des qualités d'autonomie plus ou moins développées. Ils peuvent par exemple bouger selon leur propre volonté, souffrir et se reproduire. Ces qualités les distinguent des autres types de propriété et les rendent à priori peu aptes à être traités comme de vulgaires objets.

C'est la raison pour laquelle l'Etat montre généralement un intérêt spécial envers la propriété vivante et cherche à imposer des limites à la domination absolue des propriétaires, dans l'intérêt même des choses possédées. En effet, le droit de propriété sur des biens vivants est parfois construit comme un simple droit d'utilisation ou de gardiennage, où sont par exemple prescrites des règles de bon usage prohibant la cruauté et la maltraitance[12].

Si la possession d'esclaves s'apparente ainsi à celle d'animaux, il existe des occurrences légales qui démontrent que les premiers se distinguent sur le plan pratique des seconds. Certaines dispositions des codes noirs ne sont applicables qu'aux esclaves et non aux animaux. Elles stipulent à l'encontre exclusive des esclaves des peines d'emprisonnement, de châtiments corporels ou de mort en cas d'évasion ou de délits. Il paraît alors comme aujourd'hui totalement absurde de condamner des animaux à subir de telles peines. Cette différenciation démontre qu'il n'y a pas complète analogie entre l'esclave et l'animal. Le premier se distingue du second par un niveau plus élevé de volonté et sa capacité

12 Brewer John, Staves Susan, "Introduction", in Brewer John, Staves Susan (eds.), *Early modern conceptions of property*, London and New York, Routledge, 1995, p. 11.

de prise de conscience. Cette aptitude de l'esclave à répondre de ses actes, sa « responsabilité », semble ainsi constituer le gage de son humanité.

S'il est permis ici d'énoncer des vérités qui paraissent aujourd'hui banales, elles ne le sont pas forcément à une époque où l'homme réduit en esclavage est littéralement et pratiquement traité comme une chose. Les rares exceptions à ce régime général révèlent un certain malaise des contemporains de l'esclavage quant à la nature confuse de l'esclave. Sa position d'« entre-deux », entre propriété et être humain, empêche de le situer précisément sur l'échelle de la nature. L'emploi et la disposition de l'esclave sont ainsi parfois rendus complexes, comme dans le cas d'une abolition de l'esclavage par exemple.

Une conclusion en demi teinte

Un des objectifs principaux d'une abolition consiste à atténuer, voire à supprimer l'antagonisme entre propriété et liberté, en conciliant les intérêts des uns et des autres. Il s'agit à la fois de libérer les esclaves, tout en respectant la propriété de leurs maîtres, dessein qui, à première vue, semble relever de la gageure.

Ces considérations expliquent les demi-mesures observables dans les processus abolitionnistes. Si des indemnités financières sont dans certains cas versées aux planteurs, leur montant ne représente jamais l'entier de la valeur vénale de la propriété servile[13]. Quant à la liberté des esclaves, elle n'est que fort relative.

13 La proportion du montant l'indemnité financière est rarement supérieure à la moitié de la valeur vénale des esclaves à l'exception notable de Porto Rico, voir pour les colonies britanniques Fogel Robert W., Engerman Stanley L., "Philanthropy at bargain prices: notes on the economics of gradual emancipation", in *Journal of legal studies*, 3 (1974), p. 394; pour les colonies françaises le document « Indemnité coloniale », in Archives Nationales d'Outre Mer, cote K4, *Organisation administrative de la liquidation de l'indemnité*, contenant les valeurs moyennes du prix des esclaves établies sur les dix années précédant l'abolition française et les montants de l'indemnité alloués selon les colonies; pour le district fédéral de Columbia Goldin Claudia D., "The economics of emancipation", in *Journal of economic history*, 33, 1 (1973), p. 73; pour les colonies néerlandaises Emmer Pieter C, *The Dutch in the Atlantic economy (1580-1880): trade, slavery and emancipation*, Aldershot [etc.], Ashgate Variorum, 1998, p. 230 et pour Porto Rico Curet José, "About slavery and the order of things: Puerto Rico, 1845-1973", in Fraginal Manuel Moreno, Moya Pons Frank, Engerman Stanley L. (eds.), *Between slavery and free labour: the Spanish-speaking Caribbean in the nineteenth century*, Baltimore, The Johns Hopkins University Press, 1985, p. 133.

A leur libération, les nouveaux affranchis sont généralement astreints au travail forcé pendant une période donnée[14]. De plus, ils accèdent au statut d'hommes libres dépouillés de tout capital – matériel (terres ou argent) ou intellectuel (éducation) – susceptible de leur assurer la jouissance d'une certaine autonomie face à leurs anciens maîtres. De la condition d'objet animé à celui d'homme économiquement dépendant, il reste à l'ancien esclave de nombreux échelons sociaux à gravir au lendemain des abolitions pour devenir membre à part entière de l'humanité.

Ainsi, tant le droit des maîtres sur leur propriété servile que celui des esclaves à la liberté subissent des ajustements en vue de leur conciliation. De ce choc de Titans entre deux principes constitutifs de notre société moderne ne semble ressortir qu'un semblant de match nul. S'il n'est pleinement satisfaisant pour personne, ce compromis permet cependant d'ouvrir le chemin de la liberté à des millions d'individus.

14 L'« apprentissage » stipule un temps de travail forcé pour les adultes d'une durée de trois à douze ans (colonies britanniques et danoises, Porto Rico, Cuba, Surinam), tandis que les lois du « ventre libre » prévoient l'émancipation définitive des enfants déclarés libres à la naissance entre quatorze et vingt-huit ans (Etats du Nord des Etats-Unis, Amérique latine, colonies espagnoles et Brésil).

The Italy-Libya Agreement of 2 October 1956. The Bank of Italy's Assets in Libya after World War II

Donatella Strangio

Introduction

Familiarity with the economic interests shared between the Bank of Italy and Libya can provide a good platform for a deeper understanding of the relations between these two states and two peoples in the current global context. This research was conducted mainly through documentary sources that were collected by the Bank of Italy and which are kept in its historical Archive. The Bank of Italy was called upon to operate in Libya by the Italian government during Italy's colonial period before World War II. International organizations requested that the Bank work in Libya after the war due to the specific skills and experience it had acquired in the area. The British occupation of Libya in 1943 led inevitably to a series of social, political and economic consequences, including, among others, the Anglo-Italian agreement of 1951, which called for the seizure and custody by the British authorities of different Italian companies that operated in that country. The branches of the Bank of Italy in Libya were closed when the introduction of British military authority pound destabilised the fiscal situation and effectively put them out of business. The Bank's Libyan branches reopened in 1951, when the United Nations, in accordance with Resolution no. 388, declared Libya an independent and democratic State[1]. This

1 Archivio Storico della Banca d'Italia (hereinafter: ASBI), Banca d'Italia, Studi, pratt., n. 530, fasc. 1, fasc. 2, fasc. 4. See also for the colonial event Del Boca Angelo, *Italiani Brava gente?*, Vicenza, Editori Neri Pozza, 2005; Del Boca Angelo, *A un passo dalla forca. Atrocità e infamie dell'occupazione italiana della Libia nelle memorie del patriota Moha-med Fekini*, Milano, Baldini Castoldi Dalai, 2007; St. Johns Ronald Bruce, *Libya: from colony to Indipendence*, Oxford UK, Oneworld, 2008; Calchi Novati Giampaolo, *Africa: la storia ritrovata. Dalle prime forme politiche alle indipendenze nazionali*, Roma, Carocci, 2005, pp. 233–265; Labanca Nicola, *Oltremare. Storia dell'espansione coloniale italiana*, Bologna, il Mulino, 2002, pp. 267–369.

independence ushered in a period of sour relations with Italy, which brought with it negative repercussions for the Italian community in Libya.

Libya, Italy's third possession, whose destiny was decided by the UN, became an independent kingdom combining the regions of Tripolitania, Cyrenaica and Fezzan. The new kingdom was given to the Sanusi dynasty, originally from Cyrenaica, which had a long history of opposition against the Italian presence in Italy and had eventually joined the Allied forces. Independence was proclaimed in 1951 with a federal Constitution that tried to accommodate the different characteristics of Tripolitania, which was more advanced and attracted to Tunisia, and Cyrenaica, which might be classified as more backward and was rather sensitive to Egypt's influence[2].

Among many disputes between Italy and Libya, one was finally settled: in 1956, an agreement was entered into by the two states which contemplated, under article 4, "the transfer to the Libyan State of the movable and immovable properties located in Libya which were owned by the Italian State or by autonomous state companies".

This paper will try to clarify the situation of the Bank of Italy's properties and the reason why they were not included in this and in other agreements and considered as state-owned properties. Moreover, it will explore the question of Magazzini Generali, a company established by a gubernatorial decree of 1924 to develop commercial activities[3]. In fact, this company was initially defined as a parastatal entity by the British authorities, which seized its assets. It has also been necessary to analyse carefully the legal nature of these assets. The status of Italian assets deteriorated when, after he took power, Muammar Qaddafi enacted the law of 1970 whereby all Italians were expelled from, and prohibited to return to, Libya and all their assets seized.[4]

2 Calchi Novati Giampaolo, *Il Corno d'Africa nella storia e nella politica*, Torino, SEI, 1994, p. 274.

3 ASBI, Banca d'Italia, Studi, pratt., n. 532, fasc. 6.

4 Varvelli Arturo, *L'Italia e l'ascesa di Gheddafi. La cacciata degli italiani, le armi e il petrolio (1969–1974)*, Roma, Baldini Castoldi Dalai, 2009; Varvelli Arturo, "Gheddafi e la cacciata degli italiani dalla Libia nel 1970", in *I sentieri della ricerca*, 5 (2007), pp. 179–227. See also Del Boca Angelo, *Gheddafi. Una sfida dal deserto*, Roma-Bari, Laterza, 2001; Mutti Claudio, "Gheddafi dal panarabismo al panafricanismo", in *Eurasia*, 12/06/2009. (http://www.eurasia-rivista.org/cogit_content/articoli/ EkuuZFuVFpCvSYFQIa.shtml).

The United Nations Resolution of 1950 and the Situation of Italian Assets after Libya's Independence

Based on the London agreement signed by Italy and the Allies in 1947, the end of World War II involved Italy's waiver of all its possessions in Africa, including Libya. The handover of Libya to England entailed the seizure of all the assets owned by the Italian state in Libya. This seizure was fundamental to the Anglo-Italian treaty of 28 June 1951, which was based on proclamation no. 122 of 1 December 1945. This treaty was the first of a number of agreements, draft laws and laws concerning Italian assets in Libya and, in addition to establishing the principle that "all state-owned and parastatal assets were to be seized by the British custodian", it laid down the procedures that such transfers should follow.

The transfer involved different terms and conditions, and took into account the public or private nature of the assets. Thus, public assets would be transferred at no cost while the transfer of private assets constituted compensation by the colonial administration of the Italian State. Such compensation was calculated on the basis of the current value of the assets in question. The agreement provided only for publicly-owned assets, that is assets defined by local laws as the property of citizens by way of the institutions in which they were politically organized[5].

It was important to distinguish legally between public and private property. Publicly-owned assets were intended, directly or indirectly, for public use. On the other hand, assets held by a public entity which did not represent a political organization of the community, other than a territorial entity, were considered private property. Thus, the contracting party of this treaty was the Italian State which, after the war, had to transfer to Britain its claims on its Libyan possessions, including its assets.

The question was submitted to the General Assembly of the United Nations, which adopted two Resolutions on former Italian colonies: the first on 20 November 1949 and the second on 17 November 1950. Both recognized that Libya – including Cyrenaica, Tripolitania and Fezzan – should be an independent and sovereign state and that such independence should be effective no later than 1951.

5 ASBI, Banca d'Italia, Studi, pratt. n 519, fasc. 1, p. 5.

In addition to laying down economic and financial provisions on Libya and the timing for the country's future independence, U.N. Resolution 388 also determined the final disposition of the assets of the Italian state in Libya. To this end, still with respect to the problems related to the assets owned by the colonizing State, though in relation to the private entities and institutions that were part of that State, on 2 December 1950, pursuant to article 1 of the UN Resolution, all the movable and immovable property located in Eritrea and owned by the Italian state was transferred to the successor state. The second paragraph of the same article provided that the new Eritrean state would receive the public property (demanio pubblico), the inalienable property (proprietà indisponibile), the alienable property (patrimonio disponibile) and the autonomous agencies of the State whilst letter f required that all rights of the Italian State in the capital and the property of institutions, companies and associations of a public character located in Eritrea be transferred. Thus, the principle that prevailed was that of State ownership, whereby only the State would suffer the loss while other entities, including public entities, would be exempted. In fact, considering that the rights and properties had to be located in Eritrea, the transfer did not include the State's shares in entities headquartered in Italy[6]. Article 1 of the resolution contemplated the transfer of only movable and immovable property located in Libya owned by the Italian State to the successor State[7]. The article was based on the following normative principles:

a) subjective premise: the Italian State had to own the assets to be transferred directly or in its capacity as administrator of Libya;
b) objective premise: the assets to be transferred had to be located in Libya.

The provision required the transfer of the State's property rights in establishments, companies and associations of a public character[8]. The second paragraph of the same article specified that all public property and the inalienable property had to be transferred to the Libyan State; the third paragraph added that

6 ASBI, Banca d'Italia, Studi, pratt. n. 520, fasc. 1, *Appunto sulla Banca d'Italia 14 gennaio 1953*, pp. 398 and 411.

7 ASBI, Banca d'Italia, Studi, pratt. n 535, fasc. 1 p. 68.

8 ASBI, Banca d'Italia, Studi, pratt. n 519, fasc. 1; ASBI, Banca d'Italia, Studi, pratt. n. 520, fasc. 1, pp. 399 and 412.

the alienable property and the property of the autonomous agencies located in Libya, as well as the rights of the Italian State in the capital and the property of institutions, companies and associations of a public character located in Libya, also had to be transferred.

To determine whether an item of property was public, the British authorities followed rule 432 of chapter XV of the Manual of Military Law whereby "in case of doubt as to whether a property was public or private, the property was considered private if and until evidence of its private character was established"[9]. During the years of British occupation, the Bank of Italy, as an entity operating in Libya, was involved in the process of having its assets in Libya released. Most importantly, the Bank had to provide evidence of its legal status as a private entity to the British authorities and, as such, prevent its inclusion among the entities subject to the restrictions applied in accordance with United Nations Resolution no. 388. Besides, the Anglo-Italian agreement signed in London on 28 June 1951 on Italian property in Libya, which was intended to solve various questions on the custody of certain Italian assets, did not concern the Bank of Italy, which was not included among the entities listed under article 5 of the agreement, precisely because there was no doubt, then, about its private nature. Moreover, Royal law decree no. 375 of 12 March 1936 had established that the State did not own that Bank or have any participating interest in it; it only exercised general supervision over it, as it did over all the other banks operating in Italy, including (based on the provisions of Royal law decree no. 1400 of 17 July 1937, which amended decree no. 375) the large Italian banks, which were divided into: a) public law credit institutes; and b) national interest banks. It should be clarified that this classification did not limit bank activities to specific sectors or to serving certain State purposes but simply fixed some rules, which were common to both categories, to govern their respective functions, establishing, among other things, that their articles of association had to be approved by the Head of government, upon proposal of the Committee of Ministers, having heard the technical corporative credit Committee (upon the fall of the fascist regime, Royal law decree no. 721, dated

9 ASBI, Banca d'Italia, Studi, pratt. n. 519, fasc. 1. Cf. *Memorandum on the Seizure and Requisitioning of Property in occupied Enemy Territories* Part II – Public Property – Sub-Part A: Description of Public property (ASBI, Banca d'Italia, Studi, pratt. n. 520, fasc. 1, *Appunto sulla Banca d'Italia 14 gennaio 1953*, p. 415).

9 August 1943, disbanded the central corporative Committee while article 1 of the Decree of the Provisional Head of State no. 681, dated 17 July 1947, replaced the Committee of Ministers with the Inter-ministerial Committee for Credit and Savings (CICR – Comitato Interministeriale per il Credito ed il Risparmio) chaired by the Minister of the Treasury, who therefore enacted CICR's measures with his own decrees). Thus, in terms of the control of the State over banks, it was an indirect control exercised through the supervisory authority vested in the Bank of Italy to ensure banks' compliance with the laws on credit, which were applicable to all the banks operating in the territory of the State or subject to its sovereignty. The difference between public law credit institutes and national interest banks was indeed formal but concerned their origins. Public law banks were called such since their foundation and included banks such as Banco di Sardegna (Bank of Sardinia), Banco di Napoli (Bank of Naples) and Banco di Sicilia (Bank of Sicily), which were for a long time, up to 1926, currency-issuing banks and had been established as "moral entities". National interest banks, for their part, had to be incorporated as joint-stock companies (article 25 of the banking law) and had to "have a vast organization throughout the national territory, and have to be recognized by decree of the President of the Republic, upon submission of the Ministry of the Treasury. Such qualification cannot be bestowed on banks with branches in fewer than at least thirty provinces"[10].

To prove its private nature, thus its right to keep its assets like any natural or private legal person, the Bank of Italy referred to article 20 of Royal law decree no. 375 of 12 March 1936, which set out provisions for the protection of savings and governing the credit function; this decree as subsequently amended and supplemented would eventually be termed "banking law".

Even though paragraph 1 defined it as a "Public law institute", article 20 laid down the provisions governing the activities of the Bank of Italy by establishing that "for the purposes of public credit protection and policy continuity for the central Bank, its shares are nominative and can be owned solely by: a) Savings banks; b) Public law institutes and Banks of national interest; c) Social

10 ASBI, Banca d'Italia, Studi, pratt. n. 520, fasc. 1, pp. 706–708, *Lettera del 16 marzo 1948 della filiale di Asmara al signor controllore delle banche e dei cambi*; pp. 709–712, *Lettera al ministero degli affari esteri del 5 marzo 1948 da parte degli organi della Banca Nazionale del lavoro.*

security institutions; d) Insurance companies". Moreover, the Bank of Italy was an entity headquartered in Italy and, consequently, it would be impossible to transfer its shares to the successor State. This law showed the legal prohibition for entities and persons, including the Italian State, to own shares of the Bank of Italy. Therefore, not only did the Italian State not own shares in the Bank of Italy but it was even prevented by law from owning them[11].

The foundation of the Bank of Italy as a currency-issuing institute further attested to its legal nature as a private entity. The Bank of Italy was established in 1884 as an autonomous company resulting from the merger of three pre-existing banks: Banca Nazionale del Regno (National Bank of the Kingdom), Banca Nazionale di Toscana (National Bank of Tuscany) and Banca Toscana di Credito (Tuscan Bank of Credit). These three banks were already engaged in lending activities, with the power to issue currency, as automous companies[12].

From the moment it came into being, the Italian State never had any equity interest in the Bank, directly or indirectly. Law no. 449 of 10 August 1893 on the reorganization of currency-issuing institutes authorized this merger and approved the articles of association of the Bank of Italy. The first 300,000 nominative shares were distributed to the merged banks' shareholders. Following the reform of Royal law decree no. 375 of 12 March 1936, these nominative shares were called participating interests[13].

These participating interests could be held only by certain categories of credit institutions, social security institutions and insurance companies. Thus, the State could not hold participating interests in the Bank of Italy. However, due to matters of economic order, and in exchange for the monopoly privilege

11 Paragraph 2 of article 20 provided that "The Bank's capital amounts to three hundred million lire and is represented by 300,000 shares with nominal value of one thousand lire each, fully paid in".

12 On the beginning and formation of the Central Bank see Bonelli Franco, *La Banca d'Italia dal 1894 al 1913. Momenti della formazione di una Banca centrale*, Roma-Bari, Laterza, 1991; Conte Leandro, *La Banca Nazionale. Formazione e attività di una banca di emissione 1843–1861*, Napoli, Edizioni Scientifiche Italiane, 1990. About history, duties, part and administration of the Bank of Italy see Gigliobianco Alfredo, *Via Nazionale. Banca d'Italia e classe dirigente. Cento anni di Storia*, Roma, Donzelli, 2006; Cama Giampaolo, *La Banca d'Italia. Le istituzioni politiche in Italia*, Bologna, il Mulino, 2010.

13 ASBI, Banca d'Italia, Studi, pratt. n. 520, fasc. 1, *Appunto sulla Banca d'Italia 14 gennaio 1953*, pp. 413.

granted, the State protected its citizens' interests by setting a limit to the profit that the Bank of Italy could distribute. In fact, according to article 54 of the Articles of Association of the Bank of Italy, as approved by the Royal Decree of 11 June 1936 (as amended and supplemented), which, under paragraph 8, provided that, following provisions made in accordance with the above article and the allocation of profit within a certain limit, "the remaining sum is paid to the State pursuant to article 3 of Ministerial Decree no. 1647 of 31 December 1935"[14].

That said, between 1941 and 1951, that is during the years of British occupation, based on article 4 of proclamation no. 122 of 1 December 1945, British authorities themselves did not think that the Bank of Italy could be considered state owned. Furthermore, the Anglo-Italian agreement on Italian assets in Libya did not include the Bank of Italy among public entities.

The question of Italian assets in the colony involved in particular the Italian citizens isolated after World War II by the local people, who considered Italian private assets as the property of the future Libyan state. This provision – which was common to other central banks (see e.g. the agreement between the French State and the Bank of France of 18 July 1818) – reflected an economic need in that, since the Bank of Italy exercised a monopoly over issuing currency, the State protected the interests of all its citizens by setting a limit on distributable profits. In other words, the State collected a tax in exchange for this privilege out of net profit (after provisions and allocation to reserves and payment of a dividend to shareholders). The payment of this tax, which would be governed by subsequent agreements, began in 1909, much earlier than 1936. Yet, there was no specific provision in case of liquidation, as any residual interests in liquidation would be attributed to shareholders in proportion to their holdings, as with any private company. In other words, under no circumstances could the Bank of Italy's assets be attributed to the State in case of liquidation[15].

This situation led the Italian and the Libyan States to begin negotiations that ended with the Libyan agreement dated 2 October 1956. The agreement, as indicated in its preamble and in the Italian implementation and ratification

14 ASBI, Banca d'Italia, Studi, pratt. n. 520, fasc. 1, *Appunto sulla Banca d'Italia 14 gennaio 1953*, pp. 401 and 414.

15 ASBI, Banca d'Italia, Studi, pratt. n. 535, "In Parlamento l'esame dell'accordo di trasferimento dei beni italiani al nuovo Regno Unito di Libia", fasc. 1, p. 5.

law, was designed to implement strictly the economic and financial provisions related to the new independent Libyan State laid down in the resolution of the United Nations.

The content of this Resolution was founded on a clear conception of the current conditions in Libya and the achievements of the Italian State in Libya in terms of economic and social development since 1912. In 1902 agreements had been signed by the Italian (Giulio Prinetti) and French (Theophile Delcasse) foreign ministers, in keeping with the new Italian foreign policy designed to establish closer ties with France, despite the triple-alliance treaty signed by Italy with Germany and Austria in 1882. Such agreements limited the spheres of influence of Italy and France in North Africa to Libya and Morocco respectively. With the Libyan war decided by Giolitti in September 1911, Italian foreign policy matched the move made earlier by France with its occupation of Morocco. In fact, the French initiative had put Prime Minister Giolitti in a dilemma, as he did not know whether Italy should go on and conquer Libya based on the 1902 agreement or give up the idea of establishing a presence in the only area of Mediterranean Africa that was not yet subjected to a European colonial power. Besides, the conquest of Libya by Giolitti was supported by a consensus of Italian public opinion including liberals, conservatives, radicals, industrial and financial interests and, last but not least, Catholics. The Treaty of Lausanne in October 1912, following Turkey's surrender, recognized Italy's annexation of Libya. The hostilities, however, did not cease because the "holy war" proclaimed by the Libyan population forced the Italian garrisons to limit their control to the port coastal areas[16].

The agreement – which was composed of 19 articles, 20 annexes and 14 letters – stipulated that "all the Italian assets belonging to a specific public entity shall be transferred to the Libyan state" but article 9 provided that private owners of goods in Libya were authorized to "exercise freely and directly their rights".

Eventually, the Bank of Italy learned that, based on the negotiations that preceded the agreement, its assets would be transferred to Libya in accordance with the Resolution of the United Nations of 15 December 1950[17].

16 Labanca, *Oltremare. op. cit.*, pp. 267–369.

17 ASBI, Banca d'Italia, Studi, pratt., n. 535, fasc. 1, p. 7 "Interpretazione dell'accordo italo-libico, 2 ottobre 1956".

Thus, the Bank of Italy was concerned with upholding the principle acknowledged in the various agreements to implement the Treaty that it was not one of the entities whose assets should be transferred. In other words, the Bank of Italy:

1. did not, institutionally or in fact, pursue purposes closely related to key state purposes;
2. its capital could not belong to the State if the State had in no way participated in its creation;
3. the State and other public entities did not provide any funding to the Bank;
4. there was no direct availability of the Bank of Italy's assets or profit;
5. there was no public destination, in the sense of a nationalization;
6. shareholders included a large number of unquestionably private entities (e.g. Assicurazioni Generali)[18].

As it could not be demonstrated that the Bank of Italy's assets were the property of the Italian State and, therefore, had to be turned over to the Libyan State, a fictional transaction was arranged whereby Libya would buy the Bank of Italy's assets for a nominal price of 100 lire while the Italian Treasury would pay to the Bank of Italy the difference up to the effective price of those assets.

The Italian law that ratified the agreement – no. 843 of 17 August 1957 – with the exchange of notes between the Italian Republic and the United Kingdom of Libya agreed that "the Bank of Italy's properties located in Libya shall be sold to the Libyan state for 100 Italian lire". The Bank of Italy's assets, both in Tripolitania and in Cyrenaica, included the building where its office was, the building where its employees lived and Magazzini Generali.

The agreement, however, did not mark an end to the problems between the Italian State and the Libyan State, especially after the coup d'état of 1 September 1969 and the ascent to power of Qaddafi, which led to the adoption, in the space of a few months, of increasingly restrictive measures against the Italian community and ultimately, on 21 June 1970, to the decree that ordered the seizure of all the private assets of the Italian citizens. The decree, which stemmed from the intention of the Libyan government to return to its citizens the wealth looted during the years of Italian domination, did not take into account, however, the Resolution of the United Nations of 1950, especially

18 ASBI, Banca d'Italia, Studi, pratt., n. 519, fasc. 1.

article 4 which provided that the properties, rights and interests of Italian citizens and legal persons would be respected[19]. International law qualified this violation as illegal. In fact the expropriating government, Libya, should at least have paid compensation equal to the present and potential value of the properties, rights and interests in question.

The Italian government, however, chose not to denounce before the United Nations these acts by the Libyan authorities, which so blatantly violated the UN Resolution of 1950, or to protect its citizens by trying to enforce the Libyan authorities' obligation to provide compensation for those properties, rights and interests so illegally and indiscriminately seized with the law of 21 July 1970, on the basis of a specific provision of the international law. Thus, having adopted this stance, the Italian government had knowingly abdicated its obligation – based on diplomatic protection, the instrument made available by international law – to protect its citizens and their rights and interests before a foreign State. As a second consequence, the Italian government undertook the obligation to pay the full amount – including goodwill and monetary devaluation – of the properties, rights and interests of the Italian community that was forced out of Libya. With respect to this substitutive compensation, the Italian government did enact a number of measures in favour of the citizens returned from Libya; however, such measures were completely inadequate because the sum paid to this day, more than thirty years after the seizure, amounts to 228 billion lire. This sum is a far cry from the estimated losses of 400 billion lire incurred in 1970.

Magazzini Generali and the Italy-Libya Agreement

The Italy-Libya agreement called for the transfer to the new Libyan State of all the movable and immovable properties located in Libya owned by the Italian State and by those agencies that were considered public.

The assets of the Bank of Italy as a private entity operating in Libya were not included in the Italy-Libya agreement or in the Anglo-Italian agreement of 1951, as already noted, because there was no evidence that attested to their

19 ASBI, Banca d'Italia, Affari Coloniali, 3; ASBI, Banca d'Italia, Segreteria Particolare, pratt., n. 439, fasc. 10.

public nature and, accordingly, they were considered as the property of private legal persons.

The Bank of Italy's activities during the Italian colonial period, as well as in the post-colonial one, were primarily concerned with local development. To this end, policies were adopted on farm credit, building finance and to promote import-export activities[20].

Responsibility for these matters was entrusted to Magazzini Generali and regulated by the gubernatorial decree of 7 May 1924 which, under article 1, granted the concession to build the warehousing facilities in Tripoli in cooperation with Banco di Napoli and Banco di Sicilia[21]. The decree set out how the operations and the facilities – located on the quay of the port of Tripoli – had to be managed.

The Bank of Italy would bear the cost of building the facilities[22].The concessionaire was required to pay to the Libyan government, as owner of the land, an annual rent for the area on which the facilities would be erected. Magazzini conducted a diversified operation which involved: a) Storage of imported goods until they would be delivered to importers at the customs facilities; b) Storage of goods subject to customs duties which would eventually be sold for consumption or re-exported; c) Advances against warehouse receipts issued by the warehouse's administration for goods stored with Magazzini Generali; d) Loading and unloading of ships by the company with its own employees.

Magazzini Generali gave impetus to the construction of substantial infrastructural features which could reinforce its activity, such as the railroad connections necessary for inland shipping from the port[23]. The concession to use the Magazzini was split three ways among the Bank of Italy, with 50 % of the total, and Banco di Napoli and Banco di Sicilia, with 25 % each. The length of the concession should have been 90 years, at the end of which all the equipment and infrastructure built by the Bank of Italy would have been handed over to the colonial administration[24].

20 Ercole Tuccimei, *La Banca d'Italia in Africa*, Roma-Bari, Laterza, 1998, pp. 70–79, 81–85.

21 ASBI, Banca d'Italia, Studi, pratt., n 523, fasc. 6 p. 5.

22 ASBI, Banca d'Italia, Studi, pratt., n. 532, fasc. 6, p. 351.

23 ASBI, Banca d'Italia, Studi, pratt., n. 532, fasc. 6, p. 358.

24 Tuccimei, *La Banca d'Italia, op. cit.*, p. 79. Strangio Donatella, *Decolonizzazione e sviluppo economico. La Cassa per la Circolazione monetaria della Somalia e la Banca nazionale somala: il ruolo della Banca d'Italia (1947–1960)*, Milano, Franco Angeli, 2010, pp. 18–19 note n. 18.

The consortium established by the three banks was managed by: a) A higher committee based in Rome, at the Bank of Italy's General Directorate, which consisted of 3 officials of the Bank of Italy, 3 executives from Banco di Napoli and 1 executive from Banco di Sicilia, appointed by the respective managements. The higher committee was chaired by one of the three officials of the Bank of Italy, who was designated by the Bank's director general; b) A local committee based in Tripoli, at the offices of the Bank of Italy, which consisted of the managers of the branches of the three banks of the consortium and a lending officer (consigliere di Sconto) of the Bank of Italy; c) a director of Magazzini Generali, who was appointed by the higher committee[25].

The higher committee had policy setting responsibilities, approved the accounts and allocated net profits. Magazzini operated between 1924 and 23 January 1943, when its activity was interrupted by the British occupation[26]. During the years of British occupation Magazzini Generali – as part of the assets owned by the Italian State – was seized, based on the Anglo-Italian agreement. Its facilities were rented by the British authorities. Following the measure published by the Tripolitania gazette, no. 1 of 1 January 1945, the allied authority declared Magazzini Generali of Tripoli a parastatal entity and, as such, all previous rental contracts were cancelled and all the activities of the company were transferred to the custody of the British military[27].

The categorisation of parastatal entity given to Magazzini Generali by the allies was not determined by the public nature of the Bank of Italy – as the British authorities had no doubt about its nature as a private entity – but by the legal nature of the other two institutes – Banco di Napoli and Banco di Sicilia – which held the remaining 50% of the concession.

The Bank of Italy tried to object to the conclusions reached by the British authorities by maintaining that Magazzini Generali could not be considered a parastatal entity as this company's functions were not exactly State functions but were based mainly on common commercial activities that could be performed by any private entity.

The Italian law at that time included parastatal entities among those that performed typical State-related duties, which were defined also as "minor

25 ASBI, Banca d'Italia, Studi, pratt., n. 532, fasc. 6, p. 5.

26 Tuccimei, *La Banca d'Italia in Africa, op. cit.*, pp. 255–261.

27 ASBI, Banca d'Italia, Studi, pratt., n. 532, fasc. 6, p. 111.

public entities", that is bodies performing indirect administrative state duties, existing and working to achieve public interest purposes[28].

The State attributed part of its activities to auxiliary entities, public minor entities in fact. Banco di Napoli and Banco di Sicilia did not exactly perform state functions, but were under the supervision of the State, on the basis of the Italian law on the protection of savings and the governance of the credit system (the aforementioned banking law).

Magazzini Generali had been established for a merely private purpose, that is the performance of a purely commercial activity. The fact that the company was attributed public functions did not alter its nature as a private entity which, as such, fell within the scope of article 9 of the Italy-Libya agreement and the Italian ratification law no. 843 of 17 August 1957, which called for the payment of compensation to the Italian owners of properties transferred in accordance with annex A of the Italy-Libya agreement[29].

Thus, as it demonstrated the private nature of the company, the Bank of Italy began to provide compensation to the owners of properties and the holders of rights and interests lost as a result of the peace treaty and other international agreements related to this treaty.

The amount that the Libyan State was required to pay to the Italian State was not only based on the value of the assets of Magazzini Generali but also on the early termination of the concession arrangements which, according to the agreement of 1924, should have lasted for 90 years, as already noted[30]. The loss of future profits should have been calculated on the basis of profits booked during the years of normal operations as adjusted to reflect the value that money had in those years.

Concerning properties, the Bank of Italy had a claim on all the real estate that it had built. Thus, compensation should have been calculated on the basis of the current value of these properties. This value reflected their condition, excluding changes made by the Libyan government. Clearly compensation did not cover war damage inflicted to the properties. The fate of Magazzini Generali was common to other private companies that had operations in Libya

28 ASBI, Banca d'Italia, Studi, pratt., n. 532, fasc. 6, p. 114.

29 ASBI, Banca d'Italia, Affari coloniali, pratt., n. 519 (relazione tecnica Sirolli e Palisca), n. 572, fasc. 364, n. 10, fasc. 386, n. 14, fasc. 332.

30 ASBI, Banca d'Italia, Studi, pratt., n. 532, fasc. 6, p. 92.

and that, following British occupation and the Anglo-Italian agreement, were forced to transfer their assets. After it achieved independence, following the resolution of the United Nations, the former Italian colony became the new Kingdom of Libya of Idris I al-Sanusi, who in his youth had fought against colonial Italy. The monarchy became close to Great Britain, with which it signed a twenty-year alliance, and the United States with which, in 1954, it signed an agreement for the Weelus Field military base. With the military coup of 1 September 1969, conducted when the king was in Bursa, Turkey, the situation changed abruptly. Power was taken by the revolutionary command, a council of 12 men led by Colonel Muammar Qaddafi who, at the age of twenty-seven, became the world's youngest head of state[31]. The provisional constitution adopted defined Libya as "a free and democratic Arab republic".

The new government was recognized by Egypt, Sudan, Iraq and Syria, but soon recognition came also from the Soviet Union, United States, France and Italy, which supported the demise of a corrupt regime and the pursuit by the new government of a promised modernization programme that would allegedly move the country past the tribal fights that tore apart the areas where the central power had little control. The immediate consequence of the coup was the enactment of the law of 21 July 1970 by the Revolutionary command Council, which affected relationships between Italy and Libya by calling for the seizure of all the movable and immovable properties of the Italian community in Libya and the expulsion of all the members of the community.

The main reason for this decision was the lack of recognition by the Italian State of its colonial faults. In the summer of the following year, with the seizure of the assets of Italian residents in Libya and the expulsion of twenty thousand Italian citizens, an attempt was made to erase the remnants of Italian colonialism. The seizure did not affect the companies of the ENI and FIAT groups, which had a privileged business relationship with the Libyan government. Ironically, Italy became Libya's first commercial partner because of Italy's dependence on oil imports from Libya. In fact, in October 1972, a

31 Quaddafi's coup d'état on 1 September 1969 was inspired by the free Egyptian officers and Nasserism. With the military regime, Libya became a republic, undertaking a "third way" that resulted in the closing of the English and American bases, a different oil policy and the seizure of the land still occupied by Italian farmers (Calchi Novati, *Africa: la storia ritrovata, op. cit.*, p. 153).

couple of years after the departure of the Italians from Libya, ENI avoided the fate of nationalization that befell several foreign oil companies and signed a joint venture agreement with the Libyan National Oil Company (LNOC) for the exploitation of the rich oilfield of Bu Attifel. Moreover, two years after this agreement, arrangements were made for technical, scientific and economic cooperation which confirmed Italy's role as Libya's "privileged partner"[32]. The expulsion of the Italian community and the seizure of Italian assets marked the end of the colonial experience. As noted by Rosaria Trovato Macciaro, who returned to Italy after the law of 1970, "It took years for life to go back to normal. For years we were like gypsies. We Tripolinians still have the mal d'Afrique but I would never go back to Tripoli"[33].

32 Varvelli Arturo, "L'Italia, la Libia e l'indebolimento del rapporto privilegiato", in *ISPI. Policy Brief*, 97 (2008), pp. 1–7; Vandewalle Dirk J., *Lybia Since Indipendence. Oil and State Building*, I.B., London, Tauris Pubblishers, 1998.

33 www.airl.it/accorditrattati3.php. Varvelli Arturo, "L'Italia, la Libia", *art. cit.*, pp. 1–7; Id., "Lo sviluppo economico della Libia dopo la 'riabilitazione'", in *ISPI. Policy Brief*, 46 (2006), pp. 1–7.

Expropriations qui créent des propriétaires: le cas des ventes et indemnisations de terres à Rio de Janeiro (Brésil), 1870-1910

Manoela Pedroza

Introduction

Cette contribution porte sur la zone ouest de la commune de Rio de Janeiro, dans la *freguesia*[1] de Campo Grande et analyse les expropriations ou les ventes de terres de particuliers au gouvernement fédéral brésilien à la fin du XIXe siècle. Notre analyse montre que « l'urbanisation » de Rio de Janeiro a été accomplie en s'appuyant sur le sens d'opportunité des agents locaux qui ont volontairement encouragé la rupture avec les anciens droits d'usage sur les terres. Ces opérations ont pu être menées grâce à la connexion entre les pratiques matérielles d'une part et les groupes sociaux et les solutions institutionnelles d'autre part, à l'intérieur de solutions locales variées. Les coutumes et les normes juridiques ont pu être manipulées et utilisées pour légitimer une transformation radicale de la notion et des droits de propriété.

Selon Paolo Grossi, la propriété peut être appréhendée comme une solution historique et particulière au problème de l'appartenance[2]. La tâche de l'historien serait alors celle d'historiciser la propriété moderne. D'après Rosa Congost, il importe aussi de regarder au-delà des conditions légales ou nominales de la propriété, pour se soucier des formes quotidiennes de l'accès aux ressources[3]. En d'autres termes, il s'agit de découvrir les pratiques quotidiennes de distribution sociale de la rente pouvant conditionner (ou être conditionnées

1 *Freguesia* est le nom attribué au Portugal (ainsi que dans les pays colonisés par les Portugais) à la plus petite division administrative du territoire. Chacune d'elles disposait d'un conseil et d'un comité. Au Brésil, la reconnaissance comme *freguesia* d'un groupement de population marquait autrefois la première étape de la croissance d'une agglomération.

2 Grossi Paolo, *História da propriedade e outros ensaios*, Rio de Janeiro, Renovar, 2006, p. 39.

3 Congost Rosa, *Tierras, leyes, historia: estudios sobre ‹ la gran obra de la propriedad ›*, Barcelona, Crítica, 2007.

par) différentes formes de jouissance des droits de propriété. Dans ce cadre, il importe néanmoins de rappeler que l'expérience historique brésilienne reste très éloignée de celle européenne; de ce fait, des précautions doivent être prises face à l'adoption pour la réalité luso-américaine de catégories mises au point et utilisées pour le Vieux Monde[4].

Historique de la transformation des droits de propriété au Brésil

Depuis le début effectif de la colonisation portugaise en Amérique (1534) et pendant trois siècles environ, toute personne qui s'était distinguée pour avoir une *sesmaria* n'acquérait pas un droit de propriété perpétuel et inaliénable. Le *sesmeiro* était la personne qui recevait directement du roi du Portugal les droits les plus étendus sur une portion du territoire de la colonie (la *sesmaria*). En tant que seigneur d'une *sesmaria*, le titulaire disposait de droits administratifs, judiciaires, policiers et commerciaux. Il pouvait aussi percevoir des droits et des rentes de ses censitaires. Cependant, la *sesmaria* était un droit de propriété soumis à certaines conditions, telles que le défrichage du terrain, la possession d'esclaves, la construction de moulins, les paiements de droits, la démarcation et la confirmation des aires, etc. Les *sesmarias* étaient donc moins une forme de propriété qu'une forme d'appropriation de la terre[5].

En outre, au Brésil, la possession effective s'est imposée comme une coutume ayant un appui juridique. Possession, habitation, travail et culture étaient des formes de légitimation du « dominium » et des droits de propriété sur un terrain, en dehors des chemins prévus par la législation relative aux *sesmarias*. Selon Laura Varela, elles constituaient des coutumes contre la loi, dans un univers juridique qui méconnaissait le droit de propriété selon sa conception actuelle et la notion d'État en tant que source légale et souveraine. Il ne s'agissait pas de « dominium » (ou de « possession ») considéré dans une forme abstraite, mais de « dominium » défini par son utilisation[6].

4 Fonseca Ricardo, « A Lei de Terras e o advento da propriedade moderna no Brasil », in *Anuário Mexicano de Historia del Derecho*, 17 (2005), pp. 97-112 (98-99).

5 Oliveira Marques, « Lei das Sesmarias de 1375 », in *Dicionário de história de Portugal*, Porto, Livraria Figueirinhas, 1985, p. 543.

6 Varela Laura, *Das sesmarias à propriedade moderna: um estudo de história do direito brasileiro*, Rio de Janeiro, Renovar, 2005, p. 59.

L'indépendance nationale, proclamée en 1822, imposa la définition d'un nouveau *corpus* juridique construit graduellement. En 1835, l'empereur supprima la primogéniture et institua la «Loi des Partages». En 1845, le gouvernement impérial brésilien approuva la première loi permettant l'expropriation pour cause d'utilité publique. Le statut 1664 du 27 octobre 1855 autorisait l'expropriation automatique des terres lors de l'approbation du tracé de la voie ferrée, mais l'accès à la possession n'était validé qu'après paiement de l'indemnisation au propriétaire[7]. Ces lois s'avérèrent assez utiles au moment de l'installation du réseau ferroviaire.

Avec la promulgation de la Loi sur les Terres en 1850, s'ébauchèrent les contours d'un droit de propriété moderne. Selon Lígia Osório Silva, le rôle essentiel de cette loi fut d'opérer la transition d'un système de concession à un système de propriété absolue[8]. Au cours de cette transition, la Loi essaya de régler les modalités d'accès à la propriété de la part de certains *sesmeiros* et possédants. En fait, grâce à elle, de nombreux possédants purent s'élever à la condition de propriétaires de plein droit.

Droits de propriété à Campo Grande

Après avoir esquissé les lignes générales de la problématique concernant la propriété de la terre au Brésil, nous pouvons aborder plus directement notre étude de cas. Par notre démarche, nous allons voir que le caractère historiquement non-linéaire de la transition entre deux solutions juridiques relatives à la propriété de la terre est en rapport avec les projets et les actions des sujets localement impliqués dans ce processus.

La crise de la *freguesia* se manifesta *dès la fin du* XVIIIe siècle. En 1794, aucun nouvel *engenho* ne s'installa dans la région et chez les anciens le nombre d'esclaves s'était sensiblement réduit comparé aux années précédentes. *À partir de* 1813, l'acquisition de nouvelles portions de terre à Campo Grande par des anciens et des nouveaux *sesmeiros* déclina. La seconde moitié du XIXe siècle infligea des épreuves encore plus sévères aux exploitations agricoles. La baisse

7 Loi 356 du 12 juillet 1845.

8 Silva Ligia, *Terras devolutas e latifúndio: efeitos da lei de 1850*, Campinas, UNICAMP, 1996, p. 160.

de la qualité des produits agricoles, l'interruption du trafic international d'esclaves qui fournissait la main-d'œuvre principale et une série de fléaux, finirent par annuler quasiment la commercialisation de la production agricole. Une partie des champs se vida, car l'émigration avait aussi servi d'exutoire dans un contexte de frontière fermée, de manque de main-d'œuvre servile, d'érosion du sol, d'endettement et de fragmentation des patrimoines.

Au Brésil, la législation coloniale (en vigueur depuis 1613[9]) et la nouvelle loi sur les partages (en vigueur depuis 1835[10]) imposaient l'égalité entre tous les héritiers. Toutefois, dans la pratique, même aux tropiques, le patriarche-seigneur pouvait désigner un héritier préférentiel et veiller ainsi au maintien de l'intégrité du patrimoine familial. Sur la base du dépouillement d'une série de testaments incluant des clauses relatives à la transmission des terres dans la *freguesia*, nous avons constaté que ces pratiques préférentielles liées à la culture seigneuriale d'Ancien Régime ne dépendaient pas de la taille du terroir légué. En outre, ces pratiques successorales se sont maintenues jusqu'à la fin du XIXe siècle[11].

Cependant, la faible densité démographique et l'existence de terres libres favorisèrent la mise en œuvre d'une solution originale au problème de la transmission des biens fonciers parmi les familles titulaires des terres. Celle-ci reposait sur la création d'une échelle inégale de transmission des droits entre les héritiers, qui commençait par l'héritier principal et passait par diverses gradations:

9 Les *Ordenações Filipinas* étaient le Code de lois en vigueur dans l'empire portugais à partir de 1603, et au Brésil jusqu'en 1916. Elles sanctionnaient la coutume selon laquelle les mariages étaient des contrats à moitié. Au décès de l'un des conjoints, l'autre était responsable d'entreprendre le partage, gardant pour lui sa moitié et partageant entre tous les enfants légitimes du défunt les deux tiers de la moitié restante. Il pouvait accorder librement le dernier tiers par un acte testamentaire. Cf. *Ordenações Filipinas* 1870.

10 Seules les terres nobles (*morgados*) étaient indivisibles, mais la Loi des Partages (loi du 6 octobre 1835) a supprimé l'institution du *morgadio* au Brésil.

11 Ont procédé ainsi, par exemple: Ana Maria de Jesus, avec ses 5.000 braças de testada « insuffisantes pour les satisfaire tous », en 1794; Antonio de Oliveira Galindo, sur sa situação avec 200 braças de testada, en 1871; et le capitaine-majeur José Antunes Pereira Susano, pour ses fermes Capoeiras et Pedregoso, en 1876. Cf. Archives Nationales du Brésil (ANB). Fonds: Inventaires Post Mortem (code: 3J). Disparue: Ana Maria de Jesus. Inventariante: João Pereira Lemos. Année 1795. Document numéro 10, boîte 3.636. Disparu: Antonio de Oliveira Galindo. Année 1871. Document numéro 28, boîte 3.644. Disparu: José Antunes Pereira Susano. Année 1876. Document numéro 4.458, boîte 3.610 et document numéro 35, boîte 3.610.

d'abord les héritiers de menues portions du patrimoine familial, puis les filles qui recevaient leur dot, enfin les fils exclus presque entièrement des droits d'héritage: les « exclus seigneuriaux » qui devenaient des *sitiantes*.

Ces derniers disposaient seulement d'un petit *sítio* à l'intérieur d'un plus grand domaine familial où ils pouvaient vivre avec leur famille conjugale[12]. Ils obtenaient des droits d'usage, même sans être les propriétaires formels des lopins reçus. La condition des *sítios* renvoyait à deux types de situation foncière: celle des petites exploitations agricoles dirigées par des possédants indépendants, sans titres ni règlement légal, et celle des petites parcelles dans une plus grande propriété, données en usufruit à certaines familles selon leur rapport avec la famille du propriétaire. Dans les deux cas, les *sítios* ne payaient ni rente ni loyer au seigneur du « dominium ».

De quels avantages les *sítios* profitaient-ils? Pour les agriculteurs non apparentés à la famille seigneuriale, mais rattachés par des liens de travail, de mariage ou de parrainage, la formule garantissait le droit à une demeure et à un petit champ pour cultiver des provisions pour la famille ainsi que la canne à sucre pour l'*engenho*. Les exclus de la succession n'étaient pas obligés de quitter les domaines familiaux, ni de rester célibataires comme serviteurs du frère successeur. Ils pouvaient se marier et avoir des enfants. Nos reconstructions généalogiques montrent des familles paysannes avec une fécondité élevée et un grand nombre d'enfants atteignant l'âge adulte. Autre facteur important: la plupart des titulaires d'un *sítio* restaient dans leur terroir de naissance. Les exclus qui demeuraient en tant que *sitiantes* chez leurs frères héritiers n'étaient donc pas condamnés à l'exclusion totale, soit à l'émigration ou au célibat. De plus, leur condition perpétuait un réseau de réciprocités inégales qui conférait une légitimité et une stabilité à un contexte de grandes inégalités économiques et sociales.

Si la concession d'un *sítio* faisait partie d'un ensemble de pratiques reproduisant les hiérarchies sociales et économiques, on doit aussi admettre que cela contribuait à atténuer l'exclusion complète d'une partie importante de la population de l'accès aux ressources locales. L'exclusion due à la transmission patrimoniale inégale était corrigée par la concession de droits d'usage. Cette

12 Pedroza Manoela, *Engenhocas da Moral: redes de parentela, transmissão de terras e direitos de propriedade na freguesia de Campo Grande (Rio de Janeiro, século XIX)*, Rio de Janeiro, Arquivo Nacional, 2012.

habitude empêchait l'exclusion absolue de ceux qui dépendaient de petites portions de terre pour vivre. En résumé, pour les individus les plus humbles, l'obtention d'un *sítio* représentait la clé d'accès au principal moyen de production: la terre.

Pourtant, l'inégalité socioéconomique qui portait les seigneurs au sommet de la hiérarchie sociale exigeait quelques contreparties pour se perpétuer. Les seigneurs locaux avaient coutume de concéder des *sítios* à l'intérieur de leurs domaines où vivait ainsi une couche de *sitiantes* proches de leur habitation. Il s'agissait de seigneurs appauvris et endettés, propriétaires de terres qu'ils étaient incapables d'exploiter de façon adéquate, faute d'esclaves. Grâce à la concession de *sítios,* les seigneurs se donnaient les moyens de mettre en scène leur générosité, tout en manifestant leur omnipotence. À travers cette concession, ils obtenaient des travailleurs, des fournisseurs de canne à sucre, des clients, des alliés, des témoins dans les procédures judiciaires, des débiteurs d'argent et même des amis ou des co-parrains. Les *sítios* étaient comme des collecteurs au travers desquels pouvaient s'écouler les dons et les contre-dons symboliques et matériels qui soutenaient la légitimité de la position sociale des seigneurs.

Des décennies, voire des siècles durant, les seigneurs des terres de Campo Grande n'ont pas eu la force – ou le courage – de briser les normes concernant les droits d'usage locaux. Pour eux, rompre la solution *pro indiviso* signifiait perdre leur légitimité. Ces héritiers, seigneurs, parrains de leurs voisins, pères et capitaines locaux, perpétuaient sciemment la dynamique sociale qui les reliait à des parents moins fortunés, étant donné que ce capital relationnel représentait leur principale source de légitimité sociale et de pouvoir. Dans des contextes où la puissance économique n'était pas prédominante, d'autres distinctions élevaient un individu au rang de seigneur, indépendamment de ses dettes.

Entre 1813 et 1870, la majeure partie des grands domaines de la *freguesia* fut déclarée copropriété d'un ensemble de cohéritiers, presque tous frères et beaux-frères. Les actes de partage de ces terres mentionnaient un seul propriétaire, l'héritier préférentiel, mais dans la pratique les héritiers principaux partageaient la possession du « vieux bien » avec leurs frères, cousins, oncles et co-parrains[13]

13 Le co-parrainage est le lien de parenté rituel créé entre deux personnes lors du baptême d'un enfant. Souvent c'est le père qui choisit le parrain de son enfant; le père et le parrain deviennent ainsi des co-parrains.

sitiantes[14]. Jusqu'à la fin du XIXe siècle, la gestion des biens fonciers fut conditionnée par des notions communes, localement perçues comme légitimes, qu'on peut désigner comme l'« économie morale » locale. Ce système différait, en principe et dans la pratique, à la fois des impératifs de la législation, des visées des fonctionnaires du gouvernement et des principes de la propriété privée[15]. Soutien territorial à ce système, les domaines gardés en indivision (*pro indiviso*) témoignent de la perpétuation de réciprocités inégales et de droits traditionnels sur ces patrimoines.

De fait, à Campo Grande, aucun indice n'indique la présence d'une rationalité économique libérale, l'éclosion de la propriété moderne ou la rupture de la dynamique agraire traditionnelle, ceci même plusieurs décennies après la promulgation de la Loi sur les Terres[16]. À cet égard, il convient de rappeler que le changement comme la permanence, en tant que configurations sociales, sont des processus qui impliquent des agents pour les mener à bien[17]. Dans le cas qui nous occupe, nous soutenons que la reproduction dans le temps des droits de propriété traditionnels fut possible par l'action effective de ces sujets.

Changements à partir de 1877

Dès 1870, la *freguesia* de Campo Grande fut progressivement intégrée dans la planification urbaine et dans les projets politiques de transformation économique et démographique intéressant la ville de Rio de Janeiro. Certains points de repères permettent de baliser ce processus. Tout d'abord, la décision de la mairie d'installer le nouvel abattoir de la ville à l'ouest de la commune et de tracer une route raccordant Campo Grande à cet endroit précis de la ville. L'embranchement de la voie ferrée fut inauguré en 1882. Les capitaines et seigneurs traditionnels avaient mis à la disposition du Gouvernement des terrains situés sur leurs exploitations; en échange, ils avaient sollicité la construction de la gare ferroviaire sur leurs terres[18]. En grandissant, la ville avait besoin de ter-

14 Pedroza Manoela, *Engenhocas da Moral*, *op. cit.*

15 *Ibidem.*

16 *Ibidem.*

17 Levi Giovanni, « Regiones y cultura de las clases populares », in *Relaciones*, 24 (2003), pp. 250-266.

18 ANB, Rio de Janeiro, Fonds GIFI, 4B-174 et 4B-180.

rains pour loger la population. Ses autorités transformèrent ainsi les anciennes fermes en lotissements et expulsèrent les paysans vers les terres plus à l'ouest, parmi lesquelles Campo Grande. De plus, afin de répondre aux problèmes de santé et d'approvisionnement en eau, le Gouvernement étudia une solution pour amener l'eau courante au centre-ville. Il entama ainsi une campagne d'expropriations de sources d'eau et de fermes, incluant aussi celles des montagnes de Campo Grande.

À partir du dernier quart du XIXe siècle, les habitants de la *freguesia* ont donc assisté à la soudaine valorisation des terrains, à une hausse de la pression démographique et à l'arrivée de nouveaux occupants, dont des fonctionnaires du gouvernement, des prestataires de service et des voyageurs. Ces derniers étaient au courant des initiatives et des négociations entamées par le Gouvernement en vue des expropriations pour la construction de la voie ferrée et des infrastructures s'y rattachant. Ils avaient entendu parler de forains intéressés à l'achat de terrains, voire à la cession de droits sur des terrains encore non arpentés.

Les expropriations démarrèrent en 1872. Cette année là, Antônio Carlos de Paiva, qui avait acheté des portions d'une ferme quelques années auparavant, les vendit comme parc de logements[19]. En 1877, Luiz Fernandes Barata vendit au Ministère des Transports des terrains par lesquels aurait dû passer l'embranchement de la voie ferrée; en échange, il exigea que la station ferroviaire fût bâtie sur ses terres, ce qui advint en 1905[20]. En 1879, Maria Teixeira Alves céda des terres et des eaux de sa ferme afin que le Gouvernement approvisionne l'abattoir de Santa Cruz en eau courante[21], et en 1887, son fils céda toute la ferme au Gouvernement impérial. En 1889, Manuel Miguel Martins et d'autres propriétaires monnayèrent à une industrie 3.600 acres de terre, comprenant deux anciennes fermes, deux *sítios* et deux cascades, où aurait dû se construire une fabrique textile. En 1891, Marcolino da Costa Borges et Francisco Teixeira de Souza Alves vendirent leurs terres à une autre industrie, qui les céda quelques années après[22]. En 1895, Sebastião Pinho vendit deux fermes à l'Entreprise

19 Fridman Fania, *Donos do Rio em nome do rei: uma história fundiária da cidade do Rio de Janeiro*, Rio de Janeiro, Jorge Zahar Editor, 1999, p. 157.

20 ANB, Rio de Janeiro, Fonds GIFI, 4B-174.

21 Fróes Jose et Odalea Gelabert, *Rumo ao Campo Grande por trilhas e caminhos (1565-1965)*, Rio de Janeiro, sans éditeurs, 2004, p. 199.

22 Archives Générales de la Ville de Rio de Janeiro (AGCRJ), Rio de Janeiro, 68-3-73, f. 223.

Industrielle Brésilienne, qui les revendit plus tard au Gouvernement fédéral[23]. En 1884, un autre individu acheta un *sítio* avec des bâtiments abimés[24]. En 1886, Luis Vieira de Mendanha Souto Maior commença à acquérir les terres de divers héritiers dans la région du Mendanha[25]. À partir de 1911, un autre individu se mit à acheter, petit à petit, des droits d'héritage appartenant aux héritiers de la ferme « Rio da Prata du Mendanha », morcelée au fil des générations[26]. Il n'était ni fermier, ni propriétaire de moulin, ni membre apparenté. Il apparaissait de temps en temps chez le notaire, où il payait la somme due, signait et ressortait avec un terme de cession de droits d'héritage. En 1920, il était déjà propriétaire de pas moins de 34 portions de terre dans la région[27].

La combine des titres

Jusqu'en 1870, étaient nombreux ceux qui avaient l'usufruit de droits traditionnels de propriété: d'abord les frères et les sœurs des héritiers préférentiels – surtout ceux qui continuaient à habiter, à travailler et à gérer la fabrique de sucre familiale, même sous la direction d'un successeur –; ensuite tous les « exclus seigneuriaux »[28], cousins pauvres de la branche seigneuriale, mais qui utilisaient le nom de la famille et déclaraient des portions reçues en héritage des parents

23 Fridman Fania, *Donos do Rio em nome do rei*, *op. cit.*

24 ANB, Rio de Janeiro, Fonds Inventários. Nom: Marcos Cardoso des Santos. Année 1883. Notation 448, boîte 4.283.

25 ANB, Rio de Janeiro, Fonds Processos SDJ Diversos, n. 3, boîte 1.146.

26 ANB, Rio de Janeiro, Fonds 10e Notariat: livre 32 p. 61; livre 36 p. 66-verso; livre 60 p. 77; livre 68 p. 43-verso; livre 64 p. 42; livre 75 p. 60-verso; livre 72 p. 9; 15e Notariat: livre 128 p. 14-verso. Et Archives Générales de la Ville de Rio de Janeiro (AGCRJ), Rio de Janeiro, 68-3-73 (p. 223).

27 Cens national de 1920.

28 Au sujet du concept d'« exclus seigneuriaux », cf. Dépatie Sylvie, « La transmission du patrimoine au Canada (XVIIe-XVIIIe siècles): qui sont les défavorisés? », in *Revue d'Histoire de l'Amérique Française*. vol. 54, n. 4 (2001), pp. 558-570; et Dickinson John, « Destins familiaux dans de gouvernement de Montréal sous le régime français: les Brunet », in Bouchard, Gérard et al. (sous la dir. de). *Les exclus de la terre en France et au Québec XVIIe-XXe siècles. La reproduction familiale dans la différence*, Sillery, Septentrion, 1998, pp. 175-189.

et aïeuls; puis tous ceux dont le prestige et le pouvoir local avait augmenté durant la deuxième moitié du XIXe siècle, grâce à des stratégies patrimoniales et matrimoniales traditionnelles, et qui, par conséquent, avaient obtenu l'usufruit du droit aux *sítios*, aux forêts et aux rivières; enfin, tous les anciens possédants qui, du fait d'un lien quelconque (comme fournisseurs de cannes à sucre, par parrainage ou même par mariage), s'estimaient durablement établis dans leurs possessions aux alentours des anciens moulins des domaines seigneuriaux.

À partir de 1870, la situation se modifia rapidement: pour la première fois, le marché de la terre de la paroisse s'étendit hors de la sphère locale. Dans le nouveau scénario, les acheteurs et le Gouvernement cherchaient à acquérir des terrains et des sources d'eaux. Un groupe particulier put bénéficier (plus que les autres) des opportunités qui avaient vu le jour, à savoir ceux qui possédaient des papiers concernant une portion de terre, même si sa superficie n'était pas indiquée: actes de partage mentionnant héritiers et legs, écritures d'achat de possessions (*posses*, *situações*, *datas*, *sítios*), lettres de *sesmaria*, et même écritures de cession de droits d'héritage.

Dans la mesure où seuls les droits de propriété corroborés par des papiers étaient reconnus en tant que tels, beaucoup d'autres droits furent mis en discussion. Même si cela n'est pas explicité dans les sources, l'impact de cet « aveuglement externe » à l'égard du système local de droits d'usage fut sans doute considérable. La rupture des codes locaux surprit probablement de nombreuses personnes, surtout celles qui estimaient détenir de longue date certains droits, quand bien même non formalisés par des titres de propriété.

Comment les porteurs de papiers ont-ils réussi à manipuler à leur profit le système traditionnel de droits sur la terre? En fait, les détenteurs de titres maîtrisaient les canaux de la communication entre des réalités non compatibles directement: localement ils étaient les seigneurs, les capitaines et les héritiers préférentiels, mais aussi les propriétaires de terres, selon les critères juridiques et économiques les plus amples. Les papiers étaient dans leurs tiroirs et non dans ceux des « cousins pauvres ». Historiquement, ces seigneurs avaient vu leur pouvoir de propriétaire à part entière entravé par les autres droits de propriété en vigueur, mais dans la nouvelle situation, l'expropriation les considérait comme des propriétaires, une fiction créée par les titres qu'ils possédaient. Estimant que ces papiers, jaunis et longtemps oubliés, leurs conféraient des prérogatives dans les affaires avec les forains, ils négocièrent avec l'État l'expropriation des terres.

Ce fut le cas, en 1878, de Luis Antunes Gonzaga Susano et, en 1893, de Antonio de Sousa Ribeiro[29]. Outre la ratification de leur condition de propriétaire, l'indemnisation ou la vente pure et simple leur offrit la liquidité que leurs terres ne leur donnaient plus depuis longtemps. Les expropriations ont donc représenté l'une des solutions mise en œuvre par ces agents pour devenir pleinement propriétaires.

En agissant de la sorte, des capitaines purent vendre à leur profit des terres que les usages locaux ne permettaient d'aliéner, ceci en vertu de l'utilisation d'une loi «du dehors» et d'une conception du droit étrangère à la coutume locale. Motivés par l'espoir d'un bénéfice économique, ils sont parvenus, unilatéralement, arbitrairement et impunément, à démonter l'engrenage des droits d'usage locaux, affaiblissant ainsi les droits de propriété de la plus grande partie de la population.

Ils ont sciemment transformé des droits limités sur les terres en propriété pleine et absolue, au moins vis-à-vis de leurs acheteurs. Ce faisant, ils ont définitivement exclu tous ceux qui jugeaient avoir d'autres droits sur les mêmes terres. C'est pourquoi l'on peut dire qu'au lieu de violer la propriété particulière, l'expropriation l'a créée. À Rio de Janeiro, le processus d'expropriation promu par le gouvernement sur la base de papiers de nature hétérogène a institué une propriété privée qui, dans la pratique, n'avait jamais existé.

Un élément s'est ajouté à cette dynamique «perverse»: dans la majorité des cas, les titres négociés ne contenaient pas la délimitation exacte du bien. Négociant surtout au moyen de papiers la cession des droits d'héritage, le soi-disant propriétaire-vendeur permettait à l'acquéreur d'empiéter sur les terrains voisins, qui appartenaient à d'autres exploitants. En pareil cas, outre l'abus de l'aliénation, se vérifiait aussi sur le plan moral l'abus de l'espace négocié, les deux étant certifiés par des contrats réputés comme légitimes par rapport au droit de propriété.

29 AGCRJ, Rio de Janeiro, 40-4-9, p. 9.

Conclusion

Pour clore de notre analyse, il importe de rappeler les processus de transformation économique dans lesquels elle s'insère: la modernisation de l'agriculture, la pénétration capitaliste, la formation d'un marché de la terre. Notre regard a porté sur la façon dont ces processus ont construit leur efficacité au niveau local. Si ces changements ont réellement affecté le mode de vie d'un grand nombre de personnes, nous soutenons qu'ils ont bénéficié de la collaboration d'agents locaux pour les mener à terme. Selon notre hypothèse, les buts de ces projets, quand ils n'en étaient encore qu'au stade embryonnaire, ont dû avoir une résonance sur les intérêts d'agents qui avaient la capacité de les oblitérer.

Dans la *freguesia* de Campo Grande, État et Justice ont réussi à imposer un modèle de propriété privée pleine, inexistante jusqu'alors, parce que les expropriations étaient de l'intérêt des certains seigneurs. L'action orchestrée des détenteurs de titres a créé la fiction d'un marché foncier fondé sur la circulation de propriétés totales, libres et aliénables, renforçant ainsi la thèse de Karl Polanyi selon laquelle c'est toujours à l'aide de cette fiction que s'organisent dans la réalité les marchés du travail, de la terre et de la monnaie[30]. Pour Polanyi en effet, la «calamité sociale» du XXe siècle n'a pas seulement ses origines dans le domaine économique, mais aussi dans la destruction des institutions culturelles sur lesquelles les «sociétés organiques» structuraient leur existence. En ce sens, les institutions culturelles n'ont pas été détruites par l'économie de marché extérieure, mais par un groupe spécifique de sujets qui a décidé, stratégiquement et à son profit, de se libérer du poids moral qui les accompagnait.

À partir de 1877, font leur apparition les impératifs d'un marché et d'un nouveau système qui ratifient des actions auparavant condamnées ou restreintes par la mentalité traditionnelle: nous nous référons à l'exclusion ou à l'abandon de parents et de compagnons, à la violence des expulsions, à l'accaparement des terres avec la complicité de la justice, des Gouvernements et de la Police. Les bases morales traditionnelles étant sapées, une autre morale est venue dicter la dynamique agraire dans la paroisse: une morale stratégiquement manipulée en vue de consacrer certains droits et d'en finir avec les concurrents gênants.

30 Polanyi Karl, *A grande transformação: as origens da nossa época*, Rio de Janeiro, Campus, 1980, pp. 84-85.

Contributors – Auteurs

Andreozzi Daniele, Università degli Studi di Trieste
Barbot Michela, Ecole Normale Supérieure de Cachan
Beauvois Frédérique, Université de Lausanne
Conforti Claudia, Università di Roma 2 Tor Vergata
D'Amelio Maria Grazia, Università di Roma Tor Vergata
Delleaux Fulgence, Université de Caen Basse-Normandie
Forni Marica, Politecnico di Milano
Funis Francesca, Contratto Mibac– Università di Roma Tor Vergata
Gandouet Denis, Université de Poitiers
Krautberger Nicolas, Université Pierre Mendès-France, Grenoble
Lorenzetti Luigi, Università della Svizzera italiana, Mendrisio
Mocarelli Luca, Università degli Studi di Milano Bicocca
Monti Annamaria, Università commerciale Luigi Bocconi, Milano
Nardone Paola, Unversità G. D'Annunzio Chieti Pescara
Pedrosa Manoela, Universitade federal do Rio de Janeiro
Ridolfi Natascia, Università G. D'Annunzio Chieti Pescara
Strangio Donatella, Università di Roma "La Sapienza"
Vaquero Piñero Manuel, Università degli Studi di Perugia
Viganò Marino, Università della Svizzera italiana (LabiSAlp), Mendrisio
Zaggia Stefano, Università degli Studi di Padova

www.ingramcontent.com/pod-product-compliance
Ingram Content Group UK Ltd.
Pitfield, Milton Keynes, MK11 3LW, UK
UKHW020201290926
15471UKWH00005B/1002

9 783034 306683